THE
ASSASSINATION
OF
ROBERT MAXWELL

THE
ASSASSINATION
OF
ROBERT MAXWELL
Israel's Superspy

By
GORDON THOMAS
and
MARTIN DILLON

ROBSON BOOKS

First published in Great Britain in 2002 by Robson Books,
64 Brewery Road, London, N7 9NT

A member of **Chrysalis** Books plc

British Library Cataloguing in Publication Data
A catalogue record for this title is available from the British Library.

ISBN 1 86105 558 7

Contacting the authors
Gordon Thomas e-mail: *gthomas@indigo.ie*
Martin Dillon e-mail: *violetak@earthlink.net*

Typeset by FiSH Books, London WC1
Printed by CPD Wales, Ebbw Vale

Also by Gordon Thomas:

Non-Fiction

DESCENT INTO DANGER
BED OF NAILS
PHYSICIAN EXTRAORDINARY
HEROES OF THE R.A.F.
THEY GOT BACK
MIRACLE OF SURGERY
THE NATIONAL HEALTH SERVICE AND YOU
THAMES NUMBER ONE
MIDNIGHT TRADERS
THE PARENT'S HOME DOCTOR
(with Ian D Hudson, Vincent Pippet)
TURN BY THE WINDOW (with Ronald Hutchinson)
ISSELS: THE BIOGRAPHY OF A DOCTOR
THE DAY THE WORLD ENDED *(with Max Morgan-Witts)*
EARTHQUAKE *(with Max Morgan-Witts)*
SHIPWRECK *(with Max Morgan-Witts)*
VOYAGE OF THE DAMNED *(with Max Morgan-Witts)*
THE DAY GUERNICA DIED *(with Max Morgan-Witts)*
ENOLA GAY/RUIN FROM THE AIR *(with Max Morgan-Witts)*
THE DAY THE BUBBLE BURST *(with Max Morgan-Witts)*
TRAUMA *(with Max Morgan-Witts)*
PONTIFF *(with Max Morgan-Witts)*
THE YEAR OF ARMAGEDDON *(with Max Morgan-Witts)*
THE OPERATION
DESIRE AND DENIAL
TRIAL: The Jesus Conspiracy
JOURNEY INTO MADNESS
ENSLAVED
CHAOS UNDER HEAVEN
TRESPASS INTO TEMPTATION
GIDEON'S SPIES
MAGDALENE: WOMAN OF THE CROSS/THE 13th DISCIPLE
SEEDS OF FIRE
MINDFIELD

Fiction

THE CAMP ON BLOOD ISLAND
TORPEDO RUN
DEADLY PERFUME
GODLESS ICON
VOICES IN THE SILENCE
ORGAN HUNTERS
POISONED SKY

Contents

Interviewees

Rupert Allason	author (published as Nigel West) and intelligence expert.
Meir Amit	former director-general, Mossad.
Juval Aviv	former Mossad *katsa* (field officer).
Norman Bailey	former analyst, National Security Agency.
Ehud Barak	former Head, Israeli Military Intelligence, and former Prime Minister of Israel.
John A Belton	executive stockbroker, Canada.
Ari Ben-Menashe	adviser on intelligence to Yitzhak Shamir, then Prime Minister of Israel.
Vera Butler	investigative author.
Barry Chamish	investigative journalist, Israel.
William Casey	former director, Central Intelligence Agency.
Eli Cohen	former Mossad *katsa*.
Luis Garcia Cohen	forensic pathologist, Tenerife, Canary Islands, Spain.
William Colby	former director, Central Intelligence Agency.
Nick Davies	author and journalist.
Vesna Djurovic	forensic pathologist, Guy's Hospital, London, England.
Anton Doran	senior editor, *Ma'ariv*, Israel.
Rafi Eitan	former director of operations, Mossad.
Rumyana Emanilidu	author and journalist.
John Harbison	state forensic pathologist, Republic of Ireland.
William Hamilton	president, Inslaw, Washington, DC.
Isser Harel	former director-general, Mossad.
Paul Henderson	newspaper reporter.
Barbara Honegger	senior military affairs researcher, United States Navy.

David Kimche   former assistant deputy director-general,
                                Mossad.
Lisa Kordalski   former chief stewardess, *Lady Ghislaine*.
Jules Kroll   president of Kroll Associates Inc.
Violeta Kumurdjieva   journalist and translator, New York.
Carlos Lopez de Lamela   forensic pathologist, Tenerife, Canary
                                Islands, Spain
Marin Markovski   Bulgarian lawyer.
Elizabeth Maxwell   (Betty) widow of Robert Maxwell.
Isabel Maxwell   daughter of Robert Maxwell.
Peter Michalski   London editor, Springers News Service.
Muhamad Mugraby   attorney, Beirut, Lebanon.
Daniel Nagier   former member, Israeli military intelligence.
Isabel Olivia   judge, Tenerife, Canary Islands, Spain.
John P O'Neill   executive agent-in-charge, FBI, New York.
Georgi Ormenkov   former general, Bulgarian Secret Service.
Victor Ostrovsky   former Mossad intelligence officer.
Nickolai Petrov   investigative journalist, Bulgaria.
Yitzhak Rabin   former Prime Minister of Israel.
Maria Ramos   forensic pathologist, Tenerife, Canary
                                Islands, Spain.
Paul Rodriguez   editor, *Insight* magazine.
Sergio Rodriguez   maître d'hôtel, Mencey Hotel, Tenerife,
                                Canary Islands, Spain.
Miguel Rosas   investigative journalist, *El Mundo*, Madrid,
                                Spain.
Alfred Rosenbaum   radiographer, New York.
Uri Saguy   former head of Aman, Israeli military
                                intelligence.
Jose D. Sanchez   sommelier, Mencey Hotel, Tenerife, Canary
                                Islands, Spain.
David Sorsky   former deckhand of the *Lady Ghislaine*.
Richard Tomlinson   former MI6 officer.
Colin Wallace   former senior British intelligence officer.
Noel Walsh   professor of psychiatry, University College
                                Dublin, Ireland.
Murray Weiss   investigative journalist, New York.
Stuart Winter   senior editor, *Daily Star*, London.
Efraim —   former member of Mossad *kidon* unit.

Secondary Sources

Mark Atkins	former second mate, *Lady Ghislaine*.
Dr Jordan Baev	senior fellow, Sofia Military History Institute, Sofia, Bulgaria.
Susan Bender	former stewardess of the *Lady Ghislaine*.
Tom Bower	investigative author.
Richard Brenneke	former CIA operative.
Fenton Bresler	criminologist and barrister.
David Gardner	newspaper reporter.
George Gordon	newspaper reporter.
Yehuda Hiss	forensic pathologist, Institute of Forensic Medicine, Tel Aviv, Israel.
Robert Keating	former chef, *Lady Ghislaine*.
Vladimir Kryuchkov	former chairman, KGB.
Leo Leonard	former second engineer of the *Lady Ghislaine*.
Jose F Perdoma	frogman, Spanish National Rescue Service.
Gus Rankin	captain of the *Lady Ghislaine*.
Luis Gutierrez Ruiz	judge, Tenerife.
Grahame Shorrocks	former first officer, *Lady Ghislaine*.
Martin Soothill	former deckhand of the *Lady Ghislaine*.
Werner U Spritz	forensic pathologist.
Chester Stern	investigative crime writer.
Jesus F Vaca	pilot, Spanish National Rescue Service.
Edward Verity	newspaper reporter.

Authors' Note

To the interviewees and secondary sources all we express gratitude; without their help our task would have been impossible. Many had not been questioned before but felt they could finally speak more freely because a decent interval had elapsed to tell the truth about a story before it is for ever lost to memory. Theirs, we believe, is the truth of honest recall.

The interviews with our prime sources were spread over two years. They were spoken to in person, by telephone and through email. In all, the transcriptions of their interviews came to some 4,000 pages. All the questions attributed to our prime sources are from those interviews.

There were other sources who asked for, and received, a guarantee of anonymity. They included those who are currently employed in Eastern Bloc intelligences services; they feared direct attribution could lead to retribution. That does not make their testimony less valid.

Some of those intelligence sources were close to men like the KGB chief, Vladimir Kryuchkov, Ognian Doinov and Andrei Lukanov, central figures in the story of Robert Maxwell's criminal activities in Eastern Europe. Through these sources, we were able to recreate, from their oral testimony and documents in their possession, the minutae of Maxwell's activities. Again, it was possible to check the evidence of one source against another; in the great majority their evidence tallied. In a number of cases, particularly in Bulgaria and Russia, some of those sources had been directly present at meetings Maxwell had attended. In other instances they had listened to, or read transcripts of, secretly recorded conversations. Their contemporaneous notes were invaluable to describing what he said and how he reacted. Those notes form part of our considerable documentation.

In the case of some serving members of the Israeli intelligence community they are prevented by the country's laws from allowing their names to be published. Again, it does not invalidate their contribution.

Secondary sources are based upon interviews those sources have given on repeated occasions to newspapers and magazines, and to the broadcast media all over the world. In the great majority of cases those sources gave almost identical interviews on the same subject on the same day, especially in the closing weeks of Robert Maxwell's life. We therefore decided it would be unnecessary, indeed pointless, to identify statements of those secondary sources to each publication in which they appeared.

Please refer to the notes and documents section, which contains facsimiles of important documents relating to Robert Maxwell's life and untimely death.

Prologue

The first telephone call was timed at 1.34 p.m., Israeli time, on 5 November 1991. It was from the country's ambassador in Madrid on a secure line and unscrambled in the concrete needle bristling with electronic antennae high over Tel Aviv. The tower, visible from the Judean Hills, was the electronic hub of all Israeli military, diplomatic and intelligence traffic.

The call was automatically routed to the office of Prime Minister Yitzhak Shamir.

The diminutive, gnome-faced Shamir was having a daily briefing from senior advisers about the country's worsening financial situation. The red light flashing on his phone automatically triggered a recording device in his office. Age was taking a toll on his memory. As he listened to the call, his face betrayed no emotion; he liked to say that, even if God called him, his features would never betray what the Almighty was saying.

When the ambassador finished speaking, Shamir barked two questions: 'When? Where is he?'

Those questions would be repeated all over the world within hours.

In Washington DC, it was shortly after 7.30 a.m. when a duty officer in the CIA's Langley headquarters tore a message from a high-speed fax printer. He read and marked the facsimile, 'Immediate, DCI.' He then rerouted it to the seventh-floor suite of the director of central intelligence.

In Moscow, where it was already into the afternoon, the KGB's public-affairs chief, General Alexander Karabaika, was in the Kremlin with President Mikhail Gorbachev, discussing how the spy agency might respond to *perestroika* with more openness. A call quickly ended their discussion and Karabaika hurried back to his headquarters in the Lubyanka to find out whether the KGB had any additional information on what he had just heard. Gorbachev began calling overseas in the first of a series of enquiries that would go long into the Russian night.

It was still late morning in London and frantic dispatches over the wires interrupted scores of meetings in the City, the financial heart of the capital. But it was in the clubs of Pall Mall and the newspaper offices in Fleet Street where the news had its biggest impact. People were shocked speechless by what they learned.

Across the globe, there was stunned disbelief, sometimes followed by a frisson of excitement mixed with dread.

Meanwhile in Tel Aviv, Prime Minister Shamir, who had received no response to his questions – 'When? Where is he?' – punched a button on his telephone console.

It triggered an identical light on the phone of Shabtai Shavit, Israel's *mehueme*, the country's supreme head of intelligence and director-general of Mossad.

The conversation, recorded by both the Prime Minister and Shabtai Shavit, is a model of brevity and understatement.

'Have you heard?' demanded Shamir.

'Yes, I've heard.'

'What happened?'

'He just vanished.'

'Are you sure?'

'We're looking for him.'

On that day, far out in the Atlantic, Robert Maxwell met a fate that had been decided in secret three months before.

Part I
DAYS OF THE *KIDON*

ONE

In September 1991, on one of those balmy days when its citizens liked to remind each other this was why God chose their Promised Land, four men made their separate ways towards King Saul Boulevard in Tel Aviv, Israel. Outside their closed community no one knew what they did; their success depended on secrecy. Their work had one goal. Assassination.

They worked in a $60-billion global industry employing a million people. They routinely called upon the most advanced technology to conduct their business. Their budgets were unpublished; few outsiders could begin to guess accurately what use the money had been spent on, or what was the ultimate effect.

Sovereign, proud and expansionist, this secret empire could be fiercely divided by internal strife. But to those who were charged with its control – its external political masters – it presented a united front. Its survival depended on no less. Aggressive and duplicitous, it used any means to achieve what was required: robots in the deep black of space supported other cutting-edge technology. Some of the empire's workers spent their time creating ways to exploit what the satellites told them as their mechanical ears constantly turned in all directions over the earth.

The four men on the streets of Tel Aviv on that pleasant September afternoon were part of that secret world. They also worked for Israel's defence community. Like all the community's employees they were only too aware of the changes once more surging through their empire.

The Soviet Union was unravelling. As a result, the accepted rationale behind the existence of every intelligence service for the past fifty years now required urgent rethinking. The Russian KGB would no longer be there at the sharp end of the superpower conflict.

Within Israel's intelligence community, as elsewhere, there was a scramble to deal with new challenges and reassess existing ones. The end of Soviet Communism did not mean the end of an unstable world. Two

3

millennia of terrorism, distilled by the great Chinese strategist Sun Tsu – 'kill one, frighten ten thousand' – would still be there. In many ways the new post-Cold War world would be an even more unstable one with an increase of religious terrorism and proliferation in the trafficking of nuclear materials, weapons and drugs.

For the four men the area of the threatening future that currently concerned them was international financial fraud and the effect this was having on Israel. Foreign bankers and the emerging Russian Mafia, a conglomerate of crime families with global reach, had found the country a useful conduit for money laundering. Every day rich, powerful men with foreign names flew into the country or sent their emissaries to do business. Much of it centred on huge payments in return for having Jews freed from the yoke of Soviet tyranny. It had become a growth industry defined inelegantly by one participant as 'money for flesh and freedom'.

The men making their purposeful way through the streets of Tel Aviv had been told the time had come to deal with one of those powerful figures. But that was all they had been told. The need to know, and when to know, was integral to the small and close-knit unit for which they worked. It was called *kidon* and its prime function was cold and efficient killing.

They worked for Israel's Central Institute for Intelligence and Special Duties, long shortened to its universal name, Mossad; its stated aim included covert action. One of the many unofficial titles it had acquired was Executioner to the World.

Where other services no longer allowed its secret agents to slip a Walther PPK into a shoulder holster without getting approval from an intelligence oversight committee, the men and women of *kidon* operated under no such restraint. They remained fully licensed to assassinate in the name of Israel once they had routinely convinced an incumbent prime minister of the need to do so.

On that September afternoon the men walking through Tel Aviv were being called on to perform such a service.

Physically different, the eldest separated by some ten years from the youngest man, they had no fear of arrest. Each killing was a state-approved assassination of someone who could not be brought to trial before the country's courts because the person was protected deep within the borders of one of Israel's enemies. Among these were its Arab neighbours, countries within the former Soviet Bloc, North Korea and the numerous Islamic republics. There were many such hostile nations who gave succour and security to all those persons pledged to destroy the Jewish State.

In Israel's eyes the need for *kidon* had increased in the aftermath of the collapse of European Marxism and the burgeoning of Islamic fundamentalism in all its guises: Hamas, Islamic Jihad, Islamic Solidarity Front, Palestinian Liberation Front, the groups of the drugs countries of the Golden Crescent – Iran, Pakistan and Afghanistan – the terrorists of the Philippines.

The *kidon* had killed in all those places – swift and unexpected assassinations in streets, in souks and alleys that had no names. The means had been anything from a single bullet to the nape of the neck delivered from a silenced handgun, to a garrotting with a cheese-cutting wire or a knife thrust into the larynx.

Kidon could also call upon nerve agents and a poisoner's arsenal of substances specially prepared for them. There are many ways of killing and *kidon* knew them all.

But there was more to their knowledge. They had witnessed some of Israel's leading forensic pathologists at work so as better to understand how to make an assassination appear to be an accident. They learned how a pinprick or small blemish on a victim's skin could be a giveaway. For hours they would watch the pathologists at Tel Aviv's Institute of Forensic Medicine cutting and dissecting. *Kidon* would then question carefully. How had a pathologist decided a corpse had been murdered? What more could have been done to disguise the fact? What was the significance of some small clue a pathologist had discovered that had led him to a final conclusion?

Sometimes before an assassination *kidon*, who would be using a particular form of killing, drove out to the city suburb of Nes Ziona to consult with other specialists. They were the scientists who worked at the Institute for Biological Research. Its name gave little clue as to what happened inside the twelve acres of underground laboratories and workshops. Here were tested the efficacy of the biochemical weapons of Israel's enemies, the creations of similar labs in Iraq, Iran, Libya and China.

Some of the institute's chemists had worked for the KGB and the East German Stasi intelligence service. It was these scientists in their secure underground laboratories that the *kidon* came to see to discuss the appropriate nerve agent or gas for an assassination. Some weapons smelled of new-mown grass, others of spring flowers.

In a conference room specifically reserved for the purpose, chemists and assassins would sit and discuss the merits and drawbacks of a choice for a specific assassination. Would the attack be at night or day? Some of the lethal pathogens did not work well in daylight. Would the killing be in an open or closed space? Nerve gas responded very differently in either situation. Would an aerosol spray be more effective than an injection? Where should either be aimed at on the body? These were questions that required long and careful answers. A *kidon*'s life could depend on them.

A decision made, a *kidon* – usually no more than one made the journey to Nes Ziona to discuss the requirement for any assassination – would leave the institute with the appropriate vial, aerosol or bottle of death. He would have signed a document assuming full responsibility for the nerve agent, gas or pathogen.

Increasingly such means were used against terrorists when it was important to surround their assassination with mystery. A body found with no obvious bullet or knife thrust carried its own message of fear for another terrorist. Sometimes it could be the deciding factor in 'turning' that terrorist to betray his own organisation. He then no longer became of interest to *kidon*.

But, though the four men did not yet know it, the person they would be discussing was no terrorist. Indeed, he was as patriotic as any other Jew on the nation's streets that September afternoon. He had opened companies and factories across the land. He had easy access to the nation's leaders; lesser Israeli politicians spoke his name with awe. The country's media treated him with fawning respect. He dispensed largesse and bonhomie in equal measure. Israelis liked to say, as they watched his Falstaffian figure dominate their television screens, that God had indeed been good to give them this far larger-than-life tycoon they could call one of their very own.

His name was Robert Maxwell. He was a physical giant of many roles, each of which had been carefully compartmentalised for years. But to the adoring *kibbutzim* of Israel, the ones to whom he continually proclaimed he was one of their own, he remained a magical figure like no other Jew, perhaps like no other person on earth they had heard or read about in his own newspapers, or in those of his envious rivals. Perhaps that was why he simply liked to be known as 'the Publisher' or 'Chairman' or just by his initials – 'RM'. His admirers told endless variations of the joke that he was the only bouncing Czech the banks loved.

He reflected invincibility in all he said in that rich, actory voice which brooked no challenge. In recent times he had encouraged another sobriquet he added to the others: 'Cap'n Bob'. It had become the one he liked above all others. It made him feel, he rumbled, 'like one of the people'. But always still far above them.

Few men could do what he did: spend a king's ransom on having every newspaper, television and radio station on earth monitored for any mention of him. The slightest error in broadcast tone or written word was followed by a crisply worded correction from an assistant.

Other assistants kept note of his shares in all the principal stock markets. Still more staff vetted those requiring an audience with Cap'n Bob. Like a medieval king, he would keep them waiting for hours; rumour said one luckless supplicant waited two days in an outer office until the Chairman had him removed because of the smell. He was fastidious about such matters.

He encouraged every facet of his lifestyle to be photographed and chronicled. His £2 million penthouse in the heart of London was marble-floored with ceilings supported by Doric columns, which he said came from ancient Egypt. The chandeliers he claimed had been hand-blown by the finest glass blowers in medieval Italy.

The truth was that the columns were hollow fakes, the marble from a quarry that produced it by the job lot and the chandeliers from a showroom specialising in reproductions. But no one, not for a moment, would dare even to whisper that.

After all, there was so much that was beyond challenge. There was his yacht, as beautiful as any that sailed the high seas and which he had named after his favourite daughter, Ghislaine. There were his private jets and helicopter. In another of those gestures that made him so loved by Jews everywhere, he said that he would put his aircraft at his country's disposal should war again come. The gesture had brought a wry smile from Israel's defence chiefs: they had already politely told him the offer was pointless. But he had still made it on prime-time television.

Then there was the way he treated as equals the great statesmen of the world, and its global bankers – the Rothschilds and the Morgensterns – as barely to be tolerated. That played very well among all those who found that money was hard to earn, let alone to keep. That was their Cap'n Bob doing what they would all like to do – shove it to the power brokers of Wall Street and the City of London. On a lighter side, there was the way he could awaken the secretary-general of the United Nations in the small hours to confirm he was indeed going to open some new acquisition of the Chairman's. There were so many such stories. God indeed had been good to give Israel a man like this. Others could call him theatrical, egocentric and vain beyond measure. But to his beloved Israelis he had the *chutzpah* no other Jew in living memory had displayed.

He was a deal maker like no other: where lesser mortals spoke of millions, he talked in billions. To the world he was the super tycoon, a one-man conglomerate who owned newspapers, publishing, television, printing and electronic databases from one end of the earth to another. They knew his name and power in a hundred countries where his assets, on paper, were a staggering £4.2 billion – a figure he never tired of quoting.

But.

There was another side that so far Robert Maxwell had managed to hide from all those who still admired him, who saw only the image he still liked to present: a dutiful husband to Betty, a kindly father to his sons and daughters. His family knew this to be another of his fictions but they too kept it to themselves. To begin even to hint otherwise could start other questions, to unravel a terrible truth.

His paper assets of £4.2 billion had to be matched against another even more awesome figure. Robert Maxwell, who had so openly rejoiced in creating an empire in one generation – something not one of his contemporaries, Rothermere, Sainsbury and Rupert Murdoch, could do without inherited money – had run up debts of £2.2 billion with no fewer than 44 banks. There had been nothing quite like it in the history of finance.

But there was more.

His financial mismanagement had driven him to increasingly desperate measures. The more he began to cast around for rescue, the nearer came the abyss, the closer drew his opponents, whom he had so successfully outwitted. From all sides, bankers, brokers and business enemies were closing in. Not knowing exactly how badly wounded was this still towering giant whose one hand gesture could even now intimidate them into fearful silence, they kept their distance. His batteries of lawyers and accountants continued to convince the doubters that he was infinitely bigger than any of them, and, when he recouped, he would not forget what they were doing. Revenge was, after all, an important part of his complex personality. So they watched and waited.

But there was still more.

Robert Maxwell, driven by those dark inner forces that awoke him at night and for which no sleeping tablet could bring back sleep, had decided at some point before that September day in Tel Aviv in 1991 that he would use pressure he had never exerted before to find the money he needed to get him out of trouble.

He would use his leverage to get what he wanted by threatening to reveal the most secret of all his secrets. Not even his wife, his children, his closest of business associates, *no one* apart from a handful of men in Israel, knew that he had been a powerful figure in the activities of Mossad.

No one else had opened the doors for Mossad quite as he had done. Not only in the lesser halls of power in the now unravelling Soviet Bloc, but in Moscow itself, in the very heart of the Kremlin. And not just there but in Washington, London and Paris. He had spied out secrets that no other man could obtain. He had done so with a skill and risk that the men at the top of Mossad had admired. In many ways Robert Maxwell was a spy like no other. His wealth and power had given him unique access to the most feared spymasters in the Soviet Bloc: men like Yuri Andropov of the KGB and Markus Wolff of the East German Stasi. He was also on speaking terms with the heads of intelligence agencies in Bulgaria, Romania and Czechoslovakia.

How long he might have gone on using his skills as a spy was no longer a question being discussed within the higher echelons of Mossad. Maxwell had done something they had not anticipated. He had begun to threaten them. He had told them that, unless they used their huge power and influence to find him the money he so urgently needed, then they could no longer count on his silence.

At first they thought he was testing their commitment to him but his persistence convinced them otherwise. They responded by trying to persuade him to find other ways out of his dilemma. When that did not succeed, they warned him that he was courting disaster. For himself. For Israel.

He was in no mood to listen. He was in desperate straits, needing an immediate cash injection for his empire. In his mind, it was payback time. He wanted the world's financial monkey off his back and he was unwilling to wait.

Mossad had decided it could no longer afford to ignore the threat posed by Maxwell and that was why four men made their way through the streets of Tel Aviv on that September afternoon in 1991.

They worked within strict guidelines laid down over a quarter of a century previously by a man who had become a living legend far beyond the Israeli intelligence community.

He was Meir Amit, the most innovative and ruthless director-general of Mossad. Born in King Herod's favourite city, Tiberius, Amit had shown the analytical skills and cunning and, he liked to say, 'a dose of fair-mindedness' of a true Galilean. In his long career he had used those qualities to strike terror into his country's enemies. To help do so he had created the rules for assassination.

'There will be no killing of political leaders, however extreme they are. They will be dealt with politically. There will be no killing of a terrorist's family unless they are also directly implicated in terrorism. Each execution must be sanctioned by the prime minister of the day. Any execution is therefore not state-sponsored murder but an ultimate judicial sanction by the state. The executioner is no different from the state-appointed hangman or any other lawfully appointed executioner.'

The CIA had given Amit a copy of its assassination manual. The eight-page document had been written in 1953 by a scientist Meir Amit respected but did not like, Dr Sidney Gottlieb. Gottlieb had been chief of the CIA's Technical Services Branch. To many within the agency he was the devil's apostle, a man who spent his working life devising ways to kill or maim people and, away from work, liked nothing better than milking his pedigree herd of goats.

The manual had been placed in the Mossad training academy near the coastal resort of Herzlia outside Tel Aviv. Instructors used it as part of the two-year course for agents. Known as the *midrasha*, the academy was probably the most advanced of its kind in the world. It selected graduates for its *kidon*.

For Rafi Eitan, a former deputy director of Mossad operations, 'only a handful show the human requirements. A total coldness once committed. And afterwards, no regrets.'

They included the four men making their way towards King Saul Boulevard.

Between them they spoke many of the languages of their country's enemies and possessed combat experience, interrogation skills, a well-honed ability to separate fact from conjecture and a zero tolerance of error. Their methodology was anchored in deception and the situations they created were governed by a rule that fact could not always wait for certainty.

Even among themselves they took their anonymity seriously and usually used only their first names: Zvi, Efraim, Uri, Nahum.

A year before this late summer's day, one of their own, Victor Ostrovsky, had done the unthinkable, publicly declaring that he had been 'groomed for the *kidon*'.

Ostrovsky revealed that *kidon* – in Hebrew the name means 'bayonet' – was 'responsible for executions and kidnappings'. After graduating from the training school he served seventeen months as a Mossad *katsa*, a field officer, from October 1984 to March 1986. Following his resignation, he launched the most comprehensive exposure ever of Mossad, naming scores of its members, code names of units, operational methods including that of *kidon*. He insisted his motives were idealistic, that he had a duty to expose his former colleagues who 'were out of control'.

There were some *kidon* who would have liked to kill him but the restraining words of Meir Amit diffused their emotions. 'Ostrovsky is burnt toast. A man who doesn't know the meaning of loyalty.'

The sun no doubt warm on their backs and the breeze from the Mediterranean bringing the first cooling of the day, the four men converging on the Hadar Davna Building, another of the drab office high-rises that lined King Saul Boulevard, were going to decide how best to deal finally with Robert Maxwell. They would meet in the most secure room in the building, a conference room in Mossad's Directorate of Operations that was always used for this purpose by *kidon*.

Each man entered the building separately – standard operational procedure. The lobby was large. On one side was a branch of the Bank of Israel, flanked by offices of various companies. Across from them was a small cafeteria, a handful of plastic tables and chairs set out in front of a service counter displaying a variety of snacks. At the far end of the lobby was an unmarked door.

All Mossad staff had a key that allowed them to open the door. Beyond was a corridor. At its end were two elevators. Each rose through the eight floors occupied by Mossad.

Mossad's headquarters was a building within a building with its own separate utilities of power, water and sanitation.

On the first floor was the communications centre, equipped with state-of-the-art computers, secure radio receivers and transmitters. On the floor above was the Research and Development Department with laboratories and workshops that created and updated surveillance devices, adapted weapons and forged documents. Its scientists worked closely with the Institute for Biological Research.

The third floor was occupied by the archives and the liaison offices with Israel's other intelligence services, the most important of which was Shin Bet, the equivalent of the FBI.

The fourth floor housed the 'Desks' – each a separate office with direct links to Mossad's 22 overseas stations. A part of the floor was the home of the Collections Department, responsible for collating all intelligence received. In another corner of the floor was the Foreign Liaison Unit, which maintained contact with other intelligence services that Mossad deemed to be friendly. These included the CIA and Britain's MI6 and, in September 1991, South Africa's Bureau of State Security.

The fifth floor was occupied by the Directorate of Operations. The *kidon* unit was controlled from here, as were the forty other *katsas* who formed Mossad's intelligence capability in the field. A number of *katsas* were permanently stationed overseas. Those who worked out of the fifth floor were known as 'jumpers' – case officers who could be sent to reinforce an ongoing operation in some part of the world.

On the sixth floor were the analysts, psychologists and forward planners, the men and women who tried to evaluate the data from the Collections Department to see how it could affect future military and political moves by Israel.

The seventh floor housed the Legal Department, the Library, Office of Finance, Office of Logistics, Office of Personnel. Attached to these was a small medical facility.

On the eighth floor were the suites of the director-general, the deputy directors and their staffs.

All told, some twelve hundred persons worked on the floors, making Mossad still one of the smallest global intelligence services. But in support was an operation no other agency could match. It was known as *sayanim*, a derivative of the Hebrew word *lesayeah*, to help.

Throughout the Diaspora there were tens of thousands of these 'helpers'. Each had been carefully recruited, sometimes by *katsas*, more often on the recommendation of someone who had already been recruited.

Sayanim was another creation of Meir Amit, its success a striking example of the cohesiveness of the worldwide Jewish community. For Amit, 'it is proof that no matter the allegiance a *sayan* has to his or her country, in the end there is a more emotional and mystical one, an allegiance to Israel and need when called upon to help to protect it from its enemies.' Isser Harel, another former Mossad director-general, has said that 'the contribution *sayanim* have made is beyond measure.'

In practical terms it meant a *sayan* who ran a car rental agency would provide a *katsa*, a field agent, or *kidon* with a vehicle on a no-questions basis. A house-letting *sayan* would find a building for surveillance purposes for a *kidon* on a mission. A bank-executive *sayan* could be guaranteed to provide funds; a *sayan* doctor medical assistance. Each *sayan* received only expenses and frequently did not claim them.

Sayanim sometimes found themselves being used by *kidon* teams. Each team consisted of twelve members: four were responsible for carrying out the actual assassination; the others provided backup target surveillance, driving the hit team and exfiltrating them and making sure there was no pursuit afterwards.

To maintain them at peak operational level the teams constantly practised, travelling to cities all over Europe and North America. They were accompanied by their instructors; they chose local *sayanim* who were told only that they were to be used as part of a security exercise to protect a local synagogue, school or shop. During an exercise they could be snatched off a quiet street or have their homes broken into during the night and awaken to find a *kidon* standing over them.

Input from a number of headquarters staff had been called upon to discuss the fate of Robert Maxwell.

Library staff had updated his biography. Any changes in his relationships with his wife and children were noted. Details of his latest mistress were included, along with the names of other women with whom he had casual affairs. His eating and sleeping habits were recorded, along with the names and positions of his personal staff, including his chef, valet, pilot and the captain of his yacht. Their biographical details were summarised. One of them was a *sayan*, appointed shortly after Maxwell had been recruited by Mossad.

Maxwell's business activities were documented. The names of companies he had sold or acquired were listed, along with their directors and business carried out. At least one company had a *sayan* on its staff. The Finance Office on the seventh floor had provided a current portfolio of all Maxwell holdings. There were files on his relationship with banks all over the world, showing the latest intelligence on his massive debts and the state of his share holdings. In an addendum were transcripts of electronic intercepts exposing his 'rush' for money to repay his debts.

That Mossad file on Maxwell concluded with a paragraph extracted from a Department of Trade report on his methods:

'He is a man of great energy, drive and imagination, but unfortunately an apparent fixation as to his own abilities causes him to ignore the views of others if these are not compatible.'

Those words were written in 1971 but now they would form part of the decision-making process about his fate.

Mossad desks in London, New York and Washington, as well as those in Europe, had all contributed assessments on Maxwell's relationships with a number of names prominent in Mossad files. These included Mikhail Gorbachev, then the Soviet leader; Vladimir Kryuchkov, until recently head of the KGB; and a number of Mafia bosses in Eastern Europe. Maxwell had brokered deals with all of them. The month before, August, Kryuchkov had been involved in a plot to oust Mikhail Gorbachev from office while he was engaged in creating *perestroika*, the first steps in introducing democracy to Russia.

Right-wing elements in the Red Army and the KGB were appalled at the prospect. In the utmost secrecy they had plotted in dachas outside Moscow. A key issue was what would be the response of the West to such a coup. Would they regard it, if successful, as an internal matter for the Soviet Union? Or would it precipitate a freeze in the relations Gorbachev was trying to foster with Washington and European nations?

It was Kryuchkov who had suggested he should enlist the services of Robert Maxwell to act as a thermometer to test the water. Kryuchkov believed that Maxwell, not for the first time, would have relished the opportunity to take part in such secret back-door diplomacy. Previous meetings with the KGB chief had eventually led to some 300,000 Soviet Jews being allowed to emigrate to Israel.

But the coup had failed and Kryuchkov was now, on that September day, in a Moscow prison threatening to reveal Maxwell's relationship with him. Mossad had hoped it would be enough to contain that threat by discrediting the former KGB chief. But, in the past days, Mossad had received more disturbing news. To save his own skin, Kryuchkov was going to say that, through Maxwell, Israel itself had been involved in the coup. While there was no truth in that, the repercussions from such an allegation would be serious.

Washington continued to support Gorbachev as the only hope for the Soviet Union to become democratic. Even a suspicion that Israel had been ready to stop that happening in exchange for having more Soviet Jews allowed to emigrate would endanger Mossad's own relationship with the CIA and the National Security Agency, from whom it received valuable satellite data on any hostile moves by its Arab neighbours.

Some Mossad officers had echoed the words of Meir Amit: 'Maxwell should never have got mixed up with Kryuchkov.'

This was not a time for Maxwell to come to Mossad and demand help with his own pressing financial concerns. But Maxwell once more displayed the side of his personality that courted danger. He was still famous, powerful, admired, respected and feared. So he believed. He also urgently needed at least £400 million to stave off his more pressing creditors.

He asked Mossad to use its influence with Israel's bankers to arrange a loan. He was told to try to do what his fellow tycoon, Rupert Murdoch, had done when he had faced a similar situation. Murdoch had confessed his plight to his bankers and then renegotiated his debts, which were almost twice what Maxwell owed.

Another side of Maxwell's make-up was his stubbornness and blind anger if he felt he was being thwarted. The elements had been there in all his business dealings and, there can be no doubt, they had helped him to survive.

Robert Maxwell had told those senior Mossad officers that he would not go cap in hand, begging to the bankers. He would expect Mossad to help him.

Or else.

For Ari Ben-Menashe, a former Israeli intelligence adviser, it was 'clear he was saying he would blow the whistle on all he knew about Mossad. That was a threat no one could expect to get away with.'

For the meeting the psychologists on the sixth floor had provided an evaluation drawn from a number of sources, including senior Mossad staff who had recently met Maxwell in Israel and elsewhere. The evaluation contained details of his health, his current physical and mental states and medication he was taking. His weight was included.

There was a note of his girth, a 56-inch waist and a neck size of 21 inches. The length of Maxwell's arms and even the way he 'dressed' in his trousers were recorded. The information had been obtained from the Tel Aviv tailor Maxwell sometimes used.

The names and addresses of all his doctors were attached. They included Dr Paul Gilbert, a general physician at the Mount Sinai Hospital in New York; he had been recommended to Maxwell by Henry Kissinger, but had yet to be consulted.

Details of Maxwell's personal security system were listed. This included coded swipe cards to gain entry to his inner sanctum at Maxwell House in London; the cards were changed every day. A video camera filmed everyone entering and leaving his penthouse; the tapes were reviewed every night and a detailed report sent to Maxwell for his breakfast reading next day. There was a constant search for secret microphones planted by his enemies, real or imagined; a spectrum analyser traced any unauthorised transmissions in Maxwell House. A special security team regularly swept the building. The telephone switchboard and all executive offices on the ninth floor were bugged. Maxwell's incipient paranoia was a match for any of the dictators he numbered among his friends.

All the information was contained in a buff-coloured file that bore no words on its cover. Copies had been brought to the conference room close to the office of the Director of Operations. The room's walls were painted a shade of green. The glass in the window, like all those in the building, was designed to deflect bugging devices. A fluorescent tube provided lighting. The furnishings consisted of a conference table and moulded plastic bucket seats. Metal ashtrays were scattered around the table.

As well as the four members of *kidon*, there were present senior staff from the Directorate of Operations. There was a lawyer from the Legal Department.

Also present was a member of staff from the office of the current director-general of Mossad, Shabtai Shavit. Some of the men around the table shared the view of colleagues elsewhere in Mossad that Shavit had, in the words of one still-serving officer, 'the manner of a front-desk clerk in one of Tel Aviv's lesser hotels; the same carefully pressed clothes and a handshake that never maintained its grip for long.'

Shavit had taken over from Nahum Admoni just a year before and his predecessor had been a hard act to follow. Admoni had worked undercover for Mossad in Ethiopia, Paris and Washington. The postings had helped to turn him into a soft-spoken but hard-nosed bureaucrat. The former CIA director William Casey described Admoni's personality as that 'of a man who can listen in half a dozen languages. He climbed through the ranks because of his skills at avoiding his superiors' "corns". In Mossad he ran a tight ship.'

The meeting would later be described by Victor Ostrovsky as 'one of right-wingers'. Ari Ben-Menashe would call them 'a cabal who had to move carefully. Maxwell still had powerful connections which enabled him to still open doors to the highest in the land.'

The scene inside the conference room was familiar to its occupants. Those who arrived wearing jackets quickly draped them over their chair backs; informality was a requisite for all Mossad meetings from the day of Meir Amit. The air in the room was soon thickened with cigarette smoke and ashtrays filled with butts.

Efraim, one of the *kidon*, would recall that permeating the atmosphere were two overwhelming questions: 'If the truth about Robert Maxwell surfaces and he is destroyed in the process, who else will be compromised? How great will the damage be to Israel?'

All else would depend on the answers.

TWO

On that September day in 1991, Robert Maxwell had reached the age of sixty-eight years, three months and twelve days. Like much else about himself, he had varied the actual hour of his birth as after midnight, close to 6 a.m. and at midday on 10 June 1923. The reason for the discrepancies may have been a conceit constantly to impress upon others his grasp on detail and his unchallengeable memory.

But the matter of his recall of the precise time he had arrived into the world had become a small part of the sophist's empire he had created. Its survival now largely depended on his recollection of what he had previously promised his many debtors. Bankers, he had long learned, were impressed by someone who could summon up the smallest detail, in Maxwell's case with a flick of a thick, stubby thumb against forefinger, and a vulpine smile.

In truth no record existed of the hour he arrived, one of seven children born to Mechel and Hannah in the village of Slatinske Doly, in a remote corner of what became Czechoslovakia. On that day in 1923 the infant who later became Robert Maxwell was born with small unanswered mysteries that would lead to far greater ones in his adult life. What was his birth weight? Was it an easy birth? Who acted as midwife? Who had chosen his name, Abraham Leib, shortened at home to the diminutive, Leiby? Had that been a decision of his strong-willed mother or of his father?

His mother Hannah had been a Schlomovitch, one of the long-established Jewish families in that part of Europe where the Carpathian mountains run down to the River Tiza. It was a place of folklore: of stories of strange creatures in the surrounding forests, of girls being casually impregnated and their babies left out to die in the winterscape. Superstition was rife and scores were often settled by husbands or fathers with a knife or axe.

16

There was another bloodstain on the land. Anti-Semitism had been an unabated and all-consuming tidal wave that crossed mountains and rivers, driven on by a terrible lust to seek out and destroy any Jew. No matter how young or old, he or she had been put to the sword or burned on a pyre. The stench of death once hung like a pall over forests and fields as the Magyars, the Bulgars and the Russian Orthodox priests had chanted their refrain of 'Kill the Christ Killers', and slaughtered Jews in their tens of thousands.

The survivors of the pogroms of the Polish Galicia were driven westwards into the jaws of the Austro-Hungarian empire. Murdered in their beds, raped as they were about to give birth, but still steadfast in their faith and united by a common language, Yiddish, those Jews who had somehow survived had gathered in groups, which had become ghettos where they baked their *challah* bread for the Sabbath, and said that surely one day it would be better.

And in Slatinske Doly, it had seemed it *would* be by the time Hannah gave birth on that summer's day in 1923. Her neighbours were a mixture of Hassidin, Orthodox and Marmaros Jews who had settled the village two centuries previously. It was a place where Jews were allowed to sell their goods to their Christian neighbours; some even had licences to offer alcohol. They were permitted to educate their children in the Judaic faith and to wear their traditional dress and speak their own language.

Haunted by their own cruel past – there was hardly a family in the village that had not lost relatives in the pogroms – they lived frugal lives within the sanctity of their faith; the Sabbath was the high point of the week, and religious holidays the only brief few hours to relax from their grindingly harsh existence.

The villagers knew little of the world outside, and what information did reach them was vetted and carefully presented by their rabbis, who shaped every thought and decision in the community, handing out punishments according to Scripture.

Unlike Hannah, Mechel could claim no family name that could be traced back through the generations. His ancestors arrived in Slatinske Doly when it was already settled. Like many others, they came from peasant stock and were probably illiterate.

No one could remember how Mechel's great-grandfather had earned his living. His grandfather had sold horses while his own father had made a modest income in cattle dealing. Mechel's father would set off in the pre-dawn, walking from one smallholding to another, his hide pouch filled with food and water for the day, and coins in his pocket. He always had a stout stick in his hand to ward off any of the thieves who roamed the area looking for victims. Mechel's father was a giant, well over six feet and strong; his reputation for cracking heads with his stick was renowned and he was given a wide berth by any robber. Sometimes on his journeys he would buy pelts of foxes, rabbits and forest rats. These he sold to the local Christian women to sew onto their topcoats.

Then, in the early part of the twentieth century, when the area was still under Hungarian control, an official had visited the village to conduct a census, much like the head count the Romans had held at the time of the birth of Christ. The man spoke German but no Hebrew or Yiddish. Arriving at Mechel's home to note down its members, he found it impossible to write the family name. He had solved the matter with a stroke of the pen. Henceforth the family would be known as Hoch, the German word for tall.

The name change did nothing to improve the family's social standing in the village. They still lived with all the other relative newcomers, collectively known by the long-settled families as *luft menschen*, those who had arrived on the harsh Siberian winds and still 'lived on air', using their wits, cunning and, where possible, charm to eke out a living.

A Hoch was not someone the daughter of the Schlomovitches would have been expected to marry.

How Hannah had met Mechel is another of those little mysteries lost in time: it might have been at the local synagogue or *schul* or during one of the religious holidays. Legend has it he was wide across the shoulders and endearing in the childlike way some strong men have when they seek approval of the weak.

What little else has passed down about Mechel suggests he was a man of even temper, quiet and careful in his views. It is therefore likely that Maxwell had been imbued with his mother's gifts: a woman who was outspoken about the injustices of their life just because they were Jews. The image of her which would survive would come much later from Maxwell. 'Intelligent and well informed, different from other local women. She was passionate about the need to improve the masses through greater social justice,' Isabel remembered him saying.

Certainly there is independent confirmation that Hannah was a political activist and a believer in Zionism, the movement to re-establish a Jewish nation in Palestine. She would appear to be the source for the claims her son would later make for his own staunch Zionism. Less certain is how he knew from early on that she was sure that when he reached adulthood he would 'become a great rabbi because rabbis were powerful men. She had a vision of moulding my future so that later on the family would all move to Palestine where we would live and work in dignity which had been denied her,' he told Isabel.

Hannah was not exactly pretty, though she had her fine angles. Any single photograph of her would not have done her justice. She was small and dark-eyed, with the thin lips and weathered skin that came to women

early on in life who work for long hours in the open tilling, at a wash tub
or fetching water from a nearby stream.

The children arrived at regular intervals: the eldest was named Brana,
then came Abraham Leib (the future Robert Maxwell), followed by
Chaim, Shenie, Sylvia, Zissel and Cipra – solemn-faced infants with
strong features and olive-toned skins. Two would die in infancy, taken by
the chills that became pneumonia and for which there was no medicine.
Their mother helped her husband lower the corpses into their graves.

For the surviving infants it meant more food to share, an extra spoonful
of cabbage soup and a piece of bread to wipe clean the bowl. At night it
meant a little more room in the children's bed.

In 1919 Hoch, as a family name, ceased to exist. In the realignment of
Europe after World War One, Slatinske Doly was absorbed into the new
state of Czechoslovakia. An official from Prague arrived in the village.
With another stroke of the pen, the family were henceforth to be known as
the Ludviks.

Maxwell's father – or perhaps his mother – named him Abraham. In a
land that had been ruled by the Slovaks, Ukrainians, Romanians, Germans
and now the Czechs, to call a son by one of the most treasured of all
biblical names was a reminder that no amount of pressure would destroy
the essential Jewish faith that sustained them. Nevertheless, when it came
to registering the infant, on the advice of a Czech official that it was
important for the boy also to have an undisputed Czech name in a
fledgeling nation where nationalism was rife, Abraham's parents agreed to
add a further forename, Jan. The future Robert Maxwell was, for the next
few years, Jan Abraham Ludvik.

Later, when he learned how this had happened, who can doubt that he
understood the importance of having the right name, if not exactly the
right background to make his mark on the world?

In the winters Mechel's beard froze on his face as he pulled his sledge
to and from the family field. On the outward journey he brought food for
his few calves, and wood as he made his way home. Like Henry Ford, a
man he had never heard of, for there were no cars in the area, Mechel no
doubt also believed the logs he chopped kept him twice as warm. At night
he and Hannah slept fully clothed, going to bed early to save candle wax
and before the flames flickered and died in the kitchen store. Most nights
the wind howled through the cob walls of their cottage, lifting the single
goose quilt over the children (the quilt was a gift from Hannah's family).

In spring the snow would melt, sending water flooding into the cottage,
turning its clay floor into a sodden mess until the fierce sun of summer
baked it hard. Those were the days Hannah could air the winter garments
and Mechel could go to work bare-backed. Then, around the time of
Passover, would come the autumn rains, violent storms accompanied by

lightning and thunder louder than any gunfire. And finally the annual cycle would be completed with the return of the snows. 'Slatinske Doly is one hell of a place,' Maxwell's daughter, Isabel, later recalled her father saying.

This, then, was the world the infant son of Hannah and Mechel had been born into. A lifetime later he would synthesise it into one saying he never tired of repeating. 'I and my family were observant Jews. I believe in God, the God of Israel. I believe in the ethical lessons of Judaism. I love and admire my people's devotion to the study of the Torah. I definitely see myself as a Jew. I was born a Jew and I shall die a Jew, so help me God.'

By the time he did die, he had not only hurt many others of his faith, ruining some for ever who tried to live by its rules and observations, but had also left a scar on Judaism itself, his very actions giving his many enemies an opportunity to rekindle the anti-Semitism that would exist through his life. He became a symbol for the blood lie that a Jew could not be trusted.

But all that was for the future.

An unforgettable moment in the family's life was the day after the harvest was gathered. From the time they could walk, the children helped to collect the stubble and pile it up outside the cottage. Then their mother would bring out the mattresses and strip off their covers. The sour-smelling straw was carried off to be used later as winter bedding for the family cow. The covers were boiled in a cauldron to kill the lice and hung out to dry overnight. Next day the stubble was stuffed into the covers until they resembled small hayricks. That night the family slept on their luxurious new mattresses and for a few weeks the cottage was filled with the sweet smell of straw.

Maxwell's closeness to his mother is a documented fact. She taught him to read, to understand the significance of the traditional Friday evening meal and all its attendant symbols: making sure his hands were freshly washed, that his head was properly bowed while his father said the opening grace, that he waited his turn to take the freshly cut piece of the *challah* bread. When he was old enough he was taught the prayers that would be said after the meal; by five his piping voice was joining in the singing of the final blessing, the hallelujahs and the concluding amen. On Saturdays he took his place beside his mother in synagogue.

He was a swift learner: by ten he could write better than his father; he was quick and clever in argument; years later his teacher, a Rabbi Teitelbaum, was able to remember 'his analytical ability and uncanny aptitude for learning and retaining what he was taught. He could have become a rabbi.'

His boyhood years were to encourage his passion later in life for soccer. The ball was made of rags bound with strips of cowhide. A later reporter would describe him as 'a very aggressive centre forward and the other children liked to be on his side because they invariably won the match'.

There were the usual signposts that mark the life of every Jewish boy: circumcision; his first day at *heder*, the village school; bar mitzvah; the first wedding he attended. Through Pesach, Rosa Hashanah, Yom Kippur, Succoth and Hanukkah, the Jewish holidays marked his progress from childhood to the first years of his teens.

By then he had the prominent cheekbones and strong jawline and the slightly slanting eyes of a Slav. His mouth had begun to settle in the sensuous lines of later years. Jet-black hair matched his arching eyebrows.

Every inch he grew, every pound of weight he added to his frame was noted by his mother.

Later others would emerge from the childhood of the man Robert Maxwell became, to conjure up fond memories of his mother. A nephew remembered how she 'picked up every piece of newspaper in the street to discover what was going on'. Another claimed she was 'an exception in the village because she read books. She was almost an intellectual.' A third relative would recall her as 'an exemplary cook of kosher food'.

These harmless attributes were promoted by Maxwell, who, as well as carefully and continuously nurturing his own image, set about ensuring Hannah had her place in his pantheon. She became the parent who not only gave him his socialist values but the woman who foresaw what the world's economic system would lead to: the Depression, the Weimar Republic, the emergence of Hitler. From her, he insisted, came his own driving ambition, part of which was to encourage him to master a number of languages. He would become fluent in eight.

She was the parent who warned him he would have to make his own way in life, that perhaps he should even consider going to America – going anywhere instead of staying in Slatinske Doly. To stay there was to sink slowly but inevitably into poverty. And, perhaps hardest of all for her to bear, she had told her son that he should 'try not to look so Jewish'. He stopped using the name Abraham and became Jan Ludvik.

It was an understandable protection given what was happening in neighbouring Germany. Anti-Semitism was once more on the rampage. Hitler filled the airwaves with demands of *lebensraum*. By 1938 the Sudentenland, the German-speaking part of Czechoslovakia, was in Nazi hands. A year later, under the Munich agreement, the country of Jan Ludvik's birthplace had suffered the same fate.

By then, encouraged by his mother, Maxwell was gone from Slatinske Doly. He would like to remember her parting words: 'If you are ambitious, there is nothing that is impossible.'

While that benediction may well have served as her leitmotif for him, his other personality traits that later emerged were of his own creation: his obsessive need for self-aggrandisement; the easy way he played fast and loose with the truth; his personal vanity – for many years he would dye his hair an unnatural black; his blustering manner, relentless bullying and fearful rages. He carried with him another suggestion from his mother. She is credited by him as saying that 'to behave and act like an Englishman is to be successful'. Perhaps the thought had come to her from one of those scraps of paper she picked up off the muddy streets of his birthplace.

But to be a quintessential Englishman would require a suitable biography that matched the times. As Winston Churchill's storm clouds gathered over Europe, Jan Ludvik set about burnishing his image.

If truth is always the first casualty of war, then Robert Maxwell became one of its victims in the second great conflict to engulf Europe in the twentieth century.

There is no one documented moment when his dream of becoming a heroic figure took root. Were the first seeds sown when he had to fend for himself now his mother was no longer there to protect him? She had chosen his clothes for his first step into the outside world – second-hand to be sure, but he would quickly grow into his black coat and thick woollen shirt and country-boy boots. Hannah had even found enough money to keep him going for a month.

He was taller and older-looking than his years, his face filling out, the jaw more jutting, the eyes more piercing. He looked like someone who could have been in his early twenties, not a sixteen-year-old. Perhaps it was his outward physical maturity that encouraged his heroic dreams. They were undoubtedly enhanced by listening to the older men he chose to mix with in that part of Bratislava. They were simple pious Jews who, sensing what was happening, filled their days and nights talking of how they would fight and, if needs be, die for their beloved Czechoslovakia. He had never met such patriotism before and perhaps that too contributed to his need to be a hero.

War was certainly coming, and coming closer by the day. Hitler's Germany was exerting pressure, a huge dark and ever-expanding blot. Already the villagers who had remained in Slatinske Doly had lost their Czech citizenship and had become Hungarian again, a move that had effectively stripped them of any rights: they were now part of the *untermenschen* culture of Nazi Germany.

His immediate thought had been to rescue his parents and siblings. At nights, in his iron cot bed, he dreamed his impossible dream of single-handedly whisking them out of Europe to the sanctuary of Palestine. But in the dawn that dream would fade.

Those he shared his dreams with while drinking coffee in a backstreet café had told him anyway not to be a young fool. To go back to the village would be a virtual guarantee of being caught up in the tentacles of the Third Reich, which was reaching out for not only the remains of their homeland, but also for Austria and Poland. If it was action he wanted, then there was plenty to be found. The radio was filled with diatribes against 'dirty Jew terrorists'. There was plenty of room in their ranks. That may well have been the moment when the legends that would follow took shape in his mind.

Later he would polish them with the same care and consummate skill he used to create a share prospectus or a company flotation. They were more than the boastings of a lonely teenager, though there was an element of that too: they were deliberate transgressions of the truth, the creations of a mind that needed to assure the world he was different from all others.

It was a craving that, in the end, contributed to more dangerous fabrications, more reckless deceptions, more blatant lying. Those early fictions about his derring-do deeds in the fight against Hitler in 1939, the last year of peace in Europe, were to become the props that supported his unswerving belief in his own greatness, his total invincibility and readiness to bully and destroy anyone who dared to move against him.

Even before World War Two had started, he cast himself in a role that, if true, was undeniably heroic. 'I had been tapped on the shoulder on a street corner in December 1939 in Budapest to join the local Czech resistance movement fighting the Nazis in the city. I was only sixteen but I gave my age as nineteen so I could join the fight,' he later told the BBC.

There was no Czech resistance fighting in Budapest at the time because there were no German soldiers in the city.

The story would be well received by all those accountants, bankers and lawyers who, after the war, began to fill his life. In every telling the details were somewhat different. But he understood the basic rule of a man born to perform, of never leaving time for awkward questions, of always moving quickly on to the climax, then changing the subject. It never failed.

But, like all good actors, he needed more stories to hold his audience in thrall, to show them how remarkably *different* he indeed was from them. So another element was added to the script of his early war years.

He claimed in that same BBC broadcast: 'I joined the Czech army and fought the Germans and the Russians in Eastern Europe, made a fighting retreat to the Black Sea and back to France via Bulgaria and Greece in time for another crack at the Germans. I was wounded and captured in Orleans, but escaped.

'Later I was arrested, tortured and beaten up and sentenced to death as a spy. I escaped the death penalty thanks to the intervention of the French ambassador and subsequently escaped imprisonment because my guard was handicapped with only one arm.'

For men whose war had only been a blip before they returned to the panelled comfort of their boardrooms, the words of this action man were about another world. He was not just a hero, he was *their* hero. How many times did they sit back as he told them about a wartime Europe filled with terrible danger and killing, of hand-to-hand combat, of escapades few men would ever have survived, let alone imagine? And then, the show over, he would leave, smiling his wolfish smile, their cheque in his pocket.

Having created a colourful background for himself, he finally enlisted fact in support. In 1940 he had reached the French port of Marseilles. There he joined the Second Regiment of the Czech Legion before sailing to Liverpool in May of that year. Maxwell's first glimpse of wartime Britain was the long train journey south to the legion's base outside Dover.

He spoke almost no English, but was impressed by the cheerful behaviour of the people. He sensed that, unlike the French, they were not ready to surrender. At various stations the train stopped to take on water and coal and they gave him tea and cigarettes. The first words he began to understand were 'Welcome, you are one of us.' His mother had been right. To be an Englishman was indeed to be different.

He could not feel so kindly towards his fellow Czech troopers. They made clear their dislike, hatred even, of Jews. During the journey his ears continued to ring with phrases like 'The Jews got us into this war' and 'Why should we care what happens to them?'

He hated such calumny. But he had the good sense to keep his feelings to himself. He simply smiled and promised himself that at the first opportunity he would transfer out of the legion.

In 1941 Maxwell took the unusual step of requesting to join the British Army's Pioneer Corps. Just as the *luftmenschen* of his birthplace had been at the bottom of the village social scale, so the Pioneer Corps were looked upon as 'white coolies' by the rest of the army.

But for the man who now had decided to call himself Jan Hoch, it was the first step towards fulfilling his mother's dream that he should become an Englishman. He set about achieving this in his first posting with the corps to Sutton Coldfield, near Birmingham. In between his duties he persuaded a local woman to improve his English. As well as teaching him the difference between vowels and consonants, she introduced him to the finer points of English life: that when seated a man always stood up if a woman entered a room; milk was always poured into the cup first, and tea never slurped. After a Sunday afternoon lesson, she taught him to play whist and dominoes, the staples of English social life at the time. He learned how to dance and to carry out polite small talk – something he never became good at.

He developed a sense of humour by listening to radio comedy shows such as *It's That Man Again* (*ITMA*). And, just as his mother had supposedly picked up scraps of newspapers to read, so her son digested every newspaper or magazine he could lay his hands on. He was perhaps the best-informed soldier on the base.

Slowly he assumed the mannerisms of an Englishman born and bred to serve his king and country. Week by week his guttural *mittel*-European accent faded, to be replaced by the somewhat clipped vowels of the Midlands. These he would later refine to a more polished tone. It was no doubt hard work, but, for a twenty-year-old who had grown into a tall, handsome man and who casually dropped stories about his previous combat experience, the future beckoned brightly.

In October 1943, he felt confident enough to write to the commanding officer of the Sixth Battalion of the North Staffordshire Regiment asking to enlist in its ranks. How much help his English tutor had been in couching the letter is another of those little mysteries that Maxwell would never discuss. His personal relationship with her was also something he would avoid – 'A gentleman never speaks of such matters,' he later told a young reporter.

But this may have been the time he lost his virginity. Certainly he had developed the attributes of a lady's man: a natural gallantry in opening doors and lighting a woman's cigarette, on leading her around a NAAFI dance floor to the sound of Glenn Miller. He also knew how to get hold of a pair of much-sought-after American silk stockings, extra rations and sometimes even a bottle of genuine bourbon. He was, in that respect, one of that not uncommon breed of that time in uniform: a fixer.

His first documented love affair was with a nurse. She later described him as 'enchanting, fascinating, infuriating. His character was mercurial, most exuberant but sometimes deeply melancholic. At times he appeared almost illiterate, but at others he displayed such a breadth and depth of knowledge that he might have lived a hundred years. No one who knew him could ever forget him.'

The relationship lasted two years and, by all accounts, had a deep and lasting effect on him for, through this young nurse he was introduced into the refined world of the English upper class. Her wealthy parents welcomed him into their home and turned a blind eye to their suspicion that he was sleeping with their daughter. This was wartime and the moral climate had changed beyond measure. For his part, 'I was quick to notice the standards and manners, language and behaviour of her family and copied them immediately, thereby acquiring a polish that had been lacking.'

His mother would have been proud of her son.

His letter to the Sixth Battalion made its way up to the regiment's commanding officer. He noted that Maxwell claimed he had German-language skills and combat experience. The regiment's 17th Infantry Brigade was instructed to find a place for Maxwell in its intelligence unit.

On a cold November morning in 1943, Maxwell presented himself at brigade headquarters at Clifton on the outskirts of Bristol under the name of Leslie du Maurier. In his letter of application he had explained he was using the name 'so that when I once more see action and by misfortune am captured, the Germans will not know my true background'.

It was a reason that endeared him to his new commanding officer.

The infant briefly named Abraham Ludvik, then Jan Abraham Ludvik, then Jan Ludvik and Jan Hoch, had now chosen to name himself after a cigarette. The Du Maurier brand was one of the most popular in wartime Britain among its middle and upper classes.

In 1944 the newly created Corporal du Maurier was in the second wave of Normandy landings. He was promoted to sergeant. The brigade records showed he distinguished himself both as a sniper and interrogator. During his questioning of German prisoners he began to refer to himself as Leslie Jones. In the heat of battle no one wondered at why he had once more changed his name. His former regimental sergeant major was to recall that 'people did weird things in war'.

Shortly after his 21st birthday, Maxwell was promoted to second lieutenant. Before handing out his officer's pips, his commanding officer took him aside and suggested that neither du Maurier nor Jones was a suitable name for an officer and gentleman in the North Staffs. He suggested a Scottish alias would be more acceptable. Once more he assumed a new name and became Ian Robert Maxwell. Ian was the Anglicised version of the Jan that the anonymous Czech official had indicated should be attached to the infant's name at the registration of his birth.

From now on, to the world he would be known only as Robert Maxwell. A resounding name, if not exactly an Englishman's, created by the stroke of his brigadier's pen.

Gone for ever – or at least locked away in one of the many secret compartments in Robert Maxwell's mind – were those childhood memories: of how he and his siblings had all slept in one bed; how their privy was an outside lavatory bucket in a wooden frame over a pit that was emptied once a year by the poorest of the *luftmenschen*; how the family staple diet had been potatoes in summer and, on feast days, a piece of smoked fish; how he had walked barefoot in summer and shared his shoes with his brothers and sisters in winter. 'We took turns to wear a pair to school in the morning and another of us walked home in them. We carried newspaper to stuff them to adjust the foot sizes.' Perhaps they were the scraps of newsprint their mother had picked up in the street.

But all this was in the past. In his newly tailored officer's uniform, its belt and buttons burnished, his shoes mirror-polished, Second Lieutenant Robert Maxwell was a striking figure in the officer's mess of his regiment. He could hold his gin and tonic with the best of them and he paid his mess bills on time. The man from nowhere had indeed become an insider.

There was only one item lacking. A wife.

Maxwell's war from now on required no embellishment. The regimental records show he fought with distinction in a number of fierce engagements, including the crossing of the River Orne, an especially bloody fight against an SS Panzer unit. One moment captures the mood. The Germans had launched a counterattack. British troops were fleeing. The records show that Maxwell stood there, 'gesticulating and shouting "Go back and pump bullets into those Jerries or I'll turn my machine gun on you." At that moment a mortar exploded, leaving a young soldier paralysed with fear. Maxwell rushed forward and picked him up and ran with him on his shoulder as far as the cellar of a house, where he left him to receive medical attention.'

There were other examples of his bravery and his risk-taking. Who can doubt they played a part in what he became?

In September 1944, Robert Maxwell arrived in newly liberated Paris. He was in the French capital for a few days of well-deserved rest and recreation. Like hundreds of Allied officers he had been given one address to contact, the offices of the Paris Welcome Committee in the Place de la Madeleine. Its stated aim was 'to arrange as many pairings as possible between battle-weary Allied servicemen and Parisians who want to entertain them'.

Among those who effected introductions was Elizabeth Maynard, the daughter of a silk merchant. Though pitifully thin from wartime rationing, the 23-year-old was pretty and vivacious with dark hair, a gentle smile and natural good manners.

She was working in her cubbyhole office when she was summoned to that of her superior. The memory of what followed became part of the Maxwell family history, to be preserved in its private archive in their chateau in France. Early on in life, Isabel was to recall, her mother told her how Maxwell's presence filled the room on that day in Paris. 'My dad stood there in uniform with a pistol strapped to his thigh and his beret set at a rakish angle. He was like a character Errol Flynn could have played.'

Betty swooned. She told her children it was love at first sight. 'She said her legs felt all wobbly and she thought she was going to faint.'

Catching her in his arms, Robert Maxwell decided she was hungry.

In a world of changing moral values, Betty had clung fiercely to her Protestant middle-class background, which had served her own 'moral rudder' through the long years of Nazi occupation. It had kept her, she would recall, 'still protected from the storms of life'.

But now she was embarking on uncertain seas. In a few months, shortly after Field Marshal Montgomery had personally pinned the Military Cross on Maxwell's chest for bravery under fire, the couple were married. Betty wore the white dress and veil her bridegroom had somehow procured, once again displaying his incredible skills at fixing.

It was a glorious end to his war. But, while many of his comrades were content to look forward to demobilisation, Robert Maxwell was already looking beyond, to the first steps that would make him rich and powerful beyond his wildest dreams. For the moment he shared them only with his bride.

For Betty's part, she believed fervently in his future. Love – what Baudelaire had called 'that terrible game in which one of the players loses self-control' – had taken control of her life. Isabel would say her mother was content to look into her father's face – 'that mysterious and attractive face of extraordinary mobility' – and ignore how it could change in a moment. Only much later would Betty recognise the effect those mood changes would have on her – 'a strange, steely mask, sending a chill right through you,' she told Isabel.

Like any young bride who had found her man, Betty hung on his every word. Isabel would say her father was 'a natural optimist and was already looking ahead. My mother said it all when she later wrote "the shadow of his destiny lay heavy on his strong shoulders." My mother had a way with words and she could create a picture of my dad at that time of being very manly and certain. She painted this memory of his "swiftly moving lips, thick and red like two ripe fruits". My mother was a true romantic,' Isabel recalled.

Truly, Baudelaire had been right about the perils of love blinded.

The emotions of Betty Maxwell who, despite all he had later done to her, to his children, to so many others, would not for a moment diminish her love for him.

But none of this mattered at another meeting held later in that September of 1991 in Tel Aviv.

This time, the meeting was not held within Mossad headquarters but within one of its safe houses. Such a venue was always chosen as *kidon* advanced its plans.

THREE

Ten days after the first meeting, a technician from Mossad's internal security unit, Authat Paylut Medienit (APM) had entered a building in Pinsker Street in downtown Tel Aviv. He was casually dressed and carried a shopping bag. He had been here many times and did not bother to use the box-cage elevator to reach the first floor. He made his way down a corridor to a door towards the end. The door had no handle. A metal flap concealed the keyhole.

From his bag the man produced a small gadget no bigger than a television remote. He used a finger to push aside the flap, then held the instrument to the hole. There was a click of tumblers and the door opened sideways into a wall recess. The technician entered a small lobby and pressed a button on the wall. The door closed behind him. He was now inside the Mossad safe house chosen for the second meeting to discuss Robert Maxwell.

The hall led into the apartment's four rooms. To Efraim, a former *kidon*, 'it was furnished from a garage sale. Chairs, tables and other bits and pieces: nothing seems to match. The prints on the wall are the kind you can pick up in any bazaar. The carpet on the floor is standard army issue.'

Each room had its own two single beds and an unlisted telephone. The kitchen contained a secure line to a computer and a fax machine. There was a high-speed shredder, a wall safe and a fridge.

The main living room had a video player in a corner, and a dining table that doubled as a conference area. There were chairs for half a dozen people. The room's windows, like all those in the apartment, were permanently shaded with venetian blinds. The only view through the slats was on to an alley, which ran off Pinsker Street. Fluorescent tubes gave off a hard bright light. The overall effect was cold and impersonal.

According to Victor Ostrovsky, the safe houses were mostly used by trainees from the Mossad school on field trips when they came into the

29

city to learn street craft: how to tail someone; how to set up a dead-letter box or pass on information in public concealed inside a newspaper. Day and night the trainees worked in the streets of Tel Aviv under the watchful eyes of their instructors. They learned how to sit in cafés and memorise *fibers* – precise physical descriptions of people there and what they said. They discovered the black art of *neviof*, how to break into a hotel bedroom, an office or any other given target and plant listening devices. Endlessly they practised *masluh*, the skill needed to establish whether they were being followed. They were shown the *slicks*, hiding places for documents they had been told to steal. Back in a safe house like the one on Pinsker Street the lessons continued: how to write special-ink letters and use the computer to create information capable of being sent in short-burst transmissions.

The trainees also had to decide which of the documents they had stolen were genuine and which had been created by their instructors. A mistake or a wrong answer too many abruptly put an end to a trainee's hope of graduating into the ranks of Mossad.

Sometimes a *katsa*, a field agent, coming or going from a mission stayed in a safe house, receiving a final briefing or being debriefed. One had been Eli Cohen, who had worked for a quarter of a century under cover in all parts of the world, but who never forgot 'the moment of tension you felt when you left a safe house for a mission or the relief when you came back in when it was over'.

Once a year a crew known as 'the Housekeepers' came to each safe house to give it a paint-over and replace any furnishings past their usefulness. The computer and other equipment were checked on a regular basis for any electronic interference. Those who made these checks were from *yahalomin*, Mossad's communications unit.

On that mid-September day, the APM technician had a specific task. From the shopping bag he took a black box with two short antennae at one end. He began to move them steadily over the walls, ceilings and floor, going from one room to another, including the bathroom. He pointed the box towards the shower head and against the plumbing. He was looking for what he did not expect to find, a bugging device.

When trainees used safe houses, their instructors did plant such devices. There was a strict rule that there should be no discussion between them of their own activities. Later the trainees were confronted with what they had said. Trainees were also warned when they were a mixed group that there must be no sexual familiarity. More than one recruit had broken these rules over the years and had been instantly dismissed. But it still went on. For Victor Ostrovsky, 'Everyone was tied to everyone else through sex. That was how people advanced, by screwing their way to the top.'

But in the past few days the apartment had been placed off limits to everybody. Its fridge had been stocked with bottled water and snacks; fresh sheets were on the beds. A system had been installed whereby it was possible for any telephone call being made to appear to be originating in London, New York or any other capital city. These were routine preparations for what the safe house had become: a base for the four-man *kidon* in charge of planning the assassination of Robert Maxwell.

Two of the *kidon* had returned to their base in the Negev Desert. For Ari Ben-Menashe, 'What they were doing was essential in their kind of operation. The base line is getting to know your man, getting to know his style. How he reacts to a situation, what pushes his buttons. Only then can you construct an operational plan.'

One *kidon* from the pair had settled down in one of the base's viewing rooms to watch videos of Maxwell. These had been assembled over several days by Mossad's psychological-warfare department from material obtained through a number of television and newsreel sources.

The film sequence of Maxwell's earlier business life began when he had set up Pergamon Publishing, a specialist firm that effectively launched scientific publishing in postwar Britain. The clips of this period showed a smiling young man in his demob suit. From 1959 onwards, when Maxwell had embarked on a political career with his selection as a Labour Party candidate, the footage marked his steps: displaying at the hustings the same bravado with which he had charged German positions across France and into Germany. But instead of a troop carrier he used a bright-red Land Rover to hurtle through the constituency while campaigning and he would win by a good majority.

Once in Parliament he quickly managed to move up a rung, getting himself appointed to the House's catering committee. There he had stamped out the gross abuse among the kitchen staff who routinely smuggled out legs of mutton and rounds of bacon under their clothes.

In 1970 Maxwell stood for re-election. Everything seemed set for a second Labour term in office. But an always unpredictable electorate voted in a Conservative government. Maxwell lost his seat by more than 2,000 votes. The bitterness of defeat was all too clear on the face that peered out of the television news: a man close to tears, his jowls drooping. In war, Maxwell had made a reputation for counterattack. In election defeat, he sought a scapegoat, blaming his agent, who had managed his political life for four years. It was a sign of the mood swings that could bring down that steely mask which Betty Maxwell had been among the first to notice.

Then once more the ebullience had returned to the public face of Robert Maxwell. He had rescued from financial collapse the British Printing Corporation, which comprised a substantial portion of the country's newspaper and magazine publishing industry. He renamed it the Maxwell Communications Corporation, and it became the cornerstone of his empire-building. Three years later, in 1984, he had acquired Mirror Group Newspapers. From then on he had become a regular figure on the televised news bulletins in Britain, then Europe, and finally the United States. He had achieved that part of his dream: to become one of the best-known faces in the world. 'I'm up there with the Beatles and Presley,' he had been known to say. An exaggeration, but hyperbole had become part of his life.

It went with his unbridled confidence and a need to show off. He never tired of displaying his multilinguist skills, or the trappings of his success: the most expensive hand-made suits Savile Row could tailor, a vintage Rolls-Royce, a chauffeur and a personal retinue of secretaries and assistants. He had been filmed walking down a corridor, dictating; handling two telephone conversations at one time, interrupting both only to dictate to yet another secretary.

While other businessmen wondered about taking a taxi, he jumped on planes, flying all over the world to make deals and lecturing on 'the new ethics of business'. He had summarised these as, 'If a gentleman of the Establishment offers you his word as his bond, always go for the bond.'

It brought a smile to the public, but a frown to the brows of the bankers he did business with. Yet they still lent him money. At first the sums had been modest ones, £10,000 here, £10,000 there. But soon he was borrowing a hundred times that amount, the money being loaned against his undoubted success. He really was here, there and everywhere. He was filmed arriving at and leaving some thirty airports as far afield as Auckland in New Zealand and Helsinki in Finland. Returning to England, he announced to the waiting cameras, 'In seven weeks I travelled seventy thousand miles and was interviewed by a hundred and forty reporters. And, oh yes, I also did three million pounds worth of new deals.'

When asked by a banker, Sir Charles Hambro, for details of the deals, Maxwell had roared with laughter. 'Publicity, my dear Charles, is what it is all about.' If Hambro had not quite understood, he had not pressed. For Maxwell it had been an important lesson. A quick, plausible answer was the order of this new world he was dominating.

The video tapes showed that in twenty years Maxwell had almost doubled his body weight. In the postwar era he had still been a trim figure, striding briskly, back and head erect. But by the 1960s, with food rationing fading into recent memory, he had begun to expand physically, gorging himself on huge portions of lobster, salmon, caviar and choice meats, all washed down with copious amounts of vintage wines and champagnes. He had been known to eat two full dinners in one sitting, wolfing down the food at ravenous speed. Afterwards he would smoke one of the Cuban cigars he said were specially rolled for him on the order of Fidel Castro. No one dared to challenge such a nonsense claim.

By 1980 the last sign of sveltness had gone. Maxwell's girth was the height of other men, his face enclosed in a thatch of dyed black hair and treble chins, which sagged into his mastiff neck. Although he was cavalier in the way he cancelled appointments, there was one that was unbreakable. No matter where he was, twice a month, on Sunday afternoons, his personal hairdresser, George Wheeler, would be brought into his presence to administer L'Oreal Crescendo, an expensive lotion to conceal all traces of grey in his hair. The cost of this vanity was more than the salary Maxwell paid some of his staff.

He carried everywhere a powder puff. He would use it to dab his nose and forehead quickly before going into an important meeting, checking in a small silver-framed hand mirror that no traces of powder were visible. He had an abiding belief that any hint of perspiration on his face could leave him at a disadvantage in the deal he was going to make. To cope with his body odour, a secretary always carried in her handbag a stick of anti-perspirant, which she would slip to him to roll under his armpits. He would do this up to a dozen times a day.

Another essential when he was travelling a distance was a shoehorn, which an assistant carried. Maxwell liked to take his shoes and socks off on any journey – he said going barefoot reminded him of his village days walking to and from school and how far he had come. The assistant used the horn to get Maxwell back into his shoes.

Despite his size, Maxwell had still somehow managed to maintain his fleetness of foot at the end of a punishing work schedule. On more than one occasion he had told those who asked about his physical strength that, 'It's in my genes. I'm a hard man to catch.'

There were important clues here and the *kidon* would no doubt have noted them.

As the *kidon* watched the videotape, his colleague was analysing Maxwell's empire. It was both a private and publicly quoted interlocked web, which extended from Maxwell House in London into the Channel Islands, on into Germany, Hungary and Bulgaria with an offshoot in Moscow; into Africa and on to Australia and Israel, finally across into the United States and Canada. Within the conglomerate were dozens of companies, publishing mass-circulation newspapers and magazines and bestselling books; organisations that offered no clues as to what business they carried on, with names like 'Line Nominees' (Gibraltar); 'Sindron'; 'Camberry Legionstyle' and 'Visafood Magna Cell'. There were trusts and loan-financing corporations, companies that had been created to hold shares in football clubs such as Manchester United, Reading and Oxford

United. All these multi-interests were linked by a common factor: Robert Maxwell's name appeared prominently as principal shareholder.

In all, there were more than 400 private companies as well as those that came under the umbrella of the publicly quoted Maxwell Communications Corporation. There was a story, one that Maxwell never denied, that, because of the initials MCC, he had been invited to join the bastion of the British Establishment, that other MCC, the Marylebone Cricket Club, the home of the English game. It was another of those self-serving fables made all the more unbelievable by the claim that Maxwell had told friends he saw no point in joining the crusty old club. Its members included some of Britain's most powerful businessmen.

The *kidon* was interested in who were all the other stockholders outside Maxwell and his family members. It was a step in establishing his movements to see if there was a pattern to when and where he visited his fellow company directors.

For the most part the names of Maxwell's associates would probably have meant little to the *kidon*: they were accountants and lawyers, fund managers and bankers – secretive, background men who worked directly for, or advised, Maxwell's empire and carried out his orders without question.

Their thankless task was to ensure that Maxwell survived through their continuous switching of his money in a dazzling display of juggling and manipulation. Only he, sitting at the very centre of his web, his inner sanctum in Maxwell House, knew at any given moment what was happening. In an hour he would order millions in any hard currency to be moved in and out of his companies all over the world. By the end of their long day, his orders could have resulted in a billion US dollars or pounds sterling being sent on an electronic journey through the global stock markets. A barked order down the telephone would see hands once more feverishly pounding keyboards or working phones to complete some new deal that was designed to shore up a loss or hide grand larceny.

Long ago Maxwell had created ground rules to protect his secrets. No one employee, not even his sons, Ian and Kevin, could ever discover all his financial movements: his systems of cutouts and trails that ran cold were worthy of Mossad.

Robert Maxwell was the Barnum and Bailey of the financial world, the great stock market ringmaster able to introduce with consummate speed and a crack of his whip some new and even more startling financial act. But increasingly his high-wire actions had become more dangerous – and long ago he had abandoned any idea of a safety net.

But, in that viewing room, the *kidon* may have been the first to see the linkage that now finally began to unravel the complex structure of the Maxwell empire. There were names on the *kidon*'s growing list that still showed Maxwell was operating at the highest level: the Rothschild bankers; Coopers and Lybrand, accountants; the major banks and financial institutions of the City of London, Wall Street and Switzerland – venerable names such as Lloyds, Westminster, Lehman Brothers and Goldman Sachs. They were all there, still ready to take a chance on him if only to recover the vast sums Maxwell owed them.

But there was one name that stood out on the *kidon*'s list. It was that of the managing director of Maxwell's Tel Aviv-based Citex Corporation, which manufactured hi-tech printing equipment. Its Israeli head was the son of the incumbent prime minister, Yitzhak Shamir.

The tie to the family was one that Maxwell had nurtured since the day when Shamir had welcomed Maxwell to Israel. The Prime Minister was waiting on the tarmac when Maxwell's private jet landed and, for the next few days, the two men went to all the important religious and historic sites. Close to tears, Maxwell had stood before the remaining relic of Herod the Great's Second Temple in Jerusalem, the Wailing Wall, and turned to his host and said, 'I will do all I can to protect this.'

Shamir had clutched Maxwell's arm and, for a long moment, both had just stood in silence listening to the endless prayers of the Jewish faithful. It was the moment, Maxwell said later, when he found again the faith he thought he had lost. That night over dinner in a restaurant overlooking Lake Galilee, Shamir felt sufficiently close to Maxwell to confide in him his anti-Americanism. It was rooted in the Prime Minister's belief that the United States had not done enough to ensure there would be no Holocaust; that President Roosevelt should have come to an 'arrangement' – a favourite word of Shamir's – with Hitler to allow the Jews in Nazi Germany to travel to Palestine. And Maxwell had told him of his own dream of having wanted to bring out his own family. Sipping a sweet dessert wine, the two men had agreed that all that mattered now was to ensure that the survivors of that terrible time would have a secure homeland.

The next day, Robert Maxwell had met with the country's leading financiers and told them he was there to make both them and himself richer. He received a standing ovation after he revealed his blueprint for an investment of $100 million in a country that was low on the totem pole for global investors. Moving with speed and undoubted financial skills, he soon had a portfolio of Israeli chemical, hi-tech and printing firms. Companies close to bankruptcy began to display posters. 'Please Mr Maxwell, Buy Me!' And buy he did. From Beersheba to Haifa, from Tel Aviv to the shores of Galilee, he bought with a shrewdness that left local entrepreneurs open-mouthed. They would shake their heads and say, 'Who would have thought there was money in that firm?'

Maxwell became a keynote speaker at investment conferences in Europe and the United States to urge other Jews to invest in their homeland. He told them how beleaguered Israel felt, supporting his words with films showing that, despite all the threats of their Arab neighbours, Israelis were the hardest workers in the region and the most skilled, and they were not looking for inflated pay packets, just a chance to earn a living. It was a bravura performance. He told a New York group of businessmen he had bought a Tel Aviv company for $39 million and spent another $10 million updating its equipment. Now it was worth over $300 million. Ehud Olmert, than Israel's Health Minister, would stand beside Maxwell and proclaim at the end of such meetings: 'Here is a man who can open doors anywhere!'

It became a slogan Maxwell would seize upon and revise: 'You are safe with Maxwell!'

That claim had been noted by Mossad's then director-general, Nahum Admoni. But for the moment he would wait and see how matters developed.

In 1988 Maxwell had once more flown to Israel, this time to attend a dinner hosted by the country's president, Chaim Herzog. The guests included Ya'akov Neeman, the country's most astute tax lawyer, who had guided Maxwell around the pitfalls of investing in Israel. Also present were two leading political leaders, Yitzhak Shamir and Shimon Peres. Seated opposite Maxwell was Ido Dissentchik, the editor of the country's tabloid newspaper, *Ma'ariv*. Maxwell told him he would like to see the paper become the equivalent of his own *Daily Mirror*. By the end of the evening, he would consider taking a 30 per cent stake in *Ma'ariv*. It would be two years before he would do so.

That night Maxwell had stood on the balcony of his presidential suite in the King David Hotel in Jerusalem and stared out towards the Mount of Olives. Neeman would remember how Maxwell was close to tears as he whispered, 'I feel close to my parents here. I've tried all the world and I'm only happy here.'

Then it was back to business.

One company he had acquired was Degem Computers, a software manufacturing company in Tel Aviv. It mostly sold its programs in Central and South America. Even before Maxwell bought it, Degem had proved valuable to Mossad. Posing as its salesmen and technicians, operatives had roamed through Latin America. Terror groups such as Sendero Luminsos (the Shining Path), and Colombia's ELN were infiltrated to establish whether they had links with the PLO and other Islamic groups. Particular attention was paid to contacts between the PLO and Colombia's drug cartels. It was an abiding concern for Mossad that the ultimate financiers of terrorism on the streets of Israel could be the cocaine distributors on the other side of the world.

Under Maxwell's ownership, Degem had continued providing cover for *kidon* whose travel documents identified them as company employees.

Degem also had an office in Nairobi, Kenya. From there its operatives had waged another deadly war against African-based groups such as the African National Congress (ANC), because of their burgeoning ties to the Arab enemies of Israel. Several ANC members were left out on the savannahs for lions and leopards to consume. A *kidon* had planted a bomb in the bedroom toilet cistern of an emissary from Yasser Arafat who had come to meet with ANC officials in Brazzaville in the Congo. Retaliation was equally horrendous. A *katsa* was ambushed by African guerrillas and fed to crocodiles in the Limpopo River; his thrashing last moments were filmed and the video was sent to the Israeli embassy in South Africa. Forty-eight hours later the guerrilla headquarters deep in the jungle was blown apart by what was later estimated to be one hundred pounds of dynamite. The only clue as to where it came from was that it was similar to the explosive used by mining operators in South Africa.

Degem was only one of several companies in the Maxwell empire that were listed on Mossad's computers as providing services.

The names of their directors continued to be added to the list the *kidon* was preparing. Robert Maxwell's entangled links to the great and good of Israel continued to emerge.

There were also other names, dangerously embarrassing names, that had links to Maxwell and Israel. They did not officially appear on any of the Maxwell company documents. These people held their shares through nominee attorneys or accountants. Those names had invested in Maxwell because they believed it would make it easier for them to conduct their activities: whole-scale drug running, money laundering, trafficking in humans and gun running. By 1991, investors included the heads of the Russian Mafia, who had positioned themselves for the imminent collapse of the Soviet Union.

One was Semion Yukovich Mogilevich. He was a specialist in every major crime. Maxwell had arranged for Mogilevich to enter the Western financial world in 1988. It was a time when the Bank of New York had begun aggressively to prepare to step into the post-Communist financial world. Maxwell had introduced the bank to a Swiss banker who ran an investment brokerage in Geneva with branch offices in the Middle East, west Africa and the Cayman Islands. For Mogilevich it was an ideal window through which to launder his money – into hard currency. But to keep check on what was happening, he needed a passport. Robert Maxwell had recommended he should be given one from the State of Israel. The passports had been issued to Mogilevich and 23 of his gang members.

There were others on the list who did not need such a document. One was Edmund Safra, a US-based billionaire banker who had made tens of millions of dollars managing the funds of other members of the Russian

Mafia. Safra had links to Maxwell: they had dined on board the *Lady Ghislaine* when the yacht berthed opposite Safra's home in Monte Carlo. Who can doubt they had spoken of their common wish to see those untold tens of thousands of Jews in the crumbling Soviet Union safely make their way to Israel?

That prospect had ultimately led to the most far-reaching meeting Robert Maxwell had ever hosted in Israel. Once more the venue was the King David Hotel's Presidential Suite, a suitably imposing backdrop for what was to be discussed. And coming to Jerusalem was an opportunity to escape the travails of his personal life.

It was a time of deepening strain in his marriage to Betty. She could not accept – did not want to know – that the man who had promised to be faithful to his vows in that French church had long been a philanderer, bedding one leggy secretary after another. All were tall and willowy to fit his fantasy of what his ideal woman should be. He slept with them in his penthouse and on his yacht.

His wayward behaviour had led Betty to feel excluded. In the halcyon days of their marriage he had repeatedly promised to keep her in his confidence on business matters, to give her a seat on the board of Maxwell Communications, to entrust her with responsibility, to make use of her natural gift for problem solving.

Instead he had gone his own way since 1974, when he had his first serious affair, one that lasted for several years. Then he had moved on to other women, showering them with gifts and even promises of marriage once he divorced Betty.

One woman insisted, 'My love for Robert was based on a huge respect and a deep appreciation for someone who was very important to me.'

Another lover, who once worked for MI5, recalled that Maxwell was 'a sexual predator. He had those eyes which would undress me from across a crowded room. Once he had me through the bedroom door, he was all over me. The result was he usually came to orgasm during our foreplay. But he was always very generous in his gifts. He gave me expensive jewellery at Christmas and on my birthday. Only after our affair had ended did I discover he had given other women the same gifts. I guess he must have bought a job lot to pay us off. After he had sex, he was gone in minutes. Looking back, he regarded a woman as little more than someone to satisfy his physical demands. He would often call me at all hours to come to the penthouse.'

A third lover, a journalist who worked at the time on a rival newspaper to those under Maxwell's control, said he had offered her a job as an editor of one of his tabloids. 'He was quite open. He wanted me on tap in the building whenever he felt sexy. I knew then the relationship was doomed.

I was right. In six months a couple of Asprey bracelets to the good, we had gone our separate ways. I felt sorry for Betty. She was stuck out in the country, desperately hoping he would come to her, even if he wasn't bearing gifts. But it was over for her as a wife. She had become an appendage.'

But the meeting that took place in the King David's suite was no sexual assignment.

There were three other men present. One was Shimon Peres, the second Nahum Admoni. The third was one of the politician's senior aides. He recalled the encounter as 'the ego meets the megalomaniac. Peres has this Eskimo smile which never quite unfreezes at the best of times. Maxwell was, as usual, his natural bombastic self. Admoni just listened.'

And watched.

Maxwell had recently been on another business trip to Washington and his listeners were keenly interested in his views on how the Reagan Administration saw the timetable for Russia's collapse as a superpower. Maxwell's links went back to 1978, when he had met with its then leader, Leonid Brezhnev, in the Kremlin. In an unusual honour, a photograph of the two men was published in the official party newspaper *Pravda*. Since then Maxwell had met every important member of the Politburo and those who ruled over the Soviet satellites. Maxwell had acquired a rare and privileged position in the Communist world.

This was the reason Peres and Admoni had asked for the meeting. They wanted to see initially if their host could use his connections to bring more Jews out of the Soviet Bloc.

Maxwell may well have repeated that gesture of previous times, standing at one of the suite's windows and looking out towards the Dome of the Rock, that sacred shrine for two millennia of his people, one that his own mother had told him represented all that was enduring in their faith. The great rotunda may well have rekindled his own memories about his guilt for not being able to save his impoverished family from the gas chambers. And here he was, in the presence of two of the most powerful men in Israel, himself *ein Mensch*, rich beyond their means, being asked to help. No one would ever know the emotions that coursed through Robert Maxwell.

He said he would do everything possible to bring home the Soviet Union's Jews. It was then that the second reason for the meeting was raised. There is no record of the exact words used; there never could be. But Admoni, a blunt man at the best of times, would have put it as directly as he always spoke. Mossad could use Robert Maxwell. Not as a *katsa* or as a *sayan*, but as the single most important asset Mossad had ever employed.

Maxwell's previous contacts with the intelligence world had been checked by Mossad.

Certainly it was a world in which he could feel at home, where people were both true and false, in many ways a mirror image of himself. Like his own business activities, the work of intelligence was often to frustrate the truth. Facts were manipulated, just as he manipulated balance sheets; both he and the men and women who worked in intelligence went to great lengths to leave their complicity hidden.

Maxwell's first foray into intelligence – his questioning of German prisoners at the end of World War Two – was only brief. Acting as a translator rather than interrogator did little to prepare him for his duties in Spandau Prison in Berlin. Held there were a number of leading Nazis including Rudolph Hess, Hitler's deputy; Hjalmar Schacht, the keeper of the Third Reich purse strings; and Friedrich Flick, the steel baron who had rivalled Krupp in Hitler's plan for world domination.

But here, in the cold grey granite fortress of Spandau, Maxwell showed an unexpected aptitude for asking shrewd questions based on long nights spent studying documents in his room. By the light of a naked bulb he would read and make copious notes, drinking endless cups of coffee from a pot on top of the room stove. He would memorise the questions he formed and then spend long hours putting them to a prisoner.

One was Colonel Otto Guske, an Abwehr intelligence officer. From him, Maxwell learned that MI6 had not only fed false information to the Free French forces waiting in Britain to spearhead the Normandy landings, but that the intelligence service had deliberately sent some of the French parachuting into still-occupied France having alerted, via a Resistance informer, that they were coming. The parachutists were captured and tortured by the Gestapo.

When Maxwell reported what Guske had told him, the Spandau commandant told Maxwell that it was 'all history now, old man, part of the deception that made sure the invasion worked'.

For Maxwell it was an enlightening example of 'sacrificing a few to save many'.

During his time in Spandau, he met another of those colourful figures who populate the intelligence world. In his herringbone tweed three-piece suite and stiff starched collar, Frederich Vanden Heuvel looked like a courtier at some long-gone European court. It went with his title of 'Count'. No one ever quite knew where his prefix came from, but it ensured he was always guaranteed an invitation to the parties the four Allied occupying powers held in their respective zones in Berlin.

It was at one of these functions that Maxwell, wearing his Military Cross on his best dress uniform, met Heuvel. They discovered a common interest in German literature: Maxwell was an authority on Goethe.

Over dinner Heuvel revealed he was the MI6 resident in Berlin. Like Maxwell, the Count had enjoyed a good war, though a very different one. Heuvel had run an MI6 network in Germany from his base in Bern, Switzerland, working closely with Allen Dulles, the OSS (Office of Strategic Services) chief who later became director of the CIA. Heuvel had painted a glamorous picture of his work as the wine flowed. By the end of the evening, he had proposed that Maxwell 'could find a berth with Six'. It would not be a full-time position, but one in which Maxwell would act as 'a super contact man', Heuvel would recall telling the young officer.

Maxwell had refilled his glass, saying nothing. Then he had smiled and said he would think about it. Heuvel had nodded. But he had sensed there was no point in raising the matter again. 'Maxwell was not going to become one of our Jews,' he said later.

It may also not have helped because Maxwell, like every Jew in the Diaspora, was desperately concerned about what was happening in the fledgeling state of Israel. Within days of its creation, it was on the verge of being strangled by its powerful Arab neighbours. Behind their relentless attacks Maxwell suspected the hand of Britain and its pro-Arab intelligence services. Though he was careful to keep such views to himself, the suspicion grew later in MI6 and MI5 that Maxwell could not be trusted. He was placed on their Watch List and categorised as 'a Zionist – loyal only to Israel'. It was an example of the anti-Semitism rife in both services.

For his part, Maxwell had learned enough about the methods of British intelligence to discover that truth is an acquired taste. Years later, after he had finally been recruited by Mossad, he had been told by Rafi Eitan, 'our work is to create history and then hide it. On the whole we are honourable, respect constitutional government, free speech and human rights. But in the end we also understand that nothing must stand in the way of what we do.'

In many ways that was a framework in which Robert Maxwell ran his life and work.

At the time of the meeting at the King David Hotel, Maxwell had already established his relations with many world leaders. President George Bush had early on become a founder member of the group that Maxwell liked to describe airily as 'my sources'. Margaret Thatcher was another. At the height of her prime-ministerial power, Maxwell liked nothing better than calling her to say what the main story in his morning *Daily Mirror* was going to be. Later, when John Major took over as Britain's Prime Minister, he was offered the same courtesy and politely refused. But Maxwell would still corner Major at some function and talk to him about the political state of the world. France's François Mitterand and Helmut Kohl, Germany's Chancellor, who was close to matching Maxwell's physical size, were two more leaders the Chairman would boast 'listened to me more than their own politicians'. Because he was an inveterate gossip himself, who can doubt that Maxwell passed on titbits he learned from such contacts to others within that group of exalted 'sources'.

Over the years there had also been reports that Maxwell had been approached by both MI5 and MI6 to pass on information he had gleaned from his visits to the Soviet Union. But, if that was true, he had never shared it with anyone. Just as with the legal profession, with which Maxwell had long maintained a stony silence to its probing, his 'steely mask' would drop over any questions about his links to the intelligence world. At most he would admit he had 'dabbled at it' in World War Two. Even that admission would come from somewhere deep within his mind, part of that time he had known hand-to-hand combat and had stared into what he called 'the enemy's gleaming eyes'.

But in that presidential suite in Jerusalem, with its overstuffed furnishings and ornate drapes, the man who had once told his wife he had 'known the roughness of the rifle butt on his palm, the monotonous bursts of machine gunfire, the smell of powder and of blood, who knew death all too well' – that man was about to put his life at risk again.

Robert Maxwell was asked by Admoni to become the man who would open any door for Mossad, who would himself pass through those doors to learn secrets that not even Mossad could obtain. As simply as that the proposition was put.

In the long history of intelligence, there would never be a super spy quite like Robert Maxwell. His successes had included his remarkable contact with Vladimir Kryuchkov, the chief of the KGB.

The first of their encounters took place in the Lubyanka, the massive citadel that served as KGB headquarters in Moscow. Maxwell would later say he had wanted to see inside the building where so many Jewish intellectuals had been questioned before being sent to the gulags of Siberia.

The memories of that meeting survive in Kryuchkov's memory in all their excruciating detail: the bearlike hugs they exchanged, followed quickly by Maxwell's fleshy lips brushing the KGB chief's cheeks, the longer exchange of appraising looks; the two men entering the massive building, Maxwell dressed in yards of the finest of English worsted cut into a topcoat, Kryuchkov in the uniform of his country, his chest a small field of ribbons honouring his services to Russia.

The meeting had been scheduled to last 45 minutes; in the end it lasted two and a half hours. Inevitably their conversation began with reminiscences about the days when Maxwell had been stationed in Berlin in the immediate aftermath of World War Two and when he was putting down the roots of his publishing empire, acquiring the rights to publish

German scientific publications in translation. They had been transported through the then Soviet Zone to London.

Over black coffee and brandy, host and guest explored each other's world. Kryuchkov was expansive, encouraging Maxwell to be the same. The two men laughed at each other's jokes. The meeting ended with the KGB chief telling his aides, 'Comrade Maxwell is going to be a good friend of this country.' And Maxwell replied that he would be glad to tell the world how much the Soviet Union was changing.

Robert Maxwell drove away from the Lubyanka convinced he had acquired another member for his exclusive club of sources. Kryuchkov would summon his aides and tell them, 'This man is going to be useful to us.'

One of his aides, Colonel Vyacheslav Sorokin, who worked in the KGB Foreign Intelligence Branch, made a close study of Maxwell's strengths and weaknesses. He had concluded that the former far outweighed the latter and that Maxwell's barely concealed criticism of the United States was not just a ploy to impress and flatter his Soviet hosts but a genuinely felt feeling, part of Maxwell's well-publicised view in the Moscow media that he was ready and able to help the country gain economic stability. He had reminded Moscow's reporters he had done the same for Israel.

Sorokin decided that Maxwell could be recruited. It emerged in a later report to Kryuchkov that he felt the only drawback was that it would require a great deal of time and skill to hook Maxwell and that the usual means – blackmail, bribery and coercion – were unlikely to succeed. Maxwell had to be coaxed and, with remarkable foresight, Sorokin said that in any move to bring him into the KGB fold, nothing must be said or done that Maxwell could construe as a threat to Israel.

In all his ensuing visits to the Soviet Union, Maxwell was fêted and granted his every wish. When he asked to visit his birthplace, he was taken there. For hours he walked through the village streets saying little, the tears never far away. Crowds from all over the region had been marshalled to greet him. For the most part they stared silently at this stranger in their midst, dressed expensively, smiling and waving at them as if he were running for office. That night Maxwell was taken to a *dacha* and wined and dined and toasted by his hosts. Then they all took their luxury train back to Moscow. Along the route the regime's local functionaries were brought forward to shake his hand and have their photograph taken beside the bearlike potentate.

Maxwell had learned a smattering of Russian. He would boom out at every opportunity that he felt 'a little bit Russian'.

To encourage this feeling, and hopefully prepare him for the KGB to recruit, the Kremlin began to issue exit visas for Jews to emigrate to Israel. Upon their arrival in Tel Aviv, they often referred to their benefactor as

'Moshe' – Hebrew for the biblical Moses, who had also persuaded a tyrant to let his people go.

It was another of those moments that brought tears to Maxwell's eyes. There was little doubt that his penchant for crying was genuine: it was part of his emotional make-up, going with his sudden rages, from which no one was spared.

In Moscow such matters did not pass unnoticed. Kryuchkov asked the KGB's psychiatrists to decide whether there was some deeper cause for concern beyond these constant mood swings of Maxwell's. In the end it did not really matter what the doctors concluded. Robert Maxwell had been recruited by Mossad.

Now, in September 1991, while the two *kidon* operatives had assembled their data at their unit's base in the Negev Desert, the other two who had joined them in the safe house in Pinsker Street had returned from London. Their task had been to confirm and define the extent of Robert Maxwell's personal security.

The focus of their enquiries had been his two principal homes in Britain and his various means of transport.

The penthouse in Maxwell House was a citadel. On the floor below, the ninth, was his private workplace, a number of interconnected offices, waiting rooms, kitchen and dining room, bathroom and toilets. It was from this floor that Maxwell ran his business empire – publishing, communications, printing, technology, property, currencies, gilts and shares. In a massive safe whose combination only Maxwell knew were the secrets of how he operated, at least some of them, for the Chairman liked to boast, 'I have the kind of brain that can keep a wealth of the most important information in my head.' Or perhaps it was his ever-growing paranoia that insisted he could not trust the most secure safe Chubb could manufacture.

It was on this floor, looking out over the rooftops of High Holborn, that his personal staff came and went, fixed smiles on their faces when they passed him, no doubt fear in their hearts that he would terrorise them for something they had forgotten to do. A secretary had been fired for overlooking to make sufficient copies of a memo, another sacked for forgetting he took only one spoonful of sugar in his coffee. It was on this floor that security was at its highest, where the unwritten rule was watch and be watched, and Robert Maxwell's pathological need for secrecy was in direct contrast to his continuous courting of publicity.

The penthouse was created by Jon Bannenberg, usually a designer of taste. But Maxwell had wanted high kitsch and the result was a miniature Xanadu. The elevator that only Maxwell or his guests could use, emerged into a lobby large enough to hold a family car. At the far end was a massive baronial-style fireplace, the opening large enough to roast an ox. But no flames would burn in the wrought-iron grate for, apart from the log-holder, the rest was made of fibreglass painted to resemble wood. A false chimney breast disappeared through the ceiling.

Twin mahogany doors opened into the drawing room. A stuccoed ceiling, double-lined curtains, overstuffed sofas and ottomans with piped edges were the main furnishings. Dotted across the expanse of carpet – '£50 a square inch' Maxwell had once boasted – were bronze glass-topped coffee tables holding vases of artificial silk flowers; they were a compromise to his demand that he must always 'feel nature around him'. Placed around the room were side tables supporting various *objets d'art*. Most were gifts from dictators and despots in Eastern Europe and Africa. On one table was a statue of a shrunken head; Maxwell told guests it was the skull of a victim of Congo cannibalism. It looked like a carving. More certain was the authenticity of a Russian icon. It was a gift from Mikhail Gorbachev after Maxwell had bought a stake in the *Moscow News*, an English-language newspaper that was a fervent supporter of the Russian leader. Yet a month earlier, in August 1991, Maxwell had been asked by Kryuchkov to assist in the plot to have the man Maxwell called 'my friend Gorby' removed from office.

It was what had followed that had brought the two *kidon* to England.

One of the first steps Mossad's Directorate of Operations had taken after Maxwell's recruitment was to select a *sayan* to work inside Maxwell House. He was there not to help in any unlikely emergency – Maxwell had more than enough staff to handle anything unforeseen. The *sayan* was there to keep an eye on Maxwell's behaviour and report to his controller at the Israeli embassy in London. To Ari Ben-Menashe, an old hand at such matters, 'setting a watchdog is routine when you have an asset who is known to be totally unpredictable'.

According to Victor Ostrovsky, there would have been about 2,000 *sayanim* to choose from in London. They were all handled by a *katsa*. His name was Jacob Barad and, on the list of diplomats the embassy provided the Foreign Office, he was a third secretary in the Commercial Interests section. He had full diplomatic immunity: the worst that could happen if he was caught spying was that the Foreign Office would ask for him to be formally withdrawn from his post.

Using his business contacts, Barad would have found it easy to place a *sayan* in Maxwell House. There was a constant turnover of staff. It was part of Maxwell's obsession that anyone who remained too long would learn too much about his activities. While they were employed, their salaries were unusually high, payment that Maxwell had correctly calculated would buy, if not their loyalty, at least their silence.

The *sayan* had provided Barad with a detailed description of the private quarters. Maxwell's bedroom was dominated by a bed whose mattress was almost twice the normal size and reinforced by hand-made springs. The décor was a mixture of dark-red flock wallpaper and a gold-thread carpet and bedspread. Two walls of fitted wardrobes contained years of careful tailoring: there were reputed to be fifty suits on their hangers, and twice as many shirts in the stack of drawers. There was a rack for his belts, two for his ties. These were all pressed by his Filipino maids, Juliet and Elsa.

One of their less pleasant duties was to flush the toilet in the bathroom after Maxwell had used it and to gather up the soiled face towels he had taken to use instead of toilet paper. 'These were put through the washing machine and we then ironed them for later use,' Elsa would remember. Juliet would complete the image of Maxwell's distasteful personal habits by revealing that most mornings his silk bedsheets were soiled, as were his underpants, which he dumped on the carpet before going to bed in a kaftan.

The chef, Martin Cheesman, had a standing order to make sure the kitchen was always stocked with a large plate of sandwiches in case Maxwell awoke peckish during the night. Then he would sit in bed, munching and channel-hopping across the outsize television screen in the room. In the morning he would be brought freshly squeezed orange juice, bagels stuffed with smoked salmon and a pot of coffee. Maxwell would make the first of his calls on the telephone console beside the bed, barking orders in between chewing and slurping.

All this the *sayan* had passed on to Barak at one of their regular meetings. When the *kidon* arrived in London, the *katsa* had prepared a detailed plan of the penthouse layout and its master's lifestyle.

But there was more to learn.

On the roof of Maxwell House was a strip of Astroturf. It marked the pad for Maxwell's helicopter, an Aerospatiale 335. He had not quibbled over the insurance premium for the helipad. To be able to use it was a status symbol that even Rupert Murdoch could not match. Maxwell liked nothing better than to order his pilot, Richard Cowley, to fly directly over Murdoch's newspaper headquarters as he made his way to some meeting, or to land beside the two other aircraft he owned. One was his Gulfstream-4 executive jet, with its call sign of VR-BOB (Very Rich Bob). The other was a Gulfstream-2 which he kept as a standby. Both were visible proof of his wealth and, in his own mind, his importance.

The planes were based at Farnborough in Hampshire. The *kidon* did not need to inspect either aircraft. Their details were freely available in the Gulfstream catalogue. They would have had no interest in the interior fittings – all cream cloth and lightly tanned leather – or that the personal staff who looked after him on every flight, Carina Hall the stewardess and Simon Grigg his valet, were among the best in the business. The *kidon* interest would have been in take-off weight, air speed, cruising altitude.

Those were details, if required, with which they could work.

At some point in their enquiries they gathered information on the *Lady Ghislaine*, the yacht that Maxwell had bought for £12 million from Adnan Khashoggi's brother. At 185 feet (56 metres) long, its five decks, private Jacuzzi and gymnasium were a reminder that the rich *are* different. Maxwell liked to boast that to run it cost him more than the annual salary of Britain's Prime Minister.

A detailed blueprint of the yacht had been obtained by the *kidon*. They would have been expected to have done no less.

There was one further area of interest to them. Maxwell's stately home in the pleasant setting of Oxfordshire was the imposingly named Headington Hill Hall. He had leased it at little more than a peppercorn rent. It was here that Betty had brought up their children. Between 1946 and 1961, all nine were born in the same Paris nursing home; this ensured they would have dual French–British nationality. 'Maman wanted us to have the best of both worlds,' Isabel would say.

The first, Michael, named after Maxwell's father, had died shortly after the youngest, Ghislaine, had arrived: he had been in a coma for six years as a result of a car crash. Another child, Karine, died of leukaemia shortly after her third birthday.

Years later Betty had wondered if that loss was the beginning of the foundering of her marriage. Her role was to run Headington Hill Hall and wait for his sudden appearances. Most of the time he would be closeted with his staff. Then, having eaten all she had set before him, he would be gone, usually with no more than a brief peck on her cheek. The passionate kisses from the lips she had noticed in their first encounter in a liberated Paris were now for other women.

For her, life had become supervising the gardeners, dropping in on the lodge-keepers and observing the security men who patrolled the grounds day and night. To escape she could be driven in her raspberry-coloured Rolls-Royce. But, although she was surrounded by scores of staff, Betty's loneliness could only have been a living, searing pain. It was there in her face, the smile she tried to summon when her children came calling, the reassurances that she was just fine. 'Maman was a wonderful woman in hiding her feelings,' said Isabel. Betty hid the truth from them all, from Kevin and Ian, Philip and Anne and Isabel's twin, Christine.

The family were outside the remit of the *kidon* operatives in the safe house in Pinsker Street on that September day in 1991. But from all the information now available to them would emerge a plan. Not one detail would be committed to paper. Instead it would be worked out in discussion.

For the first time it would be an assassination approved only within the closed ranks of Mossad – and then only by a handful.

Victor Ostrovsky would label them as a small group of right-wing intelligence officers who believed that Robert Maxwell had become such a threat to Mossad, and to Israel itself, that he had to die. There was no other solution.

From that moment onwards the plotters had moved the operation out of the headquarters building to one of the many safe houses to which they had access. There they continued their preparations aimed at an ultimate goal. For Victor Ostrovsky, 'making it look impossible was part of the *kidon* magic'.

Part II
CONNECTIONS

FOUR

A year before Robert Maxwell was recruited by Mossad another unit in the Israeli intelligence community had carried out a breathtaking operation under the control of Rafi Eitan.

In the history of the country's intelligence gathering there had never been anyone quite like the master spy. The squat, bull-necked man had become immortalised as one of the team that snatched off a Buenos Aires street Adolf Eichmann, a man who had organised and overseen many of the atrocities of the Holocaust. Eitan had insisted on standing in the execution chamber in Israel after Eichmann was found guilty of crimes against humanity. 'He looked at me and said, "Soon it will be your turn, Jew." I had replied, "Not today, Adolf." With that he dropped through the trap. We let him hang for an hour so his neck was properly stretched and his tongue hanging below his chin. Then we took him to a specially built crematorium oven and burnt him. Just as all those millions of Jews had died,' Eitan would recall.

Rough-hewn in speech and manner, he was what Israelis called a WASP – a White Ashkenazi Sabra Proteksia. Ashkenazi originate from Eastern and Central Europe and had built up what was then Palestine, and played an important part in creating the state of Israel. They attached special pride to the word 'proteksie' – it means someone with influence.

Maxwell had a similar label attached to him and made much of it. But, to men like Rafi Eitan, he was a WASP who 'just blew in and out, making a lot of noise. He wasn't my kind of man.'

Nevertheless, when the time came, Rafi Eitan put aside his personal distaste for Maxwell and his bombastic ways. The man the *kibbutzim* called 'our own titan' would become an integral element of Eitan's incredible operation. Maxwell would serve his purpose for the same reason everyone else had. 'For two thousand years we Jews have prayed for deliverance. In song, in prose, in our hearts, we have kept alive that dream – and the dream has kept us alive.'

If Maxwell could bring that dream closer to reality, then Eitan would forgive him anything.

Eitan had served Mossad for many years with considerable distinction. But, in one of those regular internal battles for control over the service, he had found himself out of favour. Eitan resigned and set up as a private consultant, selling his skills to companies requiring to improve their security or to some of the emerging Israeli millionaires who needed to have staff trained in how to protect them against kidnapping or a terrorist bomb. Eitan found the work boring. He let it be known within government circles he was ready to return to professional intelligence activities.

He became an adviser on counterterrorism to Prime Minister Yitzhak Rabin. When Menachem Begin replaced Rabin, he appointed Rafi Eitan as Director of the Bureau of Scientific Liaison. Its Hebrew acronym was LAKAM. Eitan intended it should become one of the most important arms of the Israeli intelligence community.

Created in 1960 as a unit to obtain scientific data, from the outset LAKAM targeted those Maxwell companies that published a number of specialist journals and foreign-language reprints.

When Eitan took charge of LAKAM, he made it his business to learn more about Maxwell's publishing background and his close ties to the Soviet Committee for Science and Technology. This had given Maxwell access to a wide range of Soviet scientific publications. Many were restricted for military use and almost never available outside the Soviet Union. Eitan was also intrigued by reports of Maxwell's contacts with the KGB. But he concluded, 'These were probably no more than someone looking for any door he could walk through to make a deal.'

Rafi Eitan would discover later that there was more to it than that. The KGB had recognised early on in Maxwell's career that he could become an important figure who, if properly handled, would serve their purposes. But the KGB would also misread Maxwell. He may have been a Jew who had no time to go to synagogue or to often observe the Sabbath, but he *was* a Jew and his emotions were governed by the past of his people. He was never more at ease than when speaking of their suffering. At those times he did not bother to hide his anger over the Nazi death camps that had claimed so many of his family. The Soviet Union had its own part in that: his cousins had been deported to the gulags in those postwar years. The KGB may well have forgotten that. But Robert Maxwell had not.

There was another link to the intelligence world Eitan discovered. Since 1946, Maxwell had worked closely with Ferdinand Springer, a German publisher who had survived the Third Reich despite his Jewish background. He and Maxwell had started a publishing venture. Two years later Maxwell, in one of those adroit moves with which he was making his reputation, merged the Maxwell-Springer company with Butterworth

Press in London. That company had long ties to MI6.

According to Eitan, Maxwell was clearly 'swimming with the sharks'. He made a mental note to file Robert Maxwell in that part of his prodigious brain where Rafi Eitan kept his future plans.

Eitan had taken over LAKAM during yet another of those periods of turbulence within the country's intelligence community. Within the Kirya, the spacious headquarters of the Israeli Defence Forces, there were renewed arguments over the intelligence services being bogged down in what had become the quagmire of Lebanon. There had been almost daily failures to predict what Arab terrorist groups would do next. The communications needle towering over the Kirya complex had bristled with outgoing traffic to commanders in the field demanding to know what Mossad and Aman, military intelligence, was doing to rectify the situation.

Already the internal conflict had claimed a powerful victim. David Kimche, long an undimmed star in the Mossad firmament, had been dismissed from handling the Lebanon 'account'.

Kimche was mild-mannered, with an accent that hovered between the English shires and the South African veldt, and his only known vanities were a toupee and customised bifocals. In that world where intelligence interacts with diplomacy and secret alliances forged, there was no one more adept at bridging the gap than the slim Kimche, a man who even his enemies said was made for a dress suit.

He had joined Mossad in those days when it had freebooted through Africa, penetrating the newly independent black African governments. Kimche had run agents with consummate skill. Later he had taken over another 'account', masterminding the Kurdish insurrection against Iraq. Then had come a spell when he regularly slipped out of the featureless building on King Saul Boulevard to visit London and the European capitals. He could be found in their most expensive restaurants, cutting his food into small bites and wiping his mouth with a napkin after each mouthful. And smiling and listening before moving a conversation along with a well-constructed question.

But it was in America that he had shown his intellectual mettle; no one better understood the subtleties of the relationship between Israel and the United States. He had himself described it as 'a very intimate dialogue, very intimate indeed'. Even when he had left Mossad, he remained a welcome figure in the intelligence communities of Washington and London, his manner epitomising the ultimate confluence of intelligence and political power.

Kimche had been among the first firm friends Maxwell had made among Israel's powerbrokers. They had first met in Kimche's office in Asia House, one of Tel Aviv's more interesting buildings, reflecting thought in design and the choice of materials. On the third floor, Kimche had introduced Maxwell to the building's owner, Shaul Nehemiah Eisenberg.

In the select group of Israel's seriously rich millionaires, Eisenberg was the richest. His business empire ran from chemical factories in Korea to mines in Chile and extensive operations in Europe. He was the only citizen to have a law named after him, the Eisenberg Law, which gave him tax relief for his operations. Central to these was the arms business, brokering deals with China, South Africa and any country that wished to purchase the latest aircraft from Israel Aircraft Industries, another of Eisenberg's companies. His senior staff were drawn from the world of intelligence and included Zvi Zamir, who had run Mossad from 1968 to 1973, and Amos Manor, the first head of Shin Beth, the country's equivalent to the FBI.

Kimche had joked to Maxwell that the 'big question is whether the State of Israel owns Eisenberg, or whether Eisenberg owns the State of Israel'.

The two tycoons had found much in common. Both came from impoverished backgrounds in Middle Europe and had risen above it by their entrepreneurial skills. Both disliked the fanatical obscurantism of ultra-Orthodox Jews; both liked good food without regard to religious dietary restrictions.

They also understood the value of connections. On that first evening of their first meeting, Kimche had invited Maxwell to his home. Over dinner, Eisenberg developed his views on the need for connections in that most important of all connected cities, Washington.

It was in the USA that Rafi Eitan planned to launch an intelligence assault on that most powerful of Israel allies, the United States of America.

It would be an opportunity to show that, while Mossad was no longer a beneficiary to his skills, LAKAM had become a serious player in the intelligence world. The scientific journals published by Robert Maxwell had convinced Eitan that America was the most advanced scientific community in the globe. For LAKAM to obtain even some of the data would be a tremendous coup.

Of particular interest to Rafi Eitan was a report on a piece of software from one of LAKAM's operatives in the United States. It was called Promis.

More formally, it was known as the Prosecutor's Management Information Systems.

On 19 December 1982, Eitan flew to the United States. He liked to travel during the onset of a holiday season because it was always a busy period and officials would not have the time to ask questions. At Kennedy Airport he presented his Israeli passport, which identified him as Dr Benjamin Orr, an assistant public prosecutor in the Ministry of Justice in Tel Aviv, Israel.

His age was given as 57 years and his status, married with no children.

In all respects the details fitted Eitan's dictum to 'lie about the truth'.

There *was* a Dr Orr. He *had* worked for the Justice Ministry. The given personal details *were* all correct. But the real prosecutor had retired and his passport was a perfect forgery, created by one of LAKAM's specialists.

Rafi Eitan strolled out into the New York night carrying the leather suitcase he had travelled with for the past twenty years. Waiting for him was one of LAKAM's men. He drove Eitan to a mid-Manhattan apartment LAKAM maintained.

Over dinner Eitan learned more about the Promis software: its staggering 570,000 lines of computer code and its ability to integrate innumerable databases without requiring any reprogramming.

Eitan was the first to admit he was no computer geek. But he quickly grasped that Promis could convert blind data into information. In Eitan's world information meant power. He saw how Promis could be a device capable of monitoring intelligence operations, agents and targets. It could do far more than it had originally been designed for: a means to follow cases through the labyrinth of the court system of the United States.

He also learned that Promis was now a prized possession of the Department of Justice. Next day Eitan took a Metroliner to Washington. He liked travelling by train: it gave him a chance to enjoy the countryside and to think. Train journeys also reminded him of the vastness of America: in almost any one state you could geographically fit the State of Israel many times.

Rafi Eitan had taken a train for his previous major operation in the United States, when he had still been working for Mossad. The journey had taken him to the unappealing industrial town of Apollo in Pennsylvania. Based in its grimy suburbs was Numec, a small company specialising in reprocessing nuclear waste. Its chief executive was Dr Salman Shapiro, a pillar of the Jewish Diaspora in America. On LAKAM's computer database Shapiro was listed as a prominent fundraiser for Israel.

But it was not the search for another donation that had brought Eitan to Apollo with three of his staff. He was travelling under the name of Dr Eli Cohen. His embossed business card described him as 'Personal Scientific Adviser, The Office of the Prime Minister of Israel'.

There was no such person or post.

His two companions were described on their cards as scientists from 'The Department of Electronics, University of Tel Aviv, Israel'.

There was no such department.

The men were LAKAM security officers whose task would be to see the best way of stealing fissionable waste from Numec. All three spent four days in Apollo, passing many hours touring the Numec plant, sitting for more hours in Shapiro's office. What they spoke about would remain a secret. On the fifth day Eitan and his companions left Apollo as unobtrusively as they had arrived.

A month later the first of nine shipments of containers of nuclear waste left Numec. Each container would bear the words: 'Property of the State of Israel: Ministry of Agriculture'. The containers would each carry a stencil stating they had full diplomatic clearance and so were exempt from customs checks before they were stowed on board El Al cargo freighters to Tel Aviv.

The containers were destined for Dimona, Israel's nuclear facility in the Negev Desert. It was sited close to where the *kidon* unit had its base.

Now, as the Metroliner pulled into Washington's Union Station on that December morning, Rafi Eitan might well have felt the calm that always descended on him at the onset of another operation.

Next morning he presented himself at the Justice Department. He met C Madison 'Brick' Brewer, who had been employed by Inslaw, the company that had developed the Promis software to its present capability. The two men had not met before. Brewer took Eitan on face value, including the letter of introduction presented from Israel's Ministry of Justice.

Eitan asked if he could have a demonstration of the software. Brewer explained that with the Christmas season about to start, that could not be arranged at such short notice. However, he suggested that, if Dr Orr could return in the New Year, he was sure that not only would a demonstration be possible, but that it could be conducted at Inslaw.

Next day Rafi Eitan flew back to Tel Aviv. He would fill in the time before returning to Washington by learning all about Inslaw and its owner, William Hamilton.

Around the time Eitan's 747 was starting its long journey to Israel, Robert Maxwell had arrived in New York in a very good mood. Shortly before leaving London he had received a phone call from one of his 'trusted sources' that his unfulfilled ambition to own a national newspaper could be about to be realised. Once before he had tried. In October 1980, the venerable *Times* was up for sale. Maxwell had expressed an immediate and very public interest in buying it. But he was rejected as being unsuitable to own Britain's most prestigious newspaper. He later told Rafi Eitan he was convinced MI6 had briefed against him in the City of London because they perceived him as an upstart Jew who was marching onto their turf, a claim he would come to repeat down the years as a reason for many of his financial problems.

In that phone call, Maxwell had learned that the Mirror Group of Newspapers could soon be coming on the market. Its flagship *Daily*

Mirror had once been the world's largest-selling daily. But years of overstaffing and outmoded printing industry practices, coupled to astronomical staff salaries, had all led to financial haemorrhaging at its Holborn headquarters. Its owners, Reed International, so his caller told Maxwell, were looking for a buyer to rid themselves of a liability that could draw them into bankruptcy.

For once Maxwell had adopted a wait-and-see policy. He knew the only way to acquire the *Mirror* was by stealth. Flying to New York on a Christmas shopping spree was one way of showing his lack of interest.

In London over Christmas in 1982, David Spedding, the deputy director of the Secret Intelligence Service, MI6, spent part of the holiday studying the latest reports from the Middle East. The head of station in Amman, Jordan, reported that Iraq was looking for a translator for a number of back numbers of specialist magazines. They included the *Journal of Nuclear Energy, Journal of Nuclear Physics, Journal of Inorganic Nuclear Chemistry* and the *Journal of Atmospheric and Terrestrial Physics*. All were owned by Robert Maxwell.

Spedding had consulted with his superior, Sir Colin McColl. What puzzled them was that the back numbers appeared to be several years old. Was it still possible that Saddam Hussein's own nuclear scientists would be able to glean sufficient data to try to build their own nuclear weapon? Another intriguing question was, how had the journals come into the hands of Iraq?

The answer was quickly established. Maxwell had sold the back numbers to Iraq for some £70,000. He may well have used the money to finance his spending spree in New York.

News of the sale was added to the thickening files the security services had developed on Maxwell.

A substantial portion of the MI6 file – according to one of its former officers, Richard Tomlinson – was devoted to Maxwell's connections with the KGB and its satellite services in the Soviet Bloc. Tomlinson was to recall that there was also 'a lot of interesting stuff about Maxwell's dealings with some very dodgy characters, heads of the Russian criminal families. Some of the stuff on file were transcripts of meetings with them in hotels in Moscow. There was also material on his ties to Israel.'

MI5's file was focused on Maxwell's financial activities in the City of London: his borrowings, his relationships with dozen of banks both in London and New York, and details about his interlinked companies.

Meanwhile in Tel Aviv, with the thoroughness that typified all he did, Rafi Eitan had briefed himself fully on Hamilton, the owner of the company that developed Promis software: how he had been sent to Vietnam to devise a network of electronic listening posts to monitor the Viet Cong as its forces moved through the jungle; how he had devised a computerised Vietnamese–English dictionary, which had proved to be a powerful aid to translating Viet Cong messages and interrogating prisoners. In many ways, Hamilton was one of the founding fathers of modern-day surveillance.

Bill Hamilton would later recall that period as 'the time when the revolution in electronic communications – satellite technology and micro-circuitry – was changing things in a big way: faster and more secure encryption and better imagery were coming on line at increasing speed. Computers grew smaller and faster; more sensitive sensors were able to separate tens of thousands of conversations. Surveillance was coming into its own.'

After Vietnam, Hamilton had joined the National Security Agency, NSA, itself at the coalface of surveillance. Driven by the exigencies of World War Two and then the Cold War, the National Security Agency was created in 1952. Hamilton found himself working in an organisation with acres of computers, electronic listening posts located around the world and a fleet of spy satellites circling overhead. NSA could eavesdrop on the communications of both friends and enemies, including American citizens.

At his introductory briefing to NSA, he was told that 'news of an invasion, an assassination or a coup overseas can be flashed from the point of interception to the President's desk in minutes. The latest performance data from Soviet missile tests can be recorded and analysed. Even the radiophone conversations of top Soviet and Chinese officials can be snatched from the atmosphere.'

All this had made the president of Inslaw and his development of the Promis software a high-priority target for Eitan.

Once more in the guise of Dr Orr, Rafi Eitan returned to Washington in February 1983. He went to the Justice Department and met with Brewer, who called Bill Hamilton.

The Inslaw president had never questioned his trust in the Justice Department or in Brewer. Both had repeatedly assured him that Enhanced Promis would guarantee Inslaw's future.

On almost every occasion he had previously telephoned, Brewer had some nugget to impart. Attorney-General Edwin Meese III had praised Enhanced Promis. Deputy Attorney-General Lowell Jensen had called it 'one of the great discoveries of this century'. Brewer himself had said that the Hamiltons should be proud of what they had achieved.

Now, on that bleak February morning in 1983, he had more good news. Hamilton would have a chance to show off Enhanced Promis. Would he give Dr Orr a demonstration of how Enhanced Promis worked? Very likely, added Brewer, Dr Orr would go back to Israel not only impressed with what he would have seen, but also ready to urge his own ministry to buy the software to keep track of Israeli criminals.

Hamilton was elated. Waiting for his visitor, he made sure that Inslaw's modest offices and research and development area was shipshape. He lived by the credo that first impressions are the ones that matter. Nancy Burke Hamilton, his wife, made sure there was fresh coffee in the pot and the china they used for visitors was laid out. There were cookies on a plate. The staff had been briefed on the importance of Dr Orr's visit. After a final check that everything was in order, Bill and Nancy sat back to await his arrival. They had never met someone from Israel before and certainly not someone as important as Dr Orr. His prominence spoke for itself in the way Brewer had arranged matters so quickly.

The company's staff were all on hand to greet their visitor and, like Bill and Nancy Hamilton, they could barely conceal their excitement. All those years of research and development, of following Bill's cheerful cry of 'back to the drawing board', and Nancy's ever-ready cups of coffee to sustain flagging energy – it all seemed to have been worthwhile.

Dr Orr arrived by cab. Muffled in a topcoat and wearing a cap with ear muffs, he was a striking figure. With the build of a wrestler and a bone-crunching handshake, he had a voice to match: guttural and heavily accented, his words broken by a smile that never seemed to go beyond his lips. But the most striking thing about Dr Orr was his eyes. They reminded Bill of 'a computer – tracking everything. It was quite uncanny and intimidating. Impressive, too.'

Dressed in his favourite chain-store suit and shoes, Eitan long ago learned that 'in my business you don't want to try and impress. My work calls for many things, but being high profile or boastful are not requirements.'

Flanked by Bill and Nancy, Dr Orr was taken on a tour of the offices where Enhanced Promis had been patiently created – chip by chip, microcircuit by microcircuit. Bill Hamilton's office had been chosen for the formal presentation. He explained to his visitor how an Enhanced Promis disc could select from myriad options the one that made most sense; how it eliminated deductive reasoning because, as Bill put it, 'there are too many correct but irrelevant matters to simultaneously take into account for human reasoning. Our program can be programmed to eliminate all superfluous lines of enquiry and collate data at a speed beyond human capability.'

It was virtually the same presentation as had hooked the senior staff of the Justice Department.

Dr Orr's questions were few and the sort the Hamiltons expected to be asked. Could Enhanced Promis be adapted to different languages? It could. Had Inslaw patented it? Of course: it was the first thing its inventor had done. Was it expensive? Yes, relatively so. But it was worth the price.

Bill Hamilton remembered that Dr Orr had given another of his quick smiles that never left his lips. Then, as swiftly as he appeared, the man from Tel Aviv had gone, driving away in a cab down 15th Street.

Only later would Bill Hamilton realise that he and Nancy had been in the presence of a 'man who knew how to act the part perfectly. Not one of us who met him would ever have guessed who he was or what was going on in his mind: how to steal Enhanced Promis.'

Leaving Inslaw, Rafi Eitan had returned to the Justice Department to tell Brewer how impressed he had been.

'Did Bill give you a copy?' Brewer had asked.

Rafi Eitan had opened his briefcase, then looked at Brewer.

'You won't believe it, Mr Brewer, I clean forgot to pick up the disc.'

He had looked at his watch and sighed. 'I guess there's not time to go back. I've got a plane connection to make in New York.'

'No problem, Dr Orr.'

Brewer had gone to an office cupboard and pulled out a computer tape and handed it to Eitan.

'Compliments of Justice. Let me know if it will work for your people.'

Eitan had smiled his thanks, shook hands and left the Justice Department. He had once said, 'Sometimes you don't have to work to get what you want.'

He arrived in Tel Aviv into yet another domestic political upheaval. The aftermath of the massacres at the Sabra and Shatila refugee camps in Beirut continued to reverberate. Ariel Sharon, who had commanded Israeli forces in Lebanon, had been castigated. Menachem Begin had resigned as Prime Minister, driven to do so because he did not want to shake hands with German Chancellor Helmut Kohl on a state visit to Israel. 'I want nothing to do with a nation that is associated with the murder of so many of our people,' he had said.

Rafi Eitan took all this in his stride. He had a more important matter to consider: how exactly should he handle Promis?

There were a number of factors. How and when should he inform Mossad of this potentially priceless intelligence weapon he had obtained? Mossad's relationship with LAKAM was still cold. Then there was his own situation. He received only a small pension from his years at Mossad, and his salary at LAKAM was equally modest. He was also getting on in years and he felt a strong obligation to his family to secure their future. In all those years in Mossad he had often been away for long periods on missions. His wife had always made sure he had a comfortable home to return to. For his part he had remained totally faithful to her, unusual in a world where casual sex was the norm. Their home on Shay Street in the north of Tel Aviv was a refuge for him and distinguished by one unusual feature. To one side of the house was a small charcoal-burning stove. He used it to fashion scrap metal into surreal sculptures. He enjoyed nothing more than scouring a refuse dump for pieces of discarded piping, rusting bicycle chains and other assorted metal junk.

He knew that some of his neighbours wondered if this was his way of escaping from his memories. They knew he had killed for his country.

But on that morning in the spring of 1983, while he fashioned another sculpture, Rafi Eitan was increasingly coming to see that the copy of Promis he had hand-carried all the way from Washington could not only make him once more a powerful force in the country's intelligence community, but also secure his family's future.

Properly handled, every disk of Promis software sold could make him a personal profit.

Over the next few months in 1983, Rafi Eitan watched a team of former LAKAM programmers – men he had chosen with the same care as he had done for all those Mossad operations that made his reputation – deconstruct the Promis program and then rearrange its various components. Then they had added several new elements. It was impossible for Inslaw or the Justice Department to claim ownership of the version of Promis that the programmers had built.

The only link to the Inslaw version was the name. Eitan had decided to retain Promis because it was 'a good tool to explain what the system was. A promise that could change the entire way intelligence could work.'

Even intelligence operatives who knew little more about computer technology beyond which keys to tap would, using Promis, be able to access information far more comprehensive than they could ever carry in their heads. A Promis disc could fit a laptop computer and choose from myriad alternatives the logical one. Promis could make millions of decisions in the blink of an eyelid. It would eliminate the need for deductive reasoning because there were too many correct but irrelevant matters to take simultaneously into account for human reasoning alone to suffice. Promis could be programmed to eliminate all superfluous lines of enquiry and amass and correlate data at a speed and scale beyond human capability.

The programmers told Eitan there was one final item that needed to be added to the new version of Promis. It required a 'trapdoor' – a microchip that would allow Eitan to know what information was being tracked by any purchaser of the system. In theory he could sit in Tel Aviv and keep tabs on the world.

Eitan was cautioned that, if they installed the 'trapdoor', it could be traced back to them. In the hostile climate prevailing towards LAKAM, that could cause a problem. They suggested Rafi Eitan should use his contacts to try to find a suitable computer expert outside Israel who could install the microchip.

Eitan consulted his 'little black book in which I keep all my most useful names'. Under 'M' he found the man he wanted – Ari Ben-Menashe.

For ten years he had held a highly sensitive post in the External Relations Department (ERD) of the Israeli Defence Forces. ERD was one of the most powerful and secret organisations in the country's intelligence community.

Suddenly his world had come tumbling down as once again political strife gripped Israel. Along the way old scores were settled. In their offices in the Kirya, the new political chiefs organised their purges of Mossad and Aman and of the lesser services. Those without a future packed their attaché cases and drove home to their families. Many suspected there would be no way back to the friendless discipline of their past work. They were right: a Mossad *katsa* found the only employment he could get was as a security guard; an Aman analyst ended up giving tutorials to schoolchildren.

Ari Ben-Menashe had been abroad when the purges started. He had felt untroubled; his conduct had never raised a doubt.

'Then suddenly I was told I was out. No reason. Just – out,' he later said.

Ben-Menashe's access to the Prime Minister's complex was terminated, along with his computer password, his secret telephone number and his use of the special credit cards, each in a different name with which he had been able 'to buy anyone and anything'.

It was those qualities that had made Rafi Eitan stop next to Ari Ben-Menashe's name in his little black book. In the times he had met Ben-Menashe, Eitan had never liked him. 'He was a womaniser, boasting of his conquests, and too back-slappy. He wanted everyone to be his friend. Not something which works in this business.'

But those other qualities in Ben-Menashe had still made Rafi Eitan decide to call him.

The meeting took place in Eitan's comfortable living room on a summer's day in 1983. Over coffee and home-baked biscuits, the old spymaster explained the background to Promis.

Seated in his armchair, his eyes noting the personal mementoes of Eitan's long career in intelligence – his favourite books, a few paintings of countries he had visited and small figurines on a shelf – Ben-Menashe reminded himself again that his host, 'like many of his generation saw the world in black and white, never grey. He was supremely committed to Israel's survival and to stamping out terrorists with no pity whatsoever. He despised the PLO and wanted nothing more than to exterminate them. A pragmatist, he was convinced there was no real peace until a solution to that problem was found.'

Eitan had led Ben-Menashe to his small study in the front of the house. It was filled with state-of-the-art electronic equipment. Eitan had slipped a disc into the maw of the computer.

They had watched in silence the data scrolling on the screen.

'What is this, Rafi?' Ben-Menashe finally asked. 'Some sort of new game?'

Eitan had smiled for the first time. 'My friend, we can use this to keep track of everyone. Every terrorist. Everybody. Friend and enemy. We can keep track of them.'

Ben-Menashe would remember: 'I stared at him for a moment. I thought, what the hell is he talking about? Tracking everyone. If it could do that, what did he need me for?'

Rafi Eitan told him about the need for the trapdoor.

'*Ben zona ata tso dek!*' Ben-Menashe said first in Hebrew, then for emphasis in English. 'Son of a bitch, you're right! A trapdoor! Of course! Put one in before it's sold to our enemies.'

'And friends,' said Eitan with emphasis.

He led the way back to the living room, poured more coffee and explained how it would work. Ben-Menashe sat there, taking careful notes to provide a good description of what Eitan intended.

In the silence, Ben-Menashe digested all he had been told. There were questions. It was one thing to sell the software to Third World countries who would not have the ability to detect a trapdoor, but what of more sophisticated nations? Surely they would have the technology to detect it. And, anyway, would they not suspect anything coming from Israel? Something like a bug, however well concealed, could still leak out.

As Ben-Menashe put each question, Eitan had nodded but said nothing. Ben-Menashe tried to conceal his concern that maybe Eitan had not thought of everything.

The two men sat in silence for another long moment. Then Ben-Menashe made a proposal. 'Look, Rafi, why don't you go America? To the NSA. It's the sort of thing they could help with if you cut them in. We both know they are still always ready to cut a deal.'

Eitan shook his head.

Ben-Menashe later recalled, 'As far as he was concerned, it was Israel's idea and would remain so. What he was really saying was it was his idea and he wanted his piece of the action. But I wondered where I still fitted into all this. He hadn't offered me anything. But I knew he hadn't invited me round just for afternoon coffee and cakes.'

Rafi Eitan eventually told him why he was there. He wanted Ari Ben-Menashe to find him a computer expert who could insert the microchip and guarantee – 'that is crucial, an absolute guarantee' – that it would never be discovered. Eitan shook his lion head and continued with emphasis, 'Even if the software is completely deconstructed there must be no trace of the trapdoor. It must be the perfect self-destruct.'

In return for doing this, Ben-Menashe could find himself returning to the mainstream intelligence fold of Israel. Rafi Eitan would also ensure his guest was suitably remunerated.

It took Ari Ben-Menashe a week to decide upon the man he would use. His name was Yehuda Ben-Hanan and he owned a small computer company in California. Ari Ben-Menashe took a plane to Los Angeles and hired a car.

On a Friday afternoon he arrived on Yehuda's doorstep shortly before the Sabbath meal would begin. He was invited to partake in the celebration. Over the *challah* bread and wine, the talk was lively and animated.

'But all the time I was trying to make a judgment. Yehuda was talkative but was he a blabbermouth? How curious was he that I had just dropped in after all those years? What were his views now on Israel? The sort of questions that are built into my work,' recalled Ben-Menashe.

In all, he spent five days with Ben-Hanan in his factory, his home, on drives around the countryside, even a stroll along the Pacific beach. Finally he decided that his host could be trusted. Ben-Menashe produced the Promis software and explained that it belonged to the Israeli government, whom he represented. He added that, the software now having been created, there was not one Israeli technician capable of producing a system that would protect it.

Ben-Menashe had anticipated the questions. He smiled and said, 'I can't tell you what it is for and why it must be protected but be assured there is a good reason.'

'Mossad?' Ben-Hanan had asked.

'Now, Yehuda, you know better than to ask that.'

For two days Yehuda Ben-Hanan had worked to create the trapdoor. He handed the microchip over to Ben-Menashe.

'Israel will thank you for this,' Ben-Menashe said, giving Ben-Hanan $5,000 in dollar bills.

Next day he was back in Tel Aviv. A LAKAM programmer took the microchip and inserted it in a copy of Promis.

Now it needed to be tested under field conditions.

Once more Rafi Eitan consulted his trusted address book and found the telephone number of the man he was seeking: Dr Earl Brian.

They had last met in Teheran when Eitan had been one of the Mossad team steering the arms-for-hostages fiasco later to be known as Irangate. Brian was in the Iranian capital to try to sell a healthcare system.

Eitan had immediately sensed there was something of the night about Brian: the way he walked close to a wall, his eyes darting ahead before glancing back over his shoulder, the way he drummed his finger on a table top. Eitan didn't share the view of others that Brian could fall into a cesspool and still come up smelling of roses.

In their days together drinking endless coffee in one of the few hotels that still knew how to brew it, Eitan had formed other views. Brian was a name dropper and ruthlessly ambitious. He had mentioned, almost with a sense of pride, that when he had been in charge of California's healthcare programme under Governor Ronald Reagan he was known as 'the man who walked over the dead'.

Eitan didn't like that: it showed a lack of respect for the job. He had returned to Tel Aviv and run his own checks on Brian, discovering that the American had been in Vietnam, where he was involved in CIA covert operations. Coincidentally, it was the same time as Bill Hamilton was creating his electronic Vietnamese–English dictionary. Like Hamilton, Brian had eventually ended up in Washington. The computer expert had vanished into the confines of the National Security Agency; Brian had found himself a berth in the White House of President Reagan.

There the traits Eitan had noticed in Teheran had continued. Brian travelled under various aliases, coming and going from the White House with the stealth of a spy on some ultra-secret mission. No one challenged him: Brian was one of the select few who had instant access to the Oval Office.

He also had an open door to the Justice Department run by another old friend, Edwin Meese, the Attorney-General, who was a devotee of Promis. They had known each other from the days they had served under Reagan's governorship. Meese and his wife, Ursula, remained close friends with Brian and it was Ursula who told him over dinner about Promis.

Brian later recalled Ursula saying, 'Now wouldn't it be great if you could get hold of marketing Promis outside of the Justice Department?'

Still working from his office in the White House, Brian had launched himself on the business world, creating a company he registered as Hadron.

Its sole asset was a copy of the Promis software that the Justice Department had agreed he could market. The arrangement had been made with the blessing of Meese. What paperwork ever existed on the matter had long gone; Meese and Brewer would remain close-mouthed on the matter.

Brian began to promote Promis using the White House switchboard to make and receive calls.

One of them was to Ira Gurston Rosenfeld, a senior member of the respected Montreal brokerage, Nesbitt-Thompson. It handled billions of dollars annually and advised thousands of rich clients on investments. Rosenfeld liked the idea of doing business with a man who conducted it from the White House, but he was also worried about a conflict of interest with his duties as a stockbroker. Brian told him he had 'the right man for fronting things'. This was Janos Pasztor, a freelance market analyst he had recently met on a trip to Wall Street to seek further funds for Hadron.

'The guy needs money and we can run him up front. If anything goes wrong, he can take the fall,' Brian told Rosenfeld.

The philosophy of all three men was subtly different. For Brian, 'Promis was an invention from which I was entitled to live off the inheritance,' he told Rosenfeld.

The quintessential stockbroker in his dark suit and soft-spoken manner, he felt 'in my heart, in my very soul, that I have responsibility not only to make deals for my investors, but to enhance the general prosperity of my company and, of course, myself'.

Pasztor was a hard-driving operator. 'I'm in a business for people who don't have money but who know someone who has money. My job is to give him a reason to part with it. And to make a few bucks for myself along the way. I'm not especially interested in the background to what I'm marketing. The bottom line is, can I sell it?'

The three men met over a weekend in Montreal. By Sunday a deal had been worked out. Pasztor would be Hadron's CEO. Brian would remain as president, to whom Pasztor would report on a regular basis. Rosenfeld would find money from Nesbitt-Thompson to kick-start the operation. Perhaps in what should have been a warning to any stockbroker, Brian casually mentioned as he prepared to take the flight back to Washington that he liked the sound of the names 'Nesbitt' and 'Thompson'.

'I might even use them as names to travel under,' he added.

If Rosenfeld was puzzled as he drove his two companions to the airport, he didn't say anything. After all, Brian was well connected in Washington and perhaps he needed to have aliases. There was about Rosenfeld something so open, so trusting, so naïve. Certainly, on that Sunday he had no idea of all that was about to be unleashed on the other side of the world, in Israel.

Pasztor started to promote Promis as a prime investment exclusively available through Hadron. Describing himself as the company's CEO, Pasztor selected his first client – the Royal Canadian Mounted Police. He flew to Ottawa and gave the RCMP a demonstration. The Mounties were impressed and agreed to test the software in 26 of their field offices across Canada.

These tests were still under way when Rafi Eitan called Earl Brian, who by now had left government service and was fully engaged in creating a raft of companies. Like Robert Maxwell, Brian was busy empire building.

But the call from Rafi Eitan made him catch the next plane to Israel.

Waiting for him at the airport was Ari Ben-Menashe, who drove him to a small office in downtown Tel Aviv. Rafi Eitan welcomed Brian like a long-lost friend: there were drinks and canapés and reminiscences about their times together in Iran.

Gradually Eitan checked what he already knew against how much Brian was telling him about his thirty contracts for his version of Promis; many of them were with US intelligence agencies, including the CIA.

Brian produced a still-secret memo prepared by the then special assistant for security planning. It ordered the National Security Agency to 'penetrate banks to combat money-laundering and other criminal activities, and illegal sales of high technology to the Soviet Union'. The NSA was instructed to install Promis in all major wire-transfer clearing houses in the United States and Europe, including the Clearing House Interbank Payment System in New York.

Brian said he had moved Hadron's facilities to Newport, Rhode Island, so that he could be closer to the navy's Undersea Systems Center. He hoped the proximity to the base would enable him one day to get the contract for Hadron to install its Promis software on board Trident nuclear submarines.

Brian explained how the software could, for example, store the unique sonar signal of every British, Chinese or Russian submarine. Artificial intelligence on board a Trident could then perform the firing calculations to destroy any hostile submarine.

Brian had said, Rafi Eitan later recalled, that Promis could also be adapted for the firing of nuclear-armed missiles from a submerged Trident, a technique known as 'over the horizon', at targets within the Soviet Union or China. The software was also programmed to include details of the defences around a target, along with the advanced physics and mathematics needed to ensure a direct hit.

And it was not only submarines that would benefit. Rafi Eitan's loose-tongued guest had rambled on, sipping the vintage whisky Rafi Eitan poured for favoured visitors. A system like Promis could automatically route the aircraft around enemy radar and missile threats and ensure that the fighter maintained its stealthness during a mission.

Finally Brian had asked, 'What can I do for you, Rafi?'

Ben-Menashe would remember that Eitan had spread his hands and smiled his most deprecating smile.

'Earl,' he said, 'after all you're involved with, I don't think I should be bothering you.'

'No bother, Rafi. That is what friends are for. So tell me.'

And Eitan had. He told Brian he had 'a piece of software I'd like to test. It seems to me that Hadron is the ideal company to do it.'

Jordan was selected as the test site because it had become a haven for terrorists targeting Israel. From the desert kingdom they continued to direct the Arab street mobs on the West Bank and Gaza.

Within a month Brian had arranged for Hadron's programmers to install

Rafi Eitan's version of Promis in Amman's military headquarters. In Tel Aviv, Eitan's programmers showed him how well the trapdoor worked. But they had expressed doubt about the abilities of Hadron's salesmen to market the software effectively on a global scale.

For all his boasting at being able to call up anybody on earth through the White House switchboard, to which he still had access – something Brian had demonstrated in setting up the Amman deal – his sales force was too small and inexperienced to operate globally.

Eitan arranged to give Brian a generous payoff and looked round for a salesman with an organisation able to do the kind of marketing he wanted. He turned to the one man above all others he still trusted: Yitzhak Shamir.

His response was immediate. There was only one person for the job: Robert Maxwell.

At 35,000 feet, the pilot, Brian Hull, began his descent into Tel Aviv airspace in the autumn of 1984. In the cabin, Robert Maxwell sat sprawled on the light-brown leather seat, his massive belly held in check by a special safety belt he always kept fastened during a flight except for the moment he had to go to the wood-panelled toilet with its own perfumed air system.

Maxwell was the only passenger and, as usual, he had taken his shoes and socks off after take-off. Boarding, he had checked with the steward, Simon Grigg, that the galley was stocked with smoked salmon, a large silver bowl of caviar, cheddar cheese and chicken. In the refrigerator was vintage Krug champagne.

Maxwell was in an ebullient mood. The Mirror Group newspaper acquisition had gone ahead he had achieved his aim of acquiring a national newspaper and was looking forward to the power it would grant him. He had not forgotten his mother's thoughts on the importance of newspapers in society – how they could be mechanisms for change. He would now be one of the opinion-makers of Britain and would use his paper in one way to promote the ailing Labour Party. Since Mossad had recruited him, he had made several trips to meet with its director-general, Nahum Admoni. It was he who had proposed Maxwell should help with the famine crisis in Ethiopia. Maxwell seized upon the idea: it not only offered an opportunity for a personal publicity coup but would gain support for his claim that the *Mirror* would return to its old ways of being a 'caring' newspaper. He had flown there with a cargo of maize.

The mercy mission played well in Israel. But the jibes of the Murdoch newspapers and *Private Eye*, the satirical UK magazine, referred to the *Mirror* as the *Daily Maxwell*.

When the Gulfstream landed, Rafi Eitan was waiting on the tarmac with a limousine. Introductions over, he had told the driver to take them to Jerusalem. Eitan knew the perfect introduction to what he planned.

Hours later he led Maxwell through Yad Vashem, the museum that is a poignant reminder of the victims of the Holocaust with its images and relics of a barely imaginable act of mass murder, a fearful crime that still affects the world's views about Israel and its people.

For Eitan it was another opportunity to explain the still little-known role of the Jewish resistance during the Holocaust; how it had piggybacked on Stalin's most secret operations to deceive Hitler; how it had uncovered Allen Dulles's wartime efforts to create a post-Hitler alliance with Germany against the Soviet Union; how the Jewish resistance had used the information to help form an underground system for smuggling Jews out of Nazi Europe. The Jewish resistance, Eitan had explained, had been the most effective spy organisation of modern times. It had played a key part in the creation of the State of Israel. Eitan knew because in that struggle he had used the survivors of the Jewish resistance. He called them 'my grandfather spies'.

And, in that quiet way he had of making his points, Eitan said that no doubt Maxwell knew how the Allied leaders had agreed at Yalta to place Jewish immigration to Palestine off limits when victory came. The spymaster was doing what he had done so many times, 'creating a mood'. He knew that there could be no doubting Maxwell's commitment to Israel: he had shown that in his willingness to assist Mossad. But Eitan wanted more.

Maxwell had already demonstrated his worth to Mossad. In those post-war years, when he had been in Berlin, he had established a network of contacts within the scientific publishing community. Later he had extended these into other Eastern Bloc satellites of Moscow. Over the years he had worked his way into their upper echelons. He spoke their languages, understood their culture and respected their ways. These assets, which he had first used to help build his own publishing empire, now became avenues along which he could travel with a new purpose: to obtain the information Mossad needed.

To do so, Maxwell continued to exploit and revel in his celebrity; it opened ever more important doors to him. He encouraged senior cadres to be photographed with him in their newspapers. In turn that led to further invitations to meet more important people. He listened carefully to all they had to say and asked his questions with a shrewdness that was part of him. In turn, he understood their jokes, recognised the food they offered him, spoke knowledgeably of their difficulties and encouraged their aspirations. Because of all this, they told him far more than they should. He learned about the military, political and economic secrets no other spy from the West could hope to acquire.

His very celebrity, increasingly ridiculed in London, was a powerful asset. The more famous he became in Eastern Europe, the more its leaders wanted to sit down with him, treat him as an honoured guest, bestow upon him their nation's highest awards and share with him still more confidences.

He was the first to learn that Soviet agents in the West were being asked to watch for sudden appeals for blood donors – a sign that a suspected nuclear attack was in the offing. He was told the full extent of Moscow's responses when a Korean airliner, KAL-007, which had strayed into a high-security airspace was shot down. Moscow had expected retaliation. None came. But his contacts had shown him the extent to which fear bred fear.

In Budapest he was shown a secret briefing paper prepared by the Soviet Foreign Minister, Andrei Gromyko, that assessed how far Moscow could push the West. Over dinner with Romania's Nicolae Ceauşescu, while discussing the biography Maxwell was to publish, the dictator revealed that the KGB Chief Yuri Andropov was on a kidney-dialysis machine in the Kuntsevo clinic outside Moscow; as well as renal failure, Andropov was acutely depressed and feared war was coming – and that the West would win. Another leading communist confided that aircraft fitted with nuclear bombs were being placed on stand-by at East German air bases.

Nahum Admoni had spotted the potential for Maxwell to be able to access this kind of information, simply because of who he was and the way he behaved. The bombast of a modern-day emperor ostentatiously talking about his wealth, and displaying it at every opportunity, was the perfect cover for a superb spy. Maxwell never took a note or spoke into a tape to record what he had been told. He depended only on his phenomenal memory.

Coming out of the museum Rafi Eitan took Maxwell on a short drive down a road and through the biblical village of Ein Karen. Beyond, he had the car stop.

Together he and Robert Maxwell walked into a small forest. The trees were conifers, alien to the rest of the landscape. Dotted among their roots were granite plaques half buried in the ground. Each bore the name of someone who had died in Israel's War of Independence.

'I served with some of them,' Rafi Eitan would recall saying. 'They served Israel in more ways than there is time to tell you.'

Then he had turned to the tycoon and asked if Robert Maxwell was ready to do the same. Maxwell said he was.

Rafi Eitan had then told him of his plans for marketing Promis and the role he wanted Maxwell to play.

FIVE

Robert Maxwell's agreement to become Mossad's spy and now the very public face of marketing Promis came at a time when Israel's intelligence community was heavily engaged on all fronts.

Its *katsas* in Cairo continued to monitor the Camp David agreement which had brought peace between Egypt and Israel and firmly removed the Egyptian government from the Moscow camp. But the Soviet Union had found a new opening for its strategies in the region. It invaded Afghanistan; the warm-water ports of the Indian Ocean and the oil wells of the Persian Gulf became only a few hours away from Russian combat troops. It was the high-water mark of the Soviet leader Leonid Brezhnev's ambitions to use the Middle East as the means to expand the Cold War; only later would it turn out to be the disastrous adventure that paved the way for the collapse of the Soviet Union.

It was Robert Maxwell who had provided Mossad with advance warning that it would happen. He had managed to be invited to the Moscow All-Union Scientific and Practical Conference. The keynote speaker had been a young *apparat* who had reminded his audience that he, like many of them, had been born into the nightmare of Soviet collectivisation. It was an era when his own family had slaughtered their livestock rather than hand them over to collective farms, a time when grain had been seized at gunpoint and fed to starving cities. It had rekindled memories for Maxwell. He had sat, transfixed, listening to Mikhail Gorbachev reminding his audience this must never happen again.

For once not trusting to memory, Maxwell had scribbled down some of Gorbachev's words. A need for 'profound transformation', a 'qualitatively higher standard of living', a 'fast developing economy', and 'a need to strengthen our position in the international arena'.

The words heralded a wind of change that would sweep from Siberia to the Polish steppes. Russia, Maxwell sensed, was about to behead itself

71

once more. Having destroyed its Tsarist rulers and ripped out its collective soul under Stalin's purges, it was now, if Gorbachev was right, once more about to lop off the past.

The highly suspect national statistics, the focus on military might at the expense of gross-national-product growth – all this would be turned on its head in a new *detente* based upon normal relations with the West.

Maxwell had hurried to Tel Aviv to report his conclusions. Mossad may have been the first intelligence service to be made aware of the coming sea change. The CIA was still briefing the US President that the Soviet economy was 'far from collapse', and ' in good shape' to take the strain of the arms race 'without cuts in living standards' and that it may even 'develop more rapidly than the US economy'.

Meanwhile the seizure of the US diplomats in their Teheran embassy in the dying days of the exhausted administration of President Jimmy Carter paved the way for Ronald Reagan to enter the White House. In London he had an ally of like mind, Prime Minister Margaret Thatcher. Together they set about resurrecting the slogan of John F Kennedy in the 1960s – 'We will stand firm against Soviet aggression' – with a triple promise: to end the defeatism that gripped Western Europe; to bolster the West's defences; to roll back the Soviet advances of the previous decade.

Mossad was deeply involved in all these areas, operating the diktat David Kimche had articulated: 'In all we do it is Israel first, last and always. Always.'

When Yitzhak Hofi had been appointed in 1974 to run Mossad, one of his first tasks had been to reinforce its presence in Moscow; until then Mossad had depended on *katsas* operating under diplomatic cover. Within two years Hofi had a deep-penetration agent in place on the staff of the Soviet Foreign Minister Andrei Gromyko. The agent provided Hofi with surprising information. Neither Gromyko nor Soviet Defence Minister Dmitri Ustinov had approved the invasion of Afghanistan.

They felt the risks were unacceptable, that, just as America had become mired in Vietnam, the Soviet Union would be drawn into an ever-deeper and full-scale military commitment.

The agent also reported that Moscow was becoming increasingly worried over the fall of the Shah of Iran and his replacement by the extremist Islamic regime of Ayatollah Khomeini. The Soviet leadership feared the mullahs would trigger unrest in their own southern Muslim republics.

The revelations diametrically opposed the view Hofi had received from the CIA on his visits to Washington: its director Bill Casey had told him that America regarded the invasion of Afghanistan as a very visible sign of an aggressive and confident Soviet Union.

Hofi had wondered how this would affect Israel's hopes to persuade

Moscow to allow Soviet Jews to immigrate. He decided there could be a better chance of that if he did not share the intelligence about Moscow's very real concerns over Afghanistan. If the United States maintained its own belligerent policy over the Soviet Union's occupation of Afghanistan, it might be possible to persuade the Kremlin to make a gesture designed to appease America's powerful Jewish lobby by allowing out a substantial number of Jews.

Now, in 1984, the new director-general of Mossad, Nahum Admoni, was a tireless promoter of the cause for allowing Jews to settle in their homeland. It went with his intellectual discipline and his flair for detail.

Admoni had been part of Israel from the very hour of its creation; he had seen how it had to fight for its place among nations. He believed with quiet conviction there was no other people who had given so much, and for so long, to enlighten others on the moral and spiritual imperatives that govern the ways of mankind. For Admoni all those qualities were brought together in trying to discover what the Kremlin was doing – and how that information could be used to bring out Soviet Jews.

In those long nights when he sat alone on the top floor of Mossad headquarters reading the flow of incoming traffic from his agents all over the world, that was the compelling force, his principal article of faith and the inexhaustible wellspring from which he drew his strength to survive the trials and tribulations of being the Mossad chief. For him the State of Israel, conceived in the hearts and minds of his forebears, was the most important thing in his life. The more Jews he could arrange to come to this still threatened land, still surrounded by a hostile environment, the happier he would be. That burning wish had underlined the briefing he had given Robert Maxwell. In the tycoon he had found someone of the same passion and commitment.

Maxwell's brief also included monitoring what could happen now that Yuri Andropov was dead. In the two years the former KGB chief had run the Soviet Union, he had failed to establish *détente* with the United States. His successor, Konstantin Chernyenko, was already a geriatric, coughing his way through Politburo meetings, constantly spitting into the kind of bottle issued to Soviet tuberculosis patients. Yet behind the walls of the Kremlin there were signs of a new course being prepared for not only Russia, but all its satellite states. Maxwell was briefed to obtain the kind of information that would enable Mossad to continue to chart what was happening.

His intelligence was to provide Admoni and Israel's political masters with an inside track on the thinking in the Kremlin. He told them that Russia still feared that the United States would try to block the introduction of the Siberian gas pipeline to Western European markets unless there was a return to the Geneva arms talks.

Among his other discoveries had been that, while the Soviet Union still possessed the world's most powerful missiles, the Energiya and the SS-18, neither had the guidance system that would make it a serious threat to the West. In Maxwell's view, Moscow's stubborn refusal to negotiate while Cruise and Pershing missiles were deployed by the United States was no more than a bluff. Once more he turned out to be right.

By using his scientific contacts, offering to publish their work on computer technology in his magazines, he was able to provide hard evidence that the Eastern Bloc was well behind the West in technology and innovation.

It gave Israel an opening to sell secretly a number of Eastern Bloc countries computers produced by Degem, Maxwell's own company. In turn that allowed Mossad to send its own electronic specialists to the Soviet Union, posing as technicians, to cast their eyes over the state of the domestic computer industry.

Step by step, while Israel had no meaningful diplomatic presence in the Soviet Union, Maxwell's intelligence gathering opened up the reality of what was happening in the Communist empire.

Meanwhile, Rafi Eitan had found common cause with Admoni. Eitan would market Promis through Maxwell's organisation; in return Mossad would receive any important intelligence that came through the trapdoor. Eitan also continued to run another important operation.

Shortly before he had recruited Maxwell, Eitan had received a call from New York. It was 2 a.m. in Tel Aviv and for once Eitan had retired early.

His caller was Aviem Sella, a colonel in the Israeli air force who was on a sabbatical to study computer science at New York University. He had just come from a party given by a wealthy Jewish gynaecologist on the Upper East Side of Manhattan. Sella was a minor celebrity among the city's Jewish community as the pilot who had led an air attack three years before that had destroyed Iraq's nuclear reactor.

At the party was a diffident young man with a shy smile who seemed ill at ease among the small set of doctors, lawyers and bankers. He told Sella his name was Jonathan Pollard and that the only reason he had come was to meet him. Embarrassed by such obvious adulation, Sella made polite small talk and was about to move on when Pollard revealed he was not only a committed Zionist, but worked for US naval intelligence. In no time the astute Sella had learned that Pollard was stationed at the Anti-Terrorist Alert Center in one of the navy's most secret establishments at Suitland, Maryland. Pollard's duties included monitoring all classified material on global terrorist activities. So important was the work that he had the highest possible US intelligence community security clearance.

Sella could not believe what he was hearing, especially when Pollard began to give specific details about incidents where the US intelligence community was not cooperating with its Israeli counterpart. Sella began to wonder whether Pollard was part of a sting operation by the FBI to try to recruit an Israeli.

'Instinctively Rafi Eitan realised it was not; that Pollard was genuine. That kind of instinct goes with the territory,' according to Ari Ben-Menashe.

Rafi Eitan ordered Sella to develop his contact with Pollard.

They began to meet: at the skating rink at Rockefeller Plaza; in a coffee shop on Forty-Eighth Street; in Central Park. Each time Pollard handed over secret documents to confirm the truth of what he said. Sella couriered the material to Tel Aviv, enjoying the frisson of being caught up in an important intelligence operation.

Sella had come to know the science attaché at the Israeli consulate in New York. His name was Yosef Yagur.

Sella invited Yagur to dinner with Pollard. Over the meal Pollard repeated that Israel was being denied information to defend itself against Arab terrorists because the United States did not wish to upset its relations with Arab oil producers.

For the next three months Yagur and Sella assiduously cultivated Pollard and his future wife, Anne Henderson. They took them to expensive restaurants, Broadway shows, first-night films. Pollard continued to hand over important documentation. Rafi Eitan could only marvel at how good the material was. He decided it was time to meet the source.

Sella and Yagur invited Pollard and Henderson to accompany them on an all-expenses-paid trip to Paris. Yagur told Pollard the vacation was 'a small reward for all you are doing for Israel'. They all flew first class and were met by a chauffeured car and driven to the Bristol Hotel. Waiting for them was Rafi Eitan.

By the end of the night, Rafi Eitan had finalised all the practical arrangements for Pollard to continue his treachery. No longer would matters continue in their free-and-easy way. Sella would fade from the picture, his role over. Yagur would become Pollard's official handler.

A proper delivery system was worked out for documents to be handed over. In the apartment of Irit Erb, a mousy-haired secretary at the Israeli Washington embassy, a high-speed photocopier had been installed in her kitchen to copy the material. Pollard would visit a number of designated car washes. While his car was being cleaned, he would hand over documents to Yagur, whose own car would be undergoing a similar process.

Both Erb's apartment and the car-wash facilities were close to

Washington's National Airport, making it easier for Yagur to fly back and forth to and from New York. From the consulate he transmitted the material by secure fax to Tel Aviv.

Rafi Eitan flew to Washington in the autumn of 1984. This time he chose to go under the alias of Eli Wiesman, a name on a passport chosen from the collection he kept updated.

On that October day Robert Maxwell was visiting John Tower, a senator who was also close to Vice-President George Bush. Tower had helped to get Bush elected to Congress and later Bush had returned the favour by lobbying for Tower to be appointed as chairman of the Armed Services Committee. Eitan had asked Maxwell to introduce him to Tower.

The three men met at Tower's spacious home in Georgetown. Next day, Tower drove them out to the National Archives storage annexe in the quiet commuter community in Suitland, Maryland. Across from the Archives was a wire-fenced facility with geodesic radar domes and low buildings. This was where Jonathan Pollard worked for Naval Intelligence.

Maxwell had expressed a desire to see the annexe, repository of, among much else, records of the Indian Wars, the American Revolution, the War of 1812, the Spanish–American War, all the wars down to the Vietnam conflict. Maxwell said he wanted to find details of villagers from Slatinske Doly who had managed to escape to America before the Nazis had stopped emigration. Using his Congressional pass, Tower had persuaded staff to go through the thousands of grey boxes neatly stacked on dark metal shelves. Maxwell had become bored waiting in a small side room and said there was probably nothing to be found.

That night Eitan travelled to New York. There he had met Yagur and Sella. They told him that, by the time he returned to Tel Aviv, there would be another shipment of documents from Pollard.

Rafi Eitan continued to obtain a clear picture of US intelligence-gathering methods, not only in the Middle East but in South Africa. Pollard had provided reports from CIA operatives that provided a blueprint for the entire US intelligence network within that country.

Mossad passed over copies of all material relating to South Africa to the Pretoria regime, virtually destroying the CIA network. Twelve operatives were forced to leave the country hurriedly.

Rafi Eitan had also been impressed with Maxwell's contact with Tower.

The danger of confrontation between the Soviet Union and the United States was inherent in the Arab–Israeli conflict. It was a contest that both superpowers had waged for three decades.

Israel's leaders had come to understand the unspoken ground rules that existed in such times of crisis. The Soviet Union was ready to advance as far as it could until it met determined American resistance. Soviet daring had increased over the years – and so had the risks of military conflict. But, each time, the United States had managed to curb any direct threat – not just to Israel but to its own interests in the region. Every war between Arab states and Israel had been halted by ceasefire orders agreed upon by Washington and Moscow. That was the reality. But to understand how long it would last, Rafi Eitan was increasingly tasking Jonathan Pollard to obtain documents that reflected the inner strategies of the United States. Uppermost in his mind was one question: how far would Washington go to protect its own interests – even at the expense of Israel?

Pollard had become a crucial factor in the success of Israeli policy-making. Rafi Eitan authorised an Israeli passport for Pollard in the name of Danny Cohen as well as a generous monthly stipend. In return he asked Pollard to provide details about the electronic eavesdropping activities of the National Security Agency (NSA) in Israel and the bugging methods used against the Israeli embassy in Washington and its other diplomatic stations within the United States.

Before Pollard could supply the information, he was arrested outside the Israeli embassy in Washington by the FBI on charges of espionage. Hours later, Yagur, Sella and the embassy secretary in Washington had all caught an El Al flight from New York to Tel Aviv before the FBI could stop them. In Israel they disappeared into the protective arms of a grateful intelligence community. Pollard was sentenced to life imprisonment and his wife to five years.

Both Rafi Eitan and Nahum Admoni believed that though he was very different from Jonathan Pollard, in Robert Maxwell they had the ideal replacement. He would use his Degem computer company to sell the Promis software. It would give him the perfect cover to conduct his spying operations for Mossad.

Maxwell had quickly proved himself to be a brilliant marketer. Using the same sales slogan, 'Promis is better and cheaper than anything else on the market', he secured his first client, President Robert Mugabe of Zimbabwe. Mugabe had been elected on a pledge to introduce reforms after years of British colonial rule. But, like other African dictators, he had developed the incipient paranoia that would remain with him all his life. Maxwell assured Mugabe that Promis would enable him to track any plotters among the white tobacco farmers who remained in Zimbabwe.

From Harare, the country's ramshackle capital, Maxwell had flown south to Pretoria to sell the software to the apartheid regime, seeking a new way to hunt down black revolutionary groups. Within days miners' leaders planning a strike were tracked down by Promis through their identity passes. The day Maxwell left South Africa, all were imprisoned without trial.

His next port of call was Guatemala. Once more Maxwell personally demonstrated how Promis could track all enemies of the regime. Some 20,000 government opponents were rounded up. They were either killed or joined the ranks of South America's legion of the 'disappeared'. Soon the security forces of Colombia and Nicaragua had all acquired the software.

In Tel Aviv, Rafi Eitan and Mossad knew who had been arrested even before the families of a regime's opponents were picked up.

Maxwell next launched his sales offensive into the very bastion of security – the Swiss banking world. He persuaded Credit Suisse to install Promis. In no time Rafi Eitan was learning sensitive secrets. The data was passed to Mossad. Sometimes the depositors were Israeli millionaires who had opened overseas accounts, illegal under the country's tight financial controls. They were approached to make a donation to help Israel. If they refused, they were threatened with exposure – a guarantee of a heavy fine and imprisonment. There were no refusals.

Promis also confirmed what Mossad had suspected for some time. The respected Credit Suisse was unwittingly being used by the CIA and Mafia in their financial transactions. Sometimes up to £300 million a day passed through the special Credit Suisse accounts set up by organised-crime families: the Mafia money came from the profits of drugs and prostitution.

Within days Promis had enabled Rafi Eitan and Mossad to have the numbers of every Mafia and CIA account.

Many were held by Richard J Brenneke, the CIA operative in overall charge of the agency's secret money-laundering operations. He worked sixteen-hour days moving covert funds in and out of Credit Suisse and sending them on complex transfers around the global banking world. Using his skills like a hacker to 'weave and loop', Brenneke made sure nobody could track his own electronic signature. But, thanks to Robert Maxwell, Mossad had it.

They noted just how Brenneke worked, how he gave instructions to certain bank officials in various parts of the world on how the money would be transferred – either by cashier's cheque or by courier. Brenneke had devised special codes for all his communications: one for a receiving bank, another for a transmitting financial house. The codes changed on a regular basis. No transaction remained in any one of his accounts for more than 72 hours. Among the banks he favoured were Banco de Panama – the Panamanian national bank – and the venerable Bank Lambert in Brussels. And, of course, Credit Suisse.

In Tel Aviv, Rafi Eitan saw how foolproof was Brenneke's method. As the first profits from the sales of the Promis software started to arrive, he began to use the same follow-the-money route the CIA operation had established. Eitan was a financial ghost walking in Brenneke's footsteps.

He told Maxwell he should adopt the same way of hiding his own profits, not only from Promis, but from any other venture he wished to keep from prying eyes. It was Robert Maxwell's first step into the criminal world of money laundering.

By then Maxwell was ready to move Promis into the Soviet Union. But the endless first-class travel and deluxe hotel suites, accompanied by fawning service, had begun to pall. His lifestyle had also affected him physically: in a year he had put on twenty pounds in weight, most of it around his waist. The first hint of a wheeze had started and he had frequent colds. He dosed himself with cough mixtures and took vitamins his newspapers advertised.

His delight at owning the *Daily Mirror* was followed by the marriage of his daughter, Isabel, to Dale Jerassi, the son of a wealthy Bulgarian inventor. When Isabel, pregnant with her first son, was rushed to hospital suffering from a rare illness, leptospirosis, Betty maintained a vigil at her bedside until Isabel recovered. The baby was later born prematurely but grew into a healthy boy.

For his grandfather, it was another reason to take a holiday. He found family crises more exhausting than any business deal.

Returning from another Promis sales trip, Maxwell chartered a yacht, the *Southern Breeze*. For once he decided to make it a family holiday, flying Betty and his sons, Ian and Kevin, with him to Athens. They set sail into the Aegean for what Maxwell had promised would be a real adventure.

It turned out to be Maxwell in the role of Captain Bligh. He constantly challenged the yacht's captain over the accuracy of his charts. He had brought on board his own compass and regularly compared what it showed with the one of the bridge.

Betty, just glad to be part of his life again, albeit briefly, spent her time sunning herself on deck with their sons. Maxwell timed how long it took a stewardess to bring them drinks, how quickly the table was cleared between courses at meal times. He argued with a steward about the quality of the champagne, how cold it should be when served. At night he would stomp out of his state cabin and patrol the deck in his night shirt, surveying passing ships through glasses.

One morning he summoned the captain. Standing over the chart table, he unrolled a course map. He jabbed with a finger.

'Here,' boomed Maxwell. 'Here is where you will take me.'

The captain blinked. 'But sir, it is forbidden to go there! That is Bulgaria!'

'I know that,' Maxwell said impatiently. 'Just take me there.'

'But sir, the Soviet navy will stop us! They may even attack us!'

'Nonsense! I am Robert Maxwell. I am known in Moscow, everywhere in the Soviet Union. Now take this boat to where I order you. Or get off!'

For Betty the 'real adventure' was turning out 'not for the first time with Bob, not as I expected'.

The yacht set sail for the Black Sea port of Varna.

As they entered Bulgaria's territorial waters, Betty noted in the diary she always kept, 'The whole place reminds me of Ovid's "Laments" of "a place alas, no fortunate man should visit".'

By now Maxwell had taken command of the yacht, standing in the wheelhouse issuing course changes to the helmsman.

Suddenly, Betty recalled, a new problem arose. 'Bob couldn't decide which flag to fly when we came closer to shore.'

He had brought with him from London the MCC Maxwell House flag and a Union Jack. But he realised neither would be appropriate.

He turned to Betty. 'Sew me a Bulgarian flag.'

She nodded, glad to be able to do something that would keep her busy and away from his tyrannical mood. She had the dining-room steward bring her remnants of linen and a sewing kit. She created the Bulgarian national flag of red, white and green.

Maxwell hoisted it at the yacht's masthead. 'Sail on,' he commanded. 'We are now fully prepared.'

Hardly had he uttered the reassurance than a Bulgarian naval gunboat raced towards them.

The officer politely asked for the *Southern Breeze* to follow him into Varna.

Standing beside the hapless yacht's captain, Maxwell continued to sweep the approaches to the harbour with binoculars. He realised that his escort was guiding him to a remote part of the quay.

Maxwell pointed at a Russian destroyer on the other side of the harbour.

'Anchor alongside her,' he commanded the terrified helmsman. Beside Maxwell the yacht's captain was shaking with fear. 'Please, sir, do not do that. It is forbidden,' he whimpered.

Maxwell ignored him. The *Southern Breeze* began to head for the destroyer. On its deck sailors were lining the rails watching in disbelief. Maxwell waved at them imperiously. It was Captain Bligh coming into dock.

Behind them the Bulgarian gunboat and a police vessel were circling. A voice in Russian came through a loud hailer.

'You are in a military zone forbidden to civilians.'

Maxwell responded in a voice that carried across the closing gap between the yacht and the destroyer.

'I am Robert Maxwell. Please inform the President I have arrived.' He ordered the yacht's anchor to be dropped.

There was a short interlude. On the destroyer armed marines appeared, standing at attention. The gunboat and police launch edged closer.

Suddenly the drama was over. From the launch came a radioed message to the yacht's bridge.

Bulgaria's dictator regretted he could not personally be on hand to welcome his guests – but he was arranging for them to be properly entertained.

Shortly afterwards a motor launch flying the presidential flag came alongside. Maxwell and his family were bowed on board. As they left the yacht, the marines on the destroyer deck snapped to attention. Cap'n Bob would have expected no less.

He returned their salute with a flap of his hand that was his way of acknowledging victory.

That night Maxwell and Betty slept in separate bedrooms – he to snore, she to lie awake to ponder how best to handle a family crisis.

Kevin had announced he wished to marry a vivacious American woman, Pandora Warnford-Davis.

Maxwell had long laid down another family rule: none of his children would be allowed to wed unless he personally approved of their partners; as a rider he added he wished also to have the final say on the day and date of any wedding.

His eldest son, Philip, had already defied him. Maxwell had forbidden the rest of the family from attending the nuptials. Betty had challenged Maxwell's orders. In the end he agreed to allow the family to go to Philip's wedding.

But now Kevin had once more brought confrontation into Betty's marriage. She had fallen asleep in the Bulgarian palace the country's President had loaned them wondering if she was going to be able to win the day over Kevin's desire to marry his American beauty. In the end she did, but it was a close call.

In Tel Aviv, the secrets gleaned from Promis continued to shape Israel's strategy. They enabled Israel to take a vigorous stand with individual governments and in international forums to promote Jewish immigration and monitor those who opposed it. The extent of the reawakening of neo-Nazism was established through Promis. It had been sold to intelligence services in Chile and Argentina and it enabled Mossad to judge the extent of that upsurge. The software also allowed Israel to gauge the extent of how far Latin American regimes would go in suppressing human rights and religious freedoms. Promis had become a credible barometer to the cycle of war and ceasefire that determined the overall rhythm of Israeli policy.

On a bright winter's morning in late 1984, while Bulgaria's King Simeon languished in exile in Spain, his self-appointed successor flew into Sofia.

Robert Maxwell was back. Years later he would wear a T-shirt Betty had given him to celebrate his birthday, on which were emblazoned the words 'King of Bulgaria'. On that day he would wear a paper crown and wave his hands in regal salute as his guests toasted him in vintage champagne at Headington Hill Hall. Beneath this bizarre display was Maxwell's belief that he had attained royal status in the tiny Balkan country. He was its first and still only international deal maker, the man who trumpeted that he would bring untold economic prosperity to Bulgaria.

The impact of his many promises in Bulgaria had both an immediate and lasting effect on the population. The judgment of many is caught in the words of a local journalist:

'Because our country had been closed for so long to foreigners, from the first the state-controlled media called him a billionaire who had come to save us from financial ruin. The idea somebody from the West was going to give big money was welcomed. But the Bulgarian character has this trait of also questioning generosity from outsiders. We're naturally conspiratorial, so people began to ask each other what Maxwell really wanted. The intelligentsia, suspicious of the corruption at the top, wondered if Maxwell had also come to plunder us.'

They were right to be suspicious. If Maxwell had won their hearts, he had come to exploit their minds – the collective creative genius that had made Bulgaria one of the jewels in the Soviet crown. The country had some of the most advanced weapons-design plants and many of the arms were exported to revolutionaries worldwide.

A nation the size of Ireland was at the apex of a concerted assault on the diminishing world still under democratic rule. Bulgaria mass-produced the machinery of terrorism: guns of every calibre, including shoulder-borne ground-to-air, heat-seeking missiles that could bring down a plane at a range of five miles; explosive devices and electronic monitoring equipment; transistors powerful enough to interdict any police frequency. Every terrorist organisation from Angola and Mozambique, from Algeria and the PLO, to the Symbionese Liberation Army in California – there was not a group that operated without its quota of Bulgarian equipment. The Germany Red Army Faction, the Tupamoros of South America, ETA in Spain – all had helped to burn, rob, kidnap and kill with the weapons the factories around Sofia turned out day and night, seven days a week, twelve months a year.

The workers in those factories had come to venerate Robert Maxwell – and he to bestow on them the munificence of the nearest person they had to a king. He could do what they would never be able to do: come and go as he pleased, fly in and out in his private jet, summon the highest in the land to meet him at any hour he chose. Just as in Israel – where he was looked upon by the *kibbutzim* as one of their own – so here, in this pimple on the rump of *mittel*-Europe, he was regarded with awe. The intelligentsia may wonder. But for the majority of Bulgaria's 8 million citizens he was a mesmeric figure, not least because he always brought good news: plans to open a new plant, to finance a new building, to give money to the poor. That these gifts were mortgaged to some future date did not matter. Bulgarians were used to waiting.

But on that winter's morning he had brought a gift: a copy of Promis for the country's secret service, Darzhavna Sigurnost. Like the Stasi in East Germany, Bulgaria's equally feared spy agency provided the KGB with the capability to kill Soviet dissidents in the West. It had done so many times, in Paris, Madrid and London, each time killing with an ingenuity that only the *kidon* could match.

Within hours of the software's installation in the grime-coated headquarters in Sofia of the secret service, Rafi Eitan was receiving the first intercepts emerging through the trapdoor. Soon Mossad would require a team of analysts to prepare reports on what was happening in Bulgaria and in all the other countries where Robert Maxwell had already sold Promis.

In only months he had achieved sales totalling £100 million, of which he had taken 15 per cent commission off the top. In Bulgaria payment for the software had been laundered through Credit Suisse from the Bank of Bulgaria. From there it had begun a journey that took it through the Bank of Montreal, on to banks in Mexico and other Latin American countries, then across the Pacific before ending up in the Discount Bank of Israel. At that stage Rafi Eitan took his share of 20 per cent; a portion of the remainder was deducted for expenses. The residue was transferred to one of many accounts Mossad held in banks in London, New York and Paris. The money would be used to finance 'black' operations, so sensitive and secret they could not even be paid for out of the Finance Office in Mossad's headquarters. Usually these were operations in which *kidon* was involved. In the instances where money was moved through the international banking systems, the banks themselves were unaware that they were being used for such a purpose.

The geographic position of Bulgaria was also important to Russia. Its port of Bourgas on the Black Sea coast offered a doorway to and from the Balkans for the movement of illegal weapons, including nuclear 'suitcase bombs'. Bourgas airport was used for the transport of terrorists to a training camp in the Bulgarian mountains. No Western intelligence service could easily penetrate this closed country dotted with Soviet nuclear launch pads and tracking stations.

The picturesque Black Sea coastline from Bourgas to the medieval town of Sozopol was where key figures from the KGB and Stasi spent their vacations. Dark-haired Bulgarian women, cheap wine and good food were the attractions for the spies and counterintelligence officers.

'Maxwell also had his woman in Bulgaria. But because of his bulk, he preferred fellatio rather than penetrative sex,' a former general of the Darzvana Sigurnost later said. It was customary when Maxwell arrived to provide a girl from the stable the secret service kept for important visitors.

Robert Maxwell's interest in Bulgaria had started before he was recruited by Mossad. In one of those earlier meetings with Vladimir Kryuchkov in Moscow, Maxwell raised the possibility that Bulgaria might be a country where he could invest his money away from prying eyes in the City of London and Wall Street.

The KGB chief had been surprised. He had assumed 'somebody like Maxwell had taken care of such matters'.

But Maxwell had persisted. He would like to use Bulgaria to store substantial sums of money in hard currency. It would, of course, have to be available to him for withdrawal on demand. In the meantime, a Bulgarian bank would become his own personal vault, even more inaccessible than those in Switzerland.

Kryuchkov had asked for time to see if this was feasible. No other entrepreneur from outside the Soviet Union, let alone someone of the status of Robert Maxwell, had been given such financial shelter. Kryuchkov had correctly assumed that the money Maxwell wanted to bury in Bulgaria would raise serious questions in the bastions of the West's financial centres.

But there could be an advantage for Russia. Moscow effectively controlled Bulgaria's banking system. Allowing Maxwell to keep money there would enable the KGB to have an inside view of how he operated. There would also be the not insignificant fact that he would be expected to pay a 'handling fee' for such a service. That would come into the KGB's own bank in Moscow.

Kryuchkov consulted with the then single most important leader in the Soviet Union, his own predecessor at the KGB and at that time General Secretary of the Communist Party's Central Committee: Yuri Andropov.

The bespectacled party chief had listened carefully to Kryuchkov in his Kremlin office. Andropov knew Maxwell better than anyone in the Soviet Union. They shared a background of poverty and each had risen to eminence by a combination of hard work, ruthlessness and duplicity. They also shared another link. Both were Jews. But unlike Maxwell, Andropov had carefully hidden his ethnic roots. To be a Jew in the Soviet hierarchy was as dangerous as being one in Hitler's Third Reich.

Maxwell had learned about Andropov's background from Rafi Eitan. Just like Eitan, he had also filed that titbit away in one of those compartments in his mind. Without telling Kryuchkov, he had called Andropov on the Jewish Day of Atonement. During the conversation he said how much he would like to help develop Bulgaria because as a Jew he had always wished to see an impoverished country begin to prosper; the pitiful state of Bulgaria's economy reminded him of what life had been like in those days when he had grown up in Slatinske Doly.

While the precise words of their conversation went unrecorded, it was left to Kryuchkov to say, 'No one can agree like two Jews united in common purpose.'

More certain is that Robert Maxwell also recognised that when Andropov finally succumbed to the kidney disease that was in an advanced stage, Kryuchkov would still be an influential figure in the Soviet archipelago – and a source of important information for Mossad.

He began to send couriered gifts to Kryuchkov's office in the Lubyanka: a cashmere coat, sets of solid golf cufflinks, the latest hi-fi set and a box of the finest opera recordings. Every week without fail the British Airways flight from London to Moscow had stowed in its hold a crate of vintage Scotch whisky or Krug champagne.

Inevitably, the gifts came to the attention of MI6. It deepened its concern that Maxwell might in the later words of one serving officer 'be doing a Blunt or Philby'. Both men had been close to the core of British intelligence and had betrayed its secrets to Moscow. But David Spedding, the MI6 chief, decided that Maxwell was purely driven by an insatiable need to promote himself so as to become a major deal maker in the Soviet Union.

By then Vladimir Kryuchkov had agreed to provide Maxwell with his financial bunker in the Bulgarian capital, Sofia. In one of those piquant twists that the KGB liked, the Bank of Bulgaria, where Maxwell's money would be safe, was one the KGB used to finance international terrorist groups and the global traffic in drugs.

To watch over Maxwell, Kryuchkov decided he needed his most trusted operative in Bulgaria. He was Andrei Lukanov. Still not fifty years of age, he had been a member of Bulgaria's Central Committee for over a decade. Soft-spoken, he bore a broad Slav face, its most noticeable feature being his expressive eyes. Like Maxwell, Lukanov had long buried his peasant background. He dressed, walked and spoke in an aristocratic manner. Those he favoured, he greeted with a hug for the men, a hand-kiss for the women. Others he no longer favoured often disappeared from one day to the next. No one would ever know how many persons he had got rid of with a few whispered words or a nod. He was cast in the mould of a Mafia godfather.

Before Maxwell had been given his special coded account in the Bank of Bulgaria, Kryuchkov had sent for Lukanov.

For a moment the Bulgar had wondered if, at long last, he was to suffer the fate of so many others – a KGB execution for some misdemeanour. His fear may well have increased when the limousine that had been waiting for him on the tarmac at Moscow's Sherementeyevo Airport drove into a side entrance of the Lubyanka, known as 'Traitor's Gate'. It was through its portals that many a dissident or Russian spying for the West had been brought.

Kryuchkov had been waiting. With only a perfunctory greeting, he had led Lukanov down into the basement, along dimly lit corridors, past closed doors with no numbers. Finally Kryuchkov had opened a door into a small office. It was furnished only with a pine table and a chair. On the table was a bulky file.

Kryuchkov would remember: 'I told him to sit. I told him to open the file. I told him to start reading. He did. I told him he had an hour to read it all. I closed the door and left him to it.'

Andrei Lukanov read the KGB's file on Robert Maxwell. There were hundreds of pages of transcripts of telephone calls from Maxwell's penthouse in London, from hotels all over the world. Interspersed with the paperwork were vivid descriptions of Maxwell's sexual peccadilloes.

It was, Kryuchkov would say, 'a standard KGB file on someone we had more than a passing interest in'.

One hour later to the minute, Kryuchkov returned. Lukanov was looking at the now closed file, transfixed by what he had read. Kryuchkov picked up the file and led him from the office to his own well-appointed suite on an upper floor. An aide served coffee and plum brandy, then closed the door on the two men. Kryuchkov later recalled he had told Lukanov, 'Maxwell has enough money to buy most countries. It is good for our image in the West the more he invests here. He has the approval of people in the highest places of power in Moscow, so help him in every way you can. If you bring someone else in on this, you must keep me informed. I want a record kept of his financial dealings and of his lifestyle. Treat him like one who is important. You know how to handle him.'

Lukanov flew back to Sofia on the aircraft the KGB reserved for those it looked upon with favour.

Next morning he had a meeting with the country's leader, President Todor Zhivkov. He told him what had been decided in Moscow.

Zhivkov had been excited. For years he had financially robbed his own country, secretly storing the money in accounts in Switzerland, using the same route out of the Bank of Bulgaria that was used to finance terrorist activities. That someone of the stature of Robert Maxwell was ready to place money in Bulgaria brought one of his braying laughs from the President.

Lukanov had cautioned Zhivkov that the biggest investor Bulgaria had ever known was no fool. While Maxwell would invest huge sums in the economy to finance a variety of projects – part of the deal that Kryuchkov had finally brokered with Maxwell – he would also hide many millions in hard currency of his own money and would watch over it like one of the predatory birds in the mountains beyond Sofia. They would not be able to touch those funds. But there would still be ample money left to skim off from the projects in which Maxwell was going to invest.

So Robert Maxwell's Bulgarian odyssey had begun.

Maxwell's arrival in Sofia for the first time was treated with the deference that would be accorded to the Chairman of the Soviet Union. A red carpet had been rolled out from the aircraft steps to the waiting ceremonial guard. Like a potentate, Maxwell had marched along their serried ranks, pausing to glance briefly into a face, then lumbering on. That night at a state banquet, guest and hosts showered each other with effusive compliments. A motorcycle escort brought Maxwell's limousine to the palace set aside for him on the slope of the Vitoshi mountain overlooking Sofia.

There, on a balcony overlooking the city, he may well have thought he now had two spiritual homes – his suite in the King David Hotel in Jerusalem, and this altogether grander one.

When Lukanov fully realised the scope of what Maxwell was planning – virtually to reinvent the Bulgarian economy – he decided to bring in someone to assist him in the management of matters.

His name was Ognian Doinov, and people said that he may once have been good-looking. But excess had bloated his face and he had a debauched look that concealed a still shrewd mind. He was Bulgaria's Minister for Industry. Like Lukanov and the country's President, Doinov had an eye for a deal from which he could personally profit.

In Maxwell he saw the proverbial milch cow. In one of his customary crude asides in a telephone call to Lukanov, the minister said, 'There are enough tits on Maxwell for all of us to have a good drink.'

The call had been recorded by the Bulgarian secret service. From now on it would assign a team to eavesdrop on Maxwell every time he came to the country.

In London, MI5 and MI6 were keeping a watchful eye on Maxwell. In Tel Aviv, Mossad was doing the same. Each had very different reasons for doing so. Robert Maxwell, consumed by both a craving for secrecy and publicity, had become one of the most watched individuals on earth.

SIX

At that hour, 6.30 in the morning, only the tip of the Washington Monument was touched by the winter sun in 1984. There had been another snowfall and the only sound, one that barely penetrated the government Lincoln Continental, was from the snow blowers clearing the capital's streets.

Whatever the weather, this was the hour William H Webster, the director of the Federal Bureau of Investigation, liked to kick-start his day. Others would complain about the fumes and the haze hiding the sky they said came from the swampy location of America's capital. But after growing up in St Louis, Missouri, Webster liked Washington because it did not pretend to be anything other than a government town.

Overnight in his home in a city suburb, he had received his copy of the NIA, the FBI's summary of the main overnight intelligence developments. Sometime before dawn a Marine courier had dropped off the sealed file of the PDB, the President's Daily Briefing. It contained the most important items from all the other US intelligence agencies.

Over his breakfast coffee, Webster carefully read the documents, making the occasional note against what he wanted to have followed up. He had done this every morning since he had been appointed director in 1978.

He had been just short of his 54th birthday, an Appellate Court judge and, before that, a lawyer. The only highlight in an unexceptional legal career had been his years as a naval lieutenant in World War Two and later in the Korean War. He had seen action but, unlike other veterans, he almost never spoke about it.

If the appointment had surprised him, as it had done many others, Webster had not shown it. That kind of public emotion did not belong in his character. He was in every sense a quiet man: in his voice, in his conservative suits, in the way he made decisions. Washington's media had watched and waited when he took over the FBI, hoping there would be more of the headline-grabbing missions that had enlivened their stories about Webster's predecessors. But the worst the reporters could write was that Webster was a safe pair of hands, never one to rush to judgment.

He was now close to his seventh year as director and had long learned to walk that ever-blowing-in-the-wind invisible tightrope tugged at one end by William Casey, the Director of Central Intelligence out at Langley and, at the other, President Reagan's National Security Adviser, Robert C McFarlane, in the White House. When they were not calling him, he had to cope with their assistants: John McMahon, deputy director of the CIA, and the agency's operational chief, Clair George; in the White House it was Chief of Staff James Baker imperiously demanding action. Sometimes the calls were from Secretary of State George P Schultz, or Secretary of Defense Casper W Weinberger. To give Webster the necessary authority to deal with these formidable people, President Reagan had appointed him to chair the Senior Interagency Group for Intelligence.

Now, on this winter's morning, in the back seat of the Lincoln, even in repose an austere figure, Webster knew that many of those men he spoke to on a daily, often hourly, basis, had been touched by an FBI investigation. It was exactly six months old and was still so secret that all field reports were routed directly to the secure fax number in Webster's own office. From there he decided who in that select group should see his latest summarised evaluation. Casey, McMahon and Clair George saw everything: national security and international intelligence operations were involved. Schultz over at State and Weinberger in Defense knew a great deal; again there were implications for diplomacy and security. James Baker was told only as much as he needed to know. But Barry Goldwater, chairman of the Senate Select Committee on Intelligence and the President's Foreign Intelligence Advisory Board – a nonpartisan group who monitored intelligence for Reagan – were still out of the loop.

There was a reason for this. One of the men who formed part of the FBI investigation was himself a powerful figure in Washington's political scene. He was the Texan Republican Senator John Tower and a close ally of the equally powerful figure James Webster had ordered to be placed under investigation – Robert Maxwell.

It was Tower who had opened the most important doors for Maxwell, including that of the Oval Office. While Britain's ambassador to the United States and government ministers from London could have their time with the President strictly rationed, Maxwell, with Tower at his elbow, had often been allowed to run over his appointment. Sometimes Attorney-General Edwin Meese and Earl Brian dropped by to chat with Maxwell. Even the President's staff, used to his easygoing ways, were astonished by the way Tower had worked the obese millionaire into the Reagan White House.

Only the First Lady, Nancy, had squirmed at the sight of Maxwell barrelling along the corridor to the Oval Office, greeting the Secret Service agents and secretaries with effusive smiles. She had told her press secretary that she didn't trust this Englishman with his avuncular smile and massive girth which was anathema to her way of life. But the President liked him; there was something larger than life about the tycoon that may have reminded Reagan of one of those B-movie characters from his days as an actor.

Among much else, Webster had learned that Maxwell's relationship with Tower began early in 1984. Maxwell's own increasing wealth, even before he had started to market Promis, had convinced him that to succeed in the United States, especially in Washington, he had to use lobbyists.

They were not wealthy from just the generous salaries they commanded, but from the bribes they collected. When corporations they represented wanted a piece of legislation passed through Congress, the lobbyists used politicians who, in return for their votes, would have their families flown on exotic vacations, or receive generous stock options. At election time money was discreetly handed over to fund campaigns and senators and congressmen routinely found that directorships and consultancy roles they held were showered with cash gifts and upgraded.

Maxwell knew he would have to follow the same path of corruption. It did not trouble him. He liked to say that everyone has their price.

While Henry Kissinger was still close to him, for Maxwell he was no longer close enough to the centre of power, the Reagan White House. But Kissinger was still useful as the maître d' of the current political scene. One night at the Four Seasons in New York, Maxwell had led Kissinger past Picasso's *Guernica* in the foyer. Kissinger had said if Maxwell was to really make his mark in Washington, then he would need to meet John Goodwin Tower. The sixty-year-old politician was one of the stalwarts of the Republican Party and past chairman of the Senate Armed Services Committee. Now, after 25 years on Capitol Hill, Tower had announced he was going to resign in a year's time. Kissinger said that Tower was looking for an opening that would allow him to maintain his lavish lifestyle.

That night, from his suite at the Helmsley Hotel in mid-town New York, Maxwell had called the private number of Rafi Eitan.

'Tower's a big fish. Wait until I check him out,' said Eitan.

Mossad had files on all senior US politicians, constantly updating them with reports from its *katsas*. Tower's file contained a wealth of detail on his political opportunities, his extra-marital activities and business dealings over two decades. There was also a reference to his role in the assassination of President John F Kennedy.

In 1962 Lee Harvey Oswald, after three years in Russia working in a factory, had written to Senator Tower from Moscow pleading with him to help him return to the United States with his wife, Marina. Shortly afterwards Oswald had assassinated Kennedy in Tower's home state of Texas. Tower later claimed he passed the letter to the State Department.

Marina Oswald, when giving evidence to the Warren Commission investigation into the murder of President Kennedy, accused Tower of complicity in the assassination.

After reviewing the Tower file, Rafi Eitan informed Nahum Admoni of Maxwell's hope to employ the senator. Admoni was understandably enthusiastic. Even when he retired, Tower would be one of the 'elders' of the Washington political scene; a man still with the President's ear and a fount of information about US policymaking in the Middle East.

There were now diverging views about the Iran–Iraq War. Israel wanted Washington to forge closer links with conservatives in Teheran by supplying them with TOW missiles to fight Iraq. Tower would know how far Washington was prepared to go – beyond what was leaked to the *Washington Post*.

Eitan had called Maxwell at the Helmsley and said he could go ahead and employ Tower.

It began as simply as that.

Robert Maxwell, mindful of the protocol in such matters, decided not to ask Kissinger to effect an introduction to Tower. He had asked a member of the American board of directors of his publishing company, Pergamon, to do so. He was Dr Paul Rosbaud, the intellectual who had created Pergamon's impressive list of scientific journals.

An Austrian who had spied for MI6 during World War Two and warned them Germany was trying to build an atomic bomb, the translucent-skinned Rosbaud was a respected figure in Washington. He had telephoned Tower in February 1984 and explained what was on offer.

'Tell him it will cost him. I don't come cheap. A lot of companies have already approached me. I'll meet him as long as we're not talking small change,' Tower had warned.

Maxwell had smiled. It was nothing less than he expected. That night he had placed another call to Rafi Eitan.

'What's the going price for a retired senator like Tower?'

'Whatever it takes, Robert,' replied Eitan.

Tower's background, as Eitan knew from Mossad's files, was impressive. Born in Houston, Texas, the son of a Methodist preacher, he graduated from Southwestern University in June 1943 and joined the US Navy. During the war he served on an amphibious gunboat in the Western Pacific. In 1946, he was discharged with the rank of seaman first class. In

Maxwell, a man with a yacht larger than the naval vessel he served on, Tower would soon find a common interest that would dominate many of their dinner conversations.

Between 1949 and 1954, Tower had pursued an academic career, studying for two years at the London School of Economics. His Master's thesis was on the organisational structure of the Conservative Party.

His entry into US politics properly began in 1961, when he became the first Republican senator elected in Texas since 1870.

Like Maxwell, he had fought his way to the top and in doing so created enemies, in Tower's case among old-money Republicans who felt someone with more social standing should have been in his Senate seat.

His blunt manners alienated even his political friends, but no one could deny he was a power base with the same energy that drove Maxwell. Rising through the ranks of the Republican Party, with seats on important Senate committees, Tower was regarded by his Democratic opponents as 'ruthless, rude and unscrupulous'. He and Maxwell also shared a liking for crude jokes. When Strom Thurmond, the Republicans' elder statesman in the Senate at the age of seventy, married a twenty-two-year-old beauty queen, Tower publicly pronounced, 'When they bury Strom, they'll have to beat his pecker with a baseball bat to keep the coffin lid down.'

Like Maxwell, Tower enjoyed alcohol and food. But, when he was asked to name his favourite dish, caviar was not on his menu. He loved Texas chilli. In 1978, he unapologetically took to the floor of the Senate to declare that Texas made the best chilli, whereupon he read his own recipe.

At their first meeting Tower told Maxwell that his fee as Maxwell's personal consultant would be $200,000. For that he would 'open doors to Capitol Hill, to defence contractors – even to the Oval Office itself'.

As then still chairman of the Senate Armed Services Committee, Tower could lift a phone and talk to anyone in any defence establishment in the United States. If Maxwell wanted to visit the White House, he could arrange it. If Maxwell had a product that could be sold to the US armed forces, he would open doors to the people with budgetary responsibility.

For Maxwell $200,000 a year, paid into whatever account Tower chose, was a good investment.

'If he is now on the payroll, ask him to open the door to Los Alamos and Sandia Laboratories. That is where we want Promis installed,' Rafi Eitan told Maxwell.

'He had better do it. I'm not paying that little bugger in telephone numbers for him to sit on his arse in Capitol Hill,' Eitan remembered Maxwell retorting.

Such details and more were in the FBI files that Director Webster had been reading these past six months. Now, on this February morning, with Tower having lived up to his promise and resigned from political life,

Webster was still pondering how far he could press the investigation. Other agencies more important than the FBI had increasingly appeared to be blocking the enquiries his agents were making, not only at Los Alamos but in New York and other parts of the United States. Webster, a man low on speculation, had nevertheless wondered who was behind that blocking. Was it the National Security Agency or the CIA? And if so, why?

It was Tower who had invited the President's men – among them Schultz, Weinberger, Meese and Vice-President George Bush – to meet Maxwell at cocktail parties at his home or to private dinner parties in some of Washington's finest restaurants. On those occasions Maxwell would wear the ribbon of his Military Cross and say he had really done no more than anyone else to defeat Hitler.

To his guests he was an intriguing figure – none more so than for the influential Jewish lobby. They sat enthralled as Maxwell once more described how he had built up Israel's ailing economy. He shrewdly said what they also wanted to hear: that even he could not have achieved that without the immense outpouring of financial help from the United States. He presented himself as the messenger, a modern version of Paul Revere, a heroic figure from America's War of Independence, who had raised the alarm and saved the day. Maxwell, a consummate public speaker, had led the laughter at the image of him on the saddle of any horse.

But Webster knew that for all his self-promotion there was another side to Maxwell, the one that had triggered the FBI's investigation.

A few hours' flying time to the southwest of Washington was the very heart of America's nuclear defences – Los Alamos. It was there the bombs were created that ended World War Two – destroying the Japanese cities of Hiroshima and Nagasaki in the blink of an eyelid. Later, from Los Alamos had come the hydrogen bomb, infinitely more powerful and a credible deterrent in the postwar years to the Soviet Union. It was also from Los Alamos that Moscow's spies – scientists such as Klaus Fuchs and Nunn May – had stolen some of its secrets.

And it was to Los Alamos that Robert Maxwell had travelled to sell Promis. William Webster did not yet know whether he would ever be able to prove that Maxwell had done this as part of the secret intelligence war Israel had begun to wage against the United States. All he did know was that it had been John Tower who had opened the door to Los Alamos.

It was once more a time of renewed sensitivity in US–Israeli relations. Part of it was over Mossad's ties to the war in Nicaragua. Israel had heatedly denied it was involved but Webster knew that no service hid its operations with greater skill than did Mossad. The CIA and the NSA had considerable leverage with Israel: both had provided reconnaissance photos and other critical intelligence for Mossad to launch attacks on terrorists all over

Europe. Would allowing Maxwell access to Los Alamos be part of that deal? In the end did it matter? Israel and the United States after all were on the same side, or so Webster thought.

Did John Tower's boast to Robert Maxwell still hold true, that as long as he was on the payroll he could protect him? Or was that only part of it? In the end could Maxwell feel secure because he was working for Israel and the Jewish state was deeply involved with America in providing arms to Iran? Webster did not know.

Shortly after 7 a.m., the director's limousine entered the underground car park of FBI headquarters in mid-town Washington. During the day Webster intended to go back over the file on Maxwell to see if he had missed anything, something that would enable him to push forward on the investigation. The starting point would once more be that spring day the previous year when Maxwell had shown up at Los Alamos.

Following Rafi Eitan's request, Robert Maxwell had asked John Tower to arrange for him to visit the Sandia National Laboratories, part of the vast Los Alamos complex. Maxwell had already arranged for Tower's fee to be paid in four $50,000 tranches into a Swiss bank account; the first sum had been deposited by the time Tower had fixed the trip to Sandia. The money was paid through one of Maxwell's private companies, PHD Investments, which was a subsidiary of Maxwell Holdings Ltd. Tower was listed as a 'consultant' to PHD.

Maxwell had been among the first to exploit the international globalisation of money transfers to enable him to pay flunkeys like Tower. In 1954 the sheer volume of such transfers had increased 70 per cent over the previous five years. While it was possible to track electronic transfers through CHIPS, an interbank system that had links to 35 countries, Maxwell discovered there was no Western system that could detect cash being moved through banks in the Soviet Bloc. That had been the route he used to pay John Tower. He had simply sent a wire transfer from PHD Investments, knowing there were no stockholders to query why, to the Bank of Bulgaria. From there it had followed the now well-travelled electronic route to a bank in Zürich.

The Sandia facility is southeast of Albuquerque, New Mexico, and is close to Roswell Air Force Base, long the Mecca for ufologists who believe aliens landed there in 1945.

Albuquerque nestles in a temperate climate guaranteed by mountains close by in Los Alamos. Protected by the most secure security systems devised, Sandia is at the core of America's nuclear defence. Here are developed weapons systems for a future world so unthinkable that few wish to contemplate their consequences.

Sandia had been part of the Manhattan Project, designing the casings for the atomic bombs dropped on Japan. In 1945 it was absorbed into Los Alamos.

On that spring morning, as Maxwell's jet began its descent towards Albuquerque, if he had looked southwest he might have seen a tiny dot in a barren landscape. It was a small town called Truth or Consequences. For Maxwell the moment of truth was fast approaching. Would the money he was investing in Tower be realised? Even Maxwell, imbued with foresight, could not have foreseen the consequences that lay ahead. All he could see was a blistering sun once more heading up the desert.

Maxwell lumbered down the aircraft steps in his customised lightweight blue suit. Behind him, carrying his bulky briefcase, came an assistant from Maxwell's company, Information on Demand (IOD). The briefcase was hand-tooled and embossed with the initials RM, and was a gift from Bulgaria's President. Inside the attaché case were two copies of the Promis software Rafi Eitan's programmers had doctored with trapdoors. The copies had been couriered from Israel in a diplomatic bag to the Israeli embassy in Washington. From there a diplomat had brought the package to Tower's home, where Maxwell was a house guest.

Behind the assistant came a tall, sun-tanned secretary from IOD's San Francisco headquarters. She carried an overnight bag in which were packed several shirts and underpants for Maxwell. In her handbag she had his essential deodorant and powder puff.

The jet had landed at Kirkland Air Force base; it served as Sandia's airport. Its security included an FBI agent. Part of his job was to log the coming and going of all visitors. He noted the details of Maxwell's entourage. At the end of his shift, details would be sent by fax to FBI regional headquarters in Albuquerque. The information would go on computer along with other movements in and out of Kirkland.

A stretch limousine had been waiting on the tarmac. The assistant sat opposite Maxwell, the secretary beside him. As instructed, she produced the deodorant for Maxwell to squirt under his armpits. She then lightly powdered his face.

The assistant then opened the well-stocked bar and poured Maxwell a soft drink.

No one had spoken, and no one did, during the rest of the journey to Sandia.

Maxwell had every reason to be preoccupied. He had sold Promis by now to a large number of intelligence services and other government agencies, but Rafi Eitan had warned that Sandia would be different. The majority of those previous sales had been to Third World countries or in the Soviet Bloc. Maxwell had not expected to arouse, nor had he aroused, any suspicion among them. But the people at Sandia he was going to see were trained to look for anything untoward. The wrong word or move, overeagerness to close a sale, a reluctance to answer questions – any of these could trigger alarm in their minds.

The limousine turned onto Gibson Boulevard, then proceeded to the Wyoming Gate, the guarded entrance to the Sandia Laboratories. A security man stepped forward. Maxwell identified himself. The guard ticked off his name on his clipboard and instructed the driver where to go.

Robert Maxwell had a well-honed presentation for selling Promis. He told the scientists, senior technicians and executives in the lecture room Sandia used for important meetings that, while he was certain his good friend John Tower would have told them who he was, he would remind them. He then proceeded to explain just how well connected he was. Powerful names from President Reagan to European leaders came and went in a travelogue through his life as he swept his listeners from the Kremlin to the palace of France's President and the official residence of Britain's Prime Minister, No. 10 Downing Street. Along the way there were stopovers at Harwell, the facility that houses Britain's own nuclear facilities, his visits to Strategic Air Command – America's nuclear air arm – and to NATO's Brussels headquarters. And, of course, he repeated his close relationship with Israel's leaders and how he continued to support that country's economy.

It was a cue for him to switch courses. He told his audience that Israel had invented a piece of software like no other.

One of his listeners would later recall how Maxwell had stopped and 'raked us with his eyes. Then, with a sweep of his hand, he said "Gentlemen, I will not ask what goes on here. Senator Tower has told me enough to know it is important. Important enough for me to come all this way to tell you about this piece of software." Maxwell had stopped and held up the disk. He was like one of those medicine men who used to pass through this part of the world in days when there were no doctors. Maxwell was saying he had a cure for any ails our system may have, or even could have at some future date. From anyone else we would have shown him the door. But this was someone different. He had the kind of connections that none of us could ignore. We agreed to give it a shot to see if it could be a new tool for our mainframe.'

Maxwell concluded his presentation by saying that negotiations would be handled by Information on Demand. Its modest offices were at 2112 Berkeley Way in San Francisco. Nearby lived Isabel Maxwell and her Bulgarian husband. She had no inkling that IOD was effectively another front for Rafi Eitan and Mossad. The money to run the office would come out of one of the Mossad accounts in Credit Suisse.

Robert Maxwell left Sandia certain he had closed a sale that would net IOD $36 million. His cut would boost his earning so far from the software by another $3.6 million. His investment in John Tower had paid off handsomely.

On the flight back to Washington, darkness fell over the desertscape. Only the twinkle of lights marked the small town of Truth or Consequences.

Sandia's technology transfer department was assigned the task of examining Promis. One of its first enquiries was to establish the chain of title to the software and determine whether Maxwell owned the copyright. Resolving ownership was vital if Sandia was going to buy Promis.

Two technicians searched their extensive database for the names and registrations of technology companies and, more importantly, the transfer of technologies around the globe. They wanted to check whether, in a nuclear industry increasingly driven by technology, the software was not being sold elsewhere.

To preclude this was essential if Sandia was to remain at the forefront of hi-tech knowledge and help America to stay ahead in the arms race. The technicians had to be certain Maxwell's offer to sell Promis to Sandia was exclusive.

Enquiries quickly established that Information on Demand was a data source company linked to 250 computer databases compiling information on business and technical issues through access to US government agencies. Subscribers to IOD paid for the information on its database, and for technical advice on how to retrieve information from US government databases dealing with Congressional hearings, the National Criminal Justice Reference Service and similar institutions. None of this material was of a classified nature but security protocol within Sandia required a further check be made with the National Security Agency, the most powerful intelligence agency in the nation. The two technicians asked their counterparts in NSA to run a security trace on IOD.

Within 24 hours the Sandia technicians were informed by NSA that IOD was being accessed by paid subscribers in the Soviet Union. Its owner was 'Robert Maxwell, the owner of Pergamon International, a British information firm'.

The two technicians, like many employees in an organisation like Sandia – where one trivial security lapse leads to dismissal – decided to cover themselves. One telephoned the FBI field office in San Francisco. The call set off alarm bells. In 1983 agents from the office had investigated IOD and questioned its president, Sue Rugge, about IOD's activities. Whatever the agents learned, the matter did not warrant further action on their part.

But now the FBI's agent-in-charge in San Francisco felt the matter had to be referred upwards and not to the FBI regional office in Albuquerque. His decision to write a memorandum to FBI Director Webster was proof of the seriousness with which he viewed the matter.

His communiqué to Webster began: 'This entire communication is classified SECRET.'

The first line read, 'San Francisco indicates negative regarding Pergamon International and Robert Maxwell.'

In the second paragraph he informed Webster that on '10/11/1983, Sue Rugge, President of IOD was interviewed and described her business as "an information and research company".'

Page 2 of the document explained the nature of the database contents that IOD provided for its subscribers. Page 3 confirmed that Rugge had cooperated with the FBI. When the heavily redacted documents finally surfaced in 1998, they contained the words, 'According to Rugge, XXXXXX [redacted words] has been a client of IOD for at least ten years and it would be impossible to recall all the information requested by them . . . '

Who was the mysterious client? Was it an American agency? Or was it Degem Computers in Israel, the front company for Mossad that Maxwell had bought? Or could it be one of his companies in Bulgaria?

Page 4 of the memo contained, 'On 1/21/1984 XXXXXXXXX [redacted words] advised that XXXXXXXX . . . '

Who was advising whom and about what on 21 January 1984?

Page 5 revealed: 'San Francisco taking no further action.'

The FBI office in the city had stopped its brief investigation into Maxwell. But the FBI regional advisory office in Albuquerque had in the meantime been conducting its own investigation at the request of Webster.

On 14 August 1984, the agent-in-charge in Albuquerque sent a communication marked 'Secret' to the FBI director about Maxwell's activities:

NM, one of the individuals who originally brought information about this matter to the attention of the FBI, and the fact that NSA might wish to establish liaison with the Bureau in this matter, indicated that he had heard no further word from NSA.

Bill Hamilton, president of Inslaw, later obtained copies of the redacted FBI documents. He himself had once worked for NSA and was certain that, 'all those redacted lines contained information relevant to a clear understanding of why the FBI and NSA were not pursuing a matter which had serious implications for America's national security. There was an agenda here that goes beyond the common enough failures of cooperation within the US intelligence community. There were some very powerful people involved in Rafi Eitan's original theft of Promis from Inslaw. With Maxwell having John Tower as his point man to open doors, it was possible to exert pressure in all kinds of places, right up to the White House and top of the CIA and NSA. No doubt about it.'

Certainly the decision by NSA not to pursue matters in that memo of 14 August 1984 to Director Webster clearly played a role in the decision-making process in the FBI field office in Albuquerque.

Its final paragraph stated:

Until such time as NSA re-establishes contact and expresses further interest in this matter, Albuquerque is taking no further action and this matter is being placed in a closed status. The personnel at Sandia National Laboratories were told that if NSA has a desire to establish contact with the FBI in this matter, a logical step would be to contact FBI HQ and pursue it through that channel. There is a chance that they will come to Albuquerque in September and possibly they may be in touch with the FBI, Albuquerque. If this occurs, FBI HQ will be apprised of any pertinent data received.

Hamilton, a cautious man of few but well-chosen words, would conclude: 'The obvious question is not so much why the FBI did not pursue the matter, but why NSA kept silent, because no one from the NSA visited Sandia or raised the matter with the FBI a month later. Why did Maxwell's sale of Promis software not strike a chord in the NSA? It would have done within the CIA, which was marketing its own version of the software and would not have taken kindly to the competition.

'Did NSA learn that John Tower was behind Maxwell's sales to Los Alamos? If they did, Tower was one man on Capitol Hill not to mess with. Did he use his contacts to Reagan White House to facilitate Maxwell?'

Hamilton also obtained a secret document that confirmed Maxwell was on the FBI's database for 38 years:

Ian Robert Maxwell, born June 10, 1923 in Czechoslovakia, who was the subject of a security investigation by the FBI 1953–1961. Attached are eight memoranda and ten reports concerning his investigation.

Hamilton had obtained the documents by using his knowledge of how 'the Washington system operates. Once you get a fix on documents, you have to be persistent. The FBI come up with a blanket answer that what you want could compromise national security.'

It was indeed the reason the agency gave Hamilton when he asked why so many of the documents he had obtained were redacted. Despite his own determined efforts to continue to find out what lay behind the blacked-out passages, they have remained secret to this day. Hamilton saw this as 'evidence there are people or issues still alive that do not want the whole truth to emerge of how Maxwell and Israel exploited Promis. What happened is not just bad faith on the part of high government officers, some of whom are still alive, but criminal conduct on the part of others. Our own attorney, the former Attorney-General of the United States, Elliot Richardson, has deposed that the implications of what happened in the gross misuse of Promis is "even more damaging to what government should represent in the United States and indeed in any democracy than Watergate or Irangate, or all the other gates in recent memory".'

A Congressional Oversight Committee found:

The Department of Justice acted wilfully and fraudulently and took, converted and stole Inslaw's Promis by trickery, fraud and deceit. These actions were implemented under the direction of high-level Justice Department officials. The Department's behavior dramatically illustrates its reflexive hostility and 'circle the wagon' approach toward outside investigation and an inability or unwillingness to look objectively at charges of wrongdoing by high-level Justice officials. The Department has shielded them from investigation and prosecution.

Never before had any government department received such a damning judgment over its conduct – one that made it clear that a crime 'of the greatest magnitude has been committed'. The judgment was couched in language even more condemnatory than the Congress verdicts handed down over Watergate and Irangate.

Censorious and comprehensive though the verdict was, it still did not deal with how the greatest secret intelligence scam ever carried out within the United States was done with the knowledge of Senator John Tower and the most senior officials of the Department of Justice – either through their ineptitude or inability to realise what was happening or because they allowed greed to motivate them. Their behaviour enabled Promis to be used to steal the most sensitive secrets of the United States by removing them from the very core of its modern-day arsenal, the Los Alamos Sandia Laboratories. There may never be an intelligence operation so dangerous to US national security in both its short- and long-term implications.

But in the case of Inslaw there has yet to be accountability. There has been no national outcry. There has been no proper media investigation. No powerful newspaper has demanded action. It is almost as if the truly shattering implications of what lies behind the House Committee verdict were so shocking that it should remain buried for ever, known to only those few in high office who, despite being censured by the committee, have yet to answer in a criminal trial for the part they played.

In 2002 the House Judiciary Committee indictment of crimes committed by the Department of Justice remain on the House Record. They cite:

Conspiracy to commit an offense. Fraud. Wire Fraud. Obstruction of proceedings before departments, agencies and committees. Tampering with a witness. Retaliation against a witness. Perjury. Interference with commerce by threats of violence. Racketeer Influenced and Corrupt Organizations (RICO) violations. Transportation of stolen goods, securities, monies. Receiving stolen goods.

At the time of writing the case languishes in the files of the Attorney-General's office.

But a decade earlier the very thought that accusations might be levelled against him were far from Robert Maxwell's mind. He was, in the parlance of the day, 'striking out in all directions'.

In early February 1985, once more accompanied by an assistant and a secretary from IOD, Robert Maxwell returned to the Sandia Laboratories. He had come to sign the contract for Sandia to purchase the exclusive rights to the Promis software. He initialled each page of the document and signed his name with a flourish on the last page. He gave as his title president and chief executive officer of Information on Demand. When it had been countersigned, he placed a copy of the contract in his briefcase. Snapping it shut, he handed the valise to the assistant, dismissing him and the secretary with the familiar wave of his hand.

Maxwell was then given a celebratory luncheon in the Sandia boardroom. Then he and his entourage drove back to the waiting private jet. As it flew out over the desert, it once more passed the township with the prophetic name of Truth and Consequences.

For an unsuspecting Sandia, the truth was that Israel now had an electronic spy in the midst of, until now, the most secure of all nuclear facilities.

It was a significant triumph for the Jewish state, for its prime intelligence service, Mossad, and for Rafi Eitan. It meant Israel would be able to depend less on the United States to ensure that its nuclear arsenal out in the Negev desert would remain at the cutting edge of developments. It would ensure that Israel would also still remain the only nuclear power in the Middle East.

Ultimately it had all been achieved by Robert Maxwell, with a great deal of help from his friend, John Tower.

Now, as the FBI director William Webster stepped out of the Lincoln Continental limousine and briskly walked the short distance to the elevator for his top-floor suite, he could only have sensed what was about to happen. The FBI investigation into Robert Maxwell was finally over.

Who closed it down would remain to this day undisclosed.

*

On the other side of the world, in 1985, in Budapest, Maxwell was furthering his contacts with the Hungarian secret service. The invitation to a preliminary meeting had come weeks before to discuss Promis. The Hungarian ambassador to the United Nations had acted as a go-between.

On the advice of Rafi Eitan, Maxwell had not left behind a copy of the software: the Hungarians were notorious for copying everything they could get their hands on.

Maxwell had demonstrated how Promis worked and had then flown out of the country. But, before doing so, he had met with the chief director of the Bank of Hungary. That introduction had been effected by Ari Ben-Menashe.

'While Robert was happy to have most of his financial eggs in his Bulgarian nest, he still needed a backup and Hungary was a good place for one,' he said later.

Maxwell had returned to Budapest to finalise the Promis deal. Once more he was met at the airport and driven to the headquarters of Hungarian intelligence some five miles outside the city, and set in deep woods. This time he was shown into the office of Kalman Cocsis, the head of the service.

Maxwell was once more asked to demonstrate the software.

He had asked whom Cocsis would like to track. The intelligence chief had handed him a piece of paper. Written on it was the name of the Bulgarian ambassador in Budapest. Maxwell had asked for Cocsis to send for his best computer technician. At their last meeting he had already demonstrated for him how Promis operated.

Now, watched by Cocsis, the technician obtained a wealth of data on the unsuspecting ambassador. Cocsis said it confirmed what his own agents knew. Sensing Maxwell's disappointment, he said that proof was all he had needed. He shook Maxwell's hand. The deal was made. By the time Maxwell left Budapest, he had deposited his £1 million commission in the Bank of Hungary. The rest of the money the Hungarian secret service paid was sent on its usual route to end up eventually in Israel.

SEVEN

Robert Maxwell's domestic behaviour had increasingly begun to unsettle Betty as mistress of Headington Hill Hall. She was house-proud and a gifted cook, but Maxwell played havoc with her domestic arrangements, which had been designed to satisfy his every whim. She would prepare lunch or dinner to meet his specific instructions, telephoned through by one of his secretaries on the ninth floor of Maxwell House. Salmon and chicken had to be the essentials of any repast but he kept on demanding they should be cooked in new ways. Betty would spend time studying her French cookbooks for recipes. The challenge of pleasing him was all she had left.

Hours before he was due to arrive, she cut flowers from the garden for the table arrangement, ensured the tableware and linen were in symmetry. Then she would shower and change into a frock and sit in the drawing room trying to read the *Daily Mirror* – knowing he would question her about the day's news – and wait for the first sound of the helicopter swooping down on the mansion.

By then she had ensured the domestic staff had vacuumed the carpets and that ledges and door frames had not a speck of dust. Maxwell had come to believe his colds were caused by mites and had insisted that his penthouse and Headington Hill Hall be regularly sprayed by a crew from a pest-control company.

Out at the helipad, a servant ensured the strip was free of leaves. Gardeners bent to their work as the appointed time of Maxwell's arrival approached, knowing that the moment the helicopter appeared, they would be under scrutiny from the cabin. Maxwell had been known to fire a worker he had spotted leaning on his fork.

But all too often, by 1985, there would be no helicopter swirling down. Betty would wait, trying to hide her fear that something had happened. But, if there had been a crash, she would have heard. The kitchen staff would be told to put the food in a warming oven. Betty would pour herself a drink and try to concentrate on Maxwell's tabloid, often with his face dominating its front page above an editorial based upon his latest meeting with an Eastern Bloc dictator or an African or South American despot; using the newspaper to curry favour was another of his ways of doing business.

If, after an hour had passed, there was still no sign of the helicopter, Betty would place a call to Maxwell House, to her husband's most senior secretary. Even his wife had no direct access to him.

The secretary would have to explain, as she had done many times before, that Maxwell was either tied up in a meeting or had flown off in his Gulfstream to Europe, or further afield.

Betty would put down the phone and, if the food was still eatable, consume a lonely meal at one end of the dining table. Elsewhere the staff would relax.

On other occasions the phone in Betty's study would ring. It would again be Maxwell's senior secretary, telling her this time he was on his way in the Aerospatiale and would be landing shortly. A sense of near-panic would sweep through the mansion. The cook would bring food from the freezer for the microwave. Maids would dust, gardeners clip and hoe; Maxwell had a near-obsession for trimmed hedges and weed-free flower beds. Betty would arrange the dining table centrepiece. A servant would hover near the helipad, ready to carry Maxwell's briefcase into the mansion.

From the moment he landed, he would be barking orders into his mobile phone, at the same time dictating to one of his secretaries who worked at Headington Hill Hall; part of the mansion was given over to Pergamon and enabled him to claim extra tax relief on the property. By the time he had entered the hallway, he would have stamped the purpose of his visit and the time he would spend there with Betty.

'Just time for a quick meal,' he would bark. 'Business waits for no man.' He had a fund of such clichés, spraying them through his conversation.

If he had brought a guest – a banker, a foreign visitor, or occasionally an editor in favour – he would devote the meal to business. Betty would sit there, nodding and smiling, but able to contribute very little. Later she would say, 'The truth was that Bob and I had forgotten what it was like to be alone in each other's company.'

She had given up trying to explain what she needed from their relationship; that she longed to have more part in his ever-expanding business.

He had cruelly told her that he wished to apply his brain only to business. Betty had swallowed back her tears and consoled herself that maybe one day he would have made enough money and achieved sufficient power and status to give her more of his time. But inwardly she was 'frustrated' by her 'intellectual inactivity'.

What had once been an attraction of opposites – he the dashing go-getter, she content to be a wife and mother, the essential anchor in the marriage – had become a union in name only. He had his women; she had Headington Hill Hall. In those lonely nights she would lie alone in the huge double bed reading one of her favourite authors, Kurt Weill. There, in his celebrated *Wie Lange Noch*, was a passage that mirrored her own life:

You promised me blue skies and I cared for you like my own father. You tormented me, you tore me apart. I would have put the world at your feet. Look at me, look at me! When will I ever be able to tell you: it's over! When that day comes, I dread it. How much longer? How much longer? How long?

If those words brought tears to her eyes, she was careful to make sure no one saw them.

While Robert Maxwell's domestic behaviour had become painful to his wife and children, his other activities continued to baffle his business associates. He had begun to operate in the shadows, wherever possible surrounding his movements with mystery.

He would have his pilot, the calm and unflappable Brian Hull, file a flight plan to some French airport. Senior executives at Maxwell House would be suddenly informed that he was taking a short break from his work. In the past they had become used to the fact that the coded signal – 'a need to recharge my batteries' – was really a sign that he was off for a few days of sexual pleasure with one of the nubile young women whose phone numbers he kept in his personal organiser.

But increasingly Hull had found there were now other reasons behind the initial flight plan he filed. Once in France he would file another, to some highly restricted military airfield in Bulgaria, Hungary or Romania. There, while Hull tried to find what relaxation he could in some uniformly drab airfield building, Maxwell would be driven to a dacha to meet with senior members of the Soviet leadership. It was he, not they, who had sought such secrecy. He had become convinced that his great rival Rupert Murdoch had assigned his investigative journalists to track him, and that they were being helped by MI6. While he had continued to attract understandable curiosity over his overpublicised behaviour in his newspapers, there was also some truth in his paranoia that he had now become a victim of British Intelligence. 'Both MI5 and MI6 were at the "watch-and-observe stage",' Richard Tomlinson would later say.

Maxwell's journeys to South America were conducted with equal secrecy. Hull would file a flight plan to Acapulco in Mexico. Then he would be ordered to request a route down to Peru, Paraguay or on to Chile or Argentina. In all those countries the pilot kicked his heels at an airport hotel, while Maxwell would be holding meetings with members of the country's intelligence services to demonstrate the effectiveness of Promis. Payment for each deal followed the familiar route: out of a local central bank, into the Bank of Bulgaria and on to Credit Suisse.

Maxwell always travelled on two passports. Both were British; one was valid for all countries, the second was only for his trips to Israel. Arab countries would have refused him entry if his passport bore an Israeli stamp. He had travelled to Egypt in April 1985 and sold the country's intelligence service a copy of Promis, explaining how it could be adapted for use in Arabic. The price was the bargain-basement one of £15 million.

Installing Promis in Cairo gave Mossad a vital 'ear' to listen to the activities of Israel's near neighbours, and Egypt's own links with Syria, the one enemy Tel Aviv feared above all others. With Jordan's intelligence service already compromised by the software Earl Brian's company, Hadron, had installed in Aman, Mossad had effectively broken into the major spying agencies in the Arab world.

These sales had all been concluded through Information on Demand, the company the FBI had given up investigating.

On a warm summer's day in 1985, Robert Maxwell had once more returned to West Berlin, checking into the Kimpinski Hotel, one of the finest, and his favourite, in the city. His customary suite was waiting, the air temperature correctly regulated, champagne on ice, along with a bowl of the hotel's finest caviar.

That afternoon, Maxwell did what thousands of visitors did. He took a taxi to Checkpoint Charlie in the American zone, one of the crossing points into East Berlin. To the American MPs he would probably have seemed just another foreign tourist wanting to experience an alien society on the other side of the Berlin Wall. To the watchful Vopo guards in East Berlin he would have been an honoured guest.

On previous visits to East Germany his photograph had appeared on every front page, towering over the figure of Erich Honecker, the leader of the very undemocratic German Democratic Republic.

Usually Maxwell would fly into East Berlin's airport and be whisked away by a government limousine.

But on this occasion he had chosen to enter the GDR the way ordinary visitors did. It may have been for no other reason than that he may have been caught up in the life of the person he was going to see.

He was Markus Wolff, the head of the country's Stasi secret service.

The meeting had taken weeks to arrange. At first Wolff had refused. It had required Honecker's personal intervention to have him finally agree.

Long before then Honecker and Maxwell had forged an unlikely friendship. Two old friends of Maxwell, West German politicians who had close ties to Honecker, had offered to help. They were Helmut Schmidt, who would become the country's Chancellor, and Hans-Dietrich Genscher, who one day would be Foreign Minister.

Maxwell's friendship with the East German leader had flowered to the point where Maxwell had proposed another of his joint-partnership ventures: he would publish East Germany's scientific magazines and produce a handsome encyclopedia of the country's achievements. Naturally, East Germany would pay to have the work promoted outside its borders.

Honecker had agreed. At a reception to celebrate the deal, Maxwell had been briefly introduced to Wolff.

As usual, Maxwell had informed Mossad of the contact. Admoni and Rafi Eitan immediately saw an opportunity too good to miss. If Maxwell could sell the Stasi a copy of Promis, Israel would be privy to the thinking of the most powerful intelligence service outside of the KGB.

Now, the meeting was finally set for that summer evening. Maxwell had taken a taxi to Under den Linden and walked a short distance down the broad thoroughfare. Waiting was a government limousine.

Maxwell would later report to Mossad that Wolff had been seated in the back.

Whatever they spoke about, Maxwell did not succeed in selling Promis. It may have been no more than the renowned suspicion of Markus Wolff that made him decline. Or it may have been that, for once, Maxwell had not been at the top of his salesmanship.

That evening he dined alone in his suite. Next day he was back in London.

By now, however, Maxwell was facing competition. The CIA had also been supplied with a copy of the original Inslaw Promis by the Department of Justice. The CIA had asked one of its prime contractors, the Florida-based Wackenut company, to deconstruct the software and create a version that would enable the CIA not to have to pay royalties. That saving, based on a fee to be charged for every time Promis was used, would later be calculated to be several billion dollars – royalties that, under the original Department of Justice contract with Inslaw, should have gone to that company.

A copy of the CIA version was, by early 1985, in the hands of the National Security Agency. But the CIA had also asked Wackenut to produce a simplified version. This it intended to sell to friendly intelligence services. Sales were made to the Australian, New Zealand and Japanese agencies as well as MI5 and MI6. But the CIA salesmen were no match for Maxwell. In the end they managed to sell only some $90 million worth of their version. Robert Maxwell would eventually achieve the staggering figure of $500 million of sales as he went about wiring up the world for Mossad.

Between the CIA, NSA and IOD, Promis became a powerful tool for intelligence services. In Holland, Intel used it to track the activities of the Russian Mafia as it shipped arms and drugs through Schipol Airport. In Germany the BND, the nation's equivalent to the CIA, used the software to follow the trail of nuclear materials out of the former Soviet Union into the Middle East. In France, the security services used Promis to track terrorists in and out of North Africa. In Spain, the software was used to keep tabs on the Basque terrorist movement. In Britain, MI5 used it to watch the movements of the scores of Middle East groups who had set up base in London. In Northern Ireland, it became a weapon for the security services tracking the IRA as its members came and went across the border with the Irish Republic. In Scotland, it formed a database for what became the long-running investigation into the terrorist destruction of Pan Am 103. In Hong Kong, Britain's MI6 used the program to track the Triads and agents from the People's Republic. In Japan, Promis was used to interdict the links between the Japanese underworld and its counterparts in North Korea and mainland China. The software allowed Sweden to maintain a watch over foreign diplomats in the country, especially those from Eastern Europe who might be using their political immunity to set up arms-traffic networks.

Ari Ben-Menashe, who had played a role in creating the most successful of all the versions, was close to the truth when he said, 'Promis changed the thinking of the entire intelligence world.'

While Rafi Eitan had been the man who conceived the idea of the secret trapdoor, it had been Robert Maxwell who had sold and sold and sold Promis. When Yitzhak Shamir would later say that no one had done more for Israel, he was not exaggerating.

Now Rafi Eitan had given Maxwell a new target.

In the late summer of 1985, a subject never far from the public consciousness had surfaced again in Israel: did its military commanders have a clear strategy to avoid another conflict with its neighbours? There had been five wars so far, the last in 1982. Israel had won each one, even though there had, at times, been unacceptable failures in intelligence. But now, three years later, Syria's rhetoric over its unyielding commitment to the Palestinian cause and Damascus's denial of Israel's legitimacy had once more divided the intelligence community. There were those at its top who believed Israel would be forced to use its ultimate deterrent – the one it still vehemently denied it possessed: the stockpile of nuclear weapons out in the Negev Desert at Dimona.

There were others like Rafi Eitan who believed the correct strategy was to sow dissent within the Arab nations. One way should be to continue secretly to supply Iran with sufficient arms to topple the altogether more powerful regime of Iraq's Saddam Hussein.

For over two years, in the utmost secrecy, Israel had been supplying weapons to Teheran to fight Iraq. The logistics were formidable, involving a long sea journey around the Cape and then on through the Indian Ocean into the Gulf of Oman, through the Straits of Hormuz and finally to Iran's refinery port of Adaban. From there the weapons were trucked to the front line with Iraq. Each shipment took six weeks to arrive. At the same time Israel was sending, in the same secrecy, arms through Turkey for the Kurds to fight against the mullahs in Iran. Before his fall from grace, Ari Ben-Menashe had been responsible for supplying both sides.

The decision to arm the Kurds had been on the advice of David Kimche: he felt doing so would act as a restraint against Iran's becoming too powerful – keeping the balance of power in the region at the correct level was always uppermost in Kimche's mind.

But, increasingly, it had become clear that Teheran was losing the war with Iraq. Saddam's air force was equipped with up-to-date Russian aircraft and missiles. One by one the towns and villages of Iran were being systematically bombed back into the Stone Age. The Kurdish rebels in the far north of the country were becoming bolder – they had launched several damaging night attacks on Teheran.

Despite their strong distaste for the Khomeini regime, Israel's leaders knew they must reinforce Iran with more weapons. But the risk was evident. So far the secret shipments had been undetected. But supposing they were discovered? Iraq now had a credible intelligence service, one that had shown itself every bit as ruthless as Mossad. If Iraq learned Israel was supplying Teheran, that would surely draw Saddam closer to Moscow. He would ask for, and very likely receive, still more weaponry from the Soviet arsenal. The last thing Israel wanted was an arms race on its doorstep.

But there was also the matter of where the weapons would come from for Israel to supply Iran. Simply to dip into its own arms dumps was no longer feasible. Israel needed all the armaments it had to maintain its own superiority against the ever-present threat of Syria.

Though he had gone from Mossad to the Foreign Ministry, David Kimche was still regarded as the most innovative thinker in Israel's intelligence community. He foresaw that the day would eventually come when the United States would also recognise the need to keep Iran fighting. But he also sensed that was still a little while off. America's preoccupation with the Middle East focused on the plight of its hostages held in Beirut by the Hezbollah terror group, a surrogate of Iran. Getting the hostages home was all that mattered to the Reagan White House.

Meanwhile Kimche had begun to put together a colourful cast of characters. One was Adnan Khashoggi, the Saudi petro-billionaire who shared Maxwell's habit of eating caviar by the pound and carried a similar list of beddable girls in his phone book. The two men had already met in London, circling each other like wary predators wondering who would strike first in some deal that interested them. Another Maxwell clone in terms of behaviour was Manucher Ghorbanifar, a former agent in the Shah of Iran's notorious SAVAK secret service; like Maxwell he still had an obsession with secrecy and holding meetings in the middle of the night. They had met on that international circuit where the rich and famous mix – the South of France in summer, Aspen in winter. Into the group Kimche brought Ya'atov Nimrodi; he had run agents for Aman, Israeli military intelligence, during his time as military attaché in Teheran during the Shah's regime.

These were men who could lay their hands on aircraft, bombs, torpedoes, mines and arsenals of other weapons and ammunition. They spoke the common language of their industry, English, and dealt only in American dollars. They were suave and sophisticated as they bought and sold their weapons systems.

Kimche knew that, when America did become involved, there would have to be a cutout system in place. Washington, any more than Israel, would not want to have its fingerprints detected. Then Kimche's cast could step on stage. But not now.

Kimche had heard that, over at Mossad, Nahum Admoni, in those long hours he had sat in his suite looking over the city towards the Judean Hills, had come to a decision. Israel could not wait for America to supply arms for Iran. Like Kimche, Admoni believed that would happen later. But the reports from Mossad's *katsas* in Teheran indicated that militarily the Iranian army was on the verge of collapse. Its tanks needed spare parts; its arms dumps were being bombed out of existence; morale among troops was low: there had been desertions and public executions. The Kurds were hammering away anew, supported now by arms from Iraq. Something had to be done – and done quickly.

In March 1985, Admoni invited Saul Nehemiah Eisenberg, the country's undisputed leading arms dealer, to come to his office. Eisenberg proposed that one way to get weapons quickly for Iran was from Poland. But any approach to the Warsaw regime would have to be cleared by Moscow. Eisenberg said he did not have the connections to do that.

Admoni had asked one question, the answer to which he already knew.

Eisenberg said the only man to use was Robert Maxwell.

Admoni had once more flown to London. In Maxwell's penthouse, he had outlined the problem.

Maxwell, in his usual flamboyant way, said Admoni should consider the matter solved. Next day his Gulfstream set a course for Moscow. He had taken the precaution of bringing with him a silver-inlay chess set he had bought from Harrods. As usual he was met on the airport tarmac and driven to the Lubyanka. Kryuchkov was waiting, embracing and kissing Maxwell on both cheeks. The handing over of the gift had been followed by a toast to their eternal friendship.

As they sat opposite each other in the pair of leather armchairs Andropov had given the KGB chief, Maxwell had come to the point. He wanted Poland to supply Israel with arms.

Not for the first time, Kryuchkov had been astonished by one of Maxwell's requests. He had spread his podgy fingers and asked why Israel, which everyone knew had a powerful arms industry, wanted to buy probably inferior weapons from Poland.

Maxwell explained that they were for Iran. Kryuchkov had nodded; he well understood Israel's policy of playing one side against the other in the drawn-out conflict between Iran and Iraq.

He would later recall saying, 'So the Iranians get to kill more Iraqis. Then, when Teheran is on top, Israel starts to supply Baghdad so as to kill more Iranians.'

Maxwell could not have put it better.

Suddenly the KGB chief was all business. Maxwell's dealings in Bulgaria were one thing; but Poland was quite another matter.

Nothing was simple about Poland. The imposition of martial law in December 1981 had led to tensions between NATO and the Warsaw Pact and even the threat of whole-scale sanctions against the Soviet Union. That had now passed, but the trade union movement, Solidarity, remained a menace, supported by the Polish Pope John Paul II, and a number of human-rights groups across the world. Kryuchkov had been derisive: the Polish Communist Party was a shambles; the country's leader, General Wojciech Jaruzelski, was no more than a puppet on Moscow's string. But, the more the Kremlin tugged for him to do something about Solidarity, the more helpless the general had become.

Now it was probably too late. The new man in the Kremlin, Mikhail Gorbachev, was planning sweeping reforms. The Soviet economy, which for half a century had based itself upon its ability to fund military power all the way to the moon, was on a different orbit. Gorbachev had begun to introduce an unfamiliar word, 'glasnost', and spoke of a coming new Soviet democracy; the very word 'perestroika' had sent a *frisson* of excitement coursing from Siberia to the other far reaches of the Soviet Union. This reform would be driven by the profit motive and lead to political democratisation through the Soviet Union.

Vladimir Kryuchkov had looked at Robert Maxwell and said that, if he wanted those weapons from Poland, he had better be ready to pay the market price.

Maxwell had smiled his vulpine smile. That would not be a problem.

But his host was not quite finished. He explained that the new chairman of the KGB, Victor Chebrikov, would want to be involved. Maxwell well understood. Chebrikov would want his cut from the deal. That would also not be a problem. Maxwell would simply factor in an extra 2 million dollars for Chebrikov into the cost. There would also be a similar amount for Kryuchkov.

Maxwell had spent the night in the KGB apartment Kryuchkov always provided. It was stocked with champagne and caviar. It also had a sophisticated surveillance system of cameras and hidden microphones. That may well have been the reason Robert Maxwell always turned down an invitation to enjoy the pleasure of one of the hookers from the KGB stock.

Next day Kryuchkov told him that Chairman Chebrikov had approved the deal.

Maxwell immediately ordered his Gulfstream to fly to Tel Aviv.

Waiting in Admoni's office with Rafi Eitan was Ehud Barak, director of Aman, military intelligence. Soft-spoken and self-deprecating, Barak was not only a brilliant military strategist, but also had a sure command of international politics. Years later he would say that he had no liking for Maxwell, but respected what he had done for Israel. He close-questioned Maxwell about how he would go about his mission to Poland. Maxwell told him there was nothing to worry about: the Poles were little different from the Bulgarians. 'They are there for the taking,' Barak would remember him saying.

Barak embarked upon his views of when and where Gorbachev could be taking the Soviet Union and that the strategy's inherent risks could lead to an internal collapse of law and order and the emergence of criminal gangs who might even try to sell-off Russia's nuclear arsenal to rogue states such as Iraq, Libya and Iran. Barak also felt that no longer would Moscow base its relations with the world through the prism of the United States and Washington's response to anything Gorbachev did. There was the evidence of the way the first leader Gorbachev had invited to the Kremlin the Italian premier, Bettino Craxi. Hard on his heels had come the veteran West German politician, Willy Brandt. Gorbachev had asked them both to open doors for him to the European Community.

Suddenly Maxwell interrupted. He turned to Barak as if studying him for the first time. 'Are you the same man who went into Beirut dressed as an Arab woman to kill that terrorist?' he asked.

Barak blinked and looked at Rafi Eitan. What was all this about?

'Well, are you?' repeated Maxwell. 'Because if you are, it would be one hell of a story for my newspaper.'

Barak contained himself enough to say there would be no story. Maxwell nodded. The moment passed. But its implications had not gone unnoticed. Robert Maxwell, for all his undoubted brilliance and service to Israel, could be a loose cannon, someone whose judgment could be faulty.

The meeting ended after Rafi Eitan suggested that Maxwell's visit to Poland could be an opportunity to sell Promis to the country's UB, its main intelligence service. Installed into UB's mainframe, it would enable Mossad to interdict all important communications between Warsaw and Moscow. Israel would have a better insight into the reality of Gorbachev's *Novoye Myshlenniye*, his New Thinking.

Maxwell said he would pack into his briefcase a copy of the doctored Promis.

Before the meeting ended, Admoni asked if he could meet his Russian counterpart, Victor Chebrikov.

Ten days later, four very different men flew into London's Heathrow Airport. From Tel Aviv came Nahum Admoni and Ari Ben-Menashe. From Moscow came Chebrikov and Mikhail Gorbachev.

Maxwell had scheduled the meeting Admoni had requested for 8.30 the next morning. Chebrikov was the first to arrive; at the last moment he had decided not to take Gorbachev along.

Admoni and Ben-Menashe were driven into the underground car park of Maxwell House. A security man escorted them up to the penthouse. Maxwell was already entertaining Chebrikov.

'Introductions over and settled over coffee and bagels, it was down to business,' Ben-Menashe would recall. His account of the meeting survives as an example of the truth that the world of intelligence knows no barriers when common interests are being discussed. Or, as Ben-Menashe put it, 'Bullshit walks when money talks.'

He continued: 'Chebrikov cut to the chase. He said the quantity of arms required from Poland would cost some five hundred million dollars. How was that money going to be transferred? Chebrikov knew, of course. But he just wanted to hear it from Maxwell. Maxwell said the money would be moved from Credit Suisse to banks in Prague. It would be released to Poland's Central Bank when confirmation came the arms were ready to be shipped to Israel. However, there would have to be a guarantee, personally backed by the Kremlin, that the money held on deposit in Prague would be safe. If any did "disappear", then the Kremlin would redeem the loss. And any loss would be repaid in American dollars, not roubles. And finally Maxwell wanted his handling fee to be paid in dollars – and up front.'

Chebrikov had pinched his nose. 'How much is your fee?' he had asked.

Maxwell had replied: 'Eight million dollars. Up front. I will let you have the details later when the deal is under way.'

Ben-Menashe would say, 'Maxwell was one hell of a cool customer. He was treating the head of the KGB as if he was a glorified bank teller.'

Chebrikov agreed to the terms. Maxwell then asked when he could go to Warsaw. The KGB chairman said as soon as he liked.

By 9 a.m. the meeting was over.

Maxwell decided he would make no secret of his Polish adventure. The *Daily Mirror* proclaimed that he was going to resolve the industrial chaos that had long held Poland in its thrall. On one side was an embattled government led by the stiff toy-soldier-like General Jaruzelski. On the other was the rugged folk hero, Lech Walesa, leading the Solidarity movement. Maxwell pronounced he was going to bring them to their senses. There was no one better to do so, fawned his tabloid editorial writer.

The words brought renewed mockery from rival newspapers. As the Gulfstream flew across Europe, it left in its slipstream a torrent of abuse. *Private Eye* called him a 'roving ambassador without portfolio'. The liberal *Guardian* castigated him for going to meet a regime that 'slaughtered workers'. The right-wing media – led by Murdoch's *Times* – demanded 'Where are his Socialist principles now?' There were questions asked on the floor of the House of Commons about his sanity.

But, no matter what abuse he suffered, Robert Maxwell was determined to get his $8 million commission from the arms deal.

Waiting in Warsaw was Ben-Menashe. He would be responsible for shepherding the weapons all the way to Israel. He relished the role. He was 'now back in the centre of things, swimming with the sharks'.

Just as in Bulgaria, and all those other Soviet Union satellites he had visited, Maxwell received a carefully stage-managed welcome in Poland. Several hundred yards of red carpeting covering the tarmac; the guard of honour had been issued with special polish to ensure their boots did not allow any rain splashes to settle. The guns they held were part of the consignment Maxwell had come to buy.

Hundreds of women and children had been issued with Union Flags to wave at this massive figure advancing towards the stiff little General Jaruzelski. Hovering to one side was Ben-Menashe, the smile on his face not unlike that of a cat who has been promised unlimited access to cream. Earlier, in a phone call, he had assured Rafi Eitan that the arms were ready for shipping. Eitan had promised Ben-Menashe he would be well rewarded.

At the airport terminal Maxwell gave the first of a succession of interviews to Polish television and state-controlled radio. He had come, he boomed, to bring calm to Poland. It deserved no less. The memories of what the Nazis had done were still 'a raw wound' in his mind. The very name of Auschwitz made him tremble. It was what the regime wanted to hear. He did not mention the anti-Semitism still rife in the country. That was what the regime would not want to hear.

Interviews over, he then went on what resembled a state visit. His cavalcade swept through the city at a speed that allowed him to wave at the marshalled crowds. If he had looked closer, he might have spotted familiar faces. Once his car had passed, the crowds were hurried into buses and driven at high speed through the backstreets to some further point down his route so that they could wave their flags at him once more.

Less than 24 hours after he arrived in Warsaw, Maxwell had settled the arms deal. Now he moved on to the sale of Promis to UB. He told Jaruzelski the software would allow the security service to keep track of Walesa and Solidarity's other leaders; it had become hard to predict where the workers' organisation would next strike. Promis would end that problem.

From the briefcase that never left his side, Maxwell produced a copy of the software. Jaruzelski looked at it quizzically. He asked a question others had asked before: just how could a disk like this achieve so much?

Maxwell repeated what he had told the staff at Sandia, what he had told intelligence chiefs all over the world. Poland's leader immediately ordered a $20 million wire transfer from the country's Central Bank to the Bank of Bulgaria's special account Maxwell held. The deposit was rerouted, a long-standing instruction, to Credit Suisse in Zürich. There, $2 million was deducted as Maxwell's commission. The balance then began its electronic journey around the world to the Discount Bank in Tel Aviv. Everyone was happy.

Business over, Maxwell could not resist the opportunity to use Poland to feed his constant need for publicity. He called a press conference and announced, 'The Solidarity problem has been solved. My newspapers will be devoting less space to the protesters.'

He had seriously misjudged the reaction in Britain. Solidarity was an increasingly popular movement. It had the support of Pope John Paul II, as well as the endorsement of the United States and the European Community.

In Moscow, Chebrikov studied the UB analysis of Maxwell's visit. Shortly afterwards he received notification that a sum of $2 million had been deposited in his newly opened account in a Paris bank. Kryuchkov's fee had gone to his already growing account in Credit Suisse. In Tel Aviv, the Mossad analysts studied what had emerged through the trapdoor in the UB mainframe. In real time they were reading the report while Chebrikov was doing so in Moscow.

*

In Headington Hill Hall, Betty Maxwell had started to assemble the chronology of a marriage that was increasingly doomed. Long ago, when he had first proposed they should go their separate ways, she had put it down to the intense pressure he was under: the Department of Trade and Industry report had condemned him over his business practices; lesser men would never have risen again as he had. Friends he had thought would be loyal to him had vanished.

But he had found new friends and they were not hers. In their presence he had started to criticise her for the plain way she dressed; for her still-strong French accent; for the food she served. She had put it all down on paper. In those long nights sitting alone in her study, she had cast herself in the role of the mythical Sisyphus, who had spent his time pushing a heavy rock up a Greek mountainside only to see it come rolling back down again. In her mind's eye, Maxwell had become that rock, a figure who had shown her that, just as he could crush anyone else, he could also crush her.

She now knew that he had brought home – to *her* home, not just to the penthouse – his other women, passing them off as his secretaries and assistants. She wouldn't deign to call them mistresses; the word presumed some kind of stable relationship. They were just his tarts.

By the summer of 1985, Ben-Menashe had shepherded the last of the weapons from Poland to Iran. But they had proved to be insufficient. Iran was still fighting a rearguard action. It could only be a matter of time before Saddam Hussein could march, all-victorious, into Teheran.

Prime Minister Shimon Peres and Foreign Minister Yitzhak Shamir asked Robert Maxwell to Israel. This time they requested he keep his visit secret. To facilitate this, the Gulfstream flew into a military airport. He was brought to a Mossad safe house in Tel Aviv. Waiting there with Peres and Shamir were Nahum Admoni and David Kimche.

The question to Maxwell was simple: could he use John Tower to persuade President Reagan to start supplying arms to Iran?

Admoni and Kimche quickly sketched in the background. The request should be presented on the basis that it was the best way to free the American hostages in Beriut. US involvement in the deal would be kept secret. Adnan Khashoggi and the others Kimche had assembled would be the front men in the transaction. Tower should tell Reagan that the long-term strategy would be that, once Iran had driven back Iraq, the moderates in Teheran would open a dialogue with Washington. There was every expectation that when that was under way the liberal-thinking mullahs would stage a coup against Khomeini and his hardliners. That would pave the way for America to become a major influence in the country.

Admoni quantified the risks. One of the men in Kimche's proposed group, Ghorbanifar, was untrustworthy. He might leak the plan. On balance, Admoni said, he did not think using the group would work. Mossad would be uncomfortable working with them.

On that note the Mossad director had left.

But Maxwell was ebullient. He said the plan would not only work, but he was the man to ensure Tower would pull it off. On that optimistic note, Maxwell was driven back to the military airfield. He ordered his pilot, Brian Hull, to set course for Washington.

Two days later, he sat down to dinner with Tower in Washington. Tower worked his way through a plate of Texan-style chilli and vintage Krug.

He asked the important question: how high did the plan go? Maxwell named Peres and Shamir as its sponsors. Tower was satisfied.

Two days later the former Senator reported to Maxwell that his meeting with President Reagan had produced a positive response.

The arms-for-hostages deal was on. Maxwell called Peres in Tel Aviv to tell him.

Events moved fast. Peres sent Kimche to Washington to nail down the 'nuts and bolts' of the deal.

Kimche met Robert C McFarlane ('Bud'), the former marine who was one of Reagan's closest aides. He told Kimche that the CIA and the State Department were both opposed to the deal, for the same reason Admoni had given.

'What about the President?' asked Kimche.

'He's still for it.'

'So it's a go?'

'A green light,' confirmed McFarlane.

For the first time since coming to Washington, David Kimche smiled. He placed a call to Maxwell in London and told him the news.

'I told you it would be OK,' Maxwell boomed. 'That's what I'm good at. Making things work.'

At Headington, Betty had sent Maxwell a comprehensive description of her role in his life:

Hotel manager, restaurant major domo, first floor manager, penthouse suites supervisor, cellar stock clerk, warehouse stock keeper, office private secretary, office typist, office filing clerk, Hall receptionist, Hall translator, Hall accountant, Hall insurance clerk, Hall driver, Hall porter, private lines day shift switchboard operator, private lines night shift operator, bell captain, night watchman and disposal unit.

It was her attempt at English humour. There was no mention of her as a wife.

Maxwell did not respond.

EIGHT

By 1985, Maxwell had established for himself multi-roles apart from being Israel's superspy. To the outside world he was a powerful publisher, a man who could sway the opinions of millions of people through his flagship titles, the *Daily Mirror*, *Sunday Mirror* and *Sunday People*, and other titles under his control. To their staffs he was a capricious owner, acting on impulse and whim, bombarding his editors with impractical ideas and stories, many of which were pure inventions.

This breathtaking deceit and conceit had allowed Maxwell to assume control wherever he went, whatever he touched. In the City of London and Wall Street, he had become the ultimate proof that money bought power and power bought money. For him there was only one worthwhile relationship: himself as the master over all others. Once that was accepted he could assume other roles: the benevolent dictator, the kindly man forced by circumstances to act harshly. Then he would say, 'I am a jungle man but in the end I only want to be of service.'

He would stand in the middle of one of his newsrooms having sacked a reporter or subeditor and announce, his eyes brimming with emotion, 'I did not want to do this. But that is the terrible thing about this world: sacrifice has to be made for the greater good of others.'

It was both a lie and his truth. But newspapers were not the only place where he ruled by aggression, cruelty and ruthlessness. His obsession with power and money had bought him factories, businesses and properties, and those who were employed in these worked under his fear. It was a living, vibrant thing that extended across the globe. For them all the normal rules of right and wrong, good and bad, were suspended from the moment he acquired them.

Perhaps the worst fear of all was knowing he was about to come charging through the front door, spraying spittle and expletives, armpits still damp from the deodorant his secretary would have handed him, his wedge of a brow newly powdered from the puff he always carried.

By then it was too late. He took no prisoners: he could fire an entire board or all the senior executives of a company he had acquired. And afterwards his dyed bushy black eyebrows would come together and he would inform those he allowed to remain, 'Change is necessary. But let me tell you this. With me what you see is what you get.'

It was, of course, his ultimate lie, which held a deal of truth. However, he had at last found someone who would not be overcome by his tactics.

His name was Victor Watson and he was chairman of Waddington, an established printing and package company. Maxwell wanted to incorporate it into his own printing corporation, BPCC. Then he would asset-strip it. What little remained, he would leave to the financial scavengers on the street. It was a tactic he had used time and again.

Maxwell told Watson he was making a £44 million cash bid for the company.

Roy Greenslade, from the vantage of his editor's chair at the *Daily Mirror* in Maxwell House, wrote in his book, *Maxwell*, how he watched his employer collect 'companies as other people do stamps, and for every company he bought, he created two or three more private companies leading to his untraceable trusts.'

BPCC was owned by Pergamon, a private company. In turn that was a wholly owned subsidiary of Pergamon Holding Foundation, a trust in the tax-free haven of Liechtenstein. The tiny European nation's laws enshrined the kind of financial secrecy designed for men like Maxwell. Every *stiftung* (a tax-free trust) or an *anstalt* (a company or foundation) was constitutionally guaranteed privacy. They were operated by one of the country's hundreds of taxation lawyers, Dr Walter Keicher.

From the upper floor of a modest building in Vaduz, the country's capital, Keicher managed the Pergamon Foundation and the Pergamon Holding Foundation. There were others with more exotic names: Kiara Foundation, Baccano Foundation, Corry Trust, Heso Trust, Jungo Foundation, Allandra Trust and the Akim Foundation.

Until then their existence had been hidden in Keicher's modest office, its walls lined with locked steel filing cabinets and the door protected by a security lock opened by a swipe card. In this protected environment Walter Keicher, a sprightly seventy-year-old, worked with his son, Werner, to protect Maxwell and all those others who paid them handsome fees.

How had Maxwell managed to establish all those trusts without any of the City of London regulators knowing? Was it simply his arrogance and contempt for the rules that had made him go ahead? Was it possible the Liechtenstein trusts were there to act as collateral for other dealings Maxwell wanted to make? Was that how he had attempted to get his hands on Waddington, the company that had created the Monopoly board game?

Was Maxwell playing an altogether more reckless game than throwing a die? Suppose those trusts had been used once too often, pledged in other deals. When Maxwell had marched into Victor Watson's office, had he been playing from an empty deck?

These still unanswered questions had led the tireless Christopher Eugster, who was employed as an analyst by Waddington's bankers, Kleinwort and Benson, to another figure in the story, one as close-mouthed as any lawyer in Liechtenstein. His name was Rowland. His few friends, among whom he numbered Maxwell, called him 'Tiny'. Maxwell had used him to buy 23 per cent of Waddington's stock six months previously. The shares had been bought in Wall Street and transferred to Pergamon Press Inc., another Maxwell private company, based in New York.

Rowland was hugely wealthy, erudite, cold and calculating and physically the antithesis of Maxwell. Slim, elegant and proud of his silvered hair, Rowland looked the part of a chairman of one of the most powerful corporations in Africa, Lonrho. It was through Lonrho's highly placed connections that Maxwell had been able to meet African leaders and sell them Promis. The software had now been installed in Kenya, Nigeria and Uganda. Rowland shared one other quality with Maxwell. He too was a financial terrorist.

Born in India, the son of a German businessman and the daughter of a pillar of the English Raj, Rowland had become a supporter of Hitler in the 1930s. As he had acquired his fortune, he had managed to divest himself of that dark time in his past. In the City of London boardrooms and the gentlemen's clubs around Pall Mall, he was now the quintessential Englishman. He could be found having a late drink on Kensington's Embassy Row, hosting a dinner party for friends and enemies in private dining rooms, leading a group into his box at Covent Garden. A few whispered words and he would discreetly tarnish a reputation, or offer a tip on next day's horse race.

No one suspected that Rowland had a secret he would not wish to share: he had played a key part in establishing Saddam Hussein's personal fortune.

In 1978 the Shah of Iran had known his rule was about to end, and the gilded Peacock throne from which he had ruled with such brutality was approaching meltdown. Entire cities in Iran had become closed citadels controlled by the clergy of the Ayatollah Khomeini.

Teams of his accountants, trained by Wall Street and the Swiss banking systems, were combing the world to try to confiscate the Shah's huge fortune. Over the years he had built up portfolios in every financial market. His investments in Wall Street alone were worth over $200 million.

Anticipating Khomeini's determination to confiscate the money in the name of the Islamic revolution, the Shah had made an astonishing move to try to protect his wealth. For months in 1978 his most trusted aides had held secret meetings in Paris and Geneva with representatives of Iran's sworn enemy – Iraq. The Shah had reasoned that even the most diligent of the ayatollah's accountants would be unable to gain access to Iraq's banks.

The deal the Shah's men were proposing was breathtakingly simple. The Shah would transfer his personal fortune, which, so far, had escaped the scrutiny of the ayatollah's accountants, into accounts to be managed by the Shah's surrogates. They would place the funds in Iraqi banks. There they would for ever be beyond the ayatollah's accountants. The Shah could draw down whenever he liked and live a life of luxury in his old age, or so he was told.

The bankers in Baghdad would receive a 'handling fee' of 1.5 per cent for arranging this unique facility.

Until he came to power in 1979, Saddam had been relatively impoverished. Raised in almost abject poverty, he had never had sufficient money to finance his grandiose schemes. The war with Iran was biting even deeper into the Iraqi economy. Loans from the United States, Britain and Europe were all tightly controlled. There was little opportunity for him to get his hands on ready cash. The deal with the Shah would change all that. In a matter of days, arrangements had been agreed. Some $1 billion was withdrawn from US banks and transferred into accounts held by the Shah's surrogates to Swiss banks, including Credit Suisse.

From there the money was routed to Saddam's personal numbered accounts in Geneva, Paris, the Cayman Islands and the City of London. The Shah was unaware of what had happened until he fled to the West in 1979. There he learned where his money had gone. His appeals to Washington to intervene and recover his money fell on deaf ears. The United States realised that it had backed the Shah against Ayatollah Khomeini and as such was left with only one card to play and that was to support Saddam against his rival, Khomeini. There was no way Washington was going to ask him to pay back the Shah. The Shah was yesterday's man.

With his $1 billion safely stashed away, Saddam turned to an unlikely source to advise him on how to enhance his new fortune.

He had heard about Rowland from his own bankers. They held Tiny in awe. More important to Saddam, Rowland was a ferocious opponent of Israel, as well as being a friend of Syria's President, Hafiz al-Assad. Iraq's ambassador in London was instructed to invite Rowland to Baghdad.

Tiny Rowland impressed the Iraqi dictator with his financial acumen. Back in London he arranged for Duncan Sandys, who was Winston Churchill's son-in-law, to visit Saddam.

They explained to Saddam how to make his money work. His portfolios began to grow. Ten years after he had acquired the Shah's money, his fortune had doubled.

Rowland made no secret of his anti-Semitism, even from Maxwell. But long ago Maxwell had learned to shrug off such talk. Rowland for him was one of those who understood the principle that governed Maxwell's business life, that of talking a seller into as low a price as possible. If talk did not succeed, there was always the option of mounting a hostile take-over. Both men well understood how to hustle some refined businessman in London or New York into meeting their price.

With Maxwell waiting for his offer for Waddington's to be accepted, public scrutiny of the Liechtenstein trust was increasing.

Newspapermen began to ring the doorbell of Keicher's office building. For a man who had lived all his life in the shadows, outside the glare of scrutiny, the sudden flash of camera bulbs and the increasingly incessant questions of reporters must have driven him close to panic.

In London Maxwell was enraged. Day by day rival newspaper reports were coming uncomfortably close to the truth that he had used Liechtenstein as a secret bolthole from which to emerge, like a thief in the night, to try to steal Waddington.

He called the one man he had come to depend on, John Tower. The former Senator listened and then told Maxwell the sensible thing to do was to cut his losses and move on to a new deal.

Hours later, on 10 December 1985, Maxwell received another call. It was Dr Keicher. Maxwell took the call in the penthouse. He ordered his senior secretary to ensure no one should be allowed to interrupt him.

While no precise record of the call would exist of who said what and when, of the finer details, of the need to justify, for expiation – while none of that is possible to recapture, there can be little doubt it was a tense conversation. Keicher would have explained he was under siege from reporters. Maxwell would have ordered him to say nothing, that he would handle it. Keicher, his voice quavering with old age, would finally have said what he intended to do: close down his office until all this unseemly interest died. That day he would travel to his mountain lodge, light a log fire and allow the snow to blot out the landscape of his own life, which had been so trampled upon.

Maxwell chose a different approach. He issued a 'Statement from the Publisher'. Over the years there had been hundreds of these self-serving documents, personally dictated by Maxwell. They were arrogant, bombastic and insulting; their only saving grace was that they were relatively short – usually designed to fill the front page of one of his tabloids.

A statement was the first warning shot of a diatribe of articles in Maxwell's newspapers. At those times he would stand over his editors, ordering the size of typeface to be used, the photograph of himself he wanted to reinforce the words. Those were the times when the ghost of the American publishing tycoon William Randolph Hearst seemed to hover over Maxwell.

But Robert Maxwell had not counted on the tenacity of Victor Watson. He issued his own statement: calm and dignified, it rebutted the hyperbole of Maxwell's claim that he had become the victim of 'smears and innuendo', that he was being presented as a financial rogue when he was just a businessman going about his daily work.

In his statement Maxwell had confirmed what Watson now knew: that he had secretly acquired 23 per cent of Waddington's shares and had received a further 15 per cent acceptances from its shareholders. His offer of £44 million still stood.

Watson knew that, despite the total of 38 per cent of stock Maxwell now owned, it was still insufficient for him to wrench control. A mere nobody, as he may well have seen Watson, was not going to stop him remaining at the top.

With the deadline Maxwell had imposed for the acquisition, 13 December 1985, approaching, Maxwell approached the Sainsbury board, who had recently bought 15 per cent of Waddington stock, to say he was ready to pay over the odds for its stake in Waddington. Sensing his urgency but not quite understanding what was behind his pressure, the board took its time. There was also the well-tried principle that Maxwell had himself often reiterated: a deal is never settled until money changes hands. Negotiations continued.

It was mid-afternoon in London and Maxwell was still waiting in an anteroom while the Sainsbury board pondered, when the call came from his senior secretary in Maxwell House. She said a vice-president of Ansbacher's in New York – where the opening bell for trading had just rung in Wall Street Stock Exchange – had called. The bank official had spoken at dictation speed. She read to Maxwell what he had said. 'The persons with ultimate entitlement to the [Liechtenstein] Trusts comprise a number of charities and relatives of Mr and Mrs Maxwell not resident in the United Kingdom.'

Maxwell's shout carried to the Sainsbury boardroom.

'Is this for public consumption?' he demanded. His secretary told him that Ansbacher's would be issuing the statement to the media even as she was reading it to him.

Maxwell's wait in the anteroom was finally over. He was summoned back to face the Sainsbury board and was informed that their stake in Waddington was not for sale – no matter what was on offer.

Waddington was safe.

*

In a bid to massage his deflated ego, Maxwell announced that within five years he would be heading a global conglomerate, producing revenues of between £3 and £5 billion. That figure would place him among the wealthiest men on earth. His newspapers filled pages with the prediction. No one queried how his current profits in 1985 of $79 million would have multiplied in five years by a staggering twenty times.

While the bruising battle with Waddington had run its course, Maxwell had been engaged on another company raid, instigated this time by Rafi Eitan and Nahum Admoni.

Since his first visit to Inslaw two years before, Eitan had continued to use his own contacts in the Department of Justice to keep abreast of what Hamilton and his small team of technicians were working on. Admoni had also assigned a *katsa* working out of the Israeli embassy in Washington to do the same. Posing as a freelance science journalist, the *katsa* had regularly called Hamilton and learned that they were creating a new and altogether more sophisticated version of Promis.

Eitan flew to London, where he had set up a small import company in the city's Docklands to trade in Cuban cigars. He brought a box of the finest Havanas to Maxwell House. In the penthouse sanctum he told Maxwell he should buy Inslaw. It would not only give Mossad control over the new Promis software and where it would be marketed, but also enable the new software to be fitted with its own trapdoor – what Rafi Eitan had taken to calling Israel's very own Trojan Horse. In return for owning Inslaw, Maxwell would be allowed to market its products through Information on Demand.

Maxwell immediately contacted one of his brokers at Ansbacher. He now had a 10 per cent stake in the bank. The broker was instructed to approach Hamilton. John A Belton, the Montreal stockbroker with Nesbitt-Thompson, who had become a close associate of Hamilton, would recall: 'The broker told Bill he was calling on behalf of an unnamed publisher who was interested in acquiring the company lock, stock and down to the last computer disk.'

Hamilton, a tough-minded man cast from the same mould as Victor Watson, brusquely told the broker that Inslaw was not for sale.

The Mossad chief told Maxwell not to pursue the Inslaw deal. Admoni knew that not only would Hamilton be a formidable foe – he was then suing the Justice Department and its senior staff for their part in the theft of Promis – but a takeover battle could bring further unwelcome attention on Maxwell, and perhaps even begin to reveal his secret links to Israel's intelligence service.

Instead Maxwell was asked to continue quietly to create more private companies that could be used as fronts for Mossad's own operations in the

United States. One company was registered as Pergamon Brassey Inc. Its articles of association covered every facet of the computer industry.

As always Israel was never far from Maxwell's thoughts. He not only maintained a deep emotional attachment to the country, but ensured it would not for a moment forget who he was. The tabloid *Ma'ariv* carried his photograph and every detail of a speech he gave to some Jewish organisation, with the same slavish consistency Saddam Hussein expected from his own media. Maxwell used the power of all his newspapers to attack Israel's enemies. When an elderly Jew was murdered by terrorists who had stormed the cruise liner *Achille Lauro*, the *Daily Mirror* led the sustained attack on the PLO.

But Maxwell was also shrewd enough not to intervene in Israel's domestic politics; he stayed well clear of the frequent tensions between its leaders. He had learned one important matter from his trips to Israel: not only Mossad but its politicians surrounded themselves with security apparatus that allowed them to monitor the activities of their employees. The surveillance was still some way from the system he had seen in Bulgaria and other Eastern Bloc countries; there, loyalty to the party was guaranteed by a spying apparatus, which extended through every level of society. Central to the system were the district committees.

A leading Bulgarian journalist, Violeta Kumurdjieva, had synthesised their role as 'looking closely into who was sleeping with whom. Who had not paid his party membership? Who was drinking excessively? Who was disseminating anti-party jokes? The penalty for transgressors was immediate dismissal from the Party, effectively making them a non-person.' This was the ultimate form of control.

Not only did Robert Maxwell approve such draconian control, but he decided to introduce it into Maxwell House. In the early hours of one morning when all but the security staff had left, a team of specialists arrived and installed hidden microphones in every office on the ninth floor of Maxwell House. Secret tape recorders stored every word.

Bugs were hidden behind wall panels, in light fittings, in the handsets of phones, in restrooms. To control this hi-tech system he hired John Pole, a former chief superintendent at Scotland Yard. His task was to collect the tapes and bring them to Maxwell's penthouse.

There, in the early hours when he could not sleep, or after he had sent home one of the women he summoned for a few hours of casual sex, Robert Maxwell would sit and listen to the recordings, or thumb through the reports of the private detectives he had hired to spy on his women or business enemies.

One of these women would later recall, 'Robert had a fixation about whether I was faithful to him. He would question me about my previous relationships in as much detail as I would give him. I think he got off on that.'

Any evidence uncovered by the detectives of extramarital activities by his competitors was passed on to his editors to investigate. Many a front-page story came from that source.

The bugging system provided Maxwell with an insight into what his staff really thought of him. A secretary he had slept with had been recorded in a restroom detailing her revulsion at his sexual demands. Another had described the state of his soiled bed. A third mentioned his gross eating habits, stuffing his fingers into a caviar bowl to wipe it clean. Given his usual fury over any criticism, they could not have remained long in his employ.

In the week before Christmas 1985, Pole was to instructed to ensure the bug was working in the office telephone of Nicholas Davies, the *Daily Mirror*'s foreign editor.

With his foppish clothes and repartee, Davies could have stepped out of *The Front Page*; there was something Runyonesque about him. His North-of-England accent had all but gone; spiteful colleagues said he spent hours practising his dulcet tones. Editorial secretaries found his good manners and the commanding way he could order dinner and select a good bottle of wine was the prelude to a night of lovemaking. Davies would regale them with stories of faraway places he had been to on assignments. The casual way he steadily worked his way through the never-ending supply of women who came and went from Maxwell House had earned him the nickname of 'Sneaky'.

Pole had presented Maxwell with the tape recording of all the day's conversations to and from Davies's phone.

Robert Maxwell may well have only wanted to be reassured about his foreign editor's loyalty; not that he was really one of the few journalists he could still trust.

Maxwell inserted into the maw of the player the tape Pole had brought. There was the familiar ring of a phone being answered, followed by the voice of Davies identifying himself.

There then followed a conversation that could only have stunned Robert Maxwell.

There was no disguising the sharpness in Ari Ben-Menashe's voice.

Who can doubt that Robert Maxwell was even more stunned – or the questions that must have filled his mind? Why was Ari Ben-Menashe calling Davies? What was ORA and this manifest that they referred to? What was going on?

No doubt desperate for answers, Robert Maxwell had also learned that, in a matter like this, to confront Davies would be a tactical mistake. He had seen that the journalist could be cool and controlled under pressure.

Perhaps he would say Ben-Menashe was another of his contacts, that the terms 'ORA' and 'manifest' were a code they had devised for Ben-Menashe to pass on information for a story. Where would that then leave Maxwell? Simply to fire Davies would be to leave him without a man he had counted on to write whatever he was told. And, if Davies went, God only knew what he would publish. Certainly he would find ample space in one of the Murdoch newspapers to reveal all he knew.

ORA had been the brainchild of Rafi Eitan and had been set up in 1981 to bypass the US embargo on arms to Iran. It had first operated from an office situated on John Street in downtown Manhattan.

ORA, meaning 'light' in Hebrew, had a workforce of fifty divided into teams of arms dealers. Their task was to scour the country for hi-tech weapons, buy them and arrange for delivery to Iran.

Word of their activities leaked to the *New York Times*, which ran a story saying that Israel was secretly supplying arms to Iran. Eitan closed down the operation.

That had not been the end of ORA. In 1983, Ari Ben-Menashe was given the task of running the company out of London. His instructions were that it would be a small, discreet operation. London would primarily be a base for setting up deals, and where documentation for weapons shipments would be prepared and sent out.

It would also be a route for payments for arms from the London branch of Iran's Bank Meli. A credit transfer would be provided by the National Westminster Bank to pay for the weapons.

It had been in London that Ari Ben-Menashe and Davies first met. On that they never have disagreed, but the relationship they subsequently developed became clouded in the following years. Ben-Menashe's version had its own ring of truth and no shade of vagueness.

He would claim he had learned of Davies through a former British Special Air Services officer.

'It was in the lobby of London's Churchill Hotel in the first half of 1983. Davies struck me as just what we had in mind – intelligent, well travelled and a charmer. In addition, he had a taste for the good life, which meant he'd always need money. I told Davies we were looking for him to work for us.'

After the meeting, according to Ben-Menashe, he was invited to Davies's home for lunch and met 'his slim, attractive wife, Janet Fielding, a star on British television'.

Davies would tell a different story:

'In the early 80s, I received a call out of the blue from a visiting Israeli, Ari Ben-Menashe. He said he was from the Israeli government and could we meet? Ben-Menashe was in fact not looking for me but another journalist with my name. We exchanged numbers.'

In the Davies version of events, Ben-Menashe had told him he could act as a contact for him in Tel Aviv. A few weeks later Ben-Menashe phoned him with information that 'had a ring of truth about it'.

'He had his finger on the pulse,' admitted Davies. 'Whenever he came to London, two or three times a year, we would meet.'

Ben-Menashe offers a radically different response. He would later repeatedly claim Davies had been recruited by Mossad as far back as the mid-1970s. If that was the case, why would Mossad need 'officially' to sign Davies up again? Certainly Rafi Eitan has no recall of Davies becoming involved with Mossad a decade before Ben-Menashe brought him on that all-expenses-paid visit to Israel.

What is not in doubt is that from 1983 onwards, Nick Davies was linked to ORA and, through that, to Mossad.

Davies's then wife, Janet, would later claim she 'had not been fooled' by her husband's relationship with Ben-Menashe. She said, 'I had known what was going on after I saw documents being faxed to and from our home and overhearing conversations between my husband and Ben-Menashe – he had become an almost permanent house guest'.

At times Davies's editors did not know where he was and why he often phoned them from foreign destinations. Davies always had an explanation: 'Maxwell sent me.'

That was enough to put an end to any further questions.

'We became very good at setting up deals, disguising them and delivering the goods. The sales and smokescreens worked brilliantly,' recalled Ben-Menashe.

From Davies's home, faxes continued to be sent to arms dealers. One, from 29 December 1984 to Ran Yegnes, 17 Montefiory Street, Petah-Tikva, read:

- Re: Request for Quotation:
- We would appreciate the best quotation and delivery times and condition for new original Soviet-made Bakelite AK 47 (Kalashnikov) magazines.
- Several thousand of the above magazines are required by our company for marketing in the United States to private users.
- Form of payment will be through letter of credit opened in a prime European bank upon signing of contract.
- Prompt action and acceptable prices may bring successful completion of this deal.
- We are looking forward to doing business with you and best wishes.

Faithfully yours,

Nicolas Davis

Davies has refused to say whether or not the incorrect spelling of his name was a deliberate attempt to hide his real identity.

A subsequent letter, also signed 'Davis' in May 1985, was to GMT Ltd in Tel Aviv. It contained details about an arms deal valued at several million dollars.

By January 1985, Janet Fielding had become concerned about his dealings with Ben-Menashe. By the time she travelled to star in a stage play in Stockholm, she had made up her mind her marriage was over. The play finished, she returned to London to pack her bags.

Nick Davies was not at home when she arrived. With the help of a friend, she began packing her personal belongings. But that was not all she decided to take with her. She sifted through ORA documents and letters, rushed to a local library, copied them, and took the copies with her. Originals were also included in her cache of evidence.

They would provide her with what she called 'ammunition' in the event of her becoming entangled in a bitter divorce.

'She left me a Dear John letter. There had been no arguments, no complaints, no discussions – nothing to suggest she wanted out of the two-year marriage,' recalled Davies.

Her departure had no effect on ORA's operations.

Meanwhile, Maxwell would continue to operate on a different level for Israel. Nahum Admoni had made it clear Maxwell would not be compromised by 'getting his hands dirty in the day-to-day workings of covert operations'.

He was told to do nothing about Nick Davies. He was to keep him on staff but also to keep him at a distance.

Admoni would ensure that Ari Ben-Menashe also remained outside Maxwell's orbit. The Mossad chief saw Ben-Menashe in much the way Earl Brian was regarded by the CIA. Both were men who liked to cream off what they could for themselves. They would never rise far in the shadowy world of intelligence.

But Robert Maxwell was different. He had the potential to make an impact on matters that had global strategic importance for the State of Israel.

NINE

On a clear-skied winter's day in 1985, the first sign that Israel's short winter would soon be over, David Kimche had left Tel Aviv. Five hours later when he reached London, the weather was cold enough to penetrate his topcoat. The atmosphere reflected the chill in relations between Washington and Tel Aviv. It was the reason he had been asked to go to London and see Robert Maxwell. If anybody could sort out the deteriorating situation over the sale of arms to Iran in return for having the American hostages released from their Beirut incarceration, it had to be Kimche. He was the point man for the deal, an uncomfortable position for a man who had carefully nurtured his own relations with Washington. The deal that had looked so promising only a few weeks ago had suddenly started to unravel. He had come to London because he needed Maxwell to help stitch it together.

The first loosening of the thread that had tightly bound Israel and the United States on the deal had begun to loosen a month previously. Nahum Admoni had picked up a hint that Robert C McFarlane, the National Security Adviser, was telling President Reagan to pull the plug. 'There had to be another way, a better way, than getting us mixed up with this bunch.' McFarlane was reported to have said.

That other 'way', Admoni quickly learned, was one where by McFarlane and his deputy, Colonel Oliver North, were pushing for direct contact between Washington and Teheran so as to cut out 'this bunch'. They were the colourful group that Kimche had put together, led by Khashoggi, Ghorbanifar and Nimrodi.

McFarlane had called them 'a liability and untrustworthy'. North, ever quick to echo his master's voice, had told McFarlane that these 'guys talk big and deliver small'.

In Tel Aviv, Admoni's news had caused consternation. The Cabinet had listened in silence to his view that, if Israel was cut out of the deal, the repercussions would be far reaching. Its own influence in Iran, little enough, would wither. Worse, the word would spread through the Arab capitals that Washington saw Israel nowadays as unimportant in *any* deal. That could be disastrous, even possibly the precursor to another war. And nobody around the Cabinet table needed to be told that, since the last conflict, the Arab nations had become even more determined in their resolve to drive Israel into the sea: a cursory listening to Radio Baghdad or Radio Damascus showed how bellicose Syria and Iraq had become.

It had been left to Kimche to offer soothing hope. In his view, one based on all those long years of close contact with Washington, if Reagan was listening to McFarlane and North – a gung-ho Marine Kimche had come to dislike privately – then it was a ploy on the President's part. Kimche reminded his listeners it was no secret that the CIA and the State Department were still smarting about being kept out of the arms-for-Iran scheme. If – and it was a big if – the President was going to do anything, it was probably no more than buy time to deal with the impasse between the CIA's director Bill Casey and Secretary of State George Schultz on one side and McFarlane and North on the other. It may be no bad thing, Kimche had concluded.

It was a shrewd assessment. But once more the thread had unravelled a little further. North was the kind of charismatic soldier Reagan liked having around. He made things happen. He was go-get-'em, in the way Reagan had been in those old movies he had starred in. McFarlane was the kind of careful man Washington created by the in-tray. It was McFarlane who had started to question the validity of keeping Israel on board. It was North who clung to his battle-cry, 'Keep Israel in the fold.'

On 4 December 1985, McFarlane resigned as National Security Adviser. He told Reagan he would, however, remain in office until the end of the year to allow his successor to come up to speed on the arms-to-Iran deal.

That same day Reagan appointed Admiral John Marlan Poindexter as his new National Security Adviser.

The news caused consternation in Tel Aviv. In a dozen and more ways in the Kirya, in the Prime Minister's compound and above all on the top floor of Mossad headquarters, two questions were asked. 'Who is Poindexter? Why has Reagan done this?'

Answers were not long in coming.

On 6 December – while Maxwell was deep into his takeover bid for Waddington – a shorter and altogether more important issue was being resolved. Reagan summoned to the Oval Office Poindexter, McFarlane and North. The President walked from behind his desk and sat between them. He told them that, 'here and now, as of this moment', he was terminating the arms-for-hostages deal. He knew as well as they did what that meant: no freedom for the hostages, and even possibly their deaths.

He wanted the Israelis to know the deal was off. The meeting had lasted less than five minutes.

In Tel Aviv, Peres, Kimche and Admoni met in the Prime Minister's office. Poindexter had told him the formal winding up of the deal should be in London.

Kimche had seized upon that as a hopeful sign. London was neutral ground. It could mean that, if a good case was made, then there was still a chance of saving the day for Israel. While McFarlane was now a lame duck with less than a month to go in office, it could still be possible to convince him that he had been in at the beginning, so why not see it through? One good push and the hostages could still pop out of that underground hole the press called the 'Beirut Hilton'.

The others had listened while Kimche had argued in his calm, controlled voice, advancing his case point by point, never leaving room for doubt. It was, even by his standards, a masterclass in persuasion. The others accepted.

Kimche then said he would like to take with him to London Manucher Ghorbanifar. Admoni objected. He said the former Iranian secret agent was a 'loose cannon'. In the Mossad director's view, Ghorbanifar fitted McFarlane's damning judgment on the group Kimche had first created as a 'liability and untrustworthy'.

Peres disagreed. He told Kimche he could take Ghorbanifar to London.

Maxwell had sent a car to collect them from Heathrow Airport, having had Tower clear with the White House his offer of holding the meeting in the penthouse. Maxwell's stature in Washington was growing and his proposal was seen as further proof that he was a good friend.

Maxwell had laid on a sumptuous buffet. Champagne had been followed by a large bowl of Beluga caviar on a mountain of ice. Maxwell had poured vodka and delivered a Russian-style toast. 'To Resolution,' he had boomed. The others had dutifully repeated the hope; more fifty-dollar mouthfuls of sturgeon eggs continued to be swallowed.

Kimche, McFarlane and North ate sparingly, smiling politely at each other, well-trained fighters waiting for the bell to go.

Ghorbanifar and Maxwell had never met before and they exchanged gossip about the Shah; most of it confirmed what Tiny Rowland had told Maxwell.

Between questions, Maxwell ate in his usual way, picking up a handful of crustless sandwiches and stuffing them into his mouth, masticating noisily before grabbing more food. North wondered whether his host had an eating disorder. McFarlane wondered that, if Maxwell could not control his appetite, what else couldn't he handle?

When Maxwell had all but cleared the buffet, he motioned for his guests to move to one of the room's seating areas.

'Well, gentlemen, let's see if you can bring a meeting of minds on the matter.' It was Maxwell in his self-appointed-chairman role. He settled back in his armchair.

McFarlane repeated what Reagan had said. The operation was over. He was here only to tidy up the loose ends.

Kimche smiled politely. No one made a 6,000-mile round trip just to deliver a message. He said his latest information was that a deal over the hostages could come soon. Iran had suffered further heavy losses in the war. The mullahs had sent him a message through the back-door channel he had established. They wanted more arms urgently. That could mean they were finally ready to trade.

'They want all kinds of weapons,' Ghorbanifar had emphasised.

McFarlane and North ignored him. They continued to focus on Kimche.

Neither of the Americans had raised the ideathat America might supply Iran directly. Kimche asked if that had been ruled out.

'A mistake if so.' Ghorbanifar broke the silence.

Everyone still ignored him. Neither McFarlane nor North answered Kimche's question. He did not put it again. He felt he knew his answer.

Maxwell realised Ghorbanifar was the loose cannon Tower had warned about. Too late, Kimche realised his mistake in bringing the Iranian along. Ghorbanifar was purely interested in what more was in it for him. He and his small group of arms dealers had already made millions of dollars from the day-to-day role as the deal's cutout men.

The meeting dragged on. Sensing it was a waste of time, Maxwell returned to the buffet table and began to mop up what remained of the smoked salmon and sandwiches.

Across the room David Kimche tossed in his final negotiating point: Israel would stop sending arms to Iran if that would make the mullahs realise they had to start releasing the Beirut hostages.

'Not a good idea,' Ghorbanifar said. 'It is better to go on sending them weapons.'

'It's a good idea, David,' McFarlane told Kimche. 'Washington will be pleased.'

'So, no more arms from your end?' North asked.

Ghorbanifar said nothing. He knew that on this very day Ya'atov Nimrodi, another member of the cutout group, was negotiating a $5 million deal for arms.

The meeting ended without any resolution. McFarlane's last words to Kimche were: 'It's dead, David.' North had echoed, 'Dead as a dodo.'

Brief handshakes and they were gone.

Kimche flew back to Tel Aviv. He told Peres that he no longer believed a deal with America was possible. His resignation was accepted. Peres immediately appointed a successor, Amiram Nir.

From London, Robert Maxwell called Nahum Admoni and said he was still there, ready to be of service.

Amiram Nir had been Peres's antiterrorism adviser; no Israeli prime minister felt comfortable without one. In previous administrations the post had been held by men like Rafi Eitan and Ari Ben-Menashe, highly experienced in carrying out what essentially was acting as a watchdog for the incumbent prime minister over the intelligence community. It was never going to be 'a job that was going to make you popular like a Miss Israel', Ben-Menashe said. 'You are supposed to stick your nose into places Mossad, military intelligence and others like to keep to themselves.'

Nir had the essential qualities to do that. He was inquisitive, exploitative and manipulative. With those attributes came a raffish charm, a lack of self-restraint, an ability to ridicule, to take imaginative leaps, to break the rules, to put a spin on any fact. Nir had been a journalist. His previous knowledge of intelligence came from his work as a reporter on Israeli television; later he had joined the staff of one of the country's largest daily newspapers, *Yediot Aharonot*. It was owned by the dynasty family, Moses, who ran a publishing empire that Maxwell could only have envied: it was the epitome of respectability and securely financed; it treated its employees on the old adage of a fair day's pay for a hard day's work. Nir had married Judy Moses, making him the husband of one of the wealthiest women in Israel. It provided him with ready access to the highest echelons of the country's political hierarchy. Whenever Robert Maxwell visited Israel, Amiram Nir was always on the guest list.

Nevertheless there was astonishment when he became Peres's anti-terrorism adviser. What was Nir going to do – devise his strategy from the evening news bulletins? Meir Amit had publicly pondered. Rafi Eitan had pointed out that Nir's only known intelligence experience was a short Israeli Defence Forces course.

Nahum Admoni had gone further. He changed the structure of the Committee of the Heads of Services – on which the chiefs of all Israel's intelligence agencies sat under Admoni's chairmanship. The new rules excluded Nir.

There was nothing Peres could do. But the resignation of Kimche gave him an opportunity to snub Admoni and show his own trust in Nir.

Barely 34 years old, Nir now became Israel's point man in the arms-for-hostages deal, which, despite all President Reagan had said, had not been killed off.

The day after his appointment, Nir sought a meeting with Admoni. The director was cool. Nir set out to charm him. He said the appointment of Poindexter 'may have significance'.

Admoni sat back in his high-backed leather chair, the one that all directors since Meir Amit had used.

Nir began to expound. Poindexter was not there to close down the deal permanently. He was there to ensure Reagan pulled off another triumph: the President had come into office charged with bringing the US diplomats out of Teheran, where they were being held hostage. Now, as the polls showed, Reagan had a fight on his hands. He could restore his popularity by extracting those other American hostages out of Beirut.

Poindexter knew that the only way still to do that was to go on with the deal. There would be a pause to give the Iranians 'a wake-up call that they could not go on messing us around for ever'. That pause would also be used to open up a new way of dealing with the mullahs. The cutout team on which Kimche had laid such store would run matters directly with a little help from Oliver North. Nir said he knew North understood his mentality; he would be able to work with North. What he would like to do was to join forces with North and Poindexter and at the same time keep Israel on board. It would all be done discreetly, Admoni could be assured of that.

Finally the Mossad chief had a question: what about the CIA? 'They are still very pissed at being kept out of the loop,' Nir would recall Admoni saying.

Nir said that was probably a good thing. If the CIA was running the arms deal, then Bill Casey would want to control every stage. And, from what he had picked up in the past few hours in his calls to Washington, Nir was certain the President would want to keep the CIA out.

Admoni wanted to know who Nir had been speaking to. 'Good sources,' Nir said. He sounded like Maxwell.

Admoni had another question. 'How would Mossad now fit into all this?'

'Wherever you want to be,' Nir had said.

Admoni returned to a previous question: how could Nir be so certain that all he was saying, those 'good sources' notwithstanding, could really be what was being thought in Washington?

Nir, displaying his boyish grin, would later recall. 'I just spread my hands and said, "OK, speculation. But give me a better reason." Admoni said he couldn't. He just wanted to know one thing. Was Israel still in the game?'

The Mossad chief contacted Maxwell to tap once more the one man who was guaranteed to know the answer: John Tower.

Next day Brian Hull's Gulfstream was fuelled for the long flight across the Atlantic to Washington. The galley was stocked with food and drink. Barefoot and waited upon like a medieval prince, Maxwell arrived refreshed and once more ready to serve Mossad.

Over dinner, Maxwell explained to the Senator his concerns that the cooling of relations between the United States and Israel could have a direct bearing on what should always be uppermost in their minds: the opportunity to expand their shared business interests.

On the advice of Rafi Eitan, Maxwell had increased Tower's stipend to almost $300,000 a year and had begun to hand out generous bonuses. Maxwell had indicated there could be more to come. But, to ensure that, he wanted the relationship between Israel and Washington back on an even keel.

Was Poindexter the kind of man who could perform the miracle of getting out the hostages? Tower replied: no question at all – Poindexter *was* the man. Maxwell sat back and listened as Tower delivered a eulogy about the admiral.

How did Poindexter feel about Israel? As far as Tower knew, Poindexter had no strong feelings either way. Neutral, he suggested, would perhaps be the best word.

Maxwell gently pressed. Could Tower find out? How neutral was neutral?

Tower was back in a couple of days. Poindexter shared Reagan's admiration for Israel: he called it a 'feisty little country kicking the shit out of all those big fellas'.

Under Poindexter things were going to be different. He would have North as his own point man. And the CIA were back in the picture. 'Purely a sweetener,' Tower confided.

That night Maxwell called Admoni and said everything was back on track.

Next day Amiram Nir flew to Washington to meet Poindexter and North. Nir said, with all the confidence of the inexperienced, that Iran would free all the hostages once it had received 1,000 TOW antitank guided missiles.

Arrangements were soon in place. The CIA were asked to purchase the weapons from the Department of Defense for an unspecified covert operation. The agency, with the full knowledge and approval of President Reagan, then sold them on to the National Security Council. North and Nir arranged their transfer to Iran.

Once more, thanks to Robert Maxwell, everybody was satisfied in the dark world of intelligence in which he roamed with ever-growing confidence.

More than any mission he had undertaken for Israel, Robert Maxwell prepared for his forthcoming trip to the People's Republic of China with the greatest care. He had read long into the night in his penthouse double bed about its geography, culture and people. He had even learned a smattering of the language and when and how to bow; in the end he decided a royal incline of the head would be appropriate. He had business cards printed in Mandarin. Every spare moment he had, he read about the largest Communist nation on earth. The Soviet Union was starting to tremble at its foundations, but China remained true to its Marxist principles.

He studied briefing papers from the Foreign Office and from the State Department, from anywhere he could learn about this most paradoxical of nations. Like others before him, he tried to make sense of how, as acknowledged masters of agriculture, China had to import grain. How, possessed of the most wonderful musical traditional, its composers still wrote some of the worst modern music in the world. How was it, he had asked himself, that their political theorists had rivalled the Greeks, and ensured a stable society, which itself had survived invasion, famine and civil war for more than two millennia? Yet their modern counterparts had created a doctrine that was both crude and derivative. With a per-capita national income less than he charged for a month's supply of his newspapers, this same country of mass illiteracy had launched satellites and developed nuclear weapons and intercontinental ballistic missiles. Child-loving to a fault, its ruler had made it a crime for a couple to have more than one baby and those who gave birth to girls were encouraged to abandon or even kill them in infancy. And there was that final curiosity: they had turned a man, Mao, into a god, and then replaced him with another human being with no real regret.

The more he read, the more Robert Maxwell saw there was much to admire in the Chinese: they were loyal, modest and ethereal. But they were also infuriating, overbearing, mendacious, mercenary and sadistic. They were quite unlike anybody else. But they were remarkably similar to him. He sensed he was going to like the Chinese.

The decision for him to go there had been Rafi Eitan's. He had said to sell China Promis would be, without doubt, the greatest coup Maxwell could achieve.

Mossad had arranged for Maxwell to have copies of their own files on the leadership and their relationship with the rest of the world. Soviet stagnation, Arab terrorism, Islamic fundamentalism – China had a position on everything.

Mossad had also provided their superspy with a portrait of the People's Liberation Army, PLA, and its multi-weapons systems. Maxwell received detailed backgrounds of military commanders he might meet, along with the senior managers in China's technology companies. There were two of particular importance, Huawei Technologies and ZTE. Both corporations were defence contractors to the PLA, providing the armed services with advanced computer technology.

Admoni had flown to London to brief Maxwell on an aspect of his visit which would require the greatest caution on his part. In China surveillance was an integral part of pacification, intimidation, obfuscation, propaganda and control. Compared with China, the Soviet Union was an open society,

Admoni had warned. In China surveillance was presented as a means to avoid prison, school suspension, eviction from public housing or an appearance in court. Surveillance was promoted with the unspoken reminder that, if you do no wrong while being watched, you would not be punished.

Maxwell was warned that he would be under close scrutiny from the time he arrived. Part of it would be the natural curiosity the Chinese had about every foreigner. Part of it would be to see how he handled the deal on Promis. He was going to Beijing not only in his capacity as publisher of a newspaper group, but as the head of a small specialist company, Information on Demand. His hosts may well offer to buy their way into the company. He should play for time, suggest that the matter of any buy-in to IOD should be a matter to be considered after the Chinese had bought Promis.

Over three days Robert Maxwell conducted a successful sales drive. In an annexe at the rear of the Ministry of Defence headquarters in Beijing's Dongcheng district, he demonstrated Promis to some of the country's leading computer experts from the PLA and China's secret intelligence service, CSIS.

There had been questions over the banquet his hosts gave Maxwell that night. Was the software powerful enough to penetrate the vaunted security systems that the United States had long placed around its most sensitive establishments? Maxwell had replied that Promis was capable of penetrating any tracking system on earth.

At the end of his visit, the Chinese had signed a contract for Information on Demand to provide Promis software to the value of $9 million.

No one had suggested buying into IOD.

Mossad now became privy to the secrets of the most closed society on earth. Their analysts learned many of the inner tensions of the Politburo between the 'old guard', the survivors of the Long March that had led to the creation of Marxist China. Tel Aviv followed the decision-making process that saw Deng Xiaoping remove himself from the day-to-day political process to devote himself to the affairs of the all-important Central Military Commission. They studied the fears that gripped the leadership over the rising prices and consequent food shortages, the shambolic way the state-run enterprises operated. Promis gave them first-hand knowledge of the loss of morale and all-important self-respect among senior cadres. The analysts had followed the arguments as to why Russian Communism had failed – and the danger this posed to the policies of the Beijing ideologues. They had also learned of the fears within the Kremlin that China would strengthen its ties with the United States.

It was knowledge Israel would put to its own use, and Nahum Admoni had been suitably grateful to Robert Maxwell.

*

Further sales of Promis followed. One was to Belgium's counter-espionage service, the Sûreté de L'Etat. The software became an essential weapon in tracking the country's most powerful spy ring – one that the KGB had been running since 1967. Promis revealed it had spread to include a prominent journalist, a senior civil servant and members of the Belgian army. Eventually, through the software, the spycatchers would, in 1992, arrest the spies and expel two diplomats from the Russian embassy.

Another sale was made to Turkish intelligence. Its trapdoor had enabled Mossad to keep track of the movements of Muslim extremists in the country.

A third sale was made to Thailand. It was mostly used to track drug traffickers.

Maxwell and Rafi Eitan decided the time had come to collect their final profits from a sales drive that had proved to be highly lucrative. Following the initial RCMP test of Promis, no fewer than a quarter of all its divisions across Canada had been fitted out with the software. A sale had also been made to the altogether more important, in terms of intelligence, Canadian Secret Intelligence Service, CSIS. Like the software installed by the RCMP, the CSIS version also had its trapdoor. In effect any operation that either service mounted was monitored in Tel Aviv by Mossad.

While the RCMP sale – valued at Canadian $80 million, had been paid in full – the Canadian $11 million from the CSIS sale was still outstanding. Both sales had been run through Janos Pasztor, the front man Earl Brian had used for his company, Hadron.

Maxwell had met Pasztor in New York and had formed an instant dislike of him. He told Eitan that Pasztor was as slippery as one of the fish Maxwell had all those years ago tried to catch as a child with his hands in the river near his home in Czechoslovakia.

In truth Pasztor was out of his depth. More used to trying to make deals on the outer fringes of the financial markets in New York and Montreal, he had found himself caught up in the world of complex international money transfers in which he increasingly saw himself as 'a string on someone else's fiddle'. Two of the players of that instrument were Ira Gurston Rosenfeld and Earl Brian. But to the hapless Pasztor, Robert Maxwell could only have appeared like a conductor demanding pitch-perfect performances. Pasztor found himself flitting between deals as far afield as Canada and Australia and New Zealand. Working often twenty-hour days, skipping meals and sustained on pills, Pasztor was becoming a mental and physical wreck by the onset of 1986.

More worrying for him, Maxwell and Eitan thought he was not paying enough attention to their commands; that he was trying to please another master, the equally demanding Earl Brian.

To Rosenfeld, Pasztor was showing all the signs of 'a man jumping at his own shadow'.

Now, by January 1986, Maxwell was looking for Pasztor to get that Canadian $11 million into the safety of the Bank of Bulgaria.

But neither Rosenfeld or Pasztor knew that the RCMP had begun to look closely at their activities and had launched an investigation code-named Operation Longshadow. Key to its success would be the stockbroker, John A Belton.

A tall, muscular man with a sharp and incisive mind behind his polite demeanour, Belton wanted revenge. He had seen his clients at Nesbitt-Thompson 'robbed blind of millions' by scams operated by Rosenfeld, Pasztor and Earl Brian. With crusading zeal, he had set out to follow the paper trail they had created to steal those millions. At first the RCMP had encouraged him. But as his investigation took him – and them – into that murky world where Rafi Eitan and Ari Ben-Menashe lurked, shielded by the massive bulk of Robert Maxwell, Belton was warned by the RCMP 'to play it cool. We don't want the CIA taking shots at you.'

Belton had rightly taken the words as a clear and present warning that Earl Brian for one was shielded by powerful people in Washington.

Belton, throughout 1985, had pressed on with his enquiries. He had discovered that Earl Brian was run by the CIA in much the same way Ben-Menashe had continued to work for Mossad. Friendly though the investigators still were, in late 1985 when they met, Belton had added another observation to the copious notes he kept in a small library of files. 'They are subject to political interference. They are getting slower in acting. I believe they are victims of electronic espionage. There is no other explanation.'

But Belton pressed on – unaware that Mossad now also had Earl Brian under scrutiny. Whenever he came to Montreal, there was a *katsa* dogging his steps.

It was the agent's report that reassured Rafi Eitan. Operation Long-shadow was grinding to a halt. One of the lead investigators, Wayne Dunn, had told Belton that the investigation had been killed off by the CIA. Dunn spoke of 'high-level political pressure'.

In Tel Aviv Rafi Eitan had called Robert Maxwell and said it was time to collect the outstanding Canadian $11 million from CSIS. They decided to do so in person. It was like something out of *The Godfather*.

They arrived in Toronto on one of those subzero days that reminded Maxwell of the time he and his brothers and sisters had lain awake in their cottage listening to the wind howling outside.

Rafi Eitan had sent word ahead that Rosenfeld and Pasztor were to be waiting in the downtown hotel lobby where Maxwell had booked the Presidential Suite.

Neither Rosenfeld nor Pasztor was there. Maxwell and Eitan rode up to the suite. Rosenfeld arrived shortly afterwards apologising that the weather had delayed him.

'Where's Pasztor?' rumbled Maxwell.

Eitan would later remember how Rosenfeld stood in the lounge, fidgeting with the buttons of his long dark coat and saying he didn't know where Pasztor was.

Rafi Eitan had seen that desperate look on a man's face before, many times – that hunted, pleading look shortly before Eitan had killed him in the name of the State of Israel. But Rosenfeld was no Nazi: he was a Jew, one of their own.

Rosenfeld confirmed that Maxwell's order regarding the Canadian $11 million from the sale to CSIS and the money accruing from the sale of Promis to Australia and New Zealand had been followed. Pasztor had ensured the money had been sent to different accounts as instructed in the Bank of Bulgaria and then transferred to Zürich.

Rosenfeld handed Maxwell copies of the wire transfer documents.

Maxwell scanned them and passed them over to Rafi Eitan. Promis had netted a further US $25 million. Total sales now exceeded US $500 million.

Maxwell told Rosenfeld to leave. Within six months he would be dead from a heart attack at the age of 58.

While they waited for Pasztor, Maxwell and Eitan continued a previous discussion. It centred on Eitan's discovering that Earl Brian was now marketing the CIA version of Promis. Eitan did not know if it also had a trapdoor, but even if it had, he was not overly concerned: the one in the Israeli version had stood the test of time and he was convinced it could not be bettered.

Janos Pasztor had done well from Promis. It had bought him a fine townhouse in Toronto and the kind of money he never had imagined.

After Rafi Eitan opened the door of the Presidential Suite, Maxwell pointed to a chair and commanded Pasztor: 'Sit! I want you to explain yourself to me.'

Years later the gist of what Maxwell wanted to know was recorded by John A Belton in a conversation he had with Juval Aviv, a former Mossad *katsa* who had resigned from the service to run a private security company in New York (his clients would include Pan Am after the Lockerbie disaster). The tape had focused on Pasztor's relationship with Earl Brian and Robert Maxwell.

Juval Aviv: 'I think there was additional funding Pasztor should have got that they promised and never gave him, and on top of that I think there was an issue that he was afraid of the people they were dealing with. He was physically worried about it.'

John A Belton: 'You mean like Earl Brian and Maxwell?'

Juval Aviv: 'Exactly. Exactly. Yeah! He was thinking that those guys would come after him and kill him if he ever opened his mouth and talked about it, and so on. So there was a physical fear that he really, really, legitimately was frightened and he said, "I don't need it. I'm too old for it and whatever money I got, I got and that's the end of it and I don't ever want to talk about it."'

John A Belton: 'And there was an account in the Cayman Islands.'

Juval Aviv: 'I understand. I cannot talk about that.'

John A Belton: 'We have Earl Brian with the stock fraud. Then he moved to selling Promis.'

Juval Aviv: 'Yup!'

John A Belton: 'And Ari Ben-Menashe.'

On that January morning of 1986, Pasztor still hoped Maxwell would see he got his fair share of the profits from the Promis sales to the CSIS, Australia and New Zealand. He had also done other favours for Maxwell, like moving funds through Nesbitt-Thompson.

Now, still anxious to please, Pasztor tried to endear himself further to Maxwell.

'Earl Brian was in Brazil, Robert. He sold the CIA version of Promis to its intelligence service. He's supposed to have made a killing.'

'What else did you hear, Janos?'

'That he was there with Oliver North.'

'What was North doing there?'

'I don't know, Robert.'

'How did you hear this?'

'On the grapevine.'

Maxwell did not push. He already knew about the deal. Nahum Admoni had learned about it from Mossad's own well-connected sources in Brazilian intelligence.

But Pasztor had not quite finished. He said the same grapevine was whispering that the CIA was going to market its version of Promis in Canada.

Maxwell said nothing, dismissing Janos Pasztor with another flap of his hand. Rafi Eitan had always thought it a curiously effeminate gesture from a man who boasted of his masculinity.

Both Eitan and Maxwell agreed it was definitely time to pull out of Canada. But Maxwell did not tell Rafi Eitan he planned to keep his own ties with Pasztor. The broker could still be a useful conduit for Maxwell's money-laundering activities. His decision fitted what was happening in those other areas where his behaviour had now cast a dark shadow.

Iran–Contra, that dark episode in American history when every rule was broken, was at its peak. Drugs, guns, money and mysterious deaths would eventually define Oliver North's operation to supply guns to the Nicaraguan Contra rebels.

To Richard Brenneke, the CIA operative at the core of the operations, 'It was simple. Money from guns sold to the Iranians was moved through CIA accounts to buy drugs in South America. Those drugs were shipped back into the US, sold to the mob to buy weapons for the Contras.'

Brenneke would eventually become concerned by the flow of drugs into the United States.

'We were bringing in drugs and receiving money which was being put into accounts which belonged to the US government. I called Don Gregg and complained. At that time he was a National Security Adviser to the President. I was told to forget my worries.'

Brenneke had by then laundered $50,000,000 through CIA secret accounts; profits from the sale of cocaine to the Gotti Mafia family of New York.

TEN

By the spring of 1986, Maxwell's star continued to shine ever more brightly in the newspaper and corporate world and he revelled in the role of powerful publisher, and on being on first-name terms with world leaders and the rich and powerful.

He travelled with an entourage the size of which many a dictator would envy. A gaggle of secretaries, uniformly young, long-legged and blonde, worked under a 'communications chief' to enable Maxwell to maintain contact with his 400 companies. There were flunkeys for even the smallest tasks: one to precheck that his hotel suite was dust-free and the temperature set at the correct level of 64.5 degrees Fahrenheit; another to carry his briefcase (he was always close to Maxwell, much as the bagman carrying the nuclear codes is close to the President of the United States); a third to carry Maxwell's deodorant and powder for his puff. The most favoured aides flew with him in the Gulfstream.

Soon he would recruit John Morgan, a former British ambassador to South Africa, Poland and Mexico, whom Maxwell would introduce to heads of state as 'my foreign minister'. From Credit Suisse – the bank he nowadays called with some truth 'my bank' – he had enticed its managing director, Jean-Pierre Anselmini. He became 'my banker'.

The entourage included a valet and a photographer seconded from the *Daily Mirror* to snap every meeting. Maxwell had seen America's presidents do the same. Tucked away, usually at the back of this ensemble, was Nick Davies, always smiling, eyes darting, notebook ready to record any worthwhile words his master spoke.

While outwardly still cordial, the relationship between them had changed since the night Maxwell had listened to the tape of Ben-Menashe and Davies. He had later sent the tape on to Rafi Eitan, in whose safe it would remain as another little memento that life in the spy business is never what it seems.

Since Maxwell had listened to the tape, Davies had been under surveillance. That had led to further confirmation that the foreign editor could not be trusted; tapes showed he was indeed living up to his nickname, 'Sneaky': Davies was bedding the same women on the staff that Maxwell was seducing. For his part, Davies noted how Maxwell 'put on the style, produced the champagne, played the tycoon billionaire with smiles and flattery once he targeted a secretary'.

There was a side to Davies that Maxwell did not know. Nick Davies had for years been a source for MI6. Colin Wallace, a former intelligence officer, would describe Davies as 'useful. He had the right cover. He could dig and nobody would think he was any more than a nosey journalist. And he was good at what he did. Having him close to Maxwell gave Six a pretty good idea what was going on.'

Whether through Davies or another source, MI6 became aware of Maxwell's involvement with international criminals such as Cyrus Hashemi. He was an Iranian banker with a taste for young prostitutes to fill his bed in his Manhattan penthouse. The New York office of the FBI had acquired a library of tapes documenting Hashemi's lascivious requests. In London, MI5 had amassed a similar collection, obtained through bugs in Hashemi's Belgravia residence. These had been passed on to MI6 to help it track Hashemi's activities outside Britain. There was a growing suspicion within both services that Hashemi was more than another of those Arab millionaire playboys who spent £100,000 on the turn of a card and gave doormen Rolex watches for parking their Porsches or Ferraris.

Cyrus Hashemi could be a bagman for Islamic terrorist groups, laundering the money they required to finance their operations through the Bank of Credit and Commerce International (BCCI).

Colin Wallace knew that the bank had been one of Maxwell's early depositories, but it was also one that Mossad and the CIA used to channel their funds. Their numbered accounts were on the same secure computers as those held by Abu Nidal, who had long rejoiced in the title of 'the grandmaster of terrorism', and those of rogue states like Syria, Iraq and Iran.

Hashemi had connections to many of them. He would play tennis in the morning with a CIA agent from the American embassy in London's Grosvenor Square; in the afternoon he would have tea at the Dorchester with an Iraqi diplomat. In the early part of the evening he would meet with an arms dealer for dinner at the Savoy Grill. Later that evening Hashemi could be found at the gambling tables in Knightsbridge. At dawn he would return to his Belgravia home with several hookers to entertain him and his friends.

One of his friends was Manucher Ghorbanifar. It was he who introduced Maxwell to Hashemi. They had found common ground: discussing new ways to avoid paying taxes and burying money in all those secret accounts across the world that accommodating banks provided.

Hashemi was garrulous. When he had drunk sufficient of Maxwell's champagne, he spoke about the arms trafficking in which he was involved. That was why, he said, he no longer took his regular seat on Concorde to the United States: the FBI wanted to question him. That was why he avoided going to the Caribbean: he feared he would be snatched and brought to Washington for interrogation.

Robert Maxwell well understood such paranoia – and what to do about it. He told Admoni. The Mossad chief told Maxwell to cultivate Hashemi. Soon Mossad was building up a clear picture of Hashemi's contacts.

He was one of several people who had passed on a piece of valuable business intelligence to Maxwell. Harcourt Brace Jovanovich (HBJ), a New York publishing conglomerate, which had also taken a stake in Florida's rapidly expanding theme park industry, had overextended its credit.

Maxwell saw that if he could buy HBJ it would provide proof that his prediction of becoming a billionaire, a public salve to his ego after his failure to grab Waddington, was no idle talk. He made discreet enquiries through Ansbacher Bank. HBJ was worth $2 billion. Maxwell instructed his bankers, the respected House of Rothschild, to open negotiations at that figure.

The news sent a surge of astonishment through the financial markets. If Maxwell had that kind of money, then all the rumours that he was himself strapped for cash were groundless. His failure to get Waddington was no more than a blip on the radar screens in London and New York. This was Maxwell at his raider's best, the financial equivalent of J P Morgan.

He had not counted on William Jovanovich, the ageing chairman of Harcourt Brace Jovanovich. Like many other company presidents, he had studied the tactics Waddington had used to fight off Maxwell. Jovanovich decided to do the same. In New York, even as Maxwell was hurtling across the Atlantic in his Gulfstream, the head of HBJ issued a crisply worded statement.

'This sudden, unsolicited and hostile offer is preposterous as to its intent and value.'

William Jovanovich did not leave it there. He hired a private investigator to probe Maxwell's business history. It provided a second thunderbolt for the American public.

'Mr Maxwell's dealings since he emerged from the mists of Romania after World War Two have not always favoured shareholders. He is unfit to control a large company like ours.'

Maxwell hastily withdrew his bid.

Hashemi commiserated. But by now the arms dealer had his own problems.

Through Ghorbanifar, Hashemi had obtained a stake for himself in the arms-for-hostages deal. But, when Poindexter and North took over, they removed Hashemi. William Casey had called both men into his office at Langley and had shown them the files the CIA had put together on Hashemi. These included wiretaps in which Hashemi had boasted he had played a crucial part in ensuring that the American diplomats held in Teheran would not be freed until Reagan had entered the White House. Was that the man, Casey asked his visitors, they would want on their team? Poindexter and North shook their heads.

In London, MI6 had established that Hashemi had set up a $3 million account in the name of Iraq's Revolutionary Guard in a BCCI account. In Tel Aviv, Nahum Admoni decided that it was a deal too many. He ordered that all past contacts with Hashemi should be terminated.

Cyrus Hashemi had managed to 'seriously upset' his ties to three of the world's most powerful intelligence services.

Now, in April 1986, Hashemi decided to become another of the whistleblowers who bedevil the intelligence world. For some time he had been acting as a bagman for a number of other arms dealers outside those who had been involved in the Iranian arms-for-hostages operation. They included a former Israeli general and two men who worked for the godfather of all Israeli arms dealers. Shaul Nehemiah Eisenberg.

Hashemi persuaded them to fly to New York to conclude what he had called 'the deal of your lifetime'. The FBI were waiting. In return for immunity against all further investigation into his own past criminal activities in the United States and elsewhere, Hashemi agreed to testify against the arrested men.

Admoni called Maxwell. 'Can you talk him out of this?' the Mossad chief asked. 'He can disappear wherever he likes as long as he disappears.'

In June 1986 Maxwell invited Hashemi to his penthouse for lunch. Maxwell explained what was on offer. Withdraw – or else. For Colin Wallace that kind of offer would have been 'standard modus operandi for Mossad. They don't like to kill unless they really have to.'

Next day Hashemi flew to a private clinic in Geneva, Switzerland, for his twice-yearly medical check. He was obsessive about his health. The tests confirmed he was in robust condition. He returned to London and resumed his lifestyle of playing tennis and jogging, eating little and avoiding alcohol. He was now 45 and, apart from his face, he showed no signs of the indulgent life he had led.

On 16 July 1986, Hashemi suddenly collapsed and was rushed to a private clinic owned by BCCI. Initial tests showed his heart was in good condition but a consultant recommended a neurological examination requiring bone-marrow tests. Two days later Hashemi was dead.

His death was sufficiently puzzling for Scotland Yard Serious Crimes Squad to investigate. They called in a forensic pathologist, Dr Iain West, who often conducted post-mortems of interest to Britain's intelligence services. He was briefed about the sensitivity of the case and Hashemi's history as an arms dealer 'with possible links to the CIA and Mossad'.

Hashemi's case, he would later say, 'was one of the strangest I ever investigated'.

Hashemi's death certificate listed the cause as 'accidental brain-stem damage due to a stroke and leukaemia'.

The American embassy in London insisted one of their staff should attend the autopsy. A Scotland Yard file on Hashemi would record 'the U.S. Embassy wanted to know if we thought he had been murdered. Were any marks on the body indicating foul play? Could leukaemia be induced with drugs or other toxins?'

From the outset West had rejected 'the induction of leukaemia as an impractical form of homicide. It required too great a time frame and there was no guarantee it would be successful.' He concluded that 'chemicals which could be leukaemogenic were not present in the body'.

However, still uncertain whether Hashemi had in fact been murdered by a method he was unable to detect, West secretly sent tissue samples to Britain's germ-warfare laboratory at Porton Down. The analysis of the samples has never been made public.

Following Dr West's verdict, Scotland Yard closed the case, citing the death as 'by natural causes'.

The New York case against the arms dealers was dropped. Hashemi's secret BCCI records were seized by MI5.

For Robert Maxwell the death of Cyrus Hashemi may well have been the first example of what Victor Ostrovsky called 'the magic of *kidon*' in eliminating the enemies of Israel.

On 14 September 1986, Maxwell called Nahum Admoni with devastating news.

A freelance Colombian-born journalist, Oscar Guerrero, had approached a Maxwell-owned Sunday tabloid newspaper, the *Sunday Mirror*, with a sensational story – one that would rip aside the carefully constructed veil to disguise the true purpose of Dimona in the Negev Desert. Guerrero claimed to be acting for a former technician who had worked at the nuclear plant. During that time the man had secretly gathered photographic and other evidence to show that Israel was now a major nuclear power, possessing no fewer than 100 nuclear devices of varying destructive force.

Admoni's staff quickly confirmed that Mordechai Vanunu had worked at Dimona from February 1977 until November 1985. He had been assigned to the most secret of all the plant's Machons – Dimona's ten production units. Machon-1 was the nuclear reactor. Machon-2 was where Vanunu had worked. The windowless concrete building externally resembled a warehouse. But its walls were thick enough to block the most powerful of satellite camera lenses from penetrating.

Inside the bunker-like structure, a system of false walls led to the elevators, which descended through six levels to where the nuclear weapons were manufactured.

His security clearance was sufficiently high to gain unchallenged access to every corner of Machon-2. His special security pass – number 520 – coupled with his signature on an Israeli Secrets Acts document ensured no one ever challenged him as he went about his duties as a *menahil*, a controller on the night shift.

Somehow he had secretly photographed the layout of Machon-2: the control panels, the glove boxes, the nuclear-bomb-building machinery. He had stored his films in his locker, number 3, and smuggled them out of what was supposedly the most secure place in Israel.

Vanunu was a Moroccan Jew, born on 13 October 1954 in Marrakech, where his parents were modest shopkeepers. In 1963, when anti-Semitism, never far from the surface in Morocco, spilled once more into open violence, the family emigrated to Israel, settling in the Negev Desert town of Beersheba.

In the summer of 1976 Vanunu replied to an advertisement for trainee technicians to work at Dimona. After a lengthy interview with the plant's security officer, he was accepted for training and sent on an intensive course in physics, chemistry, maths and English. He did sufficiently well to enter Dimona in February 1977.

Vanunu was made redundant in November 1985. In his security file at Dimona was the notation that he had displayed 'left-wing and pro-Arab beliefs'. He left Israel for Australia, arriving in Sydney in May of the following year.

Somewhere along the journey that had followed a well-trodden path by young Israelis through the Far East, Vanunu had renounced his once-strong Jewish faith to become a Christian.

The picture emerging from a dozen sources for Admoni to consider was that of a physically unprepossessing young man who appeared to be the classic loner: he had made no real friends at Dimona; he had no girlfriends; he spent his time at home reading books on philosophy and politics.

In Australia Vanunu met Oscar Guerrero, the journalist. Now a committed pacifist, Vanunu wanted his story to appear in a serious publication to alert the world to the threat he perceived Israel now posed with its nuclear capability. Guerrero contacted the Madrid office of the British *Sunday Times*. A reporter was sent to Sydney to interview Vanunu.

The Colombian began to feel he was about to lose control over Vanunu's story. His fears increased when the *Sunday Times* reporter said he would fly Vanunu to London, where his claims could be more fully investigated.

Guerrero watched Vanunu and his travelling companion board the flight to London, his misgivings deepening by the minute. He needed advice on how to handle the situation. The only person he could think of was a former member of the Australian Security and Intelligence Service (ASIS). Guerrero told him he had been cheated out of a world-shaking story.

The former ASIS operative contacted his old employer and repeated what Guerrero had told him.

There was a close working relationship between Mossad and ASIS. The former provided intelligence on Arab terrorist movements out of the Middle East to the Pacific. Since 1984, ASIS had turned a blind eye to arms shipments being routed from the United States through Australia to Iran. ASIS promptly informed the Mossad *katsa* attached to the Israeli embassy in Canberra of the call from its former employee.

The information was immediately faxed to Admoni. By then more disturbing news had reached him. On his backpacking trip to Australia, Vanunu had stopped over in Nepal and had visited the Soviet embassy in Kathmandu. He could have had only one purpose: to show his evidence to Moscow.

Increasingly desperate, Guerrero set off to London in pursuit of Vanunu. Unable to find him, Guerrero took the documents to the *Sunday Mirror*. Included was a photograph of Vanunu taken in Australia. Within hours Nicholas Davies knew they were in-house. He promptly told Maxwell. The publisher called Admoni.

Now, several hours later, when the Mossad chief again called Maxwell, Admoni received another jolt. The *Sunday Times* was taking Vanunu's story seriously. It was therefore critically important to know what the technician had photographed. Hopefully a damage-limitation response could then be fashioned.

The reports from Canberra suggested that Guerrero was clearly motivated by money. If Vanunu was shown to have a similar aspiration, then it might be possible to mount a successful disinformation campaign that the *Sunday Times* had been swindled by two conmen.

Once more the indefatigable Ari Ben-Menashe was pressed into service. He recalled: 'Nicholas Davies had arranged for Guerrero to meet this "hot" American journalist – me. At the meeting, Guerrero, eager for another sale, displayed some of Vanunu's colour photographs. I had no idea if they were significant. They needed to be seen by experts in Israel. I told Vanunu I needed copies. He balked. I said I had to know if they were real if he wanted money and that Nick would vouch for me.'

Guerrero handed over several photographs to Ben-Menashe. They were couriered to Tel Aviv.

Their arrival created further consternation. Officials from Dimona identified Machon-2 from the photographs. One of the prints showed the area where nuclear land mines had been manufactured before being sown along the Golan Heights border with Syria. There was no longer any question of being able to destroy Vanunu's credibility. Every nuclear physicist would recognise what the equipment was for.

Prime Minister Peres set up a crisis team to monitor the situation. Some of Mossad's department heads urged that a *kidon* squad should be sent to London to hunt down Vanunu and kill him. Admoni rejected the idea. The *Sunday Times* would not have the space to publish everything Vanunu told the newspaper: it would require a full-length book to contain all the information to which the technician would have had access. But, once the newspaper had finished with Vanunu, the likeliest possibility was that he would then be debriefed by MI6 and the CIA and Israel would face even more problems. It was all the more imperative to learn how Vanunu had carried out his spying activities in Dimona and whether he had worked alone or with others – and if the latter, who were *they* working for? The only way to discover all this was to bring Vanunu back to Israel to be interrogated.

Admoni needed a way to flush the technician out of wherever the *Sunday Times* had hidden him. In the open it would be easier to deal with Vanunu and in the end, if he had to be killed, it would not be the first time Mossad had done so on the streets of London. In the hunt for the perpetrators of the massacre of the Israeli athletes at the Munich Olympics, Mossad had killed one of the Black September group in a carefully staged hit-and-run road accident as he walked back to his Bloomsbury hotel.

In London, the *Sunday Times*, realising Israel would do everything possible to discredit Vanunu, had arranged for him to be questioned by Dr Frank Barnaby, a nuclear physicist with impeccable credentials who had worked at Britain's nuclear-weapons installation at Aldermaston. He concluded that the photographs and documentation were authentic and the technician's detailed recall was accurate.

The *Sunday Times* took a fateful step. Its reporter presented the Israeli embassy in London with a summary of all that Vanunu had revealed to them, along with photostats of his passport and the photographs, together with Barnaby's assessment. The intention was to force an admission from the Israeli government. Instead the embassy dismissed the material as 'having no base whatsoever in reality'.

As a result of Maxwell's earlier phone call, Admoni finally came up with a way to drive Vanunu into the open. He called Maxwell.

The next issue of the *Sunday Mirror* contained a large photograph of Mordechai Vanunu, together with a story holding the technician and Oscar Guerrero up to ridicule, calling the Colombian a liar and a cheat, and the claim about Israel's nuclear capability a hoax. The report had been dictated by Maxwell, who had also supervised the prominent positioning of Vanunu's photograph. The first shot had been fired in a major disinformation campaign orchestrated by Mossad's psychological-warfare department.

Vanunu became agitated to the point where he told his *Sunday Times* 'minders' – the reporters who had watched over him since he had been brought to London – that he wanted to disappear. 'I don't want anyone to know where I am.'

The panic-stricken technician was staying at the latest hotel his minders had chosen, the Mountbatten, near Shaftesbury Avenue in Central London.

For two days every one of Mossad's *sayanim* in London had been mobilised to find him. Hundreds of trusted Jewish volunteers had each been given a list of hotels and boarding houses to check. In each call they gave a description of Vanunu from the photograph published in the *Sunday Mirror*, each caller claiming to be a relative checking to see if he had registered.

On Thursday, 25 September, Admoni received news from London that Vanunu had been located. It was time to bring into play the next stage of his plan.

Cheryl Ben-Tov was a *bat leveyha*, one grade below a *katsa*. At the age of eighteen she had met and fallen in love with a Sabra, a native-born Israeli, called Ofer Ben-Tov. He worked in Aman as an analyst. A year after they had met the couple were married.

A month after she returned from honeymoon, she received a call from a wedding guest. They arranged to meet at a café in downtown Tel Aviv. Over coffee he came to the point, explaining for whom he worked.

He then delivered a set piece that all Mossad recruiters use. The service was always on the lookout for people who wanted to serve their country. Was she interested?

Cheryl was. For the next two years she learned how to draw a gun while sitting in a chair, to memorise as many names as possible as they flashed with increasing speed across a small screen. She was shown how to pack her Beretta inside her knickers, on the hip, and how to cut a concealed opening in her skirt or dress for easy access to the handgun. She was taught how to kill by firing a full clip of bullets into a target. She learned about the various sects of Islam and how to create a *mishlasim*, a dead-letter box. A day was spent perfecting a 'floater', a strip of microfilm attached to the inside of an envelope. Another was devoted to disguising herself by inserting cotton wadding in her cheeks to alter subtly the shape of her face. She learned to steal cars, pose as a drunk, chat up men. Finally she learned the importance of her sex – how to use it to coerce, seduce and dominate. She was especially good at that.

When she had completed her training, Cheryl Ben-Tov had been assigned as a *bat leveyha* working in Mossad's *kaisrut* department, which liaised with Israeli embassies. Her specific role was to provide cover – as a girlfriend or even as a 'wife' for *katsas* on active service. She had worked in a number of European cities.

Admoni had personally briefed her on the importance of her latest mission: with Vanunu now located, it would be up to her to use her skills to entice him out of Britain.

On Tuesday, 23 September 1986, Cheryl Ben-Tov joined a team of nine Mossad *katsas* in London, summoned there from all over Europe. They were under the command of Mossad's director of operations, Beni Zeevi, a dour man with the stained teeth of a chain smoker.

On Wednesday, 24 September, Vanunu insisted his *Sunday Times* minders should allow him to go out alone. They reluctantly agreed. However, a reporter discreetly followed him into Leicester Square. There he saw Vanunu begin to talk to a woman.

Back in his hotel Vanunu confirmed to his minder he had met 'an American girl called Cindy'. The reporters were worried. One of them said Cindy's appearance in Leicester Square might be too much of a coincidence. Vanunu rejected their concerns. Whatever Cindy had said, it had been enough to make Vanunu want to spend more time with her – and not in London, but in her 'sister's' apartment in Rome.

Beni Zeevi and four other Mossad *katsas* were passengers on the flight on which Cheryl and Vanunu travelled to Rome. The couple took a taxi to an apartment in the old quarter of the city.

Waiting inside were three Mossad *katsas*. They overpowered Vanunu, and injected him with a paralysing drug. Late that night an ambulance arrived and Vanunu was stretchered out of the building. Neighbours were told by the concerned-looking *katsas* that a relative had fallen ill. Cheryl climbed into the ambulance, which drove off.

The ambulance sped out of Rome and down the coast. At a prearranged point a speedboat was waiting, to which Vanunu was transferred. The craft liaised with a freighter anchored off the coast. Vanunu was taken on board. Beni Zeevi and Cheryl travelled with him. Three days later, in the middle of the night, the freighter docked at the port of Haifa.

Mordechai was soon facing Nahum Admoni's skilled interrogators. It was the prelude to a swift trial and eighteen years in solitary confinement. Cheryl Ben-Tov disappeared back into her secret world.

But Robert Maxwell remained very much a part of it.

ELEVEN

Once more he had come unannounced and, until the last possible moment, unnoticed. As usual he had alighted from the cab that had brought him from no one knew where – a hotel, one of those service apartments that were becoming fashionable – and walked the last short distance. In his black topcoat and homburg, he looked at first glance to be a pallbearer perhaps on the way to or from a funeral. Only his slim briefcase suggested he could be a lawyer on the way to read a will.

Then, with another of those quick little footsteps that hinted that at one time in his youth, long gone now, he may have been a dancer, he was in the lobby of Maxwell House.

In that moment he became all diffident smiles, acknowledging the uniformed commissioner's nod, and the welcome of the receptionist. They knew who he was, though they knew nothing about him. Even Nick Davies, who knew many things about most people in the building, knew next to nothing about this man with the tight bookish eyes and polished black leather shoes. He was Dr R – when there was a need to refer to him, no one called him anything but Dr R. The words spoken in the same respectful way, at least in public, that people used for Cap'n Bob, the Chairman, the Publisher or RM.

Dr R was a doctor of a kind: he treated balance sheets, disguised their shortfalls, juggled and manipulated them, made them look better than they really were.

Dr R was the most important keeper of Robert Maxwell's innermost financial secrets.

He may have been a lawyer, an accountant, a financier. He may well have been all three, and even possibly the holder of more titles. No one would ever know, as he once more stood in the lobby waiting to be shown up to Maxwell's penthouse.

There was an inviolate rule that he was never to be kept waiting. The

154

first Maxwell knew Dr R was in the building was when the lobby receptionist phoned him on his private line – the one that bypassed the switchboard – and announced, 'You have a personal caller.' On instructions she did not even mention Dr R by his initials.

Maxwell's senior secretary, whatever else she was doing, stopped and took the elevator to the lobby. Once Dr R was safely inside, she used the special button that ensured that the elevator rose nonstop to the penthouse. There she deposited him in the lobby with the massive fake fireplace with its logs that would never be burned.

Robert Maxwell would be standing before the mantelpiece. He would flap away the secretary with his curious hand motion. The last words she would hear before closing the elevator behind her were Maxwell's words.

'*Guten Tag, Herr Doktor.*'

And Dr R would reply, in heavily accented English, by asking how Robert was since he had last seen him.

From then until he left, no one knew what they spoke about.

Just as Mossad used Maxwell for only its most important work, so Dr R was retained by Maxwell in a similar capacity. Not for Dr R the daily cut and thrust of deal making, the endless demands upon Maxwell's senior executives to be at his beck and call day and night, the continuous humiliation Maxwell bestowed on them, on all his staff, on his stockbrokers, his merchant bankers, even heads of state. Dr R was kept away from all that.

He was there for one function only: he was the Great Planner, the Superb Strategist whose prime, perhaps only, role was to see Robert Maxwell's empire expanding with the same speed as his girth. It was Dr R who had orchestrated the move to have Rothschild's become Maxwell's bankers, a decision that had added to his stature in the City of London and in Wall Street. It was Dr R who had looked into, and approved, Maxwell's decision to invest in television networks in France and England. It was Dr R who had used his own equally mysterious contacts to bring Maxwell together with President François Mitterand. It was Dr R who had warned Maxwell against further investments in South Africa because the white supremacist regime was doomed. It was Dr R who had flown to Australia, to Kenya, to Japan, to look into investment possibilities; some he had recommended, others not. It was Dr R who always took an overview, a long view, a view that Maxwell respected above all others. There were no secrets between them, save one. On Rafi Eitan's advice, Robert Maxwell had not told Dr R about his relationship with Mossad.

Undoubtedly Dr R had helped to shape Maxwell's thinking about what was happening in the world, especially in Eastern Europe. Gorbachev had delivered a benchmark speech at the 27th Party Congress in February

1986. It effectively ended the Brezhnev doctrine that Moscow had the hallowed right to intervene in the domestic affairs of the Soviet satellites. Gorbachev had said that 'no country enjoys a monopoly on the truth'.

For Dr R and Maxwell, the words were a bugle call to increase their holdings in the disintegrating Soviet Union. Not even the Chernobyl nuclear disaster in April 1986 or the US air strike against Libya the following year, and the arrest of the American journalist Nicholas Daniloff in September of that year on espionage charges – none of these events had for a moment halted Maxwell's determination that in the east he had seen a star. Dr R was cast in the role of his wise man.

Together they began to put together new deals, much in the way that on the global stage Gorbachev and Reagan were stitching one together in Reykjavik about nuclear-arms control, which would remove the Cruise and Pershing missiles as a threat to mankind; the old ground rules of superpower, of incremental gains, and minimal concessions were ripped up.

With the help of Dr R, Maxwell was also rewriting the rules to fill his own pockets.

In Tel Aviv Mossad continued to use its Chinese Promis trapdoor to gauge how far Beijing was prepared to go to replace the diminishing tensions in Europe by turning East Asia into one of the most heavily armed regions on earth. There, China and Russia still maintained a nuclear presence; North Korea glowered across the 38th Parallel at South Korea. This was Asia's Iron Curtain. It was the reason why Dr R strongly advised Maxwell not to risk investing in Japan: its vulnerability was all too obvious.

The place for Maxwell to be was in Eastern Europe, his birthplace, the place where he had learned, so he boasted, how to make a deal. There was nowhere better to do that than in Bulgaria.

The Renault 25 was waiting on that blustery morning in early January 1987 when Maxwell lumbered down the steps of the Gulfstream at Le Bourget airport outside Paris. His French chauffeur hurried forward to collect the briefcase that the stewardess, Carina Hall, brought down the aircraft's few steps. Maxwell had never been known to carry anything heavier than a sheaf of documents relating to one of his companies.

He called up to the pilot, Brian Hull, to be ready to take off later that afternoon. Hull had seen that Maxwell had been in good form when he boarded the plane. He suspected it was something to do with what lay at the end of the next leg of the journey, the three-hour flight to Sofia, the Bulgarian capital.

Only the pilot and cabin crew knew their final destination. Hull had filed a flight plan only as far as Le Bourget. Now, as the Renault roared away, Maxwell flopped on the back seat and the pilot hurried across the tarmac to lodge his route to Sofia.

It would be a bumpy flight, Hull sensed, and he hoped it wouldn't change Maxwell's mood – bad weather could do so in a moment. Then he would rage because the pilot hadn't found a way around a front that it was impossible to avoid.

As the Renault swept out of the airport gates, Maxwell delivered a familiar order to the chauffeur. '*Mettez le feu!*'

Though he disliked committing a traffic violation, the chauffeur clamped a flashing blue light on the roof. The beacon symbolised for Maxwell another sign of his own importance: in his mind's eye it placed him among the heads of state who regularly flew into Le Bourget.

Maxwell was on his way to the Ritz Hotel, where he had rented a suite for the meeting with Werner Keicher and Dr R. The two advisers had been summoned to Paris after Maxwell had received a telephone call on his private night line in the penthouse. The caller had been Andrei Lukanov. He simply said: 'Robert, we are ready. Everything is in place.'

Since then Maxwell had worked his bedside console. His senior secretary had been awakened at home to get the Gulfstream ready. Maxwell had called executives to cancel a breakfast meeting. He had woken bankers with a similar message. 'This is Robert Maxwell. I cannot see you today.'

By dawn all was ready. His Filipino maids had packed his clothes and heaved the suitcases up to the helipad. A hamper of food and vintage champagne had been packed and brought up to the roof. A pilot's flight bag contained the latest videos in case Maxwell wanted to watch them during a flight. Dick Cowley had stowed everything into the Aerospatiale 315. Shortly after 7 a.m., Maxwell boarded the helicopter and they whirled away above the rush-hour traffic, heading south to the airbase in Farnborough.

Four hours later he was ensconced in his $1,000-a-night suite discussing with Keicher and Dr R what Lukanov had said.

What was on offer was a deal that Maxwell believed, properly handled, would net him up to $1 billion. The money would be sucked out of companies all over the Soviet Union and funnelled into still other companies Maxwell now owned in Bulgaria and Hungary. Wherever it was deposited, the money would be safe, needing no more than a tap of a keyboard to transfer it on.

In Tel Aviv, Rafi Eitan, who suspected he would never know the full extent of every transaction, nevertheless felt that it was 'absolutely extraordinary'.

'What was so brilliant – there can be no other word that comes close to describing the operation – was that Dr R had chosen Bulgaria as its very core,' recalled John A Belton.

Maxwell had played his part. He had used the *Daily Mirror* to promote his ties with the country. Its president, Todor Zhivkov, had been written up in the paper, the ultimate accolade that Maxwell believed he could bestow. Zhivkov's speeches had been published in Britain; even when they were translated into English there was no disguising the turgid prose. Maxwell's Pergamon Press had published a directory of Zhivkov's 'achievements'. These, of course, did not include the assassination in London of Georgi Markov, a leading Bulgarian dissident writer who regularly broadcast a well-aimed criticism at Zhivkov in the BBC's Bulgarian-language service. In an operation that would later form part of the curriculum at the Mossad training school, Markov was murdered with a poison-tipped umbrella in a crowded London street. From Sofia, trained by the Bulgarian secret service, would come the fanatic Mehmet Ali Agca, who would try to assassinate Pope John Paul II before an even more crowded arena, St Peter's Square in Rome.

Before leaving the Ritz suite to return to Le Bourget airport, Maxwell had telephoned Todor Zhivkov to say he was on his way. It was really a courtesy call. Maxwell knew that the key player in the operation he had gone over with Dr R and Keicher would be Lukanov. A sign of that was the expensive gift Maxwell had ordered Keicher to bring to the Ritz from Liechtenstein. It was a cashier's cheque with a value of $250,000. Gift-wrapped, it would be a sweetener for Lukanov, with the implicit promise that substantially greater payments would be available. For Zhivkov there was a smaller cheque.

It was snowing when the Gulfstream landed in Sofia. Flakes hid the golden dome of the Alexander Nevsky church and the surrounding buildings whose architecture represented seven centuries of history. No matter what time of the year Maxwell arrived, he always looked for the ancient clock tower of the city's synagogue. It was a visible reminder it had survived the Nazi occupation.

There was the usual guard of honour to inspect before Maxwell was escorted into the warmth of the presidential limousine. Two hours later the car passed through the suburbs of Pravets, where Zhivkov had been born, and drove on up the road he had specially ordered constructed to reach his retreat at the top of a nearby mountain. There he lived like one of the Bulgarian kings who had once ruled this ancient land. His ostentatious display of wealth was equalled only by his peasant manners. He would tear at wild pig with his hands and slurp his wine. Even to Robert Maxwell, the President was a man of appalling bad taste.

Having been handed the gift-wrapped cashier's cheque, the President insisted Maxwell join him for dinner. The meal of traditional *shopska* salad and *guevetch* was washed down by endless toasts of *rikea*, the raw local liqueur made from plums. Maxwell, long used to the finest foods and wine money could buy, hated the peasant cuisine Zhivkov always served.

He finally managed to escape the tipsy embrace and cheek kisses of the President and made his way back to Sofia.

It was time to do business with Andrei Lukanov.

Three sources would exist for the meeting. There were his transcripts of the recordings Lukanov secretly made of all his meetings. There was the record made by Ognian Doinov, the vice-president of the State Economic Council, who had been ordered by Lukanov to handle the minutae of the deal. Finally, there was Robert Maxwell's account, later passed on to Dr R before being filed in the Liechtenstein office of Werner Keicher.

The relationship between the three men at the meeting was very different. Lukanov and Maxwell regarded each other as near equals. Lukanov felt he had a political edge because of his close ties as Moscow's man in Bulgaria. Lukanov also saw Maxwell enhancing his political status: he would be seen as the Bulgarian who had persuaded Maxwell to invest on an unprecedented scale.

Maxwell saw his financial power as standing above everything. Both regarded Doinov as no more than a junior partner in their triumvirate. Doinov feared Lukanov and looked upon Maxwell as his passport to the West, as an opportunity to make money. All three were united in a common purpose: to use their talents at the expense of the Bulgarian people.

Before the meeting started, Maxwell had invited both men to join him for his second dinner that night. It would have an altogether different menu from the one Zhivkov had provided. The venue was Sofia's most prestigious hotel, the Sheraton. From Paris Maxwell had ordered a banquet of foie gras d'oie, smoked salmon, confit de canard, caviar and a main course of roast pheasant. Vintage champagne and the finest Burgundies were on offer. The cost per person was more than the average Bulgarian earned in a year.

To establish his position, Maxwell had chosen to arrive deliberately late, an old trick of his. His guests had been waiting almost an hour before his car swept to a halt in front of the red carpet last rolled out for the visit of the late Yuri Andropov.

A bevy of hotel managers escorted Maxwell and his guests to the private dining room, which Lukanov had arranged to be bugged.

At some point during the banquet, Doinov placed an envelope on the table beside Maxwell. The host ignored it.

Lukanov well understood the ploy. Maxwell was not to be rushed. Lukanov had time. In that dining room he was the most powerful of all of them, more powerful than Bulgaria's President, more powerful than anyone in Bulgaria because of his now even closer links to Moscow. Because of the way he had handled Robert Maxwell, Vladimir Kryuchkov had made Lukanov an officer in MIR, the Main Investigation Unit, the most important of all departments in Soviet intelligence, even more so than the KGB.

Maxwell finally reached for the envelope and opened it. He removed the paper and slowly began to read. When he had finished one page, he returned it to its folds and placed it in an inside pocket of his jacket. He did the same with each sheet.

Doinov would recall: 'Lukanov and myself sat there watching and waiting. When he had finished, Maxwell looked at us and said, "I am a friend of your country so we can trust each other." I looked at Lukanov. He smiled and nodded at Maxwell. He smiled at each of us in turn. Then Maxwell shook our hands. It was his way of sealing what he had read.'

The document carried the sprawling signature of President Todor Zhivkov. Above his name he had printed 'I AGREE'. The page was stamped 'Classified'.

The same restriction was stamped at the top and bottom of each successive sheet.

The preamble began with a sentence: 'This document is to give Mr Robert Maxwell the following opportunity we believe he can provide for a Second Market. To achieve that he will be allowed to operate freely in this country with no restriction, and with the full support of every government department, including the Darzhavna Sigurnost.'

The secret service was Maxwell's to command. Such unprecedented freedom had never been granted to a Bulgarian businessman, let alone a foreigner. Maxwell had effectively been given the key to the country. It would open any door.

One page contained the long list of technologies that Western companies were forbidden to sell to Soviet Bloc countries. These would now become the exclusive right for Maxwell to market in those closed-off territories.

On another page was a detailed explanation of how the Darzhavna Sigurnost would use its considerable resources 'to coordinate and control the flow of money from the Second Market'. It was as if MI5 and MI6 and the CIA had been ordered to put all their money-laundering facilities at the disposal of a single foreign businessman.

The final page was devoted to the role Maxwell would have in Bulgaria's most secret of all projects. It was called Neva. It was the creation of Lukanov – though Doinov would later claim a part in its development. Neva was designed to be the single largest programme for the mass-scale theft of US technology. It would be operated by Darzhavna

Sigurnost. Not even the KGB at the height of its power, or China's Secret Intelligence Service, CSIS, had created such a project that would eventually plunder every Western industrialised nation. The Darzhavna Sigurnost would steal the technology and it would be brought to Bulgaria, usually under diplomatic cover. The equipment would then be re-engineered by companies Maxwell would own. Those companies would then resell it to other Eastern Bloc nations. The profits from such sales would go to the three men around the dining table.

Doinov had explained the practicalities of the operation. Years later he would recall how he had his wineglass refilled and had sat back in his chair and addressed Maxwell.

'I remember starting by telling him that we had our secret service persons living and working in the United States. They were in Silicon Valley and other key technology centres. The same in Britain and other countries. They would be responsible for stealing the technology blueprints, actual software, even computers. It did not matter. Their job was to make sure our target figure was met of being able to supply seventy-five per cent of all stolen equipment for selling on. Our secret service expected to be financially rewarded for this work. That sort of kickback was routine. The Bulgarian equivalent of "what is my piece of the action?" was one of the first questions you learned in government. The other profits would be moved to shell companies in the West. It would be Maxwell's job to set them up and make sure our money was safe. He would get his commission.'

Maxwell had said he wanted 25 per cent – off the top.

Lukanov had agreed.

Doinov had asked where the shell companies would be located. Maxwell said Liechtenstein. Lukanov and Doinov had nodded.

Maxwell had raised his glass to a done deal. But now it was his turn. He outlined his own plans – ones that would run in parallel with the wholesale theft of Western technology.

Again Doinov's recall gives a flavour of that bizarre night.

'Maxwell first insisted the serving staff should leave and locked the door from the inside. He poured more wine. Raising his glass, he called for another toast. "To the future, our future," he had boomed.'

The others sat back while he explained how dazzling it would be. Doinov would remember:

'Maxwell said it was time to clear the decks. It was time for him to show us what he was really able to do. The first thing he wanted to establish was a bank. He had even toyed with the idea of calling it "Bank Maxwell", but that would cause too many questions! He was right on that! But it would still be his bank, his version of the Bank of Bulgaria. He would buy one of our major newspaper and printing groups. He would also buy into our film industry. There was no need for us to ask why. We now knew about his need for publicity. He said a biopic would be a good selling tool. He poured more wine and we had another toast. I think it was to Balkan movies conquering Hollywood. Then he looked at us both and said he had saved the best until last. He would like to service Bulgaria's foreign debt. Now we were too stunned to say anything. He just laughed and said it really was possible for him to do that. We didn't say anything but nod. When a man says he can do that and it's someone like Maxwell, you just take it seriously, especially if you are Bulgarian.'

Within six months Robert Maxwell had created an umbrella of companies to operate Neva. Some would be responsible for receiving and assessing the technology stolen by the Bulgarian secret service; in the end its spies would steal from all the major technology-producing nations in the world. Other companies in the suburbs of Sofia and elsewhere in Bulgaria would then re-engineer the technology or build it from stolen blueprints. Still other companies would spearhead an unprecedented sales drive into Russia, Ukraine, Poland, Estonia, Latvia, Georgia, Romania, Slovenia, Czechoslovakia, East Germany and Hungary. Hundreds of companies and state-run corporations found themselves being offered state-of-the-art technology identical in every way to that available in the West.

To assess, restructure and sell, Maxwell had set up the companies under the Maxwell Central and East European Partnership, a protective umbrella that shielded him from curiosity. Beneath it were companies that simply had initials, LBEM (it was a sales company); Multiart, producing stolen technology for the metal industry; Intertell; MI Engineering. Stanke Dimitrov sold software to the pharmaceutical industry; Sofia Insurance produced computers for the office-management market. Other companies gave no clue what they did: Razgrad, Bristica and Informavest were examples. Ares Dekta, Inkom and Multiagrom were equally shrouded in mystery as to what function they performed in this new empire Maxwell created. Some were obvious: Balkan Films provided stolen technology from Hollywood for the Bulgarian film industry; Business Center Ltd specialised in updating the offices of the Eastern Bloc. There was even a Bulgarian Yellow Pages company whose listing included all the companies that made and sold the equipment the country's spies were stealing.

The profits from all this went first into another bank, Agricultural Credit, in which Maxwell had acquired a 10 per cent stake. The money stayed in its keep for only a short time before being moved to more secure accounts outside Bulgaria.

The country had become, thanks to the free hand Maxwell had been given, the centre of a thriving economy based upon whole-scale theft and money laundering. When Robert Maxwell had once worn a sweatshirt emblazoned with the words 'King of Bulgaria', he could not have known how apt it would be. He was the man with the Midas touch who blew his golden trumpet and everybody danced to his tune. Fawned upon by president and commoner alike, offered anything he liked – a car, a mansion, even a king's palace – provided with anyone he liked – an actress, a dancer from a nightclub, even a pretty housekeeper who had briefly taken his fancy – Robert Maxwell was indeed the undisputed ruler of Bulgaria and, in many ways, beyond it, the first authentic tycoon of the Eastern Bloc.

But not even Robert Maxwell, in those halcyon months after that dinner at the Sofia Sheraton, could have imagined that the empire he was single-handedly creating – Lukanov and Doinov were soon no more than underlings at his beck and call – would grow into one of the most powerful crime syndicates in the world, embracing the Russian Mafia, the crime families of Bulgaria and, far away across the Atlantic, those in New York and, on the other side of the world, the crime families of Japan and Hong Kong. By then all the companies that Maxwell had formed would come under one name: Multi-Group. It would control a significant percentage of the global profits from gas, telecommunications, oil, gambling and money laundering. If Maxwell had seen it reach that stage, he might well have tried to insist that due tribute be paid to his achievement. Who can doubt as the founder godfather he would have liked his name in the title. Maxwell Multi Group would surely have had a ring which would have appealed to his overwhelming vanity.

John P O'Neill, FBI executive agent-in-charge in New York, would later say that 'in many ways Maxwell was at the heart of the global criminal network. Beginning with his Bulgarian connection he showed how to structure a network that grew into financially powerful criminal corporations whose power would extend to the South American drug cartels, the Tongs and the Triads, the Russian Mafia and the Japanese Yakuza. They were all there before. But the way Robert Maxwell set up things up, they would all come together in Multi-Group in its early years. His last contribution was not that he just robbed his pension funds. It was that he was the man who set in motion a true coalition of global criminals.'

Meanwhile, in those months of founding this great underbelly of criminality to support his very public face in London and New York, Maxwell had continued to service the needs of Mossad.

Just as Degem Computers provided cover for *katsas* to move through South America, so those in the Eastern Bloc served the same purpose. Mossad, like all intelligence services, had until then found it very difficult to operate in Russia and its satellites. While the CIA and British intelligence still found it hard to do so, Robert Maxwell ensured that Mossad could penetrate far into the economic structure of Eastern Europe and make informed judgments never before possible by working under cover of the Neva companies.

But all was not well for Maxwell's two partners in the triumvirate. Ognian Doinov had fallen victim to the paranoia of State President Zhivkov. He had begun to believe that Doinov was a member of a cabal of ministers plotting to overthrow him. The President suspected – correctly – that Lukanov was involved as well. But he dare not move against Moscow's surrogate. He focused on Doinov. To arrest him would be far too dangerous – Lukanov would then undoubtedly intervene. In 1988, Zhivkov effectively banished Doinov – by appointing him as Bulgaria's ambassador to Norway. It turned out to be a tactical mistake by the President. Oslo was only a short flight from London – and the security that Maxwell afforded. The relationship between the two men had developed. Part of it was undoubtedly the respect Doinov showed Maxwell; at times it verged on adulation. For his part Maxwell had never enjoyed such a subservient relationship even with his own children. He began to treat Doinov like a son, or perhaps a younger brother. He allowed the diplomat to stay in one of the apartments Maxwell maintained in London, what he called his 'safe houses', where Nahum Admoni and other senior Mossad officers could also stay.

For Doinov his closeness to Maxwell was an opportunity to create his own dissent within the trio, in the hope it would bring him even closer to the tycoon. He warned Maxwell that Lukanov was dangerous. Lukanov would walk over anyone to get where he wanted, to reach the stage where power and wealth were his to command.

Maxwell listened carefully. The discord suited him perfectly: he had always operated on the principle of ruling by division. Doinov had the financial acumen for removing the funds from Bulgaria to all those secret accounts in the West. But Lukanov was the political force within Bulgaria, the man who knew how to keep the lid on the system and when to allow enough steam to escape.

All that ultimately mattered to Maxwell was that he could still use both men and bask in their admiration as he laid the foundation for what would become a crime syndicate without equal. He could also count on one member of his family to dote on him. To his daughter Isabel, still living in San Francisco, not far from where IOD was doing a thriving business in servicing the contracts on the doctored Promis, her father was 'a very complex but highly gifted and caring and visionary man who put his money where his mouth and vision were, to extraordinary benefit to so many, particularly in science and education and also, yes, in business and the media.'

Isabel, of course, saw only his carefully orchestrated public face staring out of his newspapers. In one instance he was photographed with some of the children who had survived the Chernobyl disaster and whom he had flown to England; other photos of Maxwell showed him with some of the Jews he had brought out of Russia to Israel. Without a doubt that was the 'good' side of Isabel's father. But there was that ever-darkening side she did not know about, which was beginning to ring alarm bells in Mossad.

The morning after the Sheraton dinner, Maxwell sent for Doinov. They strolled through the ground of the government villa where Maxwell usually stayed. He said he had been serious about resolving Bulgaria's foreign debt. All he would require was a commission of 15 per cent. Doinov agreed that was reasonable, yet it could just have been a figure that Maxwell pulled out of the air to show how powerful he was.

Crunching over the snow, Maxwell then began to outline how it would be possible.

The first steps would be to restructure a joint venture company, BIMEX, which Maxwell had set up with Lukanov some time ago. This would now be registered in London with two addresses, Headington Hill Hall and Maxwell House. The shareholders would be those in another of Maxwell's companies, Orbit House Enterprises. The initial capital would be $1 million for 500,000 shares, equally divided between the Orbit stockholders and those in BIMEX, Bulgaria. Its board would be reinforced by a director of a Bulgarian bank registered in Beirut. It was called LITEX and was a cover for the Middle East station of the Bulgarian secret service.

This interlocking arrangement would pave the way for Maxwell to obtain a controlling interest in the Bulgarian Cooperative Bank. For years the bank had unwittingly been a conduit for money laundering by one of the major criminal families in Moscow, the Rising Sun, whose head was Simeon Mogilevich.

But, on that January day in 1987, Robert Maxwell confined himself to explaining to Doinov the finer points of international financial manipulation. Once he had his hands on the Cooperative Bank, Maxwell would quietly forget about his offer to service Bulgaria's foreign debt. The bank would provide him with a means, according to a later Bulgarian government report, to:

launder over $1 billion through Switzerland, some of it passing through Gibraltar to Liechtenstein as a consequence of joint ventures like BIMEX and others in which Maxwell was involved. As a result of Decision 53 of the Council of Ministers, $200 million of the country's monetary reserve was invested in shares and bonds via Maxwell's Bishopsgate International Investment Management PLC in England.

Vassily Koralov, director of the Bulgarian Foreign Trade Bank, was unable to explain how Maxwell had taken $500 million out of the country with simply a bank withdrawal slip.

'I cannot imagine how it was possible to do this without the signature of the head accountant. I have no desire to comment on whether the money had been money that came in from abroad,' Koralov said.

The money came from profits Neva had made in sales of computer technology to all the Eastern Bloc countries. Maxwell had set up a web of financial companies across the world that ensured those profits would never be traced. The funereal-like Dr R had seen to that. The one certainty is that they far exceeded the $1 billion that the Bulgarian government subsequently reported it was able to identify.

Credit Suisse in Switzerland, banks in Gibraltar – which serve the same purpose as do those in the Cayman Islands and Liechtenstein – were mere staging points on the electronic trail the ingenious Dr R had opened, and along which his client, Robert Maxwell, was the only man allowed to travel. It would remain so well disguised that investigators from the US Internal Revenue Service, from Britain's Inland Revenue and from all the regulatory bodies who may have suspected it existed, would never – *ever* – be able to follow it.

Like the Nazi gold spirited out of Germany at the end of World War Two, like all the other secret treasures down the centuries, the secret fortune of Robert Maxwell would, thanks to Dr R, remain a secret.

While he could publicly boast that his own children would not receive a penny of his money, he was careful not to exclude their children. Through Dr R, future generations of Maxwells had been guaranteed that, just as Neva had given Maxwell the key to Bulgaria, they too could look forward to a life of financial security. Neva was an operation like no other in financial history.

David Kimche had once said that 'the sins of the father should not be allowed to be visited on the children'. He could not have chosen a better example than Robert Maxwell.

Years later in New York, the seasoned FBI agent John P O'Neill had staff still trying to unravel the links from Maxwell's legacy.

'Maxwell had been a player like no other. He had used global trading. He had those high-level contacts among Eastern Bloc politicians. What he had done was to bring together the third element in any successful criminal operation – the criminals themselves. It was a meeting of like minds. He understood the need for internationalism in everything he did. So crime became a part of it. He set the wheels in motion as far as Eastern Europe went. Others gave them pace, gathering up Cosa Nostra, the Chinese and all the others. But Maxwell was there at the beginning. He was no John

Gotti. But Gotti would not have lived in the same space as Robert Maxwell when it came down to being an operator.'

From Sofia Maxwell flew to Moscow. A year earlier he had taken a stake in the city's English-language newspaper, *Moscow News*.

The newspaper had been Maxwell's attempt to embrace the liberating policies of Mikhail Gorbachev. Both saw the newspaper as a means to promote *perestroika*. Its editor, Yegor Yakolev, was a personal friend of not only Gorbachev but his wife, Raisa, who was heavily involved in a cultural foundation. She had sought Maxwell's help with her project but, though he promised to invest heavily in the foundation, he never did.

Maxwell also had not endeared himself to the editor of the *Moscow News* because, just as he sought to control the editorial output of his British newspapers, he did the same thing in Moscow.

Yegor Yakolev would later claim that, 'Maxwell's investment in *Moscow News* had come from money funnelled through the Soviet Press Agency for the publication of fifty thousand copies of books containing Gorbachev's writings. No one ever found out how many books had in fact been printed.'

For Yakolev, having Maxwell storm into his office to demand why a political line he had suggested had not been published was intolerable. His relationship with Maxwell was going down a slippery slope that would end in open hostility between them. But that was still a little way off. For the moment Maxwell enjoyed a friendly relationship with Russia. His other publishing ventures now included a cultural magazine and a television station. He had also publicly announced he would invest heavily in setting up companies to develop computer technology for Russians for the coming of the digital world. He promised it would bring Russian television into the new satellite-driven age.

He also told Gorbachev there should be a Gorbachev–Maxwell Institute, which would contain a repository of the writings of scientists throughout the globe. He promised to donate $50 million to start it. He never did. He promised so much – and, because long ago he had learned that the well-honed promise is always one desperate people want to hear, he was believed.

TWELVE

Maxwell's influence in Moscow had been established in 1962 when he proudly boasted he had been the only British publisher with a stall at the Moscow Book Fair. He listed his profits from the visit as £52,000. More important, he had established a relationship with Nikita Khrushchev. This had enabled him to obtain the rights to edit and print *Information USSR*, a Soviet government publication carried by libraries and academic institutions across the world. The deal had fitted into Maxwell's financial manipulations. He was establishing profits from the sale of the newsletter, which were moved through his own privately owned *nonprofit* Pergamon Institute in New York. From these, Dr R sent the money on to a trust in Liechtenstein, one of the first he had established as far back as 1951.

After visiting *Moscow News*, which was dreaded as much by the staff as their counterparts in editorial offices in London, Maxwell decided to have his customary dinner with Vladimir Kryuchkov. As always, there was much to talk about.

Since Maxwell had last been in Moscow, there had been a further rearranging of global events – not all to the liking of the men in the Lubyanka.

Gorbachev was going too fast, Kryuchkov warned. The feeling in the Army and the KGB was that the only outcome of the Reykjavik Summit was that America wanted the Soviet Union to disarm while it should still be allowed to strengthen its own defences.

As the meal progressed, Kryuchkov's criticisms of Gorbachev became sharper. His visit to Washington in December 1988, while a personal success for Gorbachev, had further weakened Moscow's position in the world. His decision to free the dissident Andrei Sakharov from his long exile in Gorky had simply started a clamour for the release of the tens of thousands of other political prisoners the KGB had shipped to the gulags of Siberia.

It was time for Maxwell to ask the question uppermost in his mind: given the opposition within the KGB and the army, how safe was Mikhail Gorbachev?

Kryuchkov would remember he had looked at Maxwell for a long moment, then shrugged. He seemed to be saying it was anyone's guess.

Maxwell pressed. How far would the KGB and the army go with *perestroika*? Maxwell knew it would be the first question he would be asked in Tel Aviv.

Another silence. Another shrug.

Suddenly in one of those switches of conversations he was known for, Kryuchkov explained how the Promis software Maxwell had sold the KGB two years earlier – a sale that allowed Mossad to eavesdrop in a way no other intelligence service could emulate – had played its part in recovering from Israel the prototype of a Russian MiG-29 fighter.

The aircraft had been flown to an airfield near Gdansk for further flight tests.

Mossad had bribed a Polish general in charge of the country's UB intelligence office in Gdansk to write off the fighter as no longer airworthy. A team of Israeli technicians, under the supervision of a *katsa*, had dismantled it. Mossad had flown the general out of the country to the United States. A $1 million dollar Citibank account was waiting for him in New York. The dismantled aircraft had been flown to Tel Aviv in crates marked 'Agricultural Machinery'.

It was weeks before the theft had been discovered by Moscow during a routine inventory of aircraft supplied to Warsaw Pact countries. That was when the KGB had been called in and had used Promis to track the paper trail that revealed its ultimate destination.

A strong protest was made to Israel – including a threat to halt the exodus of Russian Jews. By then the Israeli air force had stripped the plane down to its bare essentials and learned all they needed to know about it. On orders from the Israeli government, the aircraft was reassembled and returned to Moscow. Israel's explanation to Moscow for the theft was 'the mistaken zeal of officers who had acted unofficially'.

Finishing the story, Vladimir Kryuchkov shrugged a third time.

Maxwell had always been far-sighted in the need to have shelf companies he could dust down when the time came. He had dozens of them scattered across the world, some in unlikely places such as Kenya and Nigeria. He had a number registered in the Cayman Islands, on the Isle of Man and the Virgin Islands. One of the companies, Pergamon-Brassey, was registered in McLean, Virginia, in August 1985. Robert Maxwell and his son Kevin were listed as directors with addresses at Headington Hill Hall.

In 1987, Pergamon-Brassey underwent a transformation. The retired

Senator, John Tower, was appointed chairman and the directors now included a retired four-star US Army general who had headed the Southern Command in Panama and a retired British major general. The president of that company was a recently retired US Air Force general.

Between them they had contacts through the US defence establishment and in countries where Maxwell had military and economic interests.

The president of Inslaw, Bill Hamilton, later said, 'In 1987, Pergamon-Brassey hired two senior computer-systems executives who resigned at the same time from the Meese Justice Department's Justice Data Center. The proprietary IBM mainframe version of Promis had been operating at the Justice Data Center since the early eighties. George Vaveris resigned his estimated $90,000 a year Senior Executive Service position as director of the Justice Data Center to become vice-president for technical services at the tiny Pergamon-Brassey. He told a colleague at the Justice Department his new salary would be in excess of $200,000 a year.'

The high-profile respectability of its board of directors certainly would ensure no awkward questions would emerge in Washington about why a company with only a handful of employees – there were never more than six on the payroll at any one time – needed such a distinguished board.

Pergamon-Brassey was a specialist company trading in software. How it came by that software and where it went to is another of the mysteries surrounding Maxwell's activities at this time. Pergamon-Brassey, operating out of the pleasant Virginian countryside, may have been there to support Neva in any way Robert Maxwell wanted.

In Headington Hill Hall, Betty continued to live her life with Maxwell through the daily packages of press clippings for her to place neatly in her 'archive'. There were accounts of Maxwell as guest of honour at some banquet, addressing a fundraising dinner, opening a factory in some remote part of the world. He was here, there and everywhere, his every move around the globe recorded in print. In terms of column inches, only the Beatles surpassed him. Betty went on collating and filing the endless mound of paper. In a month the file consumed almost as much newsprint as that needed to produce one of the novels she read alone in bed. In a year the cuttings equalled a small library of volumes.

Included in this flow of paper into her study were reports of Maxwell's angry reaction that two journalists had begun to probe into his life for unauthorised biographies they were going to write. He appointed his own hagiographer to produce a carefully controlled book. It glowed with the kind of prose usually found in the advertisements in his *Daily Mirror*. It would remain significant only by what it left out.

Thankfully, Betty found no evidence in her newsclips that yet another affair had somehow made its way into print. He had a team of lawyers to stop that.

Comforted by her own upbringing and strong personal ethics, she would not for a moment have considered retaliating by indulging in an extra-marital relationship. Instead she had the archive to keep her busy assembling a collage of newsclips and letters she and Maxwell had sent each other but, which like so much in their lives, had become less and less frequent.

By 1988 she was filing away reports that Maxwell had bought Macmillan, the publishing company, for $2.6 billion. While it placed him among the world's leading media moguls, the money he paid for Macmillan was considerably more than his own Maxwell Communications Corporation was worth. Together with the acquisition of the Official Airline Guide for $750 million, it meant he now had bank repayments at a staggering level of $300 million a year.

Maxwell showed no sign that this concerned him. Macmillan had placed him at the top of the publishing world. He had also decided to convert a floor of its headquarters building in Manhattan into a penthouse with spectacular views over the East River. He eventually lost interest in the idea.

But the Macmillan deal meant he had access to the company's charitable trust. He used it to spend lavishly on events in New York, paying large sums of money, sometimes as much as $100,000, for a seat at charitable functions attended by people he wanted to impress.

Now he had given Betty another task. She was to arrange his 65th-birthday party. His instructions were clear. It was to outshine any other party that year, perhaps of any year. The great and the good of the world were to be invited. Lesser mortals – his editors, senior executives and authors – were all to be asked to contribute to a book. Its theme would be his part in world publishing, the emphasis to be on the word 'world'. It would have the title *Fetschrift* and would remain for ever as a testament to his 'pre-eminent role' in the fields of technology, science and education. No despot or dictator, not even Stalin, Mao or Hitler, had demanded such approbation for a birthday gift.

Three thousand guests were invited for five separate events spread over an entire weekend. It would be his coronation with orchestras playing at one end of a marquee that would have comfortably housed a Boeing 747.

Each guest would receive a copy of the hagiography of his life, a book that so far had been conspicuous by its modest sales.

Betty, with the kind of flare that would have suited a Roman emperor, had arranged for her husband's entrance into this theatre of the absurd to be heralded by a fanfare of trumpets. Nero could not have wished for more. In his black tie and tails, Maxwell wore around his neck the White Rose of Finland insignia and his Military Cross on his lapel.

'Just like a bloody foreigner,' a guest was heard to murmur by one of the small army of security men. 'No one wears his decorations to something like this.'

President Ronald Reagan, Prime Minister Margaret Thatcher and President Mikhail Gorbachev had all sent birthday wishes. But all also found excuses not to attend. They were represented by ambassadors, lower-ranking diplomats and the middle echelon of Rothschild's and lesser bankers. In many ways the gathering was a cross between a stockholders' meeting and a convention of moneylenders.

The men of Mossad and the representatives of the Bulgarian Connection were also conspicuous by their absence.

While the birthday festivities were in full swing, in Tel Aviv Nahum Admoni was under increasing pressure from a number of failures: the Pollard affair; Irangate; the clearing out of a Mossad cell in London after MI6 had discovered a *bodel* – a Mossad courier had left eight near-perfectly forged British passports in a phone box for a *katsa* on his way to Bulgaria on a mission using as cover one of Maxwell's Neva companies.

On the Jewish New Year, Rosh Hashanah, Admoni had gathered his staff in the Mossad canteen and said: 'I wish us all a year without mistakes. We need to all keep our eye on the ball.'

It was an injunction in the case of Robert Maxwell that Nahum Admoni should himself have heeded. The criminals Maxwell was becoming involved with would not only lead him into dangerous and uncharted waters, but would eventually pose a threat to Israel and seal Admoni's own fate. He would become the Mossad director who did not hear the alarm bells ringing.

The danger surfaced in Moscow over another of those dinners Kryuchkov gave Maxwell in the Lubyanka late in 1988. Even more fearful at the pace at which *perestroika* was accelerating, Kruychkov said that for the KGB to remain a potent force he wanted to establish 'over six hundred commercial enterprises'. They would all have links to the West. Just as Maxwell's companies provided cover for Mossad's *katsas*, Kryuchkov envisaged his companies would provide similar protection for KGB operatives. The Russian companies would operate on sound business principles, just like any other corporation in the West. The profits from the Russian concerns would go to the KGB and help fund its foreign intelligence operations. Maxwell was assured none of these would be against the State of Israel.

Kryuchkov had explained that behind his immediate plan was a long-term one. The six hundred companies would each employ a quota of senior party members to provide them with an income during the difficult days ahead in the transition from Communism to capitalism. Through genuine trading links, the companies would obtain access to the very heart of capitalism: Wall Street and the City of London and the Bourses of Western Europe. Its staffs would then learn the innermost secrets of the West's banking system, the wellspring of all capitalism. Eventually it might even be possible to destabilise Western economies – and pave the way for the return of Communism.

It was madcap scheming that Stalin would have been proud of.

But there was more.

Before that meeting Maxwell met a man in the plan Kryuchkov had created. His name was Simeon Mogilevich. He was a Ukrainian-born Jew and head of the Rising Sun, one of Moscow's major criminal families. And soon, thanks to Maxwell, he would be able to travel on an Israeli passport.

Money laundering, weapons, contract hits and drug trafficking were the staples of Mogilevich's work.

At their first meeting, again in Moscow, Mogilevich told Maxwell he would be able to get Jews out of the Soviet Union and had done so on many occasions. The truth was that Mogilevich had repeatedly robbed Soviet Jews of their last valuables in return for his promise to smuggle them to Israel.

By the time he met Maxwell, Mogilevich had established some fifty legitimate companies in Israel, Britain, the United States, Austria and Germany. Through them he laundered his criminal profits. These would grow to some $40 billion a year after he met Maxwell.

A phone call to Tel Aviv, and Mogilevich had his passport. Now he could go anywhere – and he did: to Liechtenstein to set up a new money-laundering operation; to Gibraltar, to Cyprus, the Channel Islands and the Cayman Islands. In all these places money and a no-questions policy were opposite sides of the same coin, and Simeon Mogilevich, thanks to Robert Maxwell, availed himself of new opportunities.

The second man to cross Maxwell's path, this time through an introduction by his old friend Andrei Lukanov, was Ivo Janchev.

An officer in the Bulgarian secret service, he had ambitions to be rich whatever it took. Using his contacts in Moscow and Budapest, he would be the link to organised crime figures like Mogilevich. He would also be the front man to make contact with several Russians with businesses in the West.

Within a few months of meeting Mogilevich and Janchev, Robert Maxwell had gone into partnership with them. He had now become a serious player in the world of organised crime.

Even by Maxwell's standards of being willing to enter into any arrangement that would ultimately profit him, his decision to partner these two men was extraordinary.

Maxwell was a corporate raider, a man who would breeze into a boardroom and say he had come to buy the company. His new partners' usual technique was to storm into a company with their private armies of former Soviet Spetznaz (special forces), and threaten to take apart the building unless the offer they made was accepted.

While Maxwell had a bevy of fawning secretaries to slip him his deodorant or mop his brow, his partners did not bother with such feminine niceties. They depended on their armed bodyguards to make sure no one passed comment on their body odour. At play they could be rough, publicly manhandling their women, stomping their way into a night spot and terrorising the other clients.

Their business was prostitution, drug running, traffic in humans. When MI5 discovered how Mogilevich earned his money, they informed the Home Office which expelled him from Britain and publicly branded him as 'one of the most dangerous criminals in the world'. It is hard to believe that Robert Maxwell did not know that. Yet he continued to be drawn ever deeper into the dark and evil empire Mogilevich operated. A number of people who had crossed his path had been disposed of into the Moscow River or in one of the city's back streets. He had his own team of killers never further away than a phone call.

These two were the men Maxwell had chosen as his partners. The question that would be asked was: why? Why did a tycoon still listed among the top ten publishers in the world, among men like Murdoch, not only rub shoulders with, but treat as equals, Lukanov, Janchev and Mogilevich?

Maxwell's enjoyment came from being seen in public with kings and queens, with Prince Charles and Princess Diana, with Hollywood stars. Through them he could continue to fill not only the pages of his own newspapers, but those of his rivals. But with his three new partners he dared not even be photographed by a hostess in a Sofia nightclub. He could meet his partners only in the shadows, in one of their fortified palaces where even he had to undergo a body scan before gaining access.

He could never invite them, even in the dead of night, to visit him. He could never take them for a cruise on the *Lady Ghislaine*. He could do almost nothing that he normally liked to do to show his power. He was just their business partner. No more. No less.

He knew their business was corruption and pornography of every kind: fortunes were made from prostitution and drug trafficking, from trading in men, women and children for the sex industry, from the mass marketing of obscene films, from contract killings, blackmail, extortion.

What was Robert Maxwell doing in their world? The answer would come within a few months of their alliance. Maxwell, who was not averse to hiding behind other respectable figures – the Rothschilds, the Lehman Brothers and that epitome of respectability, the governor of the Bank of England, Robin Leigh-Pemberton – would now find himself fronting for three of the world's most powerful godfathers. There is only one reason why he would do so, feel he *must* do so: the attraction of making still more money to satisfy his insatiable desire to be the richest man in the world. The obsession may have gone all the way back to that time when he walked barefoot in the summer, shared his shoes with his siblings in the winter, when he slept under a quilt smelling of sour straw – and when his mother had told him that to be an Englishman was to be different. He had become an Englishman of sorts. He was certainly different – if that meant being wealthy. But he had not yet enough money. Lukanov, Mogilevich and Janchev had offered him a means to come that much closer to getting what he wanted.

Through his own connections to international finance, where his very name could still open doors to the bankers at Goldman Sachs and the House of Morgan, he had paved the way for the godfathers to enter with him. Israel's superspy had now become an associate of criminals. Fraud by now was nothing new to Maxwell. But to be a partner with criminals on every watch list of police and intelligence services *was* something new.

It marked his fall, rise and fall again: he had fallen after the damning report by the British government's inspectors that he was not fit to be a director of any company; he had risen again to own the *Daily Mirror*. But now he had embarked on a journey that could only lead to another fall.

Nevertheless, he must have believed he could still count on the protection of Mossad. He could only have believed that because he knew so much of their own dark secrets that, if his own criminal connections had surfaced, he could depend on Mossad to help him.

In New York, the FBI chief, John P O'Neill, later identified the global threat posed by organised crime and its links to Maxwell:

'Some of Maxwell's associates were involved in narcotics, illegal weapons and contract killings, of which there may be as many as five hundred a year. They were also into smuggling precious metals and counterfeiting. They had links with the Russian military. Any Russian banker that didn't do their bidding knew what to expect. He got a grenade tossed into his car. A hit like that could be arranged for as little as two hundred bucks. People who tried to cross them had nowhere to run. They could hunt you down anywhere.

'These people had sophisticated operations for washing money in London and New York. It came from drugs, financial fraud – just one step beyond what Maxwell was doing – prostitution and extortion.

'Their operations looked something like this. In Britain it was money laundering. Same in Switzerland. Italy was drugs and traffic in people – mostly women for prostitution. In Belgium and Germany, it was stolen cars and more laundering of profits. Albania and Poland was fraud, arms and drugs. Maxwell showed how an intricate, complex web of shell companies under a group umbrella could move money around the globe. When New York became a target for Eastern Bloc criminal syndicates and we looked at how it operated, the Maxwell model was there for all to see.'

In his London penthouse, Maxwell had been asleep for some time when the night line blinked on his bedside console. His caller was one of the few privileged to have the number.

'A new dawn has arrived, Robert!' Andrei Lukanov was almost shouting down the line from Sofia in the early hours on 10 November 1988.

Ten minutes before, Lukanov continued shouting excitedly, Todor Zhivkov had been removed from office.

'Robert, we expect you to join us for the celebrations!'

Maxwell was now wide awake. He pressed a bell push. It was the signal for the night-duty maid to bring him the already prepared tray of sandwiches and a pot of coffee. He settled back on his outsize pillows stuffed with goose down and started asking questions about what had happened.

The Bulgarian Communist Party had held a closed session. In ten minutes its members agreed that Zhivkov had to go. He would not only be ejected from political life, but he would lose all his palaces and residences. He would have to exchange his eyrie overlooking his birthplace at Pravets for a small house owned by his granddaughter near the village.

Lukanov had chuckled. That particular idea had been his. Zhivkov would live out the rest of his life in the very village where he had insisted the Neva project should start. In one of the backstreets was the first factory that had re-engineered stolen American technology. The computers had become known as *pravets* through the Balkans.

'He was good to me,' Maxwell said.

'And bad for a lot of people, Robert,' Lukanov had murmured. 'Don't get soft in your time of life. He thinks you had a hand in all this.'

'You're right that he had to go, Andrei. He just had to go,' Maxwell replied.

That conversation would remain long in Lukanov's memory. Doinov would suggest later 'that Maxwell was wondering how this was going to play out and what effect it would have on his own dealings in Bulgaria. He would have known, as we all did, that Lukanov had an almost painful desire to lead Bulgaria. It would finally remove the stigma of his father having been arrested under the Stalin regime in one of those purges which occurred at regular intervals.'

Betty and Robert Maxwell on their wedding day.

Robert Maxwell with his favourite 'toy' in the background: his $19 million yacht _The Lady Ghislaine_.

Above: **Robert Maxwell with Prime Minister Margaret Thatcher, whom he would often describe as one of his trusted friends.**

Below: **Robert Maxwell with his wife and favourite daughter, the international socialite Ghislaine (*left*), after whom he named his luxury yacht.**

Both courtesy of Mirrorpix

Above: **Robert Maxwell entertaining Mikhail Gorbachev, one of the many Cold War Communist leaders with whom he had close friendships.**

Below: **With Ariel Sharon, now Israel's prime minister.**

Both courtesy of Mirrorpix

Above: **Robert Maxwell with the Prince and Princess of Wales.**

Below: **Harold Wilson looks uneasy as Maxwell emphasises a point to Mikhail Gorbachev.**

Both courtesy of Mirrorpix

Above: **Robert Maxwell, the patriarch, surrounded by his family.**

Below: **The front pages of the *Mirror* present contrasting images of their publisher.**

All courtesy of Mirrorpix

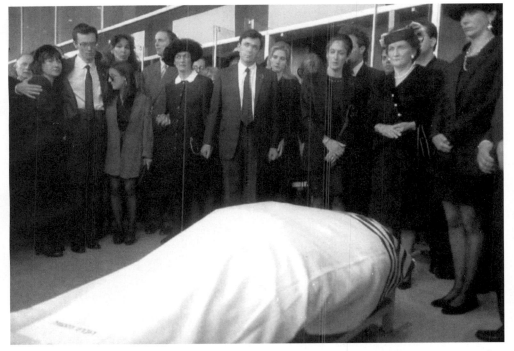

Above: **In keeping with Jewish tradition, the body of Maxwell was wrapped in a tallit. The Maxwell family and friends bid farewell to the man who, even in death, would have an impact on many of their lives.**

Below: **The body of Robert Maxwell is taken to its final resting place. Maxwell's funeral was attended by many of Israel's leading dignitaries, including the prime minister and president. The eulogy was delivered by Shimon Peres.**

Both courtesy of Mirrorpix

**Robert Maxwell's grave on the sacred ground of the
Mount of Olives in Jerusalem.**

Courtesy of Mirrorpix

Maxwell knew the demise of Zhivkov would have had the full support of Kryuchkov; nothing happened in Bulgaria without the KGB chief's approval.

In the meantime he wanted to know more from Lukanov. Who was going to head up the country? Lukanov said it would be the Union of Democratic Forces (UDF). Maxwell liked the name: it fitted with *perestroika*. But who were they? he had pressed.

'Dissidents, members of the Green Party, some of the brighter ones from Darzhavna Sigurnost and some of the Party who had seen the light,' Lukanov replied.

He repeated his invitation for Maxwell to fly at once to Bulgaria to be part of the historic revolution.

But still Maxwell hesitated. He had seen how revolutions had a nasty way of remembering the past. Heads could literally topple – perhaps even his. He had, after all, been part of the old regime. His photograph had appeared on every front page with Zhivkov each time he had flown to Bulgaria. He had lauded the former president in the country's newspapers and on television. No: to go now, while Bulgarian blood ran high, would be a risk. Best to let things cool down. First he would talk to Doinov, once more in that 'safe' apartment in London after Zhivkov had posted him as ambassador to Norway.

Doinov's account of his early-morning wake-up call from Maxwell revealed the thinking of both men.

'Robert was concerned whether it was safe for him to go to Sofia right now. I was more interested in whether Lukanov could really make the putsch [sudden overthow of government] work,' Doinov recalled.

Maxwell's third call was to Kryuchkov in Moscow. He roared with laughter at Maxwell's fears. He had nothing to worry about. Lukanov would see to that. What about Doinov? Kryuchkov had been less optimistic. There was a developing rift between the two men, and the KGB chief said that Doinov would be well advised to remain in London.

Maxwell passed on the warning. Doinov had been good to him, helping to move payments out of the Neva operation into Western banks. But Doinov felt that, if he did not make an appearance in Sofia, he would be cut out of the deals undoubtedly already being brokered. Whatever the future held, he was going to go.

Robert Maxwell decided he also had to fly to Bulgaria. As a precaution he would not offer Doinov a seat on his Gulfstream. Better to arrive without past baggage.

Maxwell was warmly greeted by Lukanov and told he would have a vital role to play in creating the new, free-economy Bulgaria in which the past would be discreetly buried. The process was already under way.

Documents dealing with Neva were being shredded by the Darzhavna Sigurnost; they included details of operations they had conducted to steal technology from the United States and Western Europe.

Just as Maxwell had been asked to help in setting up Kryuchkov's six hundred companies, so Lukanov envisaged a similar operation in which party officials and senior members of the secret service would be given positions.

'Lukanov wanted to build a new capitalist class to ensure the smooth flow and distribution of stolen money. Maxwell was to be a key player in doing that,' Doinov later said.

There were new openings to be exploited. Tobacco smuggling was one. In Spain 25 per cent of all the cigarettes smoked were contraband. In France and Germany the tax lost on smuggled cigarettes exceeded $200 million a year. There was even a market for smuggled animals. Collectors would pay huge sums for rare specimens. One of the Neva factories had installed a unit that manufactured special brassieres for carrying cockatoo eggs. There was a market for sturgeon from the Caspian Sea. Drugs, of course, would always be a prime money earner.

Until now all these sales had been under the control of the Italian Mafia, the French Mafia and their counterparts, the American crime families. But with *glasnost* and *perestroika*, there was room for Bulgaria. Why let Kryuchkov and the Russian Mafia have it all for themselves? For Lukanov and ultimately for Robert Maxwell there was room. All Maxwell had to do was to continue to do what he had done before: set up more companies through which to run the profits. The rest Lukanov would take care of. And Maxwell had replied with the words that would always be associated with him: 'I am glad to be of service.'

The Bank for Agricultural Credit (BZK), was chosen as the starting point for him once again to start performing that service.

In the past the bank had been a major outlet for the transferring of Neva's profits into the West. Maxwell had owned a 10 per cent stake in the bank, as did Lukanov and several of his associates. BZK had been a vehicle for the transfer of close to $1 billion to yet another Bulgarian bank, the LITEX, based in Beirut.

Maxwell had subsequently sold his shares in BZK for far below their market value. It may have been his first move to assist his godfather partners – Janchev, Mogilevich and Lukanov. It gave them a stake in a bank through which they could run their profits from criminal activities. From there the money could be sent on to LITEX – and to anywhere in the world. In terms of money laundering, it was crude but still effective.

All this Maxwell learned in those first few hours back in Sofia. He had brought with him a team of financial advisers, along with Nick Davies and a photographer. No one in that entourage was aware of Maxwell's criminal activities and money laundering. Lukanov had, however, assured him there would be plenty of photo opportunities for Maxwell in the new regime.

Only Doinov was not included in Lukanov's plans. Maxwell had sensed the way the wind was blowing and had also begun to wonder if he should distance himself from the now former ambassador. But for the moment Doinov remained under Maxwell's benevolent eye. Maxwell had a loyal streak; he never easily abandoned those who had helped him. Though they had been few in number, he was grateful to them. Doinov could feel secure as long as his mentor was on hand.

The night Maxwell arrived in Sofia, Lukanov gave a banquet. There was a startling moment when Maxwell placed both hands on Lukanov's face and kissed him on the lips.

It set the seal on what was to follow.

As Maxwell had sensed and warned, Doinov's return to Bulgaria was not a prudent move. His rift with Lukanov ran deep and in the Balkans revenge was a traditional way of dealing with disputes.

The heady atmosphere following the end of the Zhivkov regime encouraged hand wringing among former Politburo members who were jockeying for power. Doinov was no different in trying to play the role of Pilate and wash his hands of the crimes of the previous regime.

Documents later unearthed by Dr Jordan Baev, a senior fellow in the Military History Institute, Sofia, illustrate why Maxwell had every right to be worried about Doinov's return.

Document 4: Letter by Ognian Doinov to Delegates of the People's Assembly, 13 December 1989.

First I admit responsibility that as a former member of the Politburo I voted for the dismissal of many capable comrades whose main fault consisted in the fact that Todor Zhivkov saw them as rivals.

Second, I cannot help but be ashamed that together with others I have participated in the panegyric praising of Todor Zhivkov's personality, virtues and achievements.

Third, I bear a distinct guilt that I did not stand up against the unjust decisions concerning the plight of Bulgarian Muslims.

Fourth, I do not wish to overlook my responsibility for the sectors of which I was previously in charge.

Rumours were spread about me by the centres for disinformation at the Ministry of Foreign Affairs. It was alleged that I possessed several luxurious villas worth hundreds of thousands of dollars; that I had a great deal of money in foreign currency; that I took bribes.

I want to address A. Lukanov and ask if he feels himself the main culprit for the tremendous increase in the foreign debt.

Doinov did not stop there and called for Lukanov to resign to avoid being 'disgracefully expelled or investigated later'.

In the heat of the moment, Doinov had lost his normal caution. He not only felt embittered but his ego demanded he cleanse himself in front of his own people. It was a risky strategy that could have jeopardised Maxwell.

Lukanov waited three days to reply, dismissing the need for Politburo members to accept guilt. But, in the last section of 'Document No 5 to the Chairman of the People's Assembly', Lukanov fired a warning shot across Doinov's bows.

I come to the conclusion that he is trying to place himself ahead of truthful revelations in order to present himself as a victim once again – this time a victim of the present party and leadership. As for me, I understand really well that I am one rather 'inconvenient' witness to Ognian Doinov because I am very familiar with many of his risky projects and concrete actions due to the authority of the duties I performed.

Doinov had made an enemy of a very powerful man. From that moment he could never be certain how Lukanov would seek revenge.

At a meeting with Lukanov, Maxwell said he wanted a new stake in BZK and for his Bishopsgate Investment Trust to handle a substantial portion of Bulgaria's current $10 billion foreign debt.

He also wanted something else: the pick of Todor Zhivkov's palaces and villas, now all about to come on the market. They were being offered at bargain-basement prices. Maxwell would buy the choicest for himself and acquire the others either for resale or high rentals to the foreign investors he would bring into Bulgaria.

Accompanied by Nick Davies and his photographer, he travelled to Perla on the Black Sea. It was famous for two reasons. It produced the best *rikea* drink in all Bulgaria and was the site of the former president's most luxurious holiday palace. It had its own harbour and a cinema.

When Maxwell returned to Sofia, Doinov was anxiously waiting.

'I told him I had decided I was at risk – that I knew too much. Mr Maxwell told me to leave Bulgaria right away without telling anyone and promised to install me in Vienna as his consultant,' said Doinov.

Maxwell also promised Doinov a large salary and an ongoing secret role in laundering money from Bulgaria.

Lukanov, when he later faced scrutiny for his links to Maxwell, turned the tables on Doinov with a letter he published, within which he cited Doinov.

A Bulgarian federal prosecutor would later threaten, 'I will personally go to Vienna and bring Doinov back to Sofia in a bag if I have to.'

With no extradition treaty, that had proved impossible.

Another man who crossed Maxwell's path was Michael Chorney, a Russian Jew with an Israeli passport. Young and flashy, he impressed Maxwell as someone who would go a long way. Chorney had his own eye on setting up banks, hi-tech businesses and buying a football team in Bulgaria. In time he would learn a lot from Maxwell's flamboyant style and hard-nosed strategy. He would also subsequently become a controversial figure.

With Doinov in Vienna and Andrei Lukanov running the country, Maxwell had achieved his goal of making Bulgaria his own.

But events at home, in Russia and in Israel were about to threaten all that.

THIRTEEN

At the last moment Shabtai Shavit had ordered his driver to collect him an hour earlier than previously instructed. This was Shavit's first day as Mossad's new director-general in 1990 after his appointment in 1989 and he suspected his staff would have made it their business to know his timetable. He intended to show them they could not safely predict anything where he was concerned. For his part, he already knew a great deal about their working habits. Much of it did not impress him.

Since he had been appointed by Prime Minister Yitzhak Shamir, and was only the seventh person to hold the post in forty years, Shavit had read as much as he could, trying to find the answer to one question: what had gone so badly wrong that Israel's premier intelligence service had become a laughing stock, mocked in print and derided among the upper echelons of other agencies?

Could Admoni's constant infighting with Mossad's political handlers in the Prime Minister's cabinet, in the Foreign Ministry and in the Kirya, have all combined to bring about his downfall?

They had done so with other directors who had not fitted into their agendas. It was a risk that went with the job. A whisper at one of those poolside parties or a murmur at the end of dinner in a restaurant out in Jericho was enough to send a career on its journey out of the featureless building on King Saul Boulevard.

Had Admoni, being a proud man, decided he would resign before he was pushed? Shavit knew he would probably never know. Admoni was a naturally secretive person who kept his pride under lock and key. Even his family life he shared with few. There were no framed photographs of his wife and children on his desk; there was nothing in his office to show he even had a family. And, of course, there was no visible record of his many undoubted successes – or his failures.

Certainly in his last year on the top floor they were many. He had failed to predict the hijacking of the *Achille Lauro* cruise liner by Arab terrorists, the most spectacular act of maritime piracy the world could recall. It had happened 'in Mossad's own bathtub' – the Mediterranean – a caustic commentator had written. He had failed to anticipate that the hijackers, when they did surrender to Egypt, would be allowed to go free. He had ordered the Israeli Air Force to intercept a Lear jet flying from Libya to Damascus because he believed it was carrying terrorist leaders. Forced to land in Israel, the passengers had turned out to be pilgrims.

Had Admoni, after eight years at the helm, now lost that essential prerequisite for managing Mossad – being a skilled people handler? Was that why morale was so low throughout all the floors?

Or had Admoni simply become tired in the past year of his tenure at the constant sniping? The Israeli media – with the exception of Maxwell's *Ma'ariv* – called him 'Mr Gucci', and wrote that he spent almost as much time in Tel Aviv's male boutiques as he did poring over his case files. Was that why he had left?

Shavit had come to suspect there could be another reason. Nahum Admoni had taken his eye off the most important reason for Mossad's existence – its supreme operational capability – because he had lost the ability to take an overview, to know where to strike and when it was important. Shavit knew from his own experience that Mossad's *katsas*, its analysts and all the support staff could accept most mistakes, but they found it hard to work with a director-general who did not have an overview on everything. The more he had read, Shabtai Shavit had seen that Admoni's overwhelming preoccupation had been getting as many Jews as possible out of the Soviet Union. Anything that could further that was given a priority.

While bringing them to their spiritual homeland was still important, it was not an all-consuming concern for Shavit.

Was that why Admoni's thinking had become at times even flaccid?

There had been no sign of that in October 1985 when Shabtai Shavit had come up from the operations floor to sit with Admoni and go over his plan to assassinate a leading terrorist. Admoni had been sharp, asking the right questions, double-checking every detail.

Shavit had led the *kidon* team to Malta to assassinate Fathi Shkaki, a leader of Islamic Jihad. Lionised by his people and universally hated in Israel for his use of suicide bombers, Shkaki had long been a prime target for Mossad. The opportunity had finally come when Shabtai Shavit discovered Shkaki was stopping over in Malta on the way back from Libya.

The *kidon* team arrived on the island in late October. Shavit had masterminded the assassination from an Israeli freighter off the Maltese coast, directing the *kidon* via a short-wave radio. The two assassins shot Shkaki six times in the head and then escaped on a motorcycle to the island's harbour. Shavit had arranged for a speedboat to be waiting. In minutes the *kidon* were back on the freighter. Hours later Shavit had led them ashore in Haifa. Admoni's debriefing had been swift and thorough, that of a man on top of his job.

Both had recognised that Promis had played a key role in tracking Shkaki: his use of an American Express card to buy his airline ticket, his settlement of a hotel bill with other receipts of purchases he had made in Malta during his stopover – all had been tracked by the software installed on a Mossad mainframe computer.

Shavit, in his years in the Directorate of Operations, knew the importance of being on top of paperwork. It had made him one of the best men working on 'the dark side of the house' in Mossad headquarters. His own covert operations were examples of careful preparations. His mission reports were meticulous, so good that they were often included in the teaching curriculum at Mossad's training school. They had also helped to make Shavit the second man in the history of Mossad to rise from inside to head the service.

Now, the more he read, the more he saw with a sense of shock that Mossad had been allowed to drift since the war in Lebanon. Time and again, once so incisive, Nahum Admoni had not exerted the kind of control that was essential to run a tight ship. And, when he had tried to exert his authority, his instructions had been ignored.

Shavit knew he would never have allowed what had become a huge worldwide embarrassment to Mossad and Israel to ever have surfaced.

In 1989 news reached Mossad that Victor Ostrovsky, then living in Canada, his birthplace, was writing his memoirs about his time with Mossad. Admoni had arranged for the former *katsa* to receive a reminder that he was prohibited from doing so by the secrecy agreement he had signed. Ostrovsky had gone on writing.

Admoni called a staff meeting and said, 'We will get Ostrovsky by other means. We will break him economically.'

When word reached Ostrovsky – he still had friends in Mossad – he said, 'Israel will wage a war of attrition against me.'

He continued to set down details of operational methods and name serving officers, a move that may well have compromised them. He believed he had a duty to be a whistle-blower because he feared Mossad was 'out of control' under Admoni's tenure. There may also have been an element of revenge because Ostrovsky also felt he had been unfairly dismissed by the Mossad chief.

Prime Minister Shamir had consulted Robert Maxwell on what to do. Maxwell had advised that Ostrovsky's claims should be ignored. Shamir did not follow good advice. He launched an action in the New York courts to stop publication. The case failed. A book that might well have passed with little attention became a global bestseller. Maxwell ordered *Ma'ariv* and the *Daily Mirror* to mount a campaign denouncing Ostrovsky.

Shavit was not alone in believing Ostrovsky warranted the ultimate sanction – a *kidon* execution.

The former *katsa* would come to believe that at least one attempt was made on his life – when his house burned down. He would continue to live in fear, moving to the United States and opening an art gallery in Phoenix, Arizona, where he could display his paintings. None, of course, depicted any of the incidents he had been involved with for Mossad.

But now, on the start of his first day as director-general, Shavit believed that the damage Ostrovsky had done to Mossad was still incalculable. He blamed Admoni for allowing that to happen. Shabtai Shavit was determined it would never do so on his watch.

It was still dark when Shabtai Shavit's unmarked government car pulled away from his home in a north Tel Aviv suburb on his first morning as director-general. The Peugeot made its way into the city and down the ramp into Mossad's underground car park. Only the spaces of the night staff were occupied; the day shift would not arrive for another hour. By then Shavit would have done a great deal of work.

He rode the elevator to the top floor and used his swipe card to enter his office suite. Waiting on his assistant's desk was the stack of files he had ordered up from the Registry. Beyond, on his own desk, were the overnight reports from stations around the world. The most urgent had been flagged with red tabs.

From his briefcase Shavit produced the flask of coffee his wife had prepared for him. He poured himself a cup and settled down to read. Barring a crisis, his day would always follow this pattern. Today there was no crisis. For the next hour he could read without interruption before his 7 a.m. staff meeting.

Nineteen eighty-nine had not only been a time of change at the helm of Mossad, but also in its relationship with other intelligence services. There were indications that, with Admoni gone, Britain was ready to return Mossad to 'friendly service status'. That relationship had been withdrawn three years before when Admoni had broken an unwritten agreement with MI5 that any operation Mossad mounted on British soil would have the prior knowledge of the agency. But, in an informal meeting with the director of MI5, Israel's ambassador in London had now been told that matters could return to normal.

Mossad's Washington desk had also been given the reassuring news that the CIA had accepted that, with Jonathan Pollard locked away for life, it was time to draw a line under the matter. Shabtai Shavit was too experienced not to know this was probably no more than a polite gesture. Mossad would go on spying and America's intelligence community would not relax its vigil.

Like those of the CIA and Britain's intelligence services, the directors of those in Europe, Australia and Japan had all sent their congratulations to Shavit on his appointment. But he did not expect any dramatic changes in Mossad's relationship with any of them. Mossad would also remain securely ensconced in its European headquarters in Amsterdam's Schipol Airport. From there eighteen *katsas* monitored Continental Europe as far south as Cadiz in Spain to the northern edge of Russia's Arctic Ocean.

It was from the Schipol office – situated on the second floor of the El Al complex inside the airport – that Shavit could begin to form an overview on what was happening in Moscow and its satellites, now separating from Mother Russia with the speed an ice floe breaks away from its parent berg.

In the brief transition period between Admoni's leaving and Shavit's assuming office, the new director-general had made knowing what was happening in the Soviet Union a priority. There were specific questions he wanted answered. What was the role of the KGB going to be with Iraq and Iran and Syria? These remained the nations that still most threatened Israel. How far would Moscow go in supporting their rogue states' terrorism – despite Gorbachev's promise not to do so?

Mossad analysts had calculated that on present expectations there would be 27 new nations emerging from the collapse of the Soviet Union. Each would have a complex ethnic mixture, many of them rooted in a virulent dislike of Israel. The terrorism promoted by the USSR for almost fifty years would have new sponsors. A political redefining of the map would not itself guarantee security for Israel.

And there were those even more disturbing reports coming from Schipol station that in Moscow the old Communist bureaucrats – the *nomenklatura* – were even now beginning to think of ways they could regain power and influence under a new guise. While they would not be able to call upon the threat the Warsaw Pact had posed, or finance the now defunct Marxist terrorist organisations in Germany, Italy or France, they could cause serious problems in the Balkans. There they could exploit the ever-simmering tensions between Muslims and Serbs and Croats.

The Balkans could once more become dangerously unstable, an instability that could spill over into Albania, Turkey and Greece – reaching the very doorstep of Israel's western flank.

On its eastern border there was the growing threat of Islamic fundamentalism in Iran and the ruthless ambition of Saddam Hussein in Iraq. How far would the bureaucrats in Moscow go in supporting the mullahs and the butcher of Baghdad? How far would they promote internal revolution in Saudi Arabia and Kuwait? Both countries were highly vulnerable to such attacks: their ruling families went out of their way to maintain their privileged positions at the expense of their Bedouin poor.

These were some of the issues that Shabtai Shavit planned to explore with Robert Maxwell.

They were scheduled to meet after the director-general's morning staff briefing.

On that spring morning Robert Maxwell had arrived in Tel Aviv preoccupied and perplexed. Mikhail Gorbachev, without any warning, had sent troops storming into Lithuania. In recent weeks it had become the latest of the Soviet dependencies where nationalism had turned to open rebellion against Moscow. There had been protest marches and riots over food shortages. Gorbachev, driven by hardliners like Vladimir Kryuchkov, had ordered a crackdown. Thirteen people had been shot in the streets and scores injured. The West had been appalled. Roy Greenslade, the new editor of the *Daily Mirror*, published a page-one picture of a Soviet paratrooper attacking a cameraman. The paper's cartoon depicted Stalin looking over Gorbachev's shoulder saying, 'Now that's the way to do it, Mikhail,' and Gorbachev putting his Nobel Peace Prize in a drawer.

Maxwell had been furious at what he saw as unacceptable editorialising. There had been angry words with Greenslade. The editor had stood his ground. Maxwell had backed off. But battle lines were drawn.

Elsewhere he was facing a far more worrying situation. The strategy he had devised to manipulate the falling share prices in his two flagship corporations, Maxwell Communications Corporation (MCC), and the Mirror Group Newspapers (MGN), had run into difficulties. He had recruited to help him the bankers at Goldman Sachs, the men he called 'my trusted friends'. Their role was simple: to go to the clients who trusted them and sell shares in both companies that had been grossly inflated and appeared to be hot sellers. Once they started to buy, the share value would continue to increase. The Goldman brokers began to buy tens of millions of shares in both MCC and MGN.

Maxwell had also turned to more 'trusted friends', bankers in New York, London and in the Bourses of Europe.

To give his plan credibility – to show there was already considerable movement in the shares – Maxwell had himself bought millions of them secretly through his own trusts in the Virgin Islands, Gibraltar and Liechtenstein. He was breaking the cardinal rule of brokering: never deal in your own company shares. In doing so, he was assisted by Goldman Sachs and other brokers for whom the fees on offer were too good to turn down.

But, by the time he arrived in Tel Aviv, the downside of the strategy had begun to worry Maxwell. As long as the shares continued to boost the value of MCC, there was not a problem. But the tens of millions of shares he had purchased through his own trusts were also being used as collateral for bank loans. He needed to buy them back and to replenish the vast sums of money he had secretly withdrawn from those trusts.

The interest he was paying on top of the $300 million a year already being charged for the funding of the purchase of Macmillan and other acquisitions was spiralling. Now he did what his Balkan partners would do. Robert Maxwell began to rob the pension funds of his 24,000 employees in MGN. He had already, without their knowledge, begun to invest their hard-earned money in companies in Israel and France over which he did not have sole control, and therefore could not withdraw the invested money upon his signature.

Robert Maxwell – Cap'n Bob, the Publisher, the Chairman and RM – had now added another sobriquet to his name: The Thief They Trusted.

His business dealings had been carefully crafted to hide the truth that he could now survive only by two means. He could draw down on the considerable private fortune that Dr R had privately buried away. Or he could continue to embezzle and steal from all those who still trusted him: his employees.

On that spring morning in Tel Aviv, he had chosen to continue to plunder their savings to prop up his lifestyle and that of his children. Dr R had seen to it that future generations of Maxwells would have their financial future ensured.

But now, as he prepared for his meeting with Shabtai Shavit, Robert Maxwell began to focus on the question he was certain would be uppermost in the director-general's mind. How could more Jews be brought out of Eastern Europe before they, too, became victims of the anti-Semitism Maxwell had detected was once again on the increase?

Shavit had fully briefed himself on Maxwell's relationship with Mossad: his considerable role in the sale of the doctored Promis software all over the world; his close ties with Senator John Tower; his easy access to the Reagan White House; his contacts with European and South American heads of state; his friendship with Ari Ben-Menashe (one which had been abruptly terminated when the former national security adviser to Prime Minister Shamir had been imprisoned in New York for his part in Irangate); his open door to any banker in the world; his private life, down to the names and sexual peccadilloes of his mistresses. It was all there, and more, including the undoubtedly important role Maxwell had played in bringing Jews out of the Soviet Union and from Morocco and Ethiopia.

There was one part of Maxwell's career that Shavit later told his senior staff had caught his attention. It was Maxwell's close relationships with

Gorbachev and Kryuchkov and, more recently, his contacts with Bulgaria's new leader, Andrei Lukanov. Still more disturbing were his contacts with Mogilevich and Janchev.

Mossad had files on all three men. In each one Maxwell's name appeared. 'On the surface they appeared to be no more than contacts of the kind to be expected when doing business in the turbulent world of Bulgaria and other parts of the Eastern Bloc,' a senior member of the Israeli intelligence community would later suggest.

But Shavit now knew there could be more. His *katsa* in Moscow had filed a report that Maxwell was engaged in a growing number of business dealings with all three criminals.

A member of the 'cabal of Mossad right wingers', Victor Ostrovsky would later recall, claimed Shavit asked Maxwell to explain his association with all three men – and Maxwell had said there was nothing for Mossad to be concerned over, that they were no more than 'the type you meet in that part of the world'.

It was Maxwell once more being economical with the truth. Not only was he deeply implicated in money laundering for Neva, but his relationship with Lukanov in particular was both close and mutually financially profitable. Facing serious money problems in the 'visible' side of his empire, Maxwell may well have hoped to find the money to cover his mounting debts through his secret criminal activities with Lukanov, Janchev and Mogilevich.

Maxwell had moved the conversation on to safer ground; his plans to bring more Jews out of the Eastern Bloc.

Shavit had asked: wouldn't that now depend on *perestroika*? Wouldn't Lithuania affect that?

Maxwell had been insistent. What had happened in Lithuania was only a blip on the sea change *perestroika* was charting.

Shavit had probed further. If Gorbachev could be persuaded to act against Lithuania as he had, wouldn't the hardliners force him to do the same against other Soviet satellites?

'No, absolutely not. I know Mikhail. He is on a set course. Trust me.'

If that was the last thing Shabtai Shavit was prepared to do, he did not show it. Colleagues would later say that was when Mossad's new director-general had begun to wonder why Nahum Admoni had placed such faith in a man who numbered criminals as his associates.

Maxwell left Shavit's office with more concerns. He told Rafi Eitan over lunch that day he believed that he had been 'given the frozen mitt'.

Eitan had tried to make light of matters. He told Maxwell that was Shavit's normal limp handshake. There was something else, Maxwell said, that troubled him. When he had asked Shavit if Mossad had discovered who had killed Amiram Nir, the former assistant deputy director-general of Mossad, the only response had been a headshake. Soon afterwards Shavit had terminated the meeting.

Maxwell told Eitan he was not used to being treated in such a way. Anxious to appease his host, Rafi Eitan listened as Maxwell rumbled on about his 'close friendship with my friend Nir'.

For once he was close to the truth.

In the wake of the Irangate debacle, Nir had become one of the casualties – a scapegoat for the decisions and mistakes of others. He had resigned as Shimon Peres's counterterrorism adviser in March 1987.

By then his circle of friends had shrunk and his marriage was on the rocks. Early in 1988, Nir left Israel to live in London, where he established contact with Maxwell. He set up house in London with a pretty, raven-haired Canadian, Adriana Stanton, a 25-year-old secretary from Toronto, whom Nir had met on his travels.

Maxwell had advised him where to live and approved of Nir's decision to become the European representative of an avocado-growing company, Nucal de Mexico, based in Uruapan in Mexico. The company controlled a third of the country's export market. Maxwell, in what appeared to be one of those capricious moves that had made him endearing to some people, had treated Nir like one of his children.

There may, however, have been a motive for his behaviour. Nir was scheduled to give evidence in Oliver North's trial in the United States. North had promised friends his evidence 'would be explosive. It will be highly embarrassing for the Reagan administration and Israel.' Who can doubt that this would have concerned Maxwell? Nir was a man who had been close to Irangate and the seats of power in Washington and the United States. His testimony could not only damage North but ultimately perhaps John Tower. And that could only be a step away from embroiling Maxwell himself.

Could it have been self-protection that had motivated Maxwell's friendship towards Amiram Nir, the man he had taken to calling 'my young friend'? Had Maxwell been asked by Mossad to keep a watch on Nir? Was he reporting anything he discovered back to Admoni? Was that information being passed on to Washington because shared interests were involved?

'The questions are not fanciful. My husband, I know, felt that he was under surveillance in London,' Judy Nir had told friends.

On 27 November 1988, Nir and Adriana Stanton travelled together to Madrid en route to Mexico under false names. He called himself Patrick Weber. Stanton was listed on the Iberia passenger manifest as Esther Arriya. Why they had chosen aliases when they both travelled on their real passports would never be explained. Another mystery was why they took a flight first to Madrid when there were several scheduled direct ones to Mexico City.

Was Nir trying to impress his lover with operational techniques used by Mossad, or did he genuinely suspect he was being watched? Like so much else of what followed, those questions would remain unanswered.

They arrived in Mexico City on 28 November. Waiting at the airport was a man who would never be identified. The three of them travelled on to Uruapan, arriving there in the afternoon. Nir then chartered a T 210 Cessna from the small Aerotaxis de Uruapan.

Once more Nir behaved with strange inconsistency. He rented the plane in the name of Patrick Weber, using a credit card in that name to pay the charges, and arranged for a pilot to fly them to the Nucal processing plant in two days' time. In the local hotel where he and Stanton shared a room, Nir registered under his own name. The man from Mexico who had accompanied them disappeared as mysteriously as he had appeared.

On 30 November, Nir and Stanton turned up at the small Uruapan airport, this time with another man. On the passenger manifest he was described as Pedro Espionoza Huntado. Whom he worked for would remain another mystery. Another would be why, when they came to register their names on the manifest, Nir and Stanton had used their real identities. If the pilot noticed the discrepancy between the names and those Nir had given to charter the Cessna, it passed without comment.

The plane took off in good flying conditions. On board were the pilot, the co-pilot and their three passengers. One hundred miles into the flight, the Cessna suddenly developed engine trouble and moments later crashed, killing Nir and the pilot. Stanton was seriously injured, the co-pilot and Huntado less so.

By the time the first rescuer, Pedro Cruchet, arrived on the scene, Huntado had disappeared – another of those figures never to be seen again.

How Cruchet came to be there is yet another mystery. He claimed to work for Nucal – but the company's plant was a considerable distance away. He could not explain why he had been so close to the crash site. Asked by police to prove his identity, he pleaded he had lost his ID at a bullfight. It turned out Cruchet was an Argentinian living in Mexico illegally. By the time that had been established, he too had vanished.

At the crash site, Cruchet had recovered and identified Nir's body and had accompanied Stanton to hospital. He was with her when a local reporter called seeking details.

Joel Bainerman, the publisher of an Israeli intelligence digest, would claim: 'A young woman indicated Cruchet was present. When she went to get him, another woman appeared at the door and told the journalist that Cruchet wasn't there and that she had never heard of him. The second woman reiterated that Stanton's presence on the Cessna was purely a coincidence and that she had no connection with the "Israeli". She refused to identify herself other than to say that she was in Mexico as a tourist from Argentina.'

Stanton added to the mystery. She told investigators, according to an Israeli journalist, Ran Edelist, in 1997: 'While injured and shocked, she saw Amiram Nir a few metres away, waving and comforting her in a normal voice. "Everything will be okay. Help is on the way!" She was twice assured in the days following that Nir was alive.'

Nir's body was flown back to Israel for burial. Over one thousand mourners attended his funeral and, in his eulogy, Defence Minister Yitzhak Rabin spoke of Nir's 'mission to as-yet-unrevealed destinations on secret assignments and of secrets he kept locked in his heart'.

Had Amiram Nir been murdered to make sure he never revealed those secrets? Was it even Nir's body in the coffin? Or had he been killed before the crash? And if so by whom? In Tel Aviv and Washington a blanket of silence continues to greet all such questions.

As for Stanton, it had also appeared that she too believed her life was in danger. According to Edelist, his intelligence contacts told him 'she became a recluse, underwent plastic surgery and changed her appearance'.

Had the CIA murdered Nir? Support for that theory had come from a US Navy commander who had accompanied Nir to Teheran on the mission to free the Beirut hostages a year earlier. The commander's story revolved round his claim that Nir had met with George Bush, then Vice-President, on 29 July 1986, at the King David Hotel in Jerusalem, to brief him about the ongoing sale of US arms via Israel to Iran.

According to the writer Joel Bainerman, 'Nir was secretly taping the entire conversation. And this provided evidence linking Bush to the arms-for-hostages deal.'

Bainerman would describe a visit the commander had made to CIA headquarters in Langley, where he met Oliver North some months before the colonel faced trial. The naval officer asked North, 'What happened to Nir? North told him Nir was killed because he threatened to go public with the recording of the Jerusalem meeting.'

Journalists who tried to question North on the matter have been brushed aside. Aides who worked with Bush during that period maintained a similar attitude: anything the former president has to say about Irangate has already been said.

Later, the home of Nir's widow, Judy, was burgled. Her dead husband's recordings and documents were the only items stolen. Police said the break-in was 'highly professional'. The stolen materials have never been recovered and who the thieves were remains yet another mystery.

*

Amiram Nir's death continued to obsess Robert Maxwell. He raised it over dinner with Ognian Doinov in Vienna while they were discussing the flow of money from the Neva projects into the accounts Doinov was handling. He raised it with Andrei Lukanov several times in the brief period Lukanov had held office as Bulgaria's Prime Minister. He spoke about it to John Tower when they met in Washington and New York. But no one could provide a satisfactory answer to his question: who had killed Amiram Nir? The one growing certainty in Maxwell's mind was that the personable young Israeli had not died accidentally.

How much Maxwell knew and what role he played in the final hours of Nir's life are still unresolved. Given their friendship, it is reasonable to assume that Nir would have told Maxwell that he would be away from London – even if he did not say where he was going. There is also the real probability that the Promis software Maxwell had sold by now all over the world had been mobilised to track Nir. Certainly he had left a paper trail of hotel receipts and credit-card payments that was perfect for Promis to do its work.

To the growing ledger of Robert Maxwell's criminal investigations could now be added the possibility he was an accessory to murder.

The fear that Nir had been murdered had fuelled Maxwell's own paranoia. He became more secretive, spending hours alone in the penthouse listening to the tapes from his secret microphones on the floors below. He switched travel plans at the last moment. He called meetings with as little notice as possible.

Betty began to log his erratic behaviour: how he refused to turn up for a reception hosted by Prince Charles; another at Downing Street; a third at the Lord Mayor's dinner at the Mansion House. Soon it was becoming a regular feature of his life, accepting an invitation and then refusing to show. She noticed he would leave 'piles of mail unanswered and cheques casually lying around'.

A psychiatrist would have recognised the flowering of a clinically defined personality: the obsessive. Maxwell always had a rigid, commandeering, hard-driven personality, one in which his inner insecurities were well hidden and his perverse sexuality – an endless succession of swift, meaningless and pointless seductions – was a matter of pride. But now his behaviour was becoming expiatory, an attempt to use the mental magic, which had always been part of him, to make his deeper distress vanish. Apart from cancelling important engagements, ignoring letters and leaving quite substantial sums of money lying around – all at variance with his usual demand for perfection – there were other hints that mentally all was not well. He had started to leave his desk, walk a few paces, then return to make sure he had locked its drawers. Small things enraged him: his razor being moved in the bathroom from where he last left it; his bed not turned down exactly the way it was folded back the night before. If a table setting was not to his liking, he would tip crockery and glassware onto the floor. A psychiatrist would have identified all this as part of the *folie de doute* that was also beginning to take up space in Maxwell's mind.

At their simplest level these behaviour patterns reflected the increasing inner tensions and maladapted responses to stress. It widened his already unsatisfactory relationship with other people. Yet what appeared to be irrational and at times even frightening to others had become logical for him. For Maxwell the past was not the past. That compounded the strain on him, made him more unpredictable and therefore more frightening. The release he sought was to bury himself in the loins of a woman, preferably having consumed sufficient vintage champagne to expunge any guilt he may still have felt at once more betraying Betty.

But still she clung to the hope that her marriage could yet be salvaged. She copied into her journal the words from Jeremiah, 'I remember thee for the affection of my youth, the love of thine espousals. When thou went after me in the wilderness, in a land that was not sown.'

For her it had long been barren soil. But, proud and dignified, she made sure her tears would never as much as dampen it. They were for her alone.

In the spring of 1990, Maxwell took John Tower with him to Sofia. It was part holiday, part an opportunity to show Tower how Pergamon-Brassey could fit into the Neva project. If the Senator was shocked at the extent of Maxwell's financial ties to the country's leading criminals, there is no record he ever said so. For him it was an opportunity to indulge his appetite for good wine and the sensual young women the country's secret service maintained for Maxwell and his friends.

In those balmy spring days, it must have seemed to Tower that everybody wanted Maxwell to launder their money from a scam. A crime syndicate made up of the country's Olympic wrestling team had taken over a chain of hotels and turned them into profitable bordellos. They asked Maxwell to arrange to launder their profits through one of his companies. Another gang had a thriving business in luxury cars stolen from the West and shipped across the Black Sea to Russia. They too wanted their money laundered. In return for what was now his standard 15 per cent commission, Maxwell was always ready to oblige.

His real profits were coming from his partnership with Lukanov, Janchev and Mogilevich. But in the end he was their glorified bagman, the conduit through which their profits could travel westwards into all those banks over which the sun never set. While he could take his percentage, and did, the rest of the money he dare not touch. He knew enough by now of the way his partners operated to realise what would be his fate if he did.

The knowledge that his financial salvation was so close, yet just out of his reach, must have added to the stress coming from all sides. His own newspaper, *Moscow News*, had launched an angry attack on him accusing him of using *perestroika* to further this own interests. Elsewhere he would have issued writs. But Moscow was not London and the paper's editor was a close friend of Gorbachev. Maxwell endured his public humiliation and severed his links with the paper.

At home his repayments to his bankers had reached a staggering £415 million a year.

Once more he turned to Goldman Sachs for help. The bankers suggested he should sell shares in MCC. He said that would send 'a wrong signal to the market'. A better idea would be for the bank once more to buy the shares secretly – showing there was active trading in them. Then he would again buy them back just as secretly. The bank would make its commission on the buy-and-sell. It was another win–win situation for Goldman Sachs.

When Betty learned from her son Kevin what had happened, she would tell her daughter, Isabel, 'Kevin knows a great deal: that they sold very close to the wind. But what they did was not at the time actually illegal, although they positively ruined your father in the knowledge of what they were doing.'

Soon the bank had bought 50 million MCC shares. But Maxwell was showing no sign of buying them back. To do so he would need to borrow from other banks. He was once more caught in a vicious circle.

To break it Maxwell decided to move deeper into the mire. Lie would now beget lie. He announced he had sold two of his companies for £120 million. MCC shares began to move upwards, buoyed by this fictitious claim.

Maxwell and Senator John Tower returned to Bulgaria in December 1990, after Lukanov had resigned and Zhelyo Zhelev was appointed Prime Minister.

Maxwell had decided to establish good relations quickly with the incoming government while privately maintaining his links with Lukanov, his Neva point man.

The real purpose of his visit was to install Tower as member of the board of Maxwell's Central and Eastern European Partnership.

In Sofia, Maxwell and Tower discussed establishing a joint venture between Bulgaria and the US telecommunications giants, AT&T and Sprint. Maxwell would use Pergamon-Brassey to handle that.

Another planned project was a Bulgarian holding company with a capital of £30 million. It would purchase American and British technical equipment to upgrade Bulgaria's police and to be used in the country's prisons. The equipment would be purchased through Pergamon-Brassey.

FOURTEEN

In Vienna, the ever-inventive Doinov was working long hours putting together a plan to buy a stake in Press Group 168 Hours, a Bulgarian group of newspapers. In the meantime, Maxwell told the current rulers in Sofia he wanted them to apply for an IMF loan while he went about reducing their debts.

Tower had agreed to use his influence with President George Bush to obtain the loan, arguing that Bulgaria was an emerging democracy and should be given priority over grants to Western nations. The loan requirement was pitched at $132.4 million. Maxwell had calculated he would be able to divert some $86 million for his own use. But once more he had misjudged. The loan would take too long to process for it to be of any help in his increasingly dire financial straits.

Then came another enticing possibility. The purchase of the Macmillan publishing conglomerate had given Maxwell a foothold in New York publishing – and made him eager to expand his footprint. Back from Bulgaria, he received the news that the city's ailing *Daily News* was up for sale. For two years its owners, the Chicago Tribune Group, had suffered crippling losses. The tabloid's sales had plummeted to an all-time low. The newspaper unions had contributed to the decline by staging a strike, now in its fifth month. Maxwell announced he was ready to rescue the paper. The strikers said they wanted him as its saviour. It was a union made in hell.

In the words of one Tribune Group director, 'All our Christmases came at once.' The owners offered to pay Maxwell $60 million to take over the paper and promise to honour all pensions and pay redundancy settlements.

Maxwell said at the time he also thought Christmas had come early. He was being offered a substantial sum to give him what he would gladly have paid for – power and influence in a city he had come to like. As owner of the *Daily News*, he would have the kind of power that would reach beyond the city's mayor and the state's governor all the way to President George Bush.

Maxwell's mood swings lifted; the depressing doubts of recent weeks gave way to an almost maniacal euphoria. Just as he had once seen himself as the uncrowned king of Bulgaria, so he now cast for himself a similar role in New York. His name would be emblazoned in lights high over Broadway. The *Lady Ghislaine* would be moored at one of the East River piers. He would receive in audience the great and the good on the sun deck. The razzmatazz that had bedazzled Sofia would compare to nothing he intended to show New Yorkers.

The bankers in London would ask themselves if he had really calculated what it was all going to cost: that $60 million from the Tribune Group would be swallowed up in just getting the *Daily News* staggering off its knees. It would need much more to make it once more a viable threat to the *Post*. There would have to be a television and radio advertising campaign. There was going to be the cost of the redundancy packages. And already some key columnists were indicating they would jump ship if Cap'n Bob was on the bridge. Was it all going to end in tears?

The boardrooms of Rothschild's, Goldman Sachs and all the other banks into which Maxwell was already heavily in debt watched.

But in New York there were no such doubts. The city's all-powerful Jewish lobby took him to their collective heart. He was the Great Survivor, the boy from that pimple on the rump of Europe who had fought the Nazis, became a war hero and a man who never forgot his Jewish roots. He was given the singular honour of being the marshal in the Salute to Israel parade. Marching down Fifth Avenue past Trump Tower, St Patrick's Cathedral and Rockefeller Plaza, it would be understandable if Robert Maxwell felt at that moment he was indeed *ein Mensch* who would own a prime piece of Manhattan.

In London the bankers pondered: when was he going to redeem the 13 per cent of the MCC shares that Goldman Sachs still held – and which Maxwell was using as collateral for other bank loans? What had he done with the money? What would happen if New York's own financial scrutinisers found out he was committing a serious breach of regulations? In the language of that city, 'Is this guy a goddam fraud?'

But for the moment Maxwell was safe. The crew of the *Lady Ghislaine* could whisper stories to journalists from the other city's newspapers that Cap'n Bob was a reincarnation of Captain Queeg below decks. But the champagne and caviar still flowed for those he honoured with an invitation to party on the yacht.

Then in the midst of all the revelry, disaster struck – literally falling out of a clear blue sky. An Embraer 120 RT Turbo, cruising over the New Brunswick countryside, suddenly plummeted nose down into the ground. All 22 passengers and crew were killed.

The only death that mattered to Robert Maxwell was that of Senator John Goodwin Tower.

Once more his fears surfaced. First Amiram Nir and now John Tower had both died in plane crashes. It made no difference that the accident report indicated a design fault in the propeller unit of Tower's plane. Maxwell was certain there could be more behind the crash. Both men had been involved with him in a dark world. They both knew a great deal from all those years toiling in that secret place. Though they would of course have sworn never to reveal its workings, Nir had threatened to do so as a witness at the trial of Oliver North. And Tower was known for being garrulous. Give him enough champagne and he was more than ready to nod and wink and hint.

If both men had been killed, what about his own future? He knew so many secrets about the workings of Mossad, about Israel's secret deals. He knew so much. And so that incipient paranoia, never far nowadays from the surface, once more began to emerge in Robert Maxwell.

In London his staff saw the strange behaviour patterns they had noticed before become more pronounced. He spoke darkly of his 'enemies' and 'conspiracies' against him. It seemed to them that his mental and perceptual organisation had made him the powerful figure he was, but now he was increasingly having difficulty in distinguishing between fantasy and reality. Everything was 'black and white', 'good and bad', remembered one of the women who had briefly been his mistress.

'He was more manic in all he did,' she said. 'He seemed to have endless energy and drive. But behind this there was that fear "they" were out to get him. The last time we had dinner he was full of it. He said two of his friends had died in mysterious circumstances. But when I wanted to talk about it to try and make him feel more relaxed, the way you do when a person has had a loss, he just clammed up.'

Betty Maxwell no longer waited around for her husband to visit Headington Hill Hall. The servants had almost forgotten what it was like to panic when news reached them of his imminent arrival.

For Betty the loneliness had taken its toll but she still desperately hoped that all 'Bob's spiralling around the world' would finally end. In retirement he would recognise her worth. So she dared to hope. In the meantime she would pursue her own interests – rebuilding her family's chateau in France.

Refurbishing the chateau would cost £1 million. Betty did not have that kind of money. She had asked Maxwell to help, just as her family had helped him at the start of their marriage. He reluctantly agreed to arrange for a French bank to lend her the money. But she would be responsible for its repayment and all interest charges.

As her seventieth birthday approached, her children contacted their father and pleaded with him to attend a birthday party for her at London's Dorchester Hotel. He finally arrived late, kissed Betty, made a speech and left. Betty almost managed to hold back her tears.

Another blow was to her dream that, when he retired, they could live out their lives in the French countryside. He had said his only interest in living in France was if he could own the country. When she had looked at him in disbelief, he had told her it was about time she understood English humour.

The following day he summoned her to his office in Maxwell House. With secretaries watching and listening at a distance, he began one of the tirades she had come to know well: 'You are raving mad and I want nothing to do with you.'

She had tried to reason with him, telling him how much she loved him and had no desire to offend or hurt him. Her efforts were futile.

He wanted legal separation forthwith and one that would be made public with an advertisement in *The Times* of London. Everyone should know that their marriage was over. 'It has been a sham for a long time,' he said loudly.

She had 24 hours to present him with a list of her 'terms and conditions'.

'With that he left the office, took the elevator to the roof and boarded his helicopter,' Betty would recall.

Desperate to know what to do, she turned to her son Kevin and together they drew up a list of settlement terms. They included repayment of all her debts, money to finish the construction of her chateau, the purchase of a pied-à-terre in London, costs for removing her belongings from the family home, a lump sum to maintain her lifestyle and the right to eight days on the *Lady Ghislaine*.

The following day she went back to his office with the list. He took it. 'You can have eight days on the yacht,' he shouted. That was all he would agree to. Once more he left her sitting, fighting back the tears.

Shortly after 3 a.m. on 7 January 1991 – hours after the start of the Desert Storm conflict – seven Scuds hit Tel Aviv and Haifa, destroying 1,587 buildings and injuring 47 civilians.

Maxwell had immediately telephoned Prime Minister Yitzhak Shamir. He was unable to reach him. Next he called Shabtai Shavit. Whenever he had called Nahum Admoni, he had used a private number. When he now dialled it, he found himself talking to a Mossad duty officer. Recovering, Maxwell asked to be connected to Shavit. He was told to wait. After a while Shavit came on the line. He asked Maxwell what he wanted. Maxwell said, 'It is the duty of every Jew to offer his services at a time like this.'

Shavit replied that, if there was a need to, he would certainly call upon Maxwell. Maxwell said he could talk to Gorbachev; Russia still had influence with Saddam. Shavit said he would get back to him. He never did. A former Mossad officer who had monitored the call recalled Shavit's irritation and his decision to have the private number Maxwell had used discontinued.

The Gulf War had rekindled a fear never far from the surface in Israel. Saddam had awakened the virulent anti-Semitism in Eastern Europe and the questions had been asked with deepening anxiety: what more could be done to bring out the Jews in those countries? People had remembered how Maxwell, barely a year before, had gone to East Berlin to seek a reassurance from the head of the German Democratic Republic, Erich Honecker. As it rushed towards it first taste of real democracy, Maxwell had sat in the old man's office and said that, 'on behalf of the State of Israel and the civilised world', he was seeking an assurance that no Jew would be harmed.

Bemused and no doubt confused by what was happening elsewhere in the Soviet Union, of which East Germany had become such a powerful pillar, the 77-year-old Honecker had given such a guarantee.

In return Maxwell had presented him with a two-volume set of the *Encyclopaedia of the German Democratic Republic*. It had been published by Pergamon Press. Within weeks the books, priced at £110 a set, would become the stuff of history, its pages of ridiculous claims as outdated as the Berlin Wall would become.

Nevertheless, tens of thousands of Jews had been allowed to leave East Germany without molestation. Some of the credit for that did belong to Maxwell.

It was that knowledge that had finally caused Shabtai Shavit to decide to fly to London and meet Maxwell shortly after his return from New York. Again, like Admoni, Shavit had come to the penthouse early in the morning.

The upshot was that Maxwell agreed to contact Vladimir Kryuchkov to see if visas for Soviet Jews could be speeded up.

But events had taken on a momentum of their own. In Moscow Kryuchkov had started to say publicly that 'the party has had enough of democratisation'.

When Maxwell called, Kryuchkov suggested that instead of coming to Moscow, they could meet on the *Lady Ghislaine*. Sensing that there was something significant in the offing, Maxwell pressed for a date. Kryuchkov would merely say it would be soon.

Shabtai Shavit had arrived back in Tel Aviv to find disturbing news awaiting him. The Washington desk was reporting that, on his visit to the White House, Boris Yeltsin had told President Bush there might be a move to remove Mikhail Gorbachev.

The warning, Yeltsin had added, had come from the mayor of Moscow, Gavril Popov. Bush had immediately telephoned Gorbachev.

He had laughed at the President's concern. Moscow was the world's greatest rumour mill, he said. *Perestroika* was in safe hands.

For Shabtai Shavit there were key questions. Was Gorbachev caught up in his own publicity? Fêted in the United States and across Europe, he could continue to believe he was similarly lionised by his own people. Others had clung to a similar belief only to find to their cost the brutal reality. There was now not a leader of the Soviet satellites who had survived. Some, like Nicolae Ceauşescu had died terrible deaths.

And had Kryuchkov put off his meeting with Maxwell because he now feared Maxwell had become too close to Gorbachev? Certainly Maxwell had been hoping to use the Soviet leader to help him broker a deal to handle the trillions of dollars of foreign debts the Soviet Union had accrued. Maxwell would take his usual 15 per cent commission. If there was a coup in the offing, would Kryuchkov even hint of it to Maxwell? But then why had he suggested he should meet Maxwell on his yacht? Or was that merely to test Maxwell's reaction?

In that summer of 1991, Shabtai Shavit had no answers – not yet.

FIFTEEN

By the early summer of 1991, Robert Maxwell could look with understandable satisfaction from the picture window in his penthouse towards the financial institutions in the tower blocks huddled around the Bank of England. Returning from New York, he had faced down his most pressing creditors. One by one he had summoned them to Maxwell House as if *they* were the supplicants, not he, seeking their continued support.

He had decided which bank chairmen he would see first, which financial director would come next. Some had been kept waiting in the lobby, others had been shown directly up to the penthouse. One had been ushered into his presence by a secretary who had been commanded, 'Remember, no calls unless it is Mikhail Gorbachev,' – or some other head of state. It was an old trick of Maxwell's but it never failed to impress. Sometimes he would vary the instruction, telling a secretary to interrupt him after a few minutes with the words, 'I have the Prime Minister on the line. He says it's important.' Maxwell would leave the room, returning to say something like, 'It's always good to be able to give advice in a matter of national importance.' He never explained what that was. His visitor was too impressed to ask. Such performances helped Maxwell get his way.

Even the vintage of the champagne on offer depended on his visitor's standing. The bankers of Westminster, Lloyds and Goldman Sachs were served only Krug or Kristal; lesser directors received Pol Roger or Mumms. All were fed caviar. Then, while they supped and swallowed, he had sprayed his reassurances. They came down to six words: there is nothing to worry about.

Robert Maxwell said it in a dozen and more ways, pointing at typed balance sheets, cash-flow projections, trading figures. He had a paper for everything. They were the props for his confident reassurances.

And they believed.

He had focused their minds on his Maxwell Communications Corporation. Its profits were indeed continuing to rise and, on paper, could be expected to maintain their upward curve. However, to keep that momentum, he had continually moved funds in and out of his 400 other companies sheltering beneath the MCC umbrella, whose spokes included publishing, printing, share speculation and currency trading. No one from the City had looked closely at those companies and the role they played in keeping MCC afloat.

With the speed of a huckster performing multiple three-card tricks, Maxwell had moved funds in and out of those companies to boost MCC's overall standing in the market. It was supreme financial sleight-of-hand that required a cool head and steady nerves. Maxwell had both. To the well-shod bankers who walked towards him over the deep-pile carpet in his penthouse suite, he exuded confidence, the vulpine smile never wavering, his dark brooding eyes always filled with certainty. *Trust me. There is nothing to worry about.*

And they continued to do so. Men who had been trained to look long and hard at any set of figures, who knew the hard questions to ask, who could judge what size a loan should be with the same skill they wielded a golf club – those same men accepted at face value what Maxwell said, what he showed them.

Knowing their mindset, Maxwell had gambled they would not begin to unravel his manipulation of Bishopsgate Investment Management (BIM). Headington Hill Investments and the now renamed Mirror Group. Since he had acquired the *Daily News*, he had brought all his newspapers under a new name, the Maxwell Group.

Looking back on those summer-day meetings in the penthouse, one of those bankers from Goldman Sachs would recall there was 'something of the ringmaster about Robert. He would crack a joke as he invited us to read the paperwork. He'd been up all right checking the figures so they had better be right – otherwise he'd have to fire himself. It was Robert at his most beguiling.'

Such roustabout behaviour helped to hide from his visitors something they still had no idea about: Robert Maxwell's alliance with the criminal godfathers of Eastern Europe.

John P O'Neill, the FBI's chief agent in New York, would say, 'It is one of the great puzzles of this time that all those smart guys in London didn't just dig a little deeper and at least begin to wonder how Maxwell was continuing to operate. They just seemed to take him at his word. My experience is when someone keeps saying "trust me", you had better believe you shouldn't.'

Certainly, none of Maxwell's visitors being ushered in and out of his presence had the slightest inkling of the extent of his operations deep within the Eastern Bloc. He had been so busy developing his ties to Lukanov and Janchev that there had been no time to attend one of the Wimbledon Week parties. Night after night, while only the security guards patrolled the ninth floor, he had sat in his office and spoken to his partners-in-crime in Sofia. Even his preoccupation with listening to the tapes of his staff took second place. Nothing mattered to Robert Maxwell except shoring up his visible empire and building up his secret one in Bulgaria.

If the bankers in the City of London had been content to sip and nibble and take his assurances at face value, it was a different story with MI5 and MI6, for whom Robert Maxwell had become of more immediate interest by July 1991. His activities in Eastern Europe and his continuing contacts with the KGB chief, Vladimir Kryuchkov, at a time of deepening political and economic unrest throughout the Soviet Union, had made both services begin to look closely at Maxwell.

For intelligence officer Colin Wallace it was 'a done deal that, once Five and Six saw how deep Maxwell was into the Soviet Bloc and just who he was dealing with, they were going to put him under closer surveillance. That decision would probably have come from the top, probably from McColl. He may well have raised it with Downing Street. Putting someone like Maxwell on active surveillance would mean having his phones tapped and that sort of thing. That isn't something decided by someone in the middle ranks. That has to come from the top.'

Sir Colin McColl was chief of the Secret Intelligence Service, MI6. The Prime Minister was Margaret Thatcher.

McColl may well have been alerted about Maxwell's links to the Bulgarian underworld by David Spedding, who was then head of a joint MI5/MI6 section responsible for tracking terrorists and spies who used the Balkans as their staging ground. Or it may have been Prime Minister Margaret Thatcher, who had been warned by Mikhail Gorbachev of Robert Maxwell's close and continuing contacts with the KGB chief Vladimir Kryuchkov. In Ari Ben-Menashe's view, Maxwell may 'just have become too obvious about his links to Mossad: given he had turned down MI6, that would not have played well with the likes of Spedding and McColl.'

Meantime, Mossad's *sayan* in Maxwell House was still in place on the ninth floor and filing his reports to the resident *katsa* in the Israeli embassy. The first hint of this intelligence activity would surface only much later, and from a surprising source, Betty Maxwell.

'I was advised by a former CIA agent, Arnold Kramish, to drop everything, if I valued my life, in not pursuing the actions of the British intelligence services,' she would recall. 'My conversation with Arnold made me feel like he had lifted a corner of my carpet and the sewers of

London had started gushing in my drawing room. I felt completely nauseated and, I must add, frightened.'

The one certainty is that the fears Betty had expressed would only have fuelled the concerns Maxwell already felt about the deaths of Cyrus Hashemi, Amiram Nir and John Tower. But, on those long summer nights in 1991, he was driven by that other obsession – to make good on his boast six years before that he would by now be worth $10 billion.

Believing the dream could still come true, he had centred his financial manipulation on his Bishopsgate Investment Management (BIM). Through it he alone channelled the increasingly huge sums he stole from the pension funds of his 24,000 employees. At the same time he appointed himself chairman of BIM so that he could use it as a major money-laundering conduit for washing his activities in Bulgaria.

Having appeased the power brokers from the City of London, he now set about reassuring his staff. These past months they had all read the reports in rival newspapers, led by the Murdoch Group, that unsettled everyone in Maxwell House and employees in his other companies.

To reassure his staff, Maxwell produced a video. For fifteen minutes he sat in an outside chair and spoke directly to the camera. He told them their future was safe. He ended with a clarion call. They should go about their work secure their money was being well managed by him. He would do nothing to compromise that. 'Trust me' had been his concluding words.

In newsrooms through Maxwell House, even hard-bitten journalists had clapped.

Blissfully unaware of what was happening on the ninth floor and in the penthouse above, Maxwell's staff went about their work. Their support and cooperation was part of the intricate web Maxwell was weaving in the months of high summer.

In that summer of 1991 both Britain and the United States had slipped into recession and Japan's stock market had begun its long slow descent into a final crash. Europe's unemployment had started to climb again and in some countries 10 per cent of the labour force were jobless.

Maxwell's newspapers, like others, were filled with gloomy predictions that the world was heading back to the hard times of the previous decade.

So far Western investment in *perestroika* had failed to produce the promised results. While Gorbachev had bravely spoken of a 'new Europe becoming our common home', the reality was that while there was no longer an ideological barrier – epitomised by the prosperity on one side of the now dismantled Berlin Wall and the poverty in the East – the truth was that what passed for capitalism in the new Soviet Union was just poverty with another label.

Russia itself, which had held together the Eastern Bloc, was filled with indecision and factions. Moscow had looked to the West for economic support to create a welfare state along the lines of Britain; to offer the resources to cope with the breakdown in law and order; to fill the shortfall of food; to provide the money that the West, especially the United States, now found it impossible to provide its own recession continued to deepen. Now, as the summer progressed, there was the threat from Baltic separatists and of guerrilla war in the Caucasus to add to Moscow's fears.

Eduard Shevardnadze, Russia's Foreign Minister, had resigned. Disarmament talks slowed as Gorbachev steered closer to the Russian right while he desperately hoped to persuade the West to bail out his boat. He had looked everywhere, even offering Japan back the Kurile Islands, which had become an important Soviet military base since 1845. The asking price was $24 billion of economic aid. The Japanese had declined. Their coffers were almost empty.

Through the summer, the cut and thrust of what to do had continued both inside Moscow and elsewhere. The Harvard economist Grigori Yavlinsky proposed $30 billion a year of economic aid from the West in return for huge changes in the Soviet economy. The terms were close to what might be imposed on a defeated nation after a gruelling war. They included the transformation of the Soviet Union into a free-trade economy, the privatisation of land, housing, the retail trade, industry – and above all, massive cuts in the defence budget. It would have turned the Soviet Union on its collective head. While the debate heated up over what became known in Moscow as 'the Great Bargain – But For Who?', the seeds of deepening unrest had taken root in the Russian capital.

Increasingly lawlessness was laid at the door of *perestroika*. Opposition to it became a rallying call for the army, the veterans and a growing number of ordinary people who complained that the shortages were a betrayal of all they had fought for in the Great War. But they could not offer any alternative solution. No one wanted a return to the years of the poorly run economy of the Brezhnev era or the tyranny of Stalin's time. Angry and frustrated, they looked for a voice to coalesce all their concerns.

In Vladimir Kryuchkov they found one. He synthesised all the anger and bitterness in one repeated statement: 'The implementation of fundamental reforms in this land are not as we envisioned but as dreamed by others across the ocean. They once were our enemies. But are they our friends now?'

But Kryuchkov was doing more than give Moscow television a sound bite. He had started to meet in secret with others of a like mind. They, like him, still had power.

On his visits to Moscow, Maxwell learned of these meetings over the long dinners he shared with the KGB chief in his Lubyanka citadel.

Maxwell did not tell his 'good friend' Gorbachev of what was being discussed. But he did inform Mossad.

What he described confirmed what they were hearing through the trapdoor in the Promis software. Between Maxwell and Promis, Mossad continued to be one of the best-informed intelligence services in what was happening behind the scenes in Moscow. Israel's great fear was that Russia's formidable nuclear arsenal would find its way into the hands of rogue states like Iraq and Iran.

In one of his trips to Israel, Maxwell had been told by Prime Minister Yitzhak Shamir that his one abiding nightmare was of 'a bunch of terrorists with their hands on enough fissionable material to devastate Tel Aviv or any of our other cities'.

Soviet Scud missiles had been exported for hard currency to several Middle East countries. Soviet technicians had helped Algeria build a nuclear reactor. Russia had a large stockpile of biological weapons, including a super-plague germ that could kill millions of people.

Maxwell's help as a superspy, therefore, proved to be invaluable. His connections through the scientific publications he produced gave him ready access to Soviet scientists. He was able to judge which of them were likely to help rogue states and what their motives could be: there were those who would do it purely for cash, others for ideological reasons. He had passed on to Israel details of Russian nuclear facilities and their lax security. It was all valuable intelligence and once more showed the worth of Maxwell to Israel.

It was against this background that Robert Maxwell continued to manipulate the financial structure of his own empire.

Like many other corporations, MCC had begun to plunge so that by July 1991, its share value was almost 60 per cent below the halcyon days of two years before. Now the bankers who had been kept at bay with vintage champagne and caviar came to their senses. They asked for further securities on the loans they had advanced – almost $4 billion between some 40 banks. A year before, Maxwell had set their loans against his majority shareholding in MCC. But now, with its shares falling by the day, banks required more security.

Maxwell tried an old ploy. He secretly bought millions more MCC shares in the hope that the trading would not only halt the near freefall, but would boost the share value. The MCC freefall gathered a little speed.

He tried another familiar trick. While all around him corporations began to show signs of unease, he said he was not worried about the deepening depression. With that dismissive little wave of his hand, he would say he was inured against any blips on his financial radar: he had all those billions tucked away in trusts in Liechtenstein. It momentarily stayed his bankers. But, when they asked if they could see proof that those billions were there and available to him on demand, Maxwell shied away. No one was going to see his trusts, he thundered.

MCC's downward curve became a little steeper.

With the panache of a rogue trader on the grand scale, he now began to gamble on the international currency markets. He would invest on one day up to $10 million on the movement of the dollar, the yen, the Swiss franc. Other traders were agog. His brokers at Goldman Sachs were properly grateful for their handsome commission – whether he won or lost in an increasingly volatile market.

He may well have been planning another foray when there was a call on his private line. It was Vladimir Kryuchkov calling from the Lubyanka in Moscow.

Maxwell's tape of the call vanished in what Betty Maxwell believed was part of the 'terrifying activities' of MI5 and MI6. Her claim cannot be entirely dismissed. A former employee of the intelligence service has stated (to the authors) he was aware of two telephone calls made by Kryuchkov around this time. The then KGB chief has separately confirmed he did make a 'number of calls to Maxwell in the late summer of '91' but he could not 'recall what they were about, except they probably concerned some business he wanted my help with.'

The facts not in dispute are these. Kryuchkov had wanted to know if the *Lady Ghislaine* would be cruising in the Mediterranean in late July. Maxwell had said it would. Kryuchkov had then said he would like to join the boat.

What follows then is a matter of dispute. Victor Ostrovsky would later claim Kryuchkov wanted to use the yacht for a top-secret meeting with a senior member of Mossad to discuss what, in the end, would turn out to be an attempted coup to overthrow Gorbachev.

The facts do not support such high drama. But the truth is equally gripping.

The call from Kryuchkov was automatically reported by Maxwell to Tel Aviv.

Maxwell's call, according to Victor Ostrovsky, had been 'poorly timed'. Mossad was monitoring a peace initiative between Israel and the PLO. Every tenuous step had been threatened by attacks by extremist Islamic groups determined to wreck the process by provoking Israel into an over-reaction. In Germany, Mossad was embroiled in an operation gone badly wrong: Hamburg police had discovered a shipment of arms about to be smuggled on to an Israeli shop. Shavit had sent a fixer to smooth over the Germans. The man he had chosen for the delicate task was Efraim Halevy, the current director-general of Mossad. With 30 years of experience with the agency, he was Mossad's go-between with foreign intelligence services. Halevy had his hands full: the shipment had been arranged by the BND, Germany's secret intelligence agency, without the knowledge of the country's government or its Ministry of Defence. The arms cargo broke the federal law that forbade Germany to send weapons to a war zone. It had taken all Halevy's skill to settle matters. The arms had come from Bulgaria, from a manufacturer in which Lukanov and Mogilevich had a financial interest – namely backhanders.

In that call to Tel Aviv, Maxwell, an associate of Mogilevich, was now trying to broker a deal involving the State of Israel.

For the first time it would raise serious doubts in the minds of those Maxwell had called about his own judgment, and his ability to see beyond his own urgent requirements. It had become clear in Tel Aviv that Maxwell saw a meeting with Kryuchkov as another opportunity for him to try to solve his own financial predicament. Despite all his considerable pressure on Mikhail Gorbachev, he had not persuaded the Russian President to turn over the Soviet foreign debt for Maxwell to discount at a profit to himself. In Tel Aviv, there was no doubt that the meeting with Kryuchkov would include some attempt by Maxwell to find a new way for him to become Russia's fund manager.

Ari Ben-Menashe assessed the situation thus: 'Money. That was the bottom line with Robert at this time. He needed it to stay alive. He couldn't get it from his underworld sources. They were not in the bail-bond business. Gorbachev had enough savvy not to put Russia's debt management into Maxwell's hands. He would certainly have known about his connections to Lukanov, Janchev and Mogilevich. Gorby had good intelligence. So, whatever else Kryuchkov had in mind for his boat trip, Maxwell would have been on the lookout for a money opening.'

On that Saturday and Sunday, 20–21 July, everyone in Maxwell House knew Cap'n Bob was in the penthouse. Normally he would emerge from his elevator and rumble into the newsrooms of his tabloids, the *Daily Mirror*, the *Sunday Mirror* and the *Sunday People*. He would seize proofs and demand changes. But as edition time came and passed, there was no sign of him. Not once had he phoned down and summoned an editor to discuss a story he claimed to have acquired from his 'trusted sources'.

Roy Greenslade would say, 'My publisher liked to play reporter, though his tips always proved false.' During his tenure as editor, Greenslade fought a running battle to keep Maxwell's hot 'tips' out of his newspaper. Other editors in the group were less successful: they were bullied and dragooned into running nonsensical stories that made their papers an endless source of amusement for the satirical magazine, *Private Eye*.

But that weekend there was no sign of Maxwell stirring from the penthouse. Newspaper staff began to ask each other nervously what was happening up there. It couldn't be a secretary who was fulfilling his sexual needs for so long. Besides, the morose-faced Kevin was with him. He had even slept over on the Saturday, the first time anybody could remember. It surely couldn't be another crisis.

It was. One that could affect the future of every employee in the building. On the previous Friday night, Robert Maxwell had been told that his newly formed Robert Maxwell Group (RMG), was on the point of being declared insolvent. It needed a cash injection of £50 million to secure its immediate future – with many times that figure to follow at regular intervals.

Since he had been given the news, Maxwell and his son, like two pawnbrokers shuffling debtor slips around in their thousands, had worked the phones from dawn to midnight: they called everybody they had ever borrowed money from. By Monday there was clear war between RMG and bankruptcy. On Tuesday morning, 23 July, exhausted but triumphant, Maxwell had summoned his lawyers. With a flourish worthy of a royal proclamation he had signed a document that began, 'Since 1990 nothing has happened to materially change the condition of this company.'

It was less than the full truth but his lawyers did not know that. The future of RMG depended on a substantial cash flow. But Maxwell and Kevin had raised enough money over the weekend for the group to survive the immediate future. To live for a new day meant there was always going to be a tomorrow.

Later that day, Maxwell flew to Palma, Majorca. He told Kevin and his senior staff he was 'going to recharge my batteries'.

Carina Hall, the cabin stewardess of the Gulfstream, would remember: 'He flopped in his seat, waving away food and drink, dozing and occasionally muttering something under his breath.'

Waiting at Palma Airport was the *Lady Ghislaine*'s captain, Gus Rankin. Deeply suntanned and in immaculate whites, at six-foot-two he was almost as tall as Maxwell, but his two-hundred-pound frame was all muscle. He had skippered the yacht since May. At their first meeting, Maxwell had told him, 'Whatever decisions anyone tells you in the family, I am the one who makes the decisions.'

Maxwell began to relax once he was on board the yacht. Showered and changed into a yachtsman's shirt and shorts, he went to the bridge and ordered Rankin to set a course around the island.

They had dinner alone in the stateroom. The meal was frequently interrupted by radio phone calls and incoming faxes. Each time, Maxwell would go to his cabin and deal with them. Rankin was tempted to ask if these interruptions did not spoil the purpose of the trip, to give Maxwell a chance to relax. But he did not know him well enough for such familiarity.

The meal over, Maxwell spent time on deck, dressed in the kaftan he usually slept in, watching the other passing ships. There were no more calls or faxes. No one disturbed his reverie. Maxwell was left alone with his thoughts.

In the early afternoon Kevin called from his ninth-floor office in Maxwell House. The Investment Management Regulatory Organisation (IMRO) was once more asking questions. Its investigators had dogged Maxwell's footsteps for the past year. Each time, with the help of lawyers and accountants, he had shaken them off. Kevin was reassuring: the IMRO people had left his office once more seemingly satisfied.

The rest of the day passed uneventfully with Maxwell sunning himself and consuming substantial meals, washed down from his private supply of wine kept in a locked cupboard in the galley. Some of the bottles were worth £300 each; his finest port retailed at £150 a bottle.

That night, having checked the course and weather, he left the bridge and retired early. He was not to be disturbed unless Kevin called. Or, he added, if the caller said he was phoning from Israel.

In Tel Aviv, Mossad's analysts had continued to assess the increasingly dangerous situation in Moscow. Valentin Pavlov, the Prime Minister, had made a bizarre speech to the Supreme Soviet, suggesting Gorbachev's health was failing and that many of his presidential powers should be transferred to him.

Mossad's *katsa* in the Foreign Ministry had confirmed another development. Vladimir Kryuchkov had been holding secret meetings in the Lubyanka late at night with Defence Minister Yazov and the chairman of the Supreme Soviet, Yuri Lukyanov. The first hint of a developing conspiracy was in the air. Could this lead to a coup? Was Kryuchkov's proposed visit to Maxwell on his yacht somehow connected to this?

No one in Israel knew. But anything was possible.

For Rafi Eitan to have Maxwell and the chief of the KGB sailing around the Mediterranean on a summer's day discussing the coup was 'about as crazy as it gets'.

Ostrovsky would later insist that is what did happen. 'Mossad had helped arrange a meeting between the Mossad liaison and Kryuchkov on Maxwell's yacht. Mossad's support for the plot to oust Gorbachev was discussed. Mossad promised to bring about, through its political connections, an early recognition of the new regime, as well as other logistical assistance for the coup. In exchange, it requested that all Soviet Jews be released, or rather expelled, which would create a massive exodus of people that would be too large to be absorbed by other countries and would therefore go to Israel.'

The former Mossad officer would continue to believe he had written the truth. But the facts do not support his claims. Not one Mossad officer then – or subsequently – was prepared to offer any credence that the State of Israel would be involved in what Meir Amit would call 'this nonsensical madcap caper Victor Ostrovsky created'.

Certainly Ostrovsky does not answer important questions. For Israel to become involved in supporting any coup would have a dramatic effect on the future of the still considerable population of Soviet Jews. They could well have found themselves caught up in a modern pogrom. History had shown how easy it was for that to happen.

Equally important was the question of Israel's relationship with the United States. There had long been a clear understanding between the intelligence communities of both countries that, where a common interest was involved, there should be shared information. So far that had worked well. But to have Israel, through Mossad, providing 'logistical assistance' would wreck that, perhaps for ever. There was also the question of what form that 'logistical assistance' would take. Ostrovsky has steadfastly refused to elaborate, except to say 'I have told the truth on this.'

But there is no evidence to support him.

The scenario of a 'Mossad liaison' – presumably a sufficiently high-ranking Israeli intelligence officer to satisfy Kryuchkov – has to be set against two other issues.

One, in general terms, goes some way to supporting Ostrovsky's claim that contact between Mossad and the KGB chief was not entirely outlandish.

Meir Amit, the former director-general of Mossad, has recalled that such meetings were not unusual. When his own top spy in Syria, Eli Cohen – a man playing a not dissimilar role to Maxwell for Mossad – had been caught and was facing execution, Amit had travelled to meet his KGB counterpart at the time to try to save Cohen's life. He had failed to do so. Since then the CIA, for example, had regularly met Eastern Bloc intelligence services and, on one occasion, its then director, William Casey, met Chinese intelligence officers in the Mandarin Hotel in Hong Kong to discuss collaboration over a common threat: the drug runners of the Golden Triangle.

But the second matter that militates against Ostrovsky's claim for such a meeting is the 'deniability factor'. This is when an intelligence service, or its political masters, swear not to have any knowledge of an operation. But to try to do that when the director of the KGB was involved would simply not be believed. It was one thing for Israel to say that Rafi Eitan had been acting alone when he had been running Jonathan Pollard – a claim never seriously believed by the CIA. It would be quite another to try to pass off any meeting between Kryuchkov and a senior serving Mossad officer as a similar case.

There was no meeting on the *Lady Ghislaine*. But for Robert Maxwell his proposal to host one would change for ever the perception Shabtai Shavit and other senior Mossad officers had about him. They could tolerate his private excesses: the way he liked to be treated as a potentate whenever he came to Israel and excused all airport formalities and welcomed by an official greeter from the Foreign Office; the way he liked to have a motorcycle escort; the way he expected his favourite prostitute to be on hand when he checked into his hotel suite. This could all be tolerated. Maxwell, after all, was a valuable asset, still providing information others could not obtain for Mossad.

But becoming involved in a political coup in such a volatile situation as the one in Russia was far removed from organising a takeover of some company. Maxwell should have realised he was out of his depth. Such an error of judgment made Mossad's perception of him change. They began to see him as a loose cannon. A man desperate enough to do anything to get his hands on the vast sums of money he needed to survive.

Men like Shabtai Shavit and other senior officers in Mossad began to see that in Robert Maxwell they were dealing with an increasingly unpredictable and perhaps even unbalanced individual. As well as being an asset, he was becoming a threat.

On 26 July, Maxwell's mellowing mood on board the *Lady Ghislaine* was broken. Shortly before breakfast he received an agitated telephone call from Kevin. The visit of the IMRO investigators had not gone unnoticed by the other directors of MCC. They were demanding answers to the rumours that once more had begun to surface in the City of London that MCC was again in financial straits. Some of its directors were threatening to place their resignations on Kevin's desk. He told Maxwell they wanted a face-to-face meeting with him.

Maxwell's anger could be heard throughout the *Lady Ghislaine*. 'Get Brookes to handle them,' he finally ordered.

Basil Brookes was the acting finance director of MCC, recruited from Coopers & Lybrand. A slow-spoken man whose honesty was patent, he had been seen by Maxwell as the ideal front man to deal with troublesome situations. 'Tell Brookes to calm them,' he ordered one more time.

Hours later Kevin was back on the phone. Brookes had tendered his resignation.

Maxwell's incandescent shouting could again be heard throughout the yacht.

'Tell him I will hold a board meeting when I get back. Stall him. Keep him on board.' Maxwell's orders came at machine-gun rapidity.

Kevin was about to hang up when Maxwell remembered he had a problem closer to hand. That morning Rankin had mentioned that the crew's wages were overdue. Maxwell told Kevin to fly down with $20,000 next day. He should bring Ian Maxwell with him. It was time for a family conference.

On Sunday, 28 July, Kevin and Ian arrived in Majorca in the Gulfstream and were brought out to the *Lady Ghislaine*, moored off Palma. They had been looking forward to a day of sunbathing and using the yacht's two jet skis. Instead they found themselves taken down below to the stateroom to brief their father on the latest developments.

Kevin, knowing Maxwell's mercurial nature, gave the good news first. In the past 24 hours, he had reduced MCC's current loans to £175 million.

Maxwell grunted his appreciation. Ian added that there was, however, a further repayment on the loan of £30 million due in a week's time, on 4 August. Ian asked where was the money coming from.

His father had turned to Kevin. Well?

Kevin's response wiped away the last vestige of good humour from Maxwell's face. Over 60 banks had turned down servicing the loan. Lehman Brothers had gone further. Currently they had advanced over £80 million against the security of a portfolio of pension shares. They would not provide further loans until those shares were replaced with other securities not connected to MCC. Kevin – on the principle of 'in for a penny, in for a pound' – had told Maxwell he was certain Lehman's suspected the shares pledged with them no longer belonged to his father. 'But so far they have nothing to confirm that,' he added.

The news galvanised Maxwell. He said he would phone a 'trusted friend' in the National Westminster Bank and arrange a £150 million loan.

Kevin's task would be to organise the required collateral. There would be 20 million shares from the *Mirror* pension fund and 2 million shares from another Maxwell company, Scitex, which would come from its pension funds.

Maxwell was certain he had once more found a way out of his problems. He would call the NatWest banker first thing in the morning.

On Monday, 29 July, Maxwell was about to go up on the sun deck when Kevin called with alarming news. Two pension fund managers had been in his office demanding the actual portfolios of shares Maxwell had borrowed as collateral for part of the £80 million loan with Lehman Brothers. The managers now wanted sight of the actual share certificates.

With massive understatement, Kevin said, 'It's a tricky one, Dad.'

Maxwell this time did not explode with anger. Instead he calmly told Kevin to tell the fund managers that 'using shares as collateral is a normal function in the business world'.

Kevin's audible sigh of relief carried all the way from London.

Two hours later Kevin was back on the phone. The fund managers had accepted what Maxwell said. But Kevin was still nervous.

'Supposing they call Lehman's?' Kevin would recall asking.

His father was reassuring. That would not be a problem. He did not tell Kevin that he had structured the deal with Lehman Brothers to be another of his private arrangements with one of his 'trusted friends'.

His other 'trusted friend', Leal Bennet at National Westminster Bank, had come through for him. For the banker it had not proved to be a simple deal. Maxwell's request had exceeded the bank's ceiling of £32 million and the loan had to be decided by the most senior NatWest corporate bankers.

Leal Bennet had pressed Maxwell's case by describing him as a 'reputable and long-term client of the bank'.

But Leal Bennet's colleagues had also heard the rumours that the Maxwell empire was once more in financial difficulties. Finally Maxwell's 'trusted friend' won the day.

But Leal Bennet would have to 'monitor and record the Maxwell account every day in a special black logbook'.

The NatWest corporate bankers had themselves been confused by the number of differing accounts Maxwell had with them. Within an hour of the loan being granted, Kevin had supplied Leal Bennet with the 22 million pension shares his father had earmarked for collateral and promised that NatWest would also see £130 million lodged right away by his father.

The next morning Leal Bennet learned that Maxwell had not lodged the money. He had been betrayed.

'It was horrific,' he would later remark.

On 6 August, the anniversary of the destruction of Hiroshima by an atomic bomb, Maxwell returned to London to find himself in a mushroom cloud of his own troubles. Kevin told him that three senior executives of the Bank of Nova Scotia had been camped out in his office demanding repayment of $32 million – due on this day, and which Maxwell had promised would be repaid in the equivalent sterling. The bankers had left only moments before the Aerospatiale had clattered down onto the roof of Maxwell House – their demands assuaged by Kevin's promise that their repayment was en route from New York from the sale of 7 million shares in Scitex. What he had not told the bankers was that the shares had already been pledged to other banks also to raise money. It had been a close call for Kevin: if his visitors had asked to see the share certificates, the game would have been up, as they had been handed over as security to raise money elsewhere.

That evening Maxwell was confronted in his penthouse by a quorum of MCC directors, led by Basil Brookes. They sat opposite Maxwell, who was flanked by Ian and Kevin. The mood was tense and soon became angry. Brookes, normally a quiet and reserved man, shouted at Maxwell.

'This cannot go on, Robert. This has to stop. All the money has disappeared. We need a schedule of repayments.'

Maxwell said nothing. He turned to Kevin and nodded for him to respond.

Kevin was at his placatory best. He assured his listeners that MCC would be in funds to the value of £80 million from the sale of the Scitex shares.

Jean-Pierre Anselmini, one of the directors, made a note.

Kevin had not mentioned the guarantee he had given to the Nova Scotia bankers earlier in the day. Instead he announced, 'We will no longer use MCC as the Maxwell family bank.'

Anselmini made a further note. Suddenly Robert Maxwell broke his brooding silence. He jumped to his feet and towered over the hapless Anselmini.

'Stop that at once!' roared Maxwell, pointing at Anselmini's pen poised over his small notebook. 'How dare you take notes! I want these conspiratorial discussions to stop! Do you hear? Stop!'

No one spoke in the stunned silence. Maxwell's steely face was still working.

Anselmini slowly capped his pen and put it away with his notebook in a jacket pocket.

Maxwell sat down breathing deeply to calm himself. Brookes would say it had been a 'truly shocking display'.

After the visitors had left, Maxwell told Ian and Kevin the directors were part of a conspiracy. Now it was father and sons against the world. Kevin and Ian said nothing.

That night John Pole, still in charge of security at Maxwell House, was instructed by its owner to bug Anselmini's home phone. Pole decided to ignore the order.

Over the next few days Maxwell fought to stop the directors resigning from MCC. To lose them would be the clearest signal yet that MCC was heading for the financial rocks. For a week, using a mixture of bluster, promises and cajoling, he managed to keep most of them on board.

Then, on 15 August, the *Financial Times*, the barometer by which the financial world set its course, published the news that Goldman Sachs were sitting on a staggering 143 million MCC shares as collateral for loans. It was a near-mortal blow, revealing the massive fissure in the Maxwell empire. In hours, what had been speculation now became a distinct probability that Maxwell had overextended himself on every front. The suspicion that he had paid over $1 billion too much for the Macmillan publishing conglomerate, dismissed at the time by Maxwell's small army of publicists, now seemed all too true. The other persistent rumour – that, in paying a massive $750 million for the Official Airline Guide, he had not correctly judged its market worth – appeared also too true.

At minimum he had been foolhardy, driven by his own out-of-control ambition to outrival Rupert Murdoch, to outstrip anybody who crossed his path. In the City of London boardrooms, directors of the 40 bankers Maxwell still owed money to recalled that damning judgment of the Department of Trade inspectors 20 years earlier about Maxwell: 'He is a man of great energy, drive and imagination but unfortunately an apparent fixation as to his own abilities causes him to ignore the view of others if these are not compatible.'

To those words many a worried banker added, 'reckless to the point of criminality,'; 'a man we cannot do business with'.

But those fearsome judgments would not go beyond the boardrooms. The bankers knew that for them to precipitate a crash of the Maxwell empire would leave them with little chance to recover even the interest on their loans – now running at $415 million annually – and would see the loans approaching the size of the national debt of some countries, leading them into a financial abyss from which they could never be recovered.

But, in the hours following the news about the shares Goldman Sachs held, Maxwell made it clear he was not going to let in the auditors, something that the banks were insisting upon.

Incredibly it stopped the bankers in their collective tracks. They called each other from Rothschild's, from Lehman Brothers, Lloyds and National Westminster and, of course, from Goldman Sachs, and concluded that Maxwell did not want their own accountants and high-priced book-keepers running their calculators over his accounts for one good reason. He still had the money to pay them back. It did not matter where that financial hoard was – in Liechtenstein, in the Cayman Islands, it did not matter to them where. It had to be somewhere. The collective conclusion was they should sit tight. Hard-nosed financiers who had endured his bluster and bullying tactics, who had first believed he had lost his financial acumen, were now once more prepared to sit back and pray to whoever bankers pray to that it would come right in the end.

In Israel bankers had also read the *Financial Times*. They were not so sanguine as their London colleagues. Maxwell had borrowed heavily from them. Payback dates had come and gone. Each time, he had cajoled them into granting him another extension.

Just as in London, where bankers had their connections to MI5 and MI6, so those in Tel Aviv could reach Shabtai Shavit and other senior officers in Mossad.

They made clear their concerns. They were sufficiently real for Ari Ben-Menashe to claim later that was when the first 'informal discussions' took place about the increasing threat Robert Maxwell was beginning to pose to Mossad. 'He just knew so much,' Ben-Menashe would say. 'If he went down, a lot of people in high places might find themselves dropping with him.'

But in Russia events were under way that would focus Mossad's attention on another link Maxwell had, one in which he had tried to involve the State of Israel.

On 18 August 1991, at 4.50 p.m., Mikhail Gorbachev was relaxing with his family in their dacha when an aide answered a knock on the door. Outside was Yuri Plekhanov, a KGB officer, accompanied by internal security troops.

Gorbachev sensed danger and rushed to the special phones linking him to the Kremlin. The lines had been cut.

His Chief of Staff, Valery Boldin, entered the room and informed him he had been sent by the State Committee of Emergency. The coup Gorbachev had been warned about was under way.

Boldin outlined the plotters' demands. Gorbachev was to sign a document authorising the state of emergency. If he refused, he would be removed and replaced by his Vice-President, Gennady Yanayev.

'I will commit suicide before I sign anything like that,' Gorbachev replied.

Other KGB officers entered Gorbachev's quarters and removed the briefcase containing nuclear codes. Gorbachev and his family were placed under house arrest.

Led by Kryuchkov, plotters in Moscow ordered thousands of troops into the capital. A crucial weakness in their plot was the KGB chief's failure to arrest opposition leaders led by Boris Yeltsin, who were holed up in the parliament building when the coup began.

Next day Gennady Yanayev said he had taken over the country because Gorbachev 'had serious health problems'.

Kryuchkov announced all demonstrations were banned and the media was under control of the Committee.

Unlike Gorbachev, Yeltsin had access to the rest of the world through the parliament's telephone system. He began phoning world leaders, beginning with President George Bush.

He even phoned Gennady Yanayev and told him, 'We will never accept you and your gang of bandits.'

Yeltsin's fellow parliamentarians sent word they needed people to come onto the streets to oppose the coup. Muscovites responded in their thousands. Boris Yeltsin emerged from the parliament and spoke to over 30,000 supporters. They cheered him.

By 21 August, with the coup in its third day, the plotters went into hiding. Yeltsin issued arrest warrants for them.

Boris Pugo committed suicide. Kryuchkov and the others were hand-cuffed and marched off to prison cells to await trial. Yeltsin sent troops to Gorbachev's dacha to ensure his safe return to Moscow.

Maxwell had closely followed the coup. When he was certain of the outcome, he launched a ferocious attack on the plotters.

But there was an ominous development shortly afterwards. Boris Yeltsin told the Russian Parliament that he had ordered all KGB files to be seized. Even as he spoke, Soviet military intelligence officers were ransacking the Lubyanka for evidence to show the full extent of the plot.

Robert Maxwell could only have remembered all those times he had dined in the Lubyanka with Kryuchkov and had spoken frankly. There had also been those telephone calls asking for him to arrange a meeting between the former KGB chief and what Victor Ostrovsky had described as a 'Mossad liaison'. Maxwell did not need to be told that, if that was to surface, it could be extremely dangerous for him.

In Tel Aviv, Shabtai Shavit and that group of senior right-wing Mossad officers were also coming to a similar conclusion, with the additional concern that it could also be dangerous for Israel if those files contained evidence linking Maxwell to the failed coup.

On 25 August, Maxwell's bedside phone woke him. It was Prime Minister Andrei Lukanov calling from Sofia. His voice was pleading. Vladimir Kryuchkov had managed to smuggle out a message from his Moscow prison cell. He wanted Maxwell to call Gorbachev and have the former KGB chief set free.

Maxwell had promised he would. He never did. Vladimir Kryuchkov had joined the growing list of people who had outlived their usefulness to Robert Maxwell.

But the fear that the KGB files might implicate him continued to grow, feeding his paranoia, increasing his sleeplessness and his inability to eat regular meals. His sense of being persecuted increased; his mood swings became more pronounced. In purely psychological terms he was a dangerous person; his were often no longer the ordinary responses to stress. With his racing thoughts and his even more voluble speech, some staff members felt he was genuinely going mad and that he had no contact with reality. Those times would give way to sudden silences, when he would be morose. Perhaps, if he had been properly questioned by a psychiatrist, Maxwell might have admitted he was the victim of his own faults. But he of course would never have sought expert help.

In the last week of August 1991, he called Shabtai Shavit. Whatever Robert Maxwell said, the call ended, and according to Victor Ostrovsky, left a sense of alarm on the top floor of Mossad headquarters.

Maxwell had raised the question of his financial position but insisted it was no more than a short-term cash-flow problem.

The Mossad chief knew better. He had seen the reports from the London desk.

The *sayan* on the ninth floor in Maxwell House had indicated there was a possibility of serious irregularities in MCC. It was the first hint that Maxwell had been stealing his staff pension funds to prop up his companies. More importantly he had also made another grave error of judgment. To try to raise money, Maxwell had wanted to sell off one of his Tel Aviv-based companies. Its chief executive was the son of Prime Minister Yitzhak Shamir. Maxwell had been told by the younger Shamir that this was not the time to go to the market; further, to sell would also throw skilled people out of work when unemployment was once more a growing problem in Israel. The response had provoked a serious row, ending when Maxwell slammed down the phone. Shamir reported all this to his father. The Prime Minister had called Shavit. The incident was added to all the other pieces of information the Mossad chief was assembling.

Now, when Robert Maxwell had asked for Mossad to help, he had been told it was outside its remit.

It may well have been true, as Ostrovsky would suggest, that Robert Maxwell had finally crossed the line with Mossad.

Beset on all sides by mounting problems in London – the bankers had once more found sufficient courage to begin to ask again for their money – Maxwell decided to fly to New York. It was one way also to put some distance between himself and the investigative reporters – the ones he had dismissed as 'the dogs in the street' – snapping at his heels, taking bites out of his reputation with their barbed comments. For all the wrong reasons his photograph was dominating the financial pages.

In New York he found a new problem. Inexplicably he had not registered his name as owner of the *Daily News*. His attempts to put right the matter were a time-consuming process.

Installed in the finest suite the Helmsley Palace Hotel could provide, Maxwell was able to keep at bay the phone calls from London, where Kevin was working like a galley oarsman to keep the Maxwell man-of-war from stopping dead in the water. By any standards it was a heroic effort, though Maxwell almost never paid tribute to his sons' efforts.

For his part Maxwell, like a phantom in an opera of his own creation, would emerge into some Manhattan party, sweep through the guests, consuming glass after glass of champagne as he went, then disappear again.

Sometimes he would appear with Henry Kissinger, former US Secretary of State, now the political doyen of the fashionable rich and the Manhattan party circuit. When Maxwell, always obsessive about his health, realised he had left London without going for his regular health check-up, Kissinger had recommended he should go to his own physician, Dr Paul Gilbert, at the city's Mount Sinai Hospital. Though he could find nothing wrong physically, Gilbert, perhaps sensing Maxwell's anxieties, decided to have Maxwell's X-rays reviewed by one of New York's most respected radiologists.

A bespectacled and studious-looking man in his late fifties, Dr Alfred Rosenbaum was to remember, 'I was amazed at the sheer size of the man,' when Maxwell arrived with Kissinger in his reception area.

Rosenbaum led Maxwell into his consulting room, its walls covered with framed replicas of the radiologist's degrees and qualifications. He invited Maxwell to sit in the large chair opposite his own desk. He saw that his patient could barely squeeze into the seat. Like all good practitioners, Rosenbaum set about settling his patient, making small talk, drawing out Maxwell.

'Not that he needed much of that. He was quite boisterous and charismatic. He was a people person, someone used to being the centre of everything.'

Smiling and nodding, the radiologist began to ask his medical questions. Had anything prompted Maxwell to have his check-up in New York instead of waiting to return to London?

'I've been spitting up some blood,' replied Maxwell.

'I told him his chest X-ray showed some evidence of old surgery. But there was nothing significant. I said he was fine. Absolutely no sign he was likely to have a heart attack,' Rosenbaum would recall.

Maxwell nodded.

The radiologist had one further question. Was Maxwell taking any prescribed medication?

Rosenbaum remembered that Maxwell had shaken his head. Then, for emphasis, he had said, 'No. Nothing.'

He had struggled to his feet and lumbered out of the room. Watching him leave with Henry Kissinger, Rosenbaum had thought they looked like two old friends. Only later would Kissinger's wife dispel that notion. 'They were never friends. They just had some business dealings. That's all.'

She was not the only one wishing to put distance where Robert Maxwell was concerned.

Goldman Sachs had served notice on him that they were calling in two loans valued at $60 million. He had until 11 October to settle. If he failed to do so by that date they would sell off the MCC shares they still held. Both the bank and Maxwell knew this was a virtual death notice.

Hovering on the horizon was another even larger debt, the $755 million repayment due on other loans taken by MCC. The payback fell due shortly after Goldman Sachs's deadline.

In one of those rare moments when Maxwell confided in Betty, he told her, 'They are out to get me. They are after me.'

Not for a moment did he suspect that 'they' now included the *kidon* of Mossad.

In Tel Aviv, in the safe house in Pinsker Street, they had by now held their third meeting.

Part III
THE NIGHT OF THE *KIDON*

SIXTEEN

By early October 1991, the four *kidon* – Zvi, Efraim, Uri and Nahum – had completed their preparations.

The video clips of Maxwell's life, the breakdown of his financial holdings, his mounting debts, his mistresses, his connections to Vladimir Kryuchkov and the criminal underworld of Eastern Europe – all this and more had been studied and evaluated. A list of key people currently important in his life had been prepared. These included his sons Kevin and Ian, his lawyers in London and New York, his personal staff in the penthouse, his pilots and cabin crew for his two aircraft and helicopter. Though Maxwell never visited any of them in their homes, their private addresses were given, along with a brief description of their dwellings and their surroundings: Kevin's and Ian's homes in central London were described as being in 'easily accessible streets'. A lawyer was listed as residing in an apartment block. Others had semi-detached houses and bungalows in London's suburbia.

Maxwell's movements had been plotted: their dates, times and destinations. Mostly they had been short trips to the offices of his bankers and lawyers. He had not once visited Headington Hill Hall in the past month. He had dined in several West End restaurants. Each time he had been driven there in his car, which had brought him back to Maxwell House. Then he had flown to New York.

The New York *katsa* had taken over surveillance, logging Maxwell's visits to the *Daily News*, his partygoing, his visit to Dr Rosenbaum. Of more interest to the *kidon* were the number of telephone calls Maxwell had made to Tel Aviv from his suite in the Helmsley Palace Hotel. Transcripts had been brought to the safe house by a Mossad *bodel*.

They showed an increasing desperation by Robert Maxwell to raise money to cover his immediate debts. Some of those calls had been to bankers like senior directors at the Discount Bank of Israel, and at other financial institutions. He had met with no success. Other calls had been to fellow directors of his Israeli companies in which he had said he wished to withdraw his financial stakes. He had been told that it would either require his presence in Israel at a full board meeting or simply not be possible under the terms of his investments.

The most demanding of all his calls had been made to senior officers at Mossad: to the head of the Financial Office, the director of operations and aides to Shabtai Shavit. In those calls Maxwell had reminded them all of his considerable service to Mossad. In effect he had said it was time for reciprocation, for those officers to use their own considerable influence to persuade the banks in Israel and, if possible, in London and New York to meet his requests.

Once more he had been told, politely but firmly, that it was not possible for Mossad to do that. The words of Maxwell's responses on the transcripts, his forceful arguments giving way to anger and near threat, must have been all the more evident in the actual recorded calls.

His replies had led the *kidon* to review his medical record. When Maxwell had told Dr Rosenbaum that he was not taking any medication, that was another lie. For years he had been taking two powerful sleep-inducing drugs, Halcion and Xanax. Maxwell sometimes swallowed them together. Both had side effects.

For a man of Maxwell's age, close to his 68th birthday, and his lifestyle of overeating, incessant travel and irregular sleep patterns, swallowing both drugs together was a dangerous cocktail.

Halcion had come on to the market in 1982, sold as safer than the barbiturates Valium and Librium. By 1990, Maxwell was among over 7 million Americans who believed the claims made for Halcion. The former Secretary of State James Baker had said he found the pill helped him sleep on long flights. It was for the same reason that Maxwell had started taking the drug.

In the United States, where pharmaceutical companies wield huge political power and finance most of the drug-related research, little attention was given to the side effects of Halcion. The Food and Drug Administration ignored reports that the drug caused amnesia and agitation as well as other disturbing reactions.

Nick Davies would say that he had noticed Maxwell had developed a tendency to 'suddenly fall asleep during a meeting. He would lie back in his seat, his head reclined, his mouth wide open, and snore.'

Davies had described one of the side effects from the drug.

Maxwell continued to take Halcion even after questions started to be raised in Britain about side effects such as those Davies had witnessed. One researcher, Dr Anthony Kales, wrote that Halcion is 'a dangerous drug that acts on the brain's limbic system. Because it remains in the body for only a few hours, it can have a boomerang effect, unleashing the very anxiety it was meant to tame.' Another researcher concluded: 'In most cases where Halcion has been linked to violent behaviour, the person took more than was deemed to be safe, had been drinking alcohol, or had been on the drug for some time.'

Further, it could produce 'amnesia, hallucinations, paranoia and verbal and physical aggression'.

The clinical symptoms fitted Robert Maxwell's own behaviour at times.

The second tablet he took regularly was Xanax, which is extracted from a group of drugs known as benzodiazepines. These act as receptors in the brain, releasing a chemical called GABA (gamma amino butyric acid). Xanax was also intended to promote sleep and reduce anxiety.

It differed from Halcion in one important respect. One of its side effects was that a person could suddenly fall asleep. Like Halcion, Xanax had a high-dependency side effect. Its manufacturer cautioned that it was for 'short-term use and withdrawal should be gradual'.

Combining the two drugs, as Maxwell now did, could produce the side effects of memory impairment, abnormal behaviour and thinking, confusion, anxiety and depression.

For the *kidon*, those would be useful symptoms to consider when they came to perform Ostrovsky's 'what seemed impossible' – committing the perfect murder. For Ari Ben-Menashe, what was going on in the safe house was 'pretty standard'.

However, both intelligence officers, once thought as high fliers within the Israeli intelligence community, had by 1991 endured a sustained attack by former colleagues and would continue to do so. It largely centred on what had gone on in the Pinsker Street safe house.

David Kimche called Ostrovsky 'the man who broke all the rules'. Rafi Eitan would denounce Ben-Menashe in similar terms. Meir Amit would suggest that both men deserved to be 'locked up and the key thrown away'.

Ben-Menashe would insist: 'In all there were three murder plans. The first plan was one to sabotage Maxwell's helicopter. It would be easy to make that look like an accident. But that would have involved taking the lives of innocent others, something to be avoided in any assassination. The second plan, again considered and discarded, was to arrange for the elevator from his penthouse to suffer a cable failure and crash to the ground when he was inside. Again that had been discounted because of the risk others would be with him and die as well. The third was to stage an accident at sea where others need not be involved.'

Ostrovsky had identified that 'making it look impossible was part of the *kidon* magic'. Like highly skilled illusionists, Zvi, Efraim, Uri and Nahum had gone about their plans. They knew in that first week of October that all their preparations could come to nothing. The small group of plotters in the upper ranks of Mossad could still change their minds. Then everything that had been prepared over the past month would be destroyed. It had happened before when a target had died of natural causes. It could also be that, despite all the precautions taken, word could leak to the political masters of the plotters. Robert Maxwell was still a popular figure in Israel: ordinary people had not forgotten how much he had done for the country. If even a hint became public that there was a plot afoot to murder him, it could be sufficient to bring down the government.

But for the four men in that safe house, none of that was a consideration. They had prepared their plan. Now they must wait for the order to implement it. It was always so in their business.

When the call came, Betty could not quite believe what Maxwell was proposing: he was reminding her she had an invitation to be a guest at two important functions in the New York social calendar. One was a dinner in honour of the King and Queen of Spain. The other was a second dinner Maxwell would host at the United Nations to launch his newspaper, *The European*.

'Where am I supposed to stay?' Betty recalled asking. Maxwell said she could stay in one of the guest bedrooms in his suite at the Helmsley Palace. She had packed her favourite evening gowns and caught the next flight to New York.

The invitation to the royal dinner had been extended by Edmund Safra, the billionaire banker who owned the National Republic Bank in New York. He had been a close friend of Maxwell's for some years and had personally allowed funds to be funnelled through his bank from Eastern Europe.

'But, like so many activities the FBI were trying to link to Maxwell, the ones between Safra and organised crime was another one hard to prove,' John P O'Neill would later say.

When Betty arrived in Maxwell's suite, she was shocked by his appearance. A few months ago one of her nephews, who had briefly met Maxwell at a social occasion in France, had told Betty that her husband was suffering from hypoxaemia, which resulted in an excess of carbon dioxide in the blood. This somewhat alarming prognosis was at variance with what two of New York's most experienced medical practitioners had concluded: that, despite his size, Robert Maxwell was physically in good health.

Though their marriage was finally over in all but name – she still enjoyed being called Mrs Robert Maxwell – Betty hoped that even if she slept in the guest bedroom they could at least come to a sensible arrangement over the divorce settlement she wanted. His proposal that he would grant her a few days on the *Lady Ghislaine*, but nothing else, was unacceptable. She hoped to persuade him to go at least halfway to meeting her requirements to help her refurbish her family's chateau in France and provide an income that came somewhere near the lifestyle she had enjoyed for so many years.

His good humour in her first days in New York surprised her. The night after the dinner for the launch of *The European*, Betty had retired to her room leaving him working the phone in the lounge of the suite. She sensed he was deeply worried about something but she knew that to ask him why would have provoked an outburst.

As she fell asleep she could still hear his voice rumbling on, hectoring, demanding, insisting. She had sensed that a change of mood was in the offing. All she could hope was that it didn't come before she left New York to return home next day. So far there had been no opportunity to raise her terms for a divorce. She would try to find an opening over breakfast. Betty fell asleep trying to strategise how she could engineer what she wanted.

Next morning she came down to the penthouse suite's kitchen. Her sense of order had been deeply offended by what she saw.

'The place was in such a terrible mess, with every cup and plate dirty. Bob started ranting at me for not giving him a cup a coffee,' she remembered.

Betty had gone upstairs, finished her packing and left the suite. Her last vision of him was seated on the settee, looking miserable and grey.

The world outside the suite had once more begun to catch up with Robert Maxwell.

Robert Brown, a director of National Westminster Bank, had arrived in New York with the shares that Maxwell had pledged to the bank in return for a loan. Brown now feared that the current value of the stock no longer covered the amount of the loan. He had come to New York to discuss the matter personally with Maxwell.

But dealing with a relatively modest problem like Brown's shares was nothing like handling the battery of phone calls that had finally forced their way past the Helmsley Palace switchboard up to the penthouse. Often every extension in the suite was ringing. A harassed MCC executive in London would aptly describe the situation as 'a circus within a madhouse'.

Now, to add to the sense of unreality, Ari Ben-Menashe, one of the linchpins in the long-doomed Iran–Contra debacle, was about to return to the limelight.

While Maxwell was flying back to London to try once more to head-off his creditors – a corporate banker from Bankers Trust in London had told Kevin, 'You're dead if we don't get our fifty million back' – Ben-Menashe was being led in handcuffs from his prison cell in Manhattan's Correctional Facility and driven to the nearby US district court for trial. He was accused of trying to buy and export three planes to Iran.

Ben-Menashe had been arrested in October 1990 in the shower of a friend's apartment in Venice Beach, California, by FBI agents. They had been tracking him for some months. Dressed and handcuffed, he was brought to New York, where he was denied bail. The federal prosecutor argued that the smooth-talking Israeli who had once walked without challenge through the corridors of the Reagan White House was a flight risk.

Used to a luxurious lifestyle, Ben-Menashe found himself in a tiny cell in the Manhattan Correctional facility, furnished only by a sink, a toilet and two metal cabinets. His neighbours on the high-status white-only tier – unlike the black and Hispanic tiers – were mostly fraudsters and other white-collar criminals. The guards told him that the previous occupiers of his cell had been John Gotti, the Mafia godfather, and Joe Doherty, the Irish revolutionary who would eventually be extradited to Britain. The guards said Ben-Menashe's cell was a 'quality place' to spend time. He had not been impressed.

'The place was more like a third-class, flea-bag hotel,' Ben-Menashe would recall.

With nothing to do all day, the 37-year-old Israeli, who, remember, had once held a prestigious job in his country's intelligence community and had carried out his share of secret missions for Israel, had sat on his metal bunkhead staring up at the fluorescent lights, unable to sleep.

And thought.

The more he had thought, the more his inner anger had fuelled his determination to seek revenge on those people he was sure had betrayed and finally abandoned him. There were all those back in Israel – the politicians and the intelligence chiefs – who had denied him. There were the two lawyers acting on behalf of the Israeli government, who had come to the prison's waiting room and sat across from him at a table and chairs bolted to the floor and offered him a deal: plead guilty, serve his sentence, and Israel would find him a place in some obscure spot of the world to live out his days. He had refused. He had begged his wife, still in Israel, to come and see him. She had refused. Only his mother had stood by him. But she was also in Israel and did not have the money to fly to New York. One by one his friends in Washington had refused to take his calls or, when he reached their answering machines, had never returned them. The one man he could have counted on to help him, Amiram Nir, was dead. Ben-Menashe was convinced he had been murdered. Would he suffer the same fate in this festering federal prison?

Such thoughts had stoked his anger. And that anger he directed at only two people – Robert Maxwell and Nick Davies.

His dislike for them both was linked to the moment when his fertile mind had concocted a plan that would get him released. It was as ingenious as any of the cover stories he had dreamed up when working for Mossad. Then he had been a salesman, a tourist guide, a wine connoisseur. Now he would be a writer. He would claim that his only interest in the arms business had been to research that 'cold world, to throw a spotlight on its dealers'.

In those long nights while his cellmate slept on his bunk, Ari Ben-Menashe lay awake staring at the ceiling, honing and polishing a scheme that he hoped would get him back into the world. It would all depend, he decided, on two things: affidavits from Nick Davies that he was a bona fide author and a publishing deal from Robert Maxwell to say the book was already under contract. Armed with such 'prestigious proof', Ari Ben-Menashe was convinced he would be free.

The plan was not as simple as it sounded, but, in the Byzantine world in which Ben-Menashe had lived for so long, nothing ever was simple.

Almost eighteen months before, in May 1989, Ari Ben-Menashe had been shown into Maxwell's penthouse in London. At the least it was a charade more fitting to a stage farce than a meeting. Maxwell and Ben-Menashe already knew each other from the previous morning, when they had met with Admoni and Chebrikov, the then head of the KGB. Davies still had no knowledge of that encounter. But Maxwell also knew, from his secret bugging of Davies's phone call with Ben-Menashe, that both men had enjoyed a business relationship running arms through the company called ORA. The only person who had no inkling of any of the background was a senior executive from the *Sunday Mirror*, there to discuss a potential publishing deal of the story Ben-Menashe had proceeded to outline.

With that disarming smile that Ben-Menashe used as a weapon, he had begun to say that what he was going to outline was his personal act of atonement, his 'small way to contribute to the process of righting the terrible wrong of the 1980s and help remove from power those who were responsible'.

Who can doubt that Robert Maxwell may well have feared that in Ben-Menashe he now faced his own nemesis.

For his part, Ben-Menashe had swept his listeners along with a saga of how the United States had prevented peace in the Middle East, how Washington was still supplying chemical weapons to Saddam Hussein, how Ronald Reagan had provided arms to Iran in return for a delay in the release of the Teheran hostages until after he was elected in 1980.

It was the stuff of a hundred headlines and Ben-Menashe, sensing his moment, had said with that self-deprecating shrug that was also part of his defences, 'Is anyone going to believe me? Will the American and Israeli governments deny everything and say I am a nut?'

Davies and the *Sunday Mirror* executive both well remembered that those had been the very words used to discredit their *Sunday Times* rival over the Vanunu story. Were they to be scooped again by turning away this potential blockbuster?

Ari Ben-Menashe had concluded his presentation by saying that Davies should ghostwrite his story and that Maxwell's publishing house in New York, Macmillan, should publish it – and the *Sunday Mirror* serialise excerpts.

In return he wanted $750,000 as a down payment. The silence had been broken by Maxwell's rumbling, 'You're talking telephone numbers.'

The meeting ended with Maxwell telling Davies and Ben-Menashe to prepare a proposal.

Two weeks later Maxwell told Davies that neither Macmillan nor the *Sunday Mirror* was interested in publishing Ari Ben-Menashe's story.

Now in his prison cell, Ben-Menashe had wondered why Maxwell had changed his mind. His suspicions had hardened that Maxwell had told his still secret employer, Mossad, about what Ari Ben-Menashe was proposing.

Arrested and facing trial and the possibility of being given a long prison sentence, Ben-Menashe had once more in his desperation decided to try to persuade Davies and Maxwell to say that he had a publishing deal with them.

With the help of his lawyer, he placed a call to London. He managed to get through to Maxwell and Davies. 'Both of them told me, "You're history",' Ben-Menashe later claimed.

Not for the first time when it came to Ben-Menashe, Nick Davies would put a different spin on that contact.

'I received phone calls from apparent friends of Ben-Menashe, of whom I had never heard, asking me to go to New York and back up his story that he was simply researching the proposed book. I couldn't do so and didn't. He believed Maxwell and I should back up his story,' Davies later insisted.

More certain is that when Ben-Menashe had first arrived in the federal prison, he unburdened himself to the District Attorney's lawyers assigned to prosecute his case. The lawyer had afterwards telephoned Maxwell when he was next in the city.

Once more Davies would claim he received a telephone call on his private line in the *Daily Mirror* office in London from Maxwell from his Helmsley Palace Hotel suite.

'Maxwell called me up and asked me what I knew about Ben-Menashe. I gave him a brief outline of my knowledge of Menashe and of his ambition to become a wealthy man. Maxwell knew all about the book deal but I reminded him again. I waited for the blast. I deserved one for not warning Maxwell that in my opinion Menashe had Walter Mitty tendencies. Maxwell was surprisingly calm. He said earnestly, "You should have told me about him. You should never have let me meet him."'

Davies had never previously described Ben-Menashe as a Walter Mitty character. In fact he had done the opposite. He would later tell the veteran journalist Seymour Hersh that Ben-Menashe had amazing information.

*

Hersh would later enter the fray with deadly effect. But in the meantime, with the tireless help of his lawyer, William Schaap, support for the imprisoned one-time spy had finally come from Israel at an opportune time.

Articles had started to appear depicting Ben-Menashe as a 'fantasist', a 'real-life James Bond', a comic-book figure. Short on hard fact, they were filled with ridicule, which would follow Ben-Menashe through all his future life. But it was these attacks that finally drove colleagues in Israel to come to his defence. Israel's government had already filed a declaration with the trial prosecutor that Ben-Menashe had worked in its intelligence community only as a translator, a lowly grade worker.

Enraged by what they saw as the railroading of a competent officer, two of Ben-Menashe's former intelligence controllers, Colonel Pesah Melowanany and Colonel Arieh Shur, sent sworn affidavits to New York stating he had 'served in key positions' in Israel's intelligence community and 'was responsible for a number of complex and sensitive assignments'.

Ben-Menashe's trial lasted six weeks. Stage by stage the defence demolished the prosecution case. It took the jury only thirty minutes to find Ben-Menashe not guilty – ten years to the day since he had become involved in helping to run the arms-to-Iran operation.

But those long months in prison had, Ben-Menashe admitted, filled him with a need for another kind of justice. He wanted to see the two men he believed could have helped him, *should* have helped him, now destroyed.

He sought out Seymour Hersh. Where other journalists had walked away from Ben-Menashe and he had continued to be lampooned and ridiculed by them, Hersh was ready to listen. He had won a Pulitzer Prize for his book on the Mai Lai massacre in South Vietnam and a number of other prestigious awards. He was a careful investigative journalist with proven connections in the intelligence world. Ben-Menashe could not have made a better choice to unburden himself.

For some time Hersh had been preparing a book about Israel's role as a nuclear power for over a quarter of a century. Some of his research had by now appeared in the public domain. Like any writer, Hersh needed that 'little extra' to make his book another bestseller.

Ari Ben-Menashe was more than ready to help. The story he told Hersh was not only the one he had unfolded in Maxwell's penthouse – but now included details about the role of Robert Maxwell as a Mossad superspy. Even for Seymour Hersh, who had listened to so many startling stories in his long career, it was stunning. One of the most powerful men in the publishing world, a billionaire, a tycoon who could still appear alongside the world's leaders, here was Robert Maxwell being identified as spending part of his life in deep shadow as Israel's most important spy. What Ben-Menashe was saying, on the surface, was incredible.

There were two pressures on Hersh of the kind that face any

investigative writer. He had to check out Ben-Menashe's allegations. And he had to do it quickly. His manuscript was ready to go to the printers. To delay would affect the lucrative Christmas market and all those foreign translations that Hersh had become used to selling.

He also knew he would have to move not only with speed but with stealth. Even though he had been found not guilty, Ari Ben-Menashe would be a marked man. What he had said about Maxwell had not emerged in a court. The slightest hint now that he was sharing the details with a celebrity writer would cause consternation in Israel – and drive Maxwell to his favourite recourse when threatened: firing off numerous writs.

But Hersh knew the story must be checked. On 29 July 1991, he called Nick Davies at the telephone number that appeared on the ORA company documents Ben-Menashe had given Hersh.

Davies later recalled, 'I just told Hersh to keep on investigating Ben-Menashe. I said he was only a news source for me. But I did say he had amazing information. I agreed we had discussed collaborating on a book. But if any allegations are made about me in England, I'll be seeing my solicitor.'

Beneath Davies's dulcet tone there was a hint of panic. But he decided not to let Maxwell know about the call.

Hersh tracked down Davies's ex-wife, the actress Janet Fielding. They spoke on the phone on 6 August 1991, the day Maxwell had returned to London to find himself confronted with serious new problems with his financial manipulation of MCC shares.

The writer did not mention Maxwell. Instead he focused on what the actress knew about Davies's operations with ORA. He wrote down her response: 'She said she knew that Davies was selling arms in partnership with Ben-Menashe. She said she became appalled. "Nick would try to tell me stuff and I said I didn't want to know. I left him because of it."'

Hersh asked if she had known Ari Ben-Menashe was an Israeli agent. 'Do you think I'm bloody stupid? I shut my ears and walked,' she replied.

If not exactly the kind of copper-bottomed confirmation a lawyer might insist upon, it was sufficient for Hersh to know he had to include the data in his book.

The gun had been loaded.

Random House, Hersh's American publisher, had sold British publishing rights to Faber & Faber, known for publishing poetry and literature of high quality. They saw Hersh's book as being a worthy addition to their list. Then from New York came a message from Random House that Hersh was going to include an extra chapter. Time constraints meant it would be short. But the contents would be explosive: Robert Maxwell would be named as a Mossad spy. Nick Davies would be identified as gun running from his private phone at the *Daily Mirror*. It was enough to make any publisher salivate and the editorial team at Faber & Faber could understandably barely conceal their excitement. Here was a blockbuster that would outsell anything on their list for that winter – perhaps outsell any publishing catalogue that season.

With the secrecy of a modern-day Gunpowder Plot, plans were laid for the book to explode in Parliament. No other book would have achieved what Faber & Faber hoped for. But, as with all well-laid plans in the publishing trade, there was a leak. On 18 October, among the first to hear what was going on was Roy Greenslade. His contact told him that a book, *The Samson Option: Israel, America and the Bomb*, by Seymour Hersh, had explosive revelations that Davies and Maxwell had betrayed the Israeli technician, Mordechai Vanunu, to Mossad.

While Greenslade was on the phone with his contact from the *Sunday Times*, which had turned down serialising the book after seeing the manuscript, thousands of copies of *The Samson Option* were being flown into London from New York.

That same Friday, 18 October, Kevin Maxwell was battling with calls from bankers across the globe. In the meantime, his father had devised a scheme to deceive Citibank in New York. The bank would be told that MCC had 'millions of dollars' in their New York bank accounts from the sale of Scitex shares and wished to convert some of those millions into sterling.

In reality the money from the Scitex shares had already been used to cover even more pressing payments to other banks. Citibank agreed to transfer £20 million to London.

Two days later, on Sunday, 20 October, Maxwell flew to New York. He wanted to see what further money could be prised out of Citibank or any other bank.

On the flight he swallowed his regular Halcion pill. From the airport he was driven to the Helmsley Palace Hotel. As usual, his regular suite had been double-checked to ensure everything was dust-free and the air temperature set to his liking. A substantial buffet was waiting to be served in the dining room. That night, having demolished the food, he took a Xanax pill.

Kevin would recall that, when his father phoned him, he sounded depressed. They discussed strategy for the coming week in the money markets. Both agreed that all the signs indicated it was going to be another rough ride. Kevin tried to sound optimistic. He wondered if his father's mood had been exacerbated by the cold he seemed to be developing. Before they hung up, Kevin reminded Maxwell that he was to be the guest speaker at the Anglo-Israeli dinner in London on 4 November. Would Maxwell like Kevin to help him write a speech? Anyone who was anyone in Britain's

Jewish community, along with a number of important people from Israel, would be guests. They would include a number of bankers. It could be a chance to see if they would be able to help avert the developing crisis.

Maxwell had grunted.

In Tel Aviv the *kidon* team waited in the safe house on Pinsker Street. They passed their time reading, playing cards or watching videos.

Late on Sunday night while Maxwell slept in his hotel suite, a *katsa* in New York was placing an urgent call to headquarters in Tel Aviv. The agent had just come from dinner with diplomats. One of them had a finished copy of *The Samson Option*. The other diners had sat agog as he read excerpts.

The duty officer in headquarters switched the call directly to a more senior officer, one of the plotters who had already decided that Robert Maxwell had outlived his usefulness. What the *katsa* reported was proof of that.

The senior officer called his fellow conspirators. They had not anticipated that their well-laid plans would be wrecked by a book. Undoubtedly Hersh's revelations were even more damaging than what Ostrovsky had published. In naming Robert Maxwell, Hersh had struck a deadly blow against Mossad, and against Israel – especially in its relations with the United States, where Maxwell had used John Tower as a means to gain access to the Oval Office.

It is not difficult to imagine the barely controlled panic as the plotters called each other. It would have not been dissimilar to the one that had gripped Vladimir Kryuchkov and his cabal when it became clear their plot to overthrow Mikhail Gorbachev had failed. The plotters decided that the *kidon* team should be moved up to 'Condition Red', the stage that preceded the green light for action.

Before that was authorised, it was important to know how Maxwell would respond to the allegations. Would he surround himself with his own Praetorian guard of security men? Hire the finest lawyers in the world to stop the allegations spreading? Would he flee to the sanctuary of his criminal associates in Eastern Europe? They all had their private armies that even the *kidon* could not easily penetrate. What would he do?

Maxwell's first reaction in the early hours of Monday morning – in London it was breakfast time – when he heard the news that Seymour Hersh's revelations had caused a sensation was predictable. He ranted at his lawyers, at Kevin and Ian, at anybody he could reach. Still groggy from his sleeping tablet, he was almost incoherent.

Gradually he calmed down. His attorneys told him that no British newspaper, no television or radio station would dare to repeat Hersh's allegations. In the meantime, they would prepare libel writs against Faber & Faber, their printers and distributors. They would consult with other lawyers in New York to see what action could be taken there to protect Maxwell from the allegations. More lawyers would be retained in every European country – 'in every country in the world, Bob', one lawyer had said reassuringly.

Maxwell began to relax. But, just as he had miscalculated the bulldog mentality of Victor Watson at Waddington, so he and his attorneys had misjudged the determination of Faber & Faber.

A hint of what was afoot came from Roy Greenslade.

'We were waiting for the storm to break elsewhere,' he remembered. 'Elsewhere' turned out to be the House of Commons. Protected by privilege from the draconian laws of libel in Britain, MPs could say what they liked provided they did not break the arcane Rules of the House. Allegations made under the protection of parliamentary privilege could be reported outside.

Next day, on Tuesday, 22 October, two MPs, who had followed the story closely rose to their feet. The first was George Galloway, a truculent politician and, to many, no friend of Israel. He quoted from Hersh's deadly eight pages. He sat down to a stunned silence. Then rose the boyish-faced Rupert Allason, a writer of espionage novels under the pseudonym of Nigel West. His connections to MI5 and MI6 were well known. He completed the revelations about Maxwell, Davies and Ben-Menashe. It was devastating and the House was suitably devastated.

Rupert Allason later remembered he told the House he had found the evidence against Davies 'compelling. I conceded that Nick Davies had Walter Mitty tendencies, but the evidence of his involvement in arms dealing on behalf of the Israelis was compelling, especially as it did not come from Ben-Menashe but from documents taken by Davies's ex-wife. I had seen most of them and was able to confirm that for example the invoices to Sri Lanka for various weapons bore Davies's home address and telephone number.'

Allason was among those who received a writ for libel from Maxwell's attorneys. He brushed it aside. The writ was never pursued, but he, like Galloway, obtained substantial damages for attacks on him in the *Mirror*.

But the gun was now shooting with more deadly effect. Every major newspaper, radio station and television network reported the story that Maxwell was a Mossad spy.

The eight pages Hersh had added in fact contained few substantive allegations. There was nothing about Maxwell's links to organised crime in Eastern Europe. There was no hint of his role in the plot to overthrow Gorbachev, of his links to the KGB. Hersh had painted only broad brushstrokes.

Those details would have to wait until now, as they appear in this book.

But the few details that Hersh did provide had panicked Mossad. That panic turned to what might best be described as cold, calculating fury as, in the midst of the drama over the book, Robert Maxwell once more called Mossad, and told them he now expected them to find the vast sum of money – some £400 million – he had previously asked for. He wanted it transferred into his MCC coffers. He wanted it in full. And he wanted it now.

'He was,' Betty would recall, 'very upset at this time.'

So were the senior Mossad officers. One of them called the safe house in Pinsker Street.

Condition Red turned to Go Green.

SEVENTEEN

On Monday, 28 October 1991, one of those warm afternoons when summer seems to revisit New York, the world's foremost private detective walked into the lobby of the Helmsley Palace Hotel.

Jules Kroll was over six feet tall and dressed in an expensively tailored suit – his hallmark – and his hair was greying at the temples, making him look like a Wall Street broker rather than a feared investigator.

An assistant manager, whose nightly rate was less than Kroll charged for an hour's work, escorted him to the penthouse suite.

Maxwell was waiting at the door, smiling nervously. He gripped Kroll's hand and thanked him profusely for having agreed to the meeting.

'No problem.' Kroll's voice was measured. His eyes strayed into the spacious lounge. A woman sat there looking preoccupied. Kroll sensed Maxwell did not want her to be any part of the reason they were meeting. He was used to that. Everybody had his reason. It was partly why he existed. He didn't give the woman a second thought.

Maxwell suggested they could talk on the roof.

'No problem,' Kroll repeated. He followed Maxwell up the stairs to what passed for a roof garden. For a moment they stood and admired the view. Away to one side were the Twin Towers of the World Trade Center. Behind, in the distance, planes were on their final approach to La Guardia and Kennedy. Below, Central Park wore its autumn coat of bright hues.

Kroll was in no hurry. At the age of fifty, he had learned the importance of waiting. He had learned it in all those years he had spent investigating white-collar criminals and dealing with, among much else, kidnappers. He had synthesised his company's work as being able to anticipate the risks and mitigate them; respond immediately to a crisis; acquire the information and intelligence necessary to make the most informed and strategic decisions.

His sources and methods were his alone to know. He worked within the limits of what he uncovered, dealing always in the middle range of probability.

In 1985 a Senate Sub-Committee had hired him to track down the secret billions of dollars Ferdinand Marcos and his wife, Imelda, had hidden. Kroll located a $1 billion building in Manhattan the couple had secretly bought. A year later the Haitian government asked him to trace the fortune laundered through world banks by its former dictator, Jean Claude 'Baby Doc' Duvalier. Kroll traced the money through accounts in America and Europe. On the day he now stood on the roof with Maxwell, he was still trying to track, on behalf of the Kuwaiti government, Saddam Hussein's secret fortune.

All the qualities that had made Kroll Associates and its founder unequalled in the world of private investigation Robert Maxwell now needed.

For both men it was a bittersweet moment. Though they had never met before, both had for some time been aware of each other. On no fewer than four occasions Kroll had been called in by American companies to investigate Maxwell's methods. The detective had found nothing criminal in those cases but he had learned a great deal about how Maxwell operated. But now that he might be hired by Maxwell, that information could be used to help his new client. Essentially Kroll was a gun for hire, there to help the person who was footing his considerable retainer.

Maxwell, fearing that Kroll could turn him down, had approached the detective through an intermediary. In spite of all he had learned about Maxwell – 'that he was cunning, aggressive, abusive' – Kroll had agreed to see him. Having spent a few moments in small talk, he followed Maxwell to the roof sundeck and sat on a recliner opposite him.

'So, what can I do for you?' Kroll asked.

Maxwell told him: about the pressure from bankers, about 'all the rumours being circulated that were false and malicious and designed to ruin him financially'.

Kroll noted the phrases. They were not new; to him they were 'the standard opening gambits of people in trouble, blaming others'.

He continued to listen as Maxwell took him deeper into his financial maze. Kroll did not expect it would be the full story. Maxwell would be holding back details, putting his own interpretation on others. That was natural. But there were still some surprises. He had expected Maxwell to be 'bombastic and with the rage I had heard all about from others'. Instead Maxwell was conciliatory and self-deprecating. Kroll would later recall: 'He kept saying "I'm an amateur at this game, Mr Kroll. You're the professional." The whole tenure of our conversation was that he had been putting together information for months about what he said were his business enemies who were out to get him. He said he wanted me to put all the evidence together so that he could bring a legal action before they destroyed him.'

The detective well understood this kind of assignment. But it would not be easy. Maxwell operated in the upper strata of the financial world. The equally powerful people who worked there would have their own built-in defence systems. On their staffs were men who had held high office in the CIA and FBI; technicians who had worked for the National Security Agency, who knew how to make a room bugproof; private detectives who had worked for other security services like Mossad: at least two former Israeli *katsas* operated in New York who specialised in financial investigations. Maxwell's enemies would most certainly know which ones to have called.

At this stage Kroll wanted to gather an overview of Maxwell's problem. He asked him for the names of those he suspected were plotting against him. Kroll remembered his saying, 'I don't want to name names at this time, Mr Kroll. But will you take the case?'

Kroll was not short of work. Apart from the Kuwaiti government investigation, he and his staff were involved in a number of other high-level enquiries. But there was something about Maxwell that intrigued him. He was not like his public image. There was a vulnerability about him. If not exactly frightened of those enemies, he was pensive about what they would do next. It was almost as if his wish not to name them was out of fear that it might lead to their doing further damage.

The detective said he would take the case. He quickly laid down his terms of engagement. He would want to know where to reach Maxwell at any time. He would want a list of all those people he feared were working against him. He would need to appoint a lawyer through whom Kroll would liaise. The detective suggested three leading New York attorneys, one of whom should be retained. Maxwell did not know any of them. Kroll proposed an attorney he had worked closely with in several cases. Maxwell said that was fine by him.

Kroll remembered that Maxwell had not raised any threat to his personal security. 'He was insistent that I should target his business enemies. The threat he faced was from them, not to his personal self.'

Maxwell's dismissal of the notion that there was a threat to his life meant Kroll would not need to hire round-the-clock bodyguards to protect his new client.

Shaking hands with Maxwell, Kroll was clear in his own mind that the investigation was going to focus on what had gone on in the boardrooms in Wall Street and elsewhere.

Coming back down into the penthouse, Kroll noticed that the woman was still seated in the suite. She did not look up as he left. At the door of the penthouse they agreed to meet again when Maxwell would next return to New York. He would call him the following week.

*

Next day Robert Maxwell flew back to London. He was met by his chauffeur, John Featley, who found his employer in good humour. Featley, a wise-cracking Cockney, was relieved. There had been times when Maxwell would stumble off an aircraft snapping at anyone who caught his eye.

There were several reasons for Maxwell's relaxed manner. Before leaving New York, his lawyers had said all the writs in the Hersh case had been served. There had been no worrying calls from Kevin. Kroll had begun his enquiries. Featley had brought no urgent messages for Maxwell to phone his son as soon as he cleared customs.

The trip to New York had been heartening. It had enabled Maxwell to be seen in the flesh rather than have his voice echoing over the trans-atlantic phone link, and this had paid dividends. Sitting in one Wall Street boardroom after another, or facing a banker in his hotel suite, Maxwell had been able to work his magic: there was conviction in his voice, a sureness in the way he quoted figures, a certainty his borrowings would be covered by shares he held. And they had listened.

Promises had been extracted to look again at call-in dates. There had even been hints of more money being available. Given all the circumstances – the Hersh bombshell and the refusal of Mossad to help – New York had been a success. In his own mind Maxwell had even thought it was a turning point. If New York was with him, then it might not be impossible to bring London's lending community to heel.

It was only when Maxwell had settled in the back of the Rolls that the spell had been broken.

'The barbarians', Kevin said on the car phone, were once more threatening to breach the defences he had constructed in Maxwell House.

All weekend the financial generals had strategised in their country mansions in Surrey and deep Sussex talking on the phone, faxing each other, briefing their field commanders, the men who would lead the next assault on Fortress Maxwell. Their shock troops were warned to expect heavy resistance. Those chosen to lead the assault were the battle-hardened managers from Lehman Brothers and Credit Suisse. Theirs would be a frontal attack.

They had launched it that Tuesday morning, October 29, while Maxwell was still in the air and not in contact with his own field commander on the ground, the now hollow-eyed Kevin Maxwell. He had hardly slept during the weekend, shoring up the defences. His office on the ninth floor on that Tuesday resembled a front-line command post; the ammunition was the stacks of files and mounds of paper. Faxes came and went in a nonstop whirr. The phones had rung far into the night. This was Kevin's finest hour.

Credit Suisse had launched the first assault. Two of its most experienced senior managers arrived in Maxwell House on the stroke of 9 a.m. Their briefcases were filled with proof that the shares pledged to their bank were not worth the paper they were written on in terms of loan cover, as those same shares had been pledged to so many other banks.

Kevin had fought back. Like any seasoned defender, he had fallback positions. He would need to have more proof than in those briefcases. He would have to talk to MCC's lawyers. And above all he would have to consult his father.

The first wave had been driven off. Next came the storm troopers of Lehman Brothers. They had a reputation for not taking prisoners; the City was full of stories of their hard-nosed approach. Confronting Kevin, they did not bother with niceties. They simply said the time had come for them to dump the MCC shares they held as collateral. In survival terms for MCC it was the equivalent of being flattened by an artillery barrage.

Kevin had one answer. In a clear and confident voice he had delivered his father's immortal words: 'Trust me.'

Incredibly, they had. They had fired at him their biggest salvo – sell the shares they held at fire-sale prices – and he had not flinched. In a reasoned, calm voice, exuding quiet authority, he had repeated, 'Trust me.'

The Lehman storm troopers retired.

That was the position when Robert Maxwell arrived back in the penthouse from New York.

On the floor below in Kevin's office, the other directors of MCC were seated. They too were like combat troops who had been shelled once too often. Their talk was of surrender, of suing for what was the equivalent of peace in the financial world: getting out how best they could. If that meant selling off some still profitable companies in the MCC portfolio, it should be done. The important thing, the only one that mattered, was to walk away with what they could salvage.

'You are speaking like directors and not seeing the full picture,' Kevin said. 'We Maxwells don't surrender.'

Upstairs Robert Maxwell sat next to a wall panelling behind which a speaker was relaying the conversation. Though he had given Kroll an insight into how Maxwell House operated, he had not told the detective about the bugging systems.

Late that afternoon a fresh attack was launched, this one by the Swiss Bank Corporation (SBC). Its financial director arrived in Kevin's office to say that the bank felt that MCC's idea of how to use stocks as collateral offended their ideas. They had discovered that shares they thought were pledged to them alone now appeared to be also held by other institutions. Given that SBC was now owed £55 million, Kevin would readily understand this was now a serious matter. In that punctilious way that Swiss bankers like to assume in a crisis, Kevin's visitor had then laid out what the future could be. The bank would eventually have to inform the Department of Trade and Industry – whose investigators were known as the 'Rottweilers' – and the equally ferocious Fraud Squad at Scotland Yard. The SBC executive had bidden Kevin a good evening and left.

Next it was the turn of Goldman Sachs to occupy the front line. It sent in the men Maxwell had called 'my trusted friends' to lay siege to Kevin's office. They came to the point with the equivalent of close-combat fire. They had heard that Citibank was now going to sell at market all the shares it held, placing a value on them sufficient to cover the £40 million they were owed. The men from Goldman Sachs said they would have to do the same.

Kevin was told he had 24 hours to find the money.

In the penthouse, Robert Maxwell sat and listened and brooded. This was a feeding frenzy. He was being financially devoured alive. Soon he would be nothing but a penniless skeleton.

Then his private telephone rang. A voice said it was the Israeli embassy in Madrid calling. In the brief pause before he was connected, he may well have dared to hope that Mossad had, after all, done what he had asked and found a source for the £400 million he knew would stave off disaster. With that money he could see off his most pressing creditors, put out the word that he was solvent and launch the counterattack. Kevin had done well to hold the line, but then it would be time for Maxwell to advance with the same flamboyant courage he had shown all those years ago on the battlefield in France, when he had earned his Military Cross. If all went well, he could award himself a Bar to his decoration.

The voice in his handset asked him to identify himself. Once Maxwell had done so, the caller gave very precise instructions. Maxwell was to fly to Gibraltar. There he would board the *Lady Ghislaine* and sail for Madeira. When he reached the island he would receive further instructions. The final words of his caller were that Maxwell's situation had been carefully studied in Tel Aviv and there was no need for him to panic.

For Robert Maxwell his caller had thrown the lifeline for which he had so long waited. Mossad, like the United States Cavalry, were coming to his rescue. It must have been a glorious moment as he put down the phone and looked out over the lights of the City of London. Soon he would be free of all those men in their boardrooms who, even now, were plotting new ways to destroy him. On that at least he was correct.

The four-man *kidon* team had selected their cover identities. They were to be friends with a common passion for deep-sea fishing and were going to cast out their lines in the Atlantic between Madeira and the Canary Islands. As well as rods and tackle, they were taking diving equipment – wet suits and air bottles for underwater exploration.

All would travel on French passports. They each spoke the language fluently; two were also proficient in Spanish. Through a travel agent in Madrid they had arranged for a local *sayin* to rent them an ocean-going boat for two weeks. They would pick up the craft in Las Palmas in the Canary Islands.

Independent of the *kidon*, a group from the *yahalomin* unit had made their travel arrangements. Each two-man team would also pose as tourists, who were never quite able to leave work behind them. That would account for the laptop computers they would be carrying, along with their mobile phones.

The equipment had been converted so that the laptops could serve as jamming devices or call interceptors. Each mobile phone was adapted to allow its user to appear to be calling from different locations, even as far away as London.

On the same day that Maxwell received the call from Israel's Madrid embassy, the *kidon* and communications team arrived at Ben-Gurion Airport in Tel Aviv. They were there two hours before take-off. The *yahalomin* were booked on a scheduled flight to Madrid. From there they would take a plane to the Moroccan port of Rabat. Two boats, each with a powerful engine, would be waiting for them. These had also been hired by the Madrid *sayin*.

The *kidon* team boarded a flight to Zürich in Switzerland. At Koten Airport they took another flight to Las Palmas, arriving late on 30 October. There they waited.

The fishing equipment had all come from a Mossad storeroom that resembled a flea market. There were garments from all over the world. Most had been obtained by *sayanim* and sent on in diplomatic bags by Israeli embassies. Some items had been brought out of hostile Arab countries by pro-Israeli visitors. A few were actually made by the wardrobe mistress who presided over the storeroom. Over the years she and her small team of seamstresses had developed a reputation for detail, down to using the right sewing stitch to mimic one used in the *souks* of some particular country.

The passports and aliases had come from the *kidon*'s own operations room at their base in the Negev Desert. Rafi Eitan had introduced the idea of stockpiling travel documents and a list of aliases after the Eichmann operation. Shalom Weiss had, at the time, been one of the best forgers in Mossad; his documents had played an important part in helping the kidnap team to operate in Buenos Aires, where they had tracked down Eichmann. Weiss had died of cancer in 1963. But his name had been assumed by several operatives down the years.

Control of the operation now under way was in the hands of men Victor Ostrovsky would later state 'were high up in the Operations Department. Beyond that I am not prepared to go. I am not prepared to identify persons.'

Believing he had already come close to death at the hands of his former colleagues, Ostrovsky had become cautious and fearful. His reaction was understandable: like Ari Ben-Menashe, Ostrovsky knew that others – Amiram Nir and Cyrus Hashemi – had met their deaths when they were about to break their silence.

The operation now would be controlled by those senior officers on the seventh floor of the building on King Saul Boulevard. Through the *yahalomin* they would be linked by secure communications to the *kidon* team. At all stages any one of those officers could halt the operation. It was one of them who had made the initiating call to the Israeli embassy in Madrid that now led to Maxwell's making his own travel arrangements to travel to board his yacht.

On Wednesday, 30 October, Robert Maxwell had been woken by his butler, Joseph Caetano Pereira, with his usual tray of freshly squeezed orange juice, coffee and bagels filled with smoked salmon. There was no sign that any woman had stayed overnight. Usually the perfume of any female visitors would still be in the air when the butler arrived with the breakfast tray. Joseph opened the curtains and made sure one of the Filipino maids had left fresh towels in the bathroom before going off duty the night before.

It was another of those grey mornings, when the view towards St Paul's and beyond, the City of London, was hazy. For Maxwell it could only have been a good feeling to know that, in a few hours, he would be on the deck of the *Lady Ghislaine* and sailing out into the Atlantic. There would be nothing to see but the waves breaking against her prow and her wake fading behind her stern. The only contact with the world would be through the yacht's communication room at the back of the bridge. He could decide whom he spoke to.

During the night there had been no calls on his private bedside line. It was a further sign that down on the ninth floor Kevin had continued to manage to keep the 'barbarians' at bay.

They would be back. It was in their nature, Maxwell had told his son. But now he would be ready for them. That call from Madrid could only have buoyed him. Just as soon as there would be clear blue water between him and land, so there would be an even larger gap between him and the problems that had threatened to sink him. He did not know any details of the rescue package he was confident lay behind the words of the caller from Madrid. No doubt there would be conditions: a schedule of repayments and interest charges. But they were a matter for negotiation and, when it came to that, he knew there was no one better. In his mind's eye he may well have begun to spend the £400 million he expected would come to him through his Mossad connection.

That could explain Maxwell's cheerful mood as later that day he sat down with his editors for their weekly luncheon. He told them Kroll was on the case, and that Rupert Allason and George Galloway would rue the day they smeared him.

He reminded his editors that in this dining room – with its hidden microphones so that he could later hear what they really thought – he had created the 'Mirror Train', which had carried him across Britain on a kind of royal tour. It was here he had concocted the idea, during Britain's national coal strike, for readers to send their donations for pit workers close to the breadline directly to him.

Money had come. But so had a torrent of abuse, accusing him of exploiting the plight of miners. Instead of being a fund giver he was only a mere fund-raiser. It was here in the dining room that Maxwell had written the editorial for the front page of the *Daily Mirror* over a beaming photo of himself standing over a pile of banknotes. He was 'itching to give £1 million to one of our readers', read the caption.

Those days would come again, he promised, raising a glass to his editors before lumbering out.

Hours later he assembled the directors of MCC in the penthouse. There were no drinks or caviar on offer. This was showdown time, to remind them who was in command.

'Gentlemen, I am up to speed with what has been going on. But you know my reputation. I don't give in . . . '

For some minutes he was like a pitch salesman. What had happened these past weeks had been a bad dream. Too quickly they – and he had indicated them all with a wave of his hand – had stepped through a looking glass where reality was suspended, where the old rules, their financial reasoning, all he had taught them, had been forgotten.

Money was paper and paper was money, he said, using one of his familiar phrases.

For a moment he had stared out of a picture window towards the City of London. Over there, he continued, they understood only money. They didn't know the true value of paper: the stocks and shares still under his control. That was reality.

From now on whatever the 'barbarians' tried to do, they would fight them off with that reality.

'Trust me,' he had concluded.

Despite all they knew, had witnessed, had been shown proof of – despite all they had. They had still trusted him.

In Gibraltar, Captain Gus Rankin had supervised the preparation of the *Lady Ghislaine* for its coming journey to New York. A month ago Maxwell had told him he wanted the yacht there so that he could use it as a base for his Christmas holiday in the city.

At that time of the year, the Rock was quiet and the waterfront chandlers and victuallers were glad of the substantial orders needed to prepare the yacht for its long Atlantic voyage.

The chief engineer, Roy Whiteford, and his second engineer, Leo Leonard, had checked the twin 1,400-horsepower Caterpillar engines and the three generators, each capable of producing 100 kilowatts of energy for running the galley and on-board lighting. The radar and communications systems had been tested by First Officer Grahame Shorrocks. The portholes were locked down. The four deckhands had caulked and varnished the decks. Jet skis and windsurfers had been stowed, along with the two twin-tank sets of scuba gear and the ship's two mopeds. And, for shore excursions, Second Officer Mark Atkins had checked the lashings on the Boston whaler; at 22 feet long, it was the same length as the Mercruiser. But the whaler had a more powerful engine, 170 horsepower, as opposed to the motorboat's 140 horsepower.

The housekeeper, and one of the two stewardesses, Lisa Kordalski, along with two stewards, under the watchful eye of the chef Robert Keating, had stored supplies for the long journey. Gibraltar was equipped for every need, and day after day trucks had brought food, wines and crates of bottled water to the quayside to the *Lady Ghislaine*, riding at anchor beneath the towering rock. For the journey Lisa Kordalski had been promoted to chief stewardess as her colleague was on holiday.

The original ship's manifest from the Annels, who built the *Lady Ghislaine,* called for a captain and thirteen crew. But Maxwell had reduced the overall number by one, so that he always sailed with thirteen – his lucky number from the day he bought the *Mirror* newspaper group. Like all those who worked in the industry, the crew were transient: some signed on for a season, others sought longer berths. A few had been with the yacht before Captain Gus Rankin took over. Others he had selected to serve under him. He was regarded as a fair but firm skipper, dining with the crew when Maxwell was not on board and often going ashore with them for a drink.

Some of the crew found Rankin a martinet. A deck hand, Martin Soothill, thought him 'difficult and a nit-picker'. Stewardess, Susan Bender, found when they went ashore for a meal that the captain often boasted 'of doing big deals in the States'.

Rankin had taken over at a salary of £50,000 a year, the fifth captain in command of the yacht.

Born in the London suburb of South Woodford, he was the son of a civil engineer and a graduate of the prestigious Merchant Marine Training College in Kent. Later he had gained his Yachtsman's Ocean Certificate at the London Polytechnic, qualifying him to skipper the largest private yachts in the world.

But, instead of spending all his working life at sea, Rankin had worked for a company in Greece running diving and snorkelling trips, and later acted as a consultant, rebuilding a four-masted tall ship. 'I then drifted into commanding luxury yachts by delivering them between Europe and America,' he had told the crew.

Just as he took little interest in their lives onshore, so he told them little about his own background. The most they could glean was that he was married to an English schoolteacher and that he had taken out American citizenship, and chose to live in the backwoods of Arkansas, in a 'modest, single-storey house half a mile from any neighbours, in the township of Pocahontas,' he told Susan Bender.

'He said it was the kind of town you see in the movies about the badlands. But it was there he said he did his big land deals,' she added.

While his crew recognised that Rankin had superb sailing skills, Susan Bender was not alone in thinking the *Lady Ghislaine* was a strange ship.

Part of the reason, she suspected, was Maxwell. Like Rankin, he could be distant 'and always very demanding. The slightest thing out of place and you'd get that look in his eyes,' said Bender. The succession of women Maxwell brought on board was also something the crew did not like. 'We respected Mrs Maxwell; she was a real lady,' recalled the deck hand, Soothill. 'But some of Maxwell's women were very bossy and full of airs and graces.'

But the crew saw that Maxwell liked Rankin. The captain was blunt and not given to the social chatter of other previous skippers. 'He was there to do a job; as long as he was paid he did it superbly,' recalled Bender.

Before Maxwell had gone to lunch with his editors, he had telephoned Rankin. The captain had taken the call on the bridge. Maxwell wanted to know what the crossing would be like to New York. Rankin knew that Maxwell was no foul-weather sailor. The captain had assured him the weather was set fair. The trip to New York was on.

Then at nine o'clock on that Thursday evening, Maxwell's senior secretary in Maxwell House had called the yacht's skipper. He had gone up to Gibraltar's Main Street for a curry dinner. One of the stewardesses was sent to find him.

Breathlessly she told Rankin 'London says we're not going to New York.'

The captain looked at her in disbelief. Then, not bothering to finish his meal, he hurried back to the yacht.

Rankin's first calls had been to Maxwell's two pilots. He could not reach Brian Hull, but managed to get David Whiteman. He told Rankin Maxwell had told him to move the Gulfstream to Luton Airport, north of London, ready for an early-morning take-off for Gibraltar.

Whiteman added, almost casually, that he understood from Gibraltar that Maxwell would sail to Madeira.

Rankin was stunned. Everything had been prepared for the three-week voyage to wintry New York. Now Maxwell was heading for the sunnier climate of Madeira. There would have to be a great deal of unpacking and repositioning.

But, before that was done, Rankin had to be certain that the New York trip was off. He placed a call to a secretary at MCC. She had not heard of any change of plan. He called Maxwell House. The switchboard operator put him through to the ninth floor. It was 10.30 at night there. The security guard said all the staff had gone home. He asked to be connected to the penthouse. The night man said Mr Maxwell was not there.

While Rankin waited, the operator checked with the night news desk of the *Daily Mirror*. Maxwell had not been seen for some hours; he had left no number where he could be contacted.

For Gus Rankin and everyone else in Maxwell House, Robert Maxwell had vanished.

The two *yahalomin* were already at sea off the coast of Morocco. To test their equipment they had electronically zoned in on the *Lady Ghislaine*. The Rock was filled with state-of-the-art electronic equipment controlled by Britain's Government Communications Headquarters (GCHQ), which monitors and decodes radio, telex and fax traffic in and out of the United Kingdom. Based at Cheltenham, GCHQ is regularly tasked by MI5 and MI6. To reduce to a minimum any risk of discovery, the *yahalomin* had picked up only some of the conversations about Maxwell's change of plans. But they had heard enough to know he was going to Madeira.

The news was relayed by one of the boats in a short-wave burst transmission to the *kidon* on Gran Canaria.

In London no one would ever know where Robert Maxwell had gone to that night. There are two possibilities. He had either gone to keep a personal assignation in the apartment where he had allowed Ognian Doinov to stay. Or he had gone to meet the resident *katsa* at the Israeli embassy. If such a meeting did take place, it may have been at the instigation of the *katsa*, acting on instructions from one of the senior Mossad officers running the operation. He may have wanted to ensure that Maxwell did not change his travel plans about going to Madeira. Or the meeting could have been requested by Maxwell, in the hope of finding out more about the £400 million he needed to get him out of financial trouble.

On board the *Lady Ghislaine*, Rankin spent a restless night. He had ordered the crew to work to make sure the yacht was in perfect condition for the voyage to Madeira. At the back of the captain's mind was the possibility that, when he did arrive on Gibraltar, Maxwell would change his mind again and once more set them on a course for New York.

Next morning at 5.30 Gibraltar time, Rankin placed another call to the penthouse. He was immediately answered by Maxwell. Rankin would recall he was bright and cheerful and confirmed their destination to be Madeira. Rankin warned him the yacht was not in shape for a cruise, adding that the regular chief stewardess, who was one of Maxwell's favourite crew members, would not have been joining them until they had planned to reach New York.

If Rankin had hoped this would change Maxwell's plan to sail to Madeira, he was disappointed. Maxwell said he was not bringing his personal secretary or his butler, Joseph. In Maxwell's life that was tantamount to travelling light. The absence of a stewardess was not going to change his plans.

At 11.30 a.m. Gibraltar time on Thursday 31 October, the Gulfstream swept in over Cadiz, on Spain's southern tip, and crossed the Straits to land in Gibraltar.

Waiting on the tarmac was Rankin and a deck hand to deal with the luggage. Nearby were two cars and a customs officer.

They all moved forward as Maxwell came down the aircraft steps. He was followed by a stewardess carrying his briefcase, who handed it to Rankin. The deck hand began to unload the aircraft luggage bay. He stowed it in the second car. He was finished by the time customs formalities were completed.

Maxwell and Rankin sat in the first car, the crewman and baggage filled the other.

They were driven to the quayside, where the *Lady Ghislaine* was tied up.

Set against the midday sun and the Spanish mountains behind Cadiz, she was a sight that never failed to excite Maxwell. More than anything else he owned, this was his most prized possession from that day, 23 April 1987, when he had bought her from Adnan Khashoggi's brother. From stern to prow she was 180 feet and nearly 30 feet wide amidships. She weighed 500 tons and had a speed of almost 17 knots, close to a destroyer, he had said, with justifiable hyperbole for once. She cruised in comfort two knots below her flank speed. Her range of 3,200 miles was enough to follow the sun, winter and summer, without having to refuel tanks that held 78,000 litres. The hull was of steel – 'as strong as any warship' – and the superstructure was finished in the finest aluminium. She was brand-new and, Maxwell said proudly, he had bought her for a 'bargain price', a mere £12 million.

There was state-of-the-art Faruno radar, magnetic gyro compasses, an echo sounder and wind-speed indicator. For Maxwell the attraction had been the communications system: there was a telephone switchboard large enough for a medium-sized land company, three separate fax machines, the latest IBM computer, a sophisticated VHF system and a powerful high-frequency receiver and transmitter. Maxwell would never be out of touch, and on any ocean the *Lady Ghislaine* would take him in luxurious comfort.

Betty had turned the salon and stateroom into a floating palace. Once more the designer, Jon Bannenberg, who had given Maxwell the kind of penthouse he wanted, had this time the good fortune to have Betty at his elbow, picking out pattern and colour schemes.

Betty's impeccable taste had given the yacht a feeling of being a home from home. Now, however, she was limited to sailing on it eight days a year. It was still all she had managed to negotiate so far for her divorce settlement.

The captain's log noted that 'owner on board' was at 1.15 p.m. on Thursday, 31 October.

Accompanied by Rankin, Maxwell performed his first on-board routine to a long-determined pattern: he went to the communications room behind the bridge to check if there were any messages – there were none; he then conducted a ship's inspection, poking his nose into the gymnasium – the weights, exercise bicycle and massage table were exactly where he had last seen them. He never worked out himself, but he encouraged his guests to do so.

Outside the gym was a refrigerator. He checked that it was correctly stocked with Dom Perignon and Kristal champagnes. The door shelves were filled with beer bottles.

From time to time he would run a finger along a ledge to make sure it was dust-free. The housekeeper and the stewardess had ensured this was so.

He opened and closed the dining-room door. He rarely ate in this dark panelled room during the summer, preferring to dine on the upper sun deck.

Having checked the two salons and observation lounge, he told Rankin everything was in order. Maxwell never ventured down to the crew's quarters: they were Rankin's responsibility. While Maxwell on the whole was civil to them, he knew little about the crew or what went on in their private lives. They were just 'my crew', just as others were 'my bankers', 'my trusted staff'. It was Maxwell's way of saying the crew were as beholden to him as anyone else.

He finally entered his stateroom – a massive en suite bedroom, with an adjoining study. There were separate dressing rooms for himself and, originally, Betty, though for some time these had been used by many other women in his life.

His wardrobes were filled with all the clothes he would need at any time of the year and for any occasion: a rail of topcoats and suits for formal meetings; another rail of lightweight jackets and trousers; a rack of shoes. Every item had been newly pressed or polished.

Betty's wardrobe was all but empty: he had ordered most of her belongings to be packed and sent back to Headington Hill Hall.

Waiting on a table in the centre of the stateroom was a bottle of champagne on ice and a plate of seafood.

He had told Rankin he would have lunch on the sun deck once they were under way.

Shortly before 1.30 p.m. the *Lady Ghislaine* eased her way through the Straits of Gibraltar, passing Royal Navy ships riding at anchor. Under Rankin's watchful eye, the yacht entered the shipping lane that would take them out into the Atlantic towards Madeira.

Tangier and the coast of Africa were fading into the afternoon haze on the port side and Maxwell was about to go up on the sun deck for lunch. The phone call came to the stateroom.

It was Kevin. There was no mistaking the fear in his voice as he relayed the news he had just received from New York. Goldman Sachs were going to dump 2 million shares in MCC on the market unless they were paid back 'in full, Dad; in full is what they said. They want every cent we've borrowed from them. They've given us 48 hours to settle or they'll do it,' he added.

Maxwell knew that the time frame had nothing to do with Goldman Sachs being generous: it was required by law before they could sell off the shares. The decision to sell the 2 million shares was also a calculated move. Goldman Sachs, all told, held a staggering 24 million other shares in MCC. To dump them all at once would see their value plummet. To sell off only 2 million stock and at the same time demand payment in full was hard-nosed banking.

There was more grim news. Bankers from Lehman Brothers had taken up station in the foyer of Maxwell House. They were demanding to see Maxwell. Kevin had kept them at bay by saying he had full authority to deal with them. He had sent down a message to say he would see them when he was ready. Maxwell's son had learned much of his father's *chutzpah*.

While Lehman's storm troopers fumed nine floors below, Maxwell House was once more under attack from other quarters. The Swiss Bank Corporation had cast aside its last vestige of politeness. In a terse call to Kevin, its financial director had told him that unless the bank was also paid in full it would be calling in Scotland Yard's Fraud Squad.

Others were spitting blood and making threats. On that Friday Kevin had received no fewer than twenty demands from brokers and corporate bankers saying they were going to foreclose.

Kevin told Maxwell he had done his sums. At this hour, 3 p.m. in

London, just after the markets closed, MCC was in danger of imminent collapse that would leave it owing £2 billion.

Maxwell had told Kevin to keep the 'barbarians' at bay.

In two more days, when he had reached Madeira, he expected there to be further news of the £400 million Mossad would have found for him. That he had not heard from them may, in his own sense of reality, have been a good thing. That no news is good news had long been a philosophy of his.

Kevin promised to do all he could to hold the line. On that optimistic hope Robert Maxwell hung up and made his way to the sun deck for lunch.

The sun was lower in the sky, burnishing the water, giving the impression that the *Lady Ghislaine* was surging through a fiery seascape.

On Gran Canaria the *kidon* waited. Out at sea the two *yahalomin* teams had cast an electric net between the Canary Islands and Madeira.

Part IV
A FINAL VOYAGE

EIGHTEEN

Robert Maxwell had decided the spray blowing off the Atlantic swell would make it too cool for dinner to be eaten on deck; it would be served in the panelled dining room where he had invited Rankin to join him.

The chef, Robert Keating, had made his way up to the sun deck to hand Maxwell the menu. There was, as usual, an emphasis on seafood along with a well-hung rib steak and selection of vegetables. The choice of wine would begin with the one Maxwell always drank: a bottle of Petrus. Other choice vintages would follow. At the end there would be a bottle of hundred-year-old port.

Having taken the dinner order, Keating had gone below to start cooking. In the dining room Lisa Kordalski and Susan Bender laid the table. They both knew the story of what had happened in a London restaurant when Maxwell had swept china, glasses and cutlery to the floor because he did not like the way the table was laid. He had told the stewardesses that as the plates smashed he had shouted, 'Get rid of this! It's not what should be done.' They knew it was his way of reminding them of what he expected: every knife and fork had to be set the same distance apart and the napkins similarly creased. It was another reason for Susan Bender to think it was a strange ship.

Lisa Kordalski was friendly with the first officer, Grahame Shorrocks, and off duty they would often wonder what lay behind the whims and tantrums that would sweep over Maxwell from one moment to the next; like an Atlantic squall they could come and go in an instant. The moods were another version of that 'strange steely mask, sending a chill through you', which Betty had first noticed all those years ago.

Among the crew, the second officer, Mark Atkins, probably had the closest contact with Maxwell. The former policeman had a respect for authority.

While dinner preparations were under way, Rankin sat with Maxwell in the lee of the sun deck. As always the captain was in immaculate white with his rank tab on his epaulettes. Maxwell was barefoot with a sweater draped over his shoulders.

Rankin later could not remember what they spoke about. 'He may have touched on his problems. I may have given him an insight into my world. He was good on world events and I guess there was a strange affection and mutual regard between us.'

After dinner Maxwell retired to his study, which formed part of the master suite. Lisa Kordalski brought him the unfinished port bottle and noticed he had several open briefcases on the floor beside his desk. Its top was covered with papers. Beyond, in the bedroom, she saw that the wall safe door was open. She knew it was where Maxwell stored substantial sums of money in various currencies. The stewardess assumed it was for spending when he went ashore.

As she left the study she heard Maxwell again remind the bridge that any incoming calls should be switched there. Over dinner he had done the same, sending her to the bridge to tell the watch officer he was to put through any calls to his study. Lisa wondered who could be so important for Maxwell to keep reminding the bridge.

Maxwell may well have been waiting for further instructions from Tel Aviv, or a call-back from Ognian Doinov. He had left messages for him at both Doinov's Vienna and London numbers. At that time Maxwell was describing the former Bulgarian politician as 'my Soviet Union and Socialist companies' director'.

It was not altogether fanciful.

With Andrei Lukanov gone from power, Doinov had been instrumental in introducing Maxwell to Zheylo Zhelev, Bulgaria's new Prime Minister. In return Doinov would later claim, 'I received from Mr Maxwell a salary of £100,000 a year, a free apartment in London, a car, telephone and retirement package.'

Doinov had come a long way since that night he had sat with Maxwell in the Sheraton Hotel in Sofia and listened as Lukanov had outlined the plan that would eventually allow Maxwell to become the financial godfather of the Eastern Bloc and its criminal associates in New York.

Much as Ari Ben-Menashe had introduced Nick Davies as ORA's glorified bagman, so Maxwell cast Doinov in a similar role. Using his contacts in African and Arab countries that had maintained close relations with Socialist regimes throughout the world, Doinov had travelled to Nigeria, Zimbabwe and Kenya to seek business openings for Maxwell. He arranged for Mozambique's President Karavela to travel to London and stay as Maxwell's guest. Yemen, Somalia, Ethiopia, Libya and Syria were other countries where the energetic Doinov flew to and promoted the advantages of doing business with Maxwell.

Like other underlings seeking to cultivate their employer, Doinov had started to jot down in a notebook the collected sayings of his master. It included such observations as, 'Mister Maxwell had a specific way of expressing himself. For example he used to say "Don't expect justice from fate – it's always unjust" and "Even the best man has to order a grave while alive."' And, 'Mr Maxwell stood out because of his extraordinary sense of humour – even among his employees. When Chernyenko asked him what would have happened if Khrushchev had been assassinated instead of Kennedy, he replied that one thing was certain. "Aristotle Onassis would not have married Nina Khrushchev."'

That Maxwell enjoyed such fawning adulation cannot be doubted. More importantly, Doinov had now become the link between Maxwell and Ivo Janchev, a Bulgarian secret service officer tied to the country's crime families. Meanwhile, Simeon Mogilevich had set up his base in Budapest.

Unknown to Maxwell, Doinov was also keeping a second and more secret book: it was a day-to-day account of his dealings on behalf of his employer. In a self-serving note, he had written: 'Mister Maxwell hired me because I was not a corrupt official – someone likely to take bribes or presents.'

Maxwell's reason for trying to reach Doinov may well have been as a result of the silence from Tel Aviv. Given the intense pressure Kevin had reported from London, it would be reassuring for Maxwell to have known if Doinov could arrange for backup funding for the £400 million he expected from Mossad. Mogilevich and Janchev, with his secret service bosses also owning a slice of the action, might well baulk at providing that kind of money which would have to come from joint ventures in which they were engaged with Maxwell. But if anybody could, then Doinov was the man to smooth-talk the money out of them.

But where was he? Where was Mossad? Where was his rescue package?

In London the first hours of a new day, Saturday, 2 November, dawned with Kevin still on the phone. The creditors had struck on all fronts. Lehman Brothers had seized shares in one of the Maxwell companies, Berlitz. Kevin had been told that, 'possession being nine-tenths of the law', Lehman's was quite prepared to resist anyone who tried to take the shares out of its hands. Goldman Sachs had done what it said it would do: dumped 2 million MCC shares onto the market.

In Headington Hill Hall, Betty Maxwell still felt part of the story. In just two days' time, this coming Monday, 4 November, she was due to sit beside Maxwell as he spoke to the Anglo-Israeli Association dinner in London.

Without having any idea that he was sailing towards Madeira, she expected him to be at the dinner.

*

In New York, where it was still late evening on Friday, Jules Kroll was ending his first week as Maxwell's highly paid investigator. What progress he had so far made, he would share with no outsider.

Hours before, one of the *yahalomin*, a two-man team, had made their way into the marina at Funchal harbour in Madeira. Having cleared customs and immigration, they had taken a taxi to the town's most elegant accommodation, Reid's Palace Hotel, overlooking the bay and the calm Atlantic beyond.

Some 260 miles to the south in the port of Las Palmas in Gran Canaria, the *kidon* waited. To any onlooker, they were just four more fishermen.

Dawn was breaking over the sea on that second day of November as Robert Maxwell clambered to the upper sun deck. Around his neck were slung a powerful pair of Zeiss binoculars. He began to sweep the sea for sight of any ships. Just as train spotters would spend hours identifying locomotive numbers, so Maxwell liked to note the names of ships and boats. It was always a moment of satisfaction when he would spot a cruise liner or tanker he had seen in some other part of the ocean.

Despite being a deep-water harbour, Funchal had only a small marina filled with fishing and pleasure craft. Boats the size of the *Lady Ghislaine* tied up at the harbour wall.

The yacht had timed her arrival in Madeira for when the island was at its most enchanting. To the west of Funchal rose the majestic Cabo Girao, the world's second highest sea cliff, towering almost 2,000 feet out of the sea.

Gus Rankin stood on the bridge, slowly guiding the yacht into the bay. The mountains behind the town were a blaze of lush vegetation and flowering shrubs. Rising above the cobbled streets of Funchal and its colonial-style buildings was the whitewashed tower of Se Cathedral; built in 1486, its Baroque Sacramento chapel was a mecca for tourists.

On this Saturday morning for Robert Maxwell, standing on the sun deck waving to fishermen and sightseers on the harbour wall, there was another attraction: Reid's Palace Hotel.

During the early hours of the morning he had been woken by telephone calls. One was logged as coming from Kevin: he had brought the latest news about the deteriorating financial position. But the other caller had not given his name. Complying with Maxwell's new instructions to the bridge that from now on any caller who did not identify himself should still be connected to the master bedroom, the night watch officer had done so.

Was that the call that, the night before, Lisa Kordalski had seen Maxwell so anxious to receive? Was the caller bringing new instructions, reassuring ones, from Mossad? Certainly Maxwell had come on deck in a cheerful mood. To Mark Atkins he was like someone who had 'heard he'd won the pools'.

As the *Lady Ghislaine* prepared to moor against the harbour wall, Maxwell used his binoculars to see if there were any photographers among the watching crowd. Kevin had said there was a strong possibility that local reporters from the London newspapers might be waiting to pounce, trying to get Maxwell to comment on Hersh's allegations.

Maxwell turned to Second Officer Mark Atkins and said he wanted him to come ashore with him. A powerfully built man, the former policeman would be able to brush off any newspaperman who tried to accost Maxwell.

Lumbering down the gangway, Maxwell squeezed himself into a waiting taxi. Atkins sat beside the driver. They entered the town's narrow streets, passing the sixteenth-century Church of Santa Clara and the old Brandy Wine Lodge. Maxwell ordered the driver to take him to a newsagent; he bought all the London newspapers, most of them a day or more old. There were no fresh allegations from Seymour Hersh. Maxwell then told the driver to take him to Reid's Palace Hotel.

A little after 9 a.m., the taxi drove up to the entrance of the hotel. Maxwell clambered out. As Atkins was about to do the same, Maxwell ordered him to wait in the car. Then, newspapers under his arm, he walked into the lobby of one the great hotels of the world.

Atkins was puzzled. Journalists could still be waiting inside to ambush Maxwell. And the decision to go to the hotel had not been mentioned until the last moment. The second officer wondered if Maxwell was going to meet somebody he did not want Atkins to see. It wouldn't be a woman, for Maxwell usually had one brought to his boat, to the privacy of his cabin. It was, in Atkins's view, very unusual.

Thirty minutes later, Robert Maxwell emerged from the hotel no longer carrying his newspapers. He did not say a word to Atkins, only ordering the driver to take them to a bar. There, in silence, the two men drank a beer each.

Used to Maxwell's mood changes, Atkins had dismissed the silence as nothing unusual. Long ago the former policeman had learned the rich and famous were indeed different.

What had happened inside the hotel? Maxwell had not given Rankin or anyone else among the crew any indication he knew anybody on the island. Had he met one of the *yahalomin*? Was he the mystery caller who had been put through to his cabin? Had Maxwell received new instructions relating to the payout he had come to believe Mossad would provide? Was that why he had ordered Mark Atkins to remain outside?

There is no record that Maxwell made any telephone calls from the hotel. He was not given to sightseeing. While Reid's Palace Hotel is undoubtedly magnificent, Maxwell had stayed in other great hotels. He had once told Betty they were all the same. There is only one reasonable conclusion, borne out by all that was to follow: that Robert Maxwell had been ordered to go there by one of the Mossad officers in Tel Aviv.

It was the beginning of a sequence of events that, even at the height of his mood swings, Robert Maxwell could never had imagined.

Returning to the quayside, Maxwell found himself confronted by reporters and photographers. He glowered at them and lumbered back on board the *Lady Ghislaine* as Atkins shouldered aside the journalists. One of the deck hands mounted guard at the top of the gangway.

'Find me some other place,' Maxwell ordered Rankin.

Then he went below to his master cabin. He placed another call to Doinov. There was no reply.

Rankin decided the small island of Desertas to the south would suit Maxwell's purpose. The *Lady Ghislaine* slipped her moorings under a final fusillade of flashbulbs.

Out in the bay Maxwell appeared back on deck wearing brightly coloured shorts and a baseball cap. He now began to display another familiar trait, talking like a small child: Russia would become 'Wussia'. Like an angry infant Maxwell lisped to Rankin that the chef 'needed wessons in how to cook the way I like things'.

That morning Maxwell had consumed the huge breakfast that Keating had prepared.

The crew were not alone in noticing this infantile affectation. Nick Davies had noted in the times he had sailed with Maxwell that he 'loved making up names, especially for those whose identities he wanted to keep secret. Jesse Jackson, the American black politician, was always "Mr White". One of his lawyers was "Mr Morning Star", a banker named Chalk was always called "Mr Cheese".'

But even Davies did not know what Maxwell called Mossad, or that he was known in its upper echelons as 'the Little Czech'.

Atkins had told Rankin what had happened at Reid's Palace and the captain wondered if Maxwell's latest tantrum about the cook was really a reaction to something he had been told at the hotel. Or was it just Maxwell having to lash out at somebody? That was often the case: a telephone call that did not please Maxwell could lead to a complaint to the captain about some unfortunate member of the crew who had failed to do something. Whatever the reason, Maxwell's mood had once more changed and he was smiling and waving to people on the dockside as the yacht headed out into the bay.

Up on the sun deck Maxwell had smothered himself with some of the twenty sun lotions one of the deck hands brought up in a small hamper.

Lisa Kordalski had set up a table for mid-morning champagne and caviar. Maxwell had finished both by the time the yacht docked off Desertas.

His decision to go for a swim required another well-rehearsed ritual. The yacht stopped and the deck hand Soothill went to the stern and dropped a large rubber ring into the water, which was attached to a 50-foot line. Then he helped the totally naked Maxwell down the stern ladder into the sea. The deck hand took up station beside the telephone on its stand near the stern, ready to use it to summon help and then plunge into the sea if Maxwell was in difficulty. But he was a good swimmer and liked to float with the waves, though always staying within a few strokes of the rubber ring. As an additional precaution he wore a life jacket. After a while he waved to Soothill to start pulling in the line. Clutching the ring, Maxwell was then towed back to the stern and helped on board.

'Very good exercise,' he said. Dripping water, he picked up the stern phone and ordered Keating to prepare another of his 'fine snacks'.

After his snack – a mound of lobster in mayonnaise had been delivered to the sun deck and Maxwell had eaten only a few mouthfuls – he hurried down to his stateroom to make more telephone calls. Smothered in sun cream, his pale skin glistened in the cabin lights as he tried and failed to locate Doinov and Kevin. He picked up the phone one more time and dialled the bridge.

'Tell Whiteman to take the G-4 to London and bring Kevin and Ian down here,' he ordered.

Rankin called the Gulfstream's pilot in Gibraltar.

Ten minutes later Maxwell was back on the phone to the bridge.

'Cancel that order,' he barked.

'Will do, Mr Maxwell.'

Minutes later the bridge phone rang again. 'Take me back to Funchal.'

'Will do, Mr Maxwell,' Rankin said one more time.

Next Maxwell buzzed Lisa Kordalski to tell her to switch on his favourite Gershwin tape. Moments later the cabin filled with soft music. Then Maxwell ordered Kordalski to switch it off.

From the engine room came the sound of the twin motors starting. Again Maxwell called the bridge.

'How long before we get under way?' he demanded.

'Right away, Mr Maxwell,' Rankin replied.

What the captain was witnessing was another bout of Maxwell's omnipotent control, the baseline for what psychiatrists define as 'private reality'. That condition is most frequently seen in someone with manic tendencies: when nothing is beyond him; when wild, grandiose schemes are commonplace; when everything is done to excess, orders given and countermanded; when everything is seen in black and white and nothing in between. The manic can become elated, boisterous, even lewd.

In the coming hours Maxwell would display many of those symptoms: trotting out his fund of risqué stories, ordering a meal, then calling to say he had changed his mind. He would go up on deck, lie in the sun for a few minutes, then hurry down to his stateroom to make further phone calls.

Suddenly Maxwell's anger erupted. Approaching Funchal harbour, the *Lady Ghislaine* began to slow down. Maxwell demanded to know why. Rankin told him that the harbour master, who had total control over the port, has asked that the yacht should remain anchored in the bay because of the volume of sea traffic already coming and going from Funchal.

Maxwell said he wanted to call the harbour master. 'He had better understand who I am,' he thundered.

But Rankin stopped Maxwell by saying that if they remained out in the bay they would avoid any newspapermen waiting on shore.

'Good, good idea,' said Maxwell, his good humour restored. 'Exactly my thought.'

That night the *Lady Ghislaine* eased back to her harbour-wall berth. Having made sure there were no waiting journalists, Maxwell and Atkins left the yacht for the town's casino. Once more his cheerful mood at the prospect of winning changed when he was told that, if he was to gamble, the casino would require his passport and only cash was accepted. While he fumed at the bar, Atkins was sent back to the yacht with Maxwell's key to the stateroom bedroom safe and told to remove £3,000 and Maxwell's passport. Two hours later Maxwell walked away with a small profit from the roulette table.

Back on board he stashed the money and passport back in the safe, then called the bridge.

'I'm considering leaving for London in the morning. So have Whiteman ready to pick me up. Then you can make your way to New York.'

Rankin logged the new orders. He then called Whiteman and told him to be on standby to fly to Madeira.

Close to midnight, Maxwell made the last of several calls he had placed during that Saturday evening. It was to the New York lawyer Jules Kroll had appointed to act as the conduit between himself and Maxwell.

The detective later remembered he was told by the attorney that Maxwell planned to fly to New York in the coming week, 'to sit down and plan a strategy. He wanted to move things up a gear. That was fine by me.'

In Las Palmas decisions had also been taken by the *kidon*. Madeira was unsuitable for their purpose. Moored alongside the harbour wall, the *Lady Ghislaine* had become a target even beyond what Victor Ostrovsky called 'their magic'. For that to work, the yacht would have to be moved to a different location. If Robert Maxwell went through with his plan to return to London, then the plan to assassinate him would have to be abandoned. The *kidon* passed another night of waiting.

The sound of Funchal's church bells awoke Maxwell on Sunday morning, 3 November. He came up on deck in his night kaftan, a flowing robe that hid his huge potbelly. Breakfast over, he swept the port and shore front with his binoculars. Churchgoers for early-morning Mass were making their way towards the cathedral. It was a scene that had probably changed little down the centuries.

That tranquillity may well have contributed to yet another change of plan by Maxwell. He would not fly to London, he told Rankin. But he had seen enough of Madeira.

'Where would you like to go?' the captain asked. Together they pored over charts.

'There's Bermuda,' suggested the captain.

'How long will it take?'

'Nine days. Maybe a little less if I push it,' said Rankin.

'Still too long. Anywhere closer?'

'Well, there's the Azores. We could still go on from there to New York.'

Maxwell didn't fancy the Azores. He had heard it was 'just a rock with nothing to do'.

Rankin had jabbed a finger over the Canary Islands. They were a comfortable day's sailing. They could be there in time for lunch next day.

'Right, that's it, then. Tell Whiteman to make his way there to meet me,' ordered Maxwell.

'Will do, Mr Maxwell.'

The *Lady Ghislaine* prepared once more to get under way.

Alone on the sun deck, Robert Maxwell continued to train his binoculars over the town and up towards the Reid's Palace Hotel, where he had spent those mysterious thirty minutes the previous morning.

In London, Nick Davies, the journalist who had boasted he knew so much about Maxwell's dealings that he would never be sacked from the *Daily Mirror*, had just suffered that fate for lying about his claim that he was not involved in any of the allegations made by Seymour Hersh. The *Mirror*'s new editor, Richard Stott, had ordered that the foreign editor should be immediately escorted from the building by two security guards who told Davies, that he was not allowed to go to his desk, not allowed to speak to anyone and to leave immediately.

Since then he had spoken to Maxwell several times by telephone and had been told, 'Just keep your head down and say nothing to anyone until I sort it out.'

Davies's case rested on the fact that Stott had accepted he was not an Israeli spy and that he had nothing to do with the Vanunu case. He believed he had been sacked only because the paper had been made to look foolish.

Roy Greenslade, the *Mirror*'s former editor, could not understand why Davies had denied Hersh's allegations, 'since he could have openly admitted meeting arms dealers and knowing Ben-Menashe very well without there being any proof of being an arms dealer himself'.

Davies had written a letter of appeal for him to be reinstated. Maxwell had told him to come to his office at 10 a.m. the coming Friday, 8 November, to discuss the matter.

Now in London, not knowing where Maxwell was, Nick Davies, like so many others looking for the tycoon, could do nothing but wait.

In anticipation that Maxwell might change his mind again and decide to fly back to London, Rankin had summoned the Gulfstream from Gibraltar to Madeira. Whiteman had arrived earlier that Sunday.

Not expecting them to be on the move so quickly again, Rankin had given most of the crew a brief shore leave. Atkins and Lisa Kordalski were sent to round them up. All were back on board by early afternoon.

By then Maxwell had indicated a further change of plan. Once the yacht reached Tenerife – the island in the Canaries where Rankin had suggested they should drop anchor – he planned to fly back to London.

Rankin had called Whiteman, parked out at Madeira's small airport. The pilot had begun to work on a flight plan that would take him from Tenerife to London. He was still doing his calculations when he received another call from Rankin. Maxwell wanted the Gulfstream to 'do a fly-over' as they left Funchal.

At 3 p.m. the *Lady Ghislaine* eased her way out into the bay, powerful engines creating a propeller wash that had other boats bobbing on their anchor chains. Standing on the upper sun deck, this time in blazer and white trousers, a baseball cap on his head, Maxwell watched Whiteman execute a low pass, then bank and repeat the manoeuvre. The plane then turned south, heading for the Canary Islands.

Shortly afterwards Maxwell made a telephone call to his French lawyer, Samuel Pisar. He said he wanted advice on what he should say in his speech in London the following night when he was due to address the Anglo-Israeli dinner. Pisar had started to tell him what he could say when Maxwell interrupted.

'Any news on the other matter?' he asked.

For weeks Maxwell had been told he could be going to receive the highest honour France can bestow, the Légion d'Honneur. Pisar now confirmed it was going to be awarded and the decoration would be personally presented by François Mitterand. The French President was not only one of Maxwell's 'trusted friends', but also a 'trusted source' – one of many who had helped Maxwell to plague his editors with dubious stories.

Maxwell ordered up more champagne and toasted himself.

He then called Ian in London and told his son he would be back in time to make his after-dinner speech on Monday night. They had spoken for a few minutes about 'nothing much', Betty recalled Ian telling her. He had told Betty he was relieved his father had not cancelled.

There was one further call Maxwell made as the *Lady Ghislaine* reached her cruising speed. It was to Ernie Burrington, then the managing director of MCC. His background was unusual for such office. Burrington, a quietly spoken man from the north of England, had spent most of his working life in newspapers. He had been deputy editor, then editor of Maxwell's *Sunday People*, a down-market tabloid. He had served Maxwell well: in his tenure as editor, Burrington had shown himself a shrewd judge of what tittle-tattle readers liked. His style was non-confrontational, relying on gentle persuasion and common sense to get his way. He was one of the few MCC directors Maxwell still trusted.

That Sunday afternoon Burrington gave Maxwell his estimate on what the coming week would bring. For once Maxwell listened without interruption. He was 'considerate, polite and even apologetic' for the position in which MCC found itself. The conversation ended with Maxwell's assurance, 'I will deal with everything on my return.'

As he headed towards the Canaries, the weather was warm enough for Maxwell to have dinner on deck. His favourite Gershwin was piped up for his pleasure and the crew heard him humming along with the tunes. For a person who was in dire financial straits according to the English newspapers they had read, he seemed a man without a care in the world.

Monday, 4 November, in London was another of those Black Mondays that financiers dread. For Kevin and Ian, who had joined his brother in Fortress Maxwell, it was the darkest of mornings. The worst-kept secret over the weekend was now on the lips of every messenger boy in the City of London. Goldman Sachs and Lehman Brothers had carried out their threats. Who would be next?

The question was being asked in every bank boardroom. Attempts by Kevin to use pension-fund shares had been blocked. Lehman Brothers had coldly refused other shares, independent of MCCs, as security. The opinion was that any paper coming out of Maxwell House was useful only to light a fire. As the morning passed, the flames licked closer to the building. Banker after banker refused to take calls from Kevin or Ian. The ninth floor had become 'like a waiting room to hell', recalled one secretary.

Into the flurry of increasingly outgoing calls from Kevin and Ian – 'searching for money, searching for salvation', was how one employee recalled it – came an incoming call from Robert Maxwell.

Ian took it. When he started to try to describe how the situation was close to meltdown, Maxwell brushed him aside. He was sorry but he wouldn't be returning to address the Anglo-Israeli dinner that night. He wanted a couple of more days to think.

Ian looked across at Kevin and shrugged. There was nothing more to say. Both Maxwell's sons bent to the task of trying to save the remains of the Maxwell empire.

On board the *Lady Ghislaine*, Maxwell placed a second call, this one to Betty. In Headington Hill Hall there was also a sense of mounting crisis. Staff were eyeing each other nervously as they arrived for work. All wondered where their next pay cheque was coming from. Maxwell had already sold the cornerstone of his empire, Pergamon, for a remarkable £440 million. Gone too was Scitex for £120 million; along with his stake in the French TV channel, DFI, for £80 million; his shares in Britain's Central Television for £30 million; his interest in MTV (Europe) sold for £40 million. In all he had sold off assets that had brought him in £960 million. But that had not been enough to stop the haemorrhaging.

There had also been private settlements on those who had left his empire: men such as Peter Walker, a former government minister; Lord Donoghue, who had been a financial adviser; an MCC director, Jean-Pierre Anselmini, and Mark Boothe, who was executive director of the Maxwell Entertainment Group.

But Maxwell had wanted to speak of none of those matters with Betty. His call was to tell her to deputise for him at the Monday night dinner. She had agreed to do her best.

'Yes, I know you will,' he replied. He hung up before she could say goodbye.

As usual when entering a harbour, Maxwell joined Rankin on the bridge as they approached the port of Santa Cruz in Tenerife.

Rankin and the crew noticed that Maxwell was calmer than he had been for some time. His erratic behaviour had passed. There was nothing manic about him, nor for that matter did he show any signs of being concerned, let alone depressed. Whatever was going on in his mind was for him alone. If that inner, punitive, unrelenting voice of his conscience – reflected in his near abject apology to Burrington the previous day – had any part to play in his outward mood, he showed no one. If he felt, even for a moment, that what he had heard from London was no more than he deserved, that too was for him alone.

A clue that all was not well came when Maxwell once more reverted to baby talk. He was going to have 'a twim in the sea later'. Were there any 'minkeys on the island?' He disliked monkeys. 'You could get losted [lost] in one that size.' His infantile vocabulary included 'trightened' for frightened and 'deaded' for tired.

It was as if he had found the strain too great to continue for the moment behaving as an adult. The crew thought it once more the affectation of another of those wealthy eccentrics they had sailed with before.

Not for a moment did they realise his behaviour was an essential part of his defence mechanisms: it went with his lack of insight into family values, his denial of his family's emotional needs, his destruction of Betty's confidence, and that of his children, the creation of a carapace around the inner reality in which he lived, one in which the psychodynamics of the family and his working relationship with others had no place.

Instead, Robert Maxwell had chosen to face the responsibility of life alone and along the way he had abandoned the socially acceptable guidance system for his own feelings.

But none of this showed as he began to sweep the approaching coastline with his binoculars, while beside him Rankin continued to use the VHF radio to talk to the harbour master.

The *Lady Ghislaine* cruised slowly past the city of Santa Cruz, to the picturesque fishing port of Darsena Pesquera, three miles to the north. There she berthed.

It was a little after 10 a.m.

To the east of the island, in the Gran Canaria port of Las Palmas, the crew of a small motorised yacht ostensibly prepared for going fishing at sea. Food and crates of bottled water were stowed below in the cabin. On deck, fishing tackle was laid out with wet suits and air bottles. There was a small dinghy lashed to the deck at the stern of the yacht. Beside it was a small but powerful outboard motor. It had been fitted with baffles to muffle its sound. These could be removed before the yacht was returned to the rental agency.

Sails furled and using its motor, the yacht made its slow way out of port. The *kidon* were going to work.

Somewhere over the horizon the two *yahalomin* units had cast their electronic nets over the Canary Islands. One of the units had isolated and locked onto the radio frequency the *Lady Ghislaine* was using for international telephone calls and the Channel 9 VHF frequency channel Rankin had tuned to in order to communicate with the shore. Through their powerful laptop computer, it had been a simple matter for the two-man unit to establish the precise location of the yacht.

Waiting on the quayside at Darsena Pesquera was the pilot David Whiteman and Emma, the Gulfstream stewardess. They had driven up from the airport in the south of the island through pretty villages, each with its tiny harbour, to meet the *Lady Ghislaine*. Maxwell, like most visitors to the island, had been fixated by its towering Teide volcano, rising to almost 10,000 feet.

He motioned the pilot and stewardess to join him on deck. Whiteman learned there had been another change of plan. Maxwell told the pilot that he would probably fly back to London the next day.

Whiteman nodded: he had already prepared the paperwork for that flight. But Maxwell had not finished.

'Events may dictate that I have to go to New York.' He paused, then added, 'Or Jerusalem.'

White was the first to learn that Israel had now been added to Maxwell's travel plans. But he had become used to the way Maxwell could switch his itinerary at the last moment.

Meanwhile, Emma had sought and been given permission by Maxwell to use her camera to photograph the yacht, including its crew: it was her first time on board and she wanted a memento of her visit. For good measure she also took snaps of other boats moored in the harbour. From her vantage point on the upper sun deck, the *Lady Ghislaine* towered over them. Emma went to the bridge where Rankin was completing the paperwork for the harbour authorities. She photographed the kitchen, which Keating was leaving to go ashore to find lobsters for Maxwell's lunch. Within an hour the energetic Emma had used a complete roll of film. Her last shot was from the quay of Maxwell standing on the sun deck, once more using his binoculars to sweep the slopes of the volcano. In her brief time on board, Emma had thought it had been 'a fairy-tale experience' and that Maxwell had not been at all like she had expected. 'He was a gentleman'.

The young stewardess looked forward to tending to his every need on the flight next day.

In the drama that was slowly gaining pace, Emma's film would have its part.

Robert Keating had been berated by Maxwell for failing to find any lobsters. Maxwell had made do with Scottish salmon. After lunch he had told Rankin he wanted to find a place where he could swim naked as usual and secluded from any possible camera lens. He was concerned that photographers and reporters could have tracked him down to Tenerife.

Rankin pored over the local sea charts. He finally settled on Poris de Abona to the south of their present mooring. The small fishing village was on an inlet, guaranteeing calm water, and sufficiently inaccessible for any journalist to be quickly spotted.

On the sun deck Maxwell had one of the deck hands carry up his briefcase. Stripped to his sun trunks, Maxwell spent the ninety minutes it had taken the yacht to reach Poris de Abona reading papers.

It was a little after 2 p.m. when the *Lady Ghislaine* dropped anchor at the mouth of the inlet. Through his binoculars Maxwell would have seen that its few amenities included a bank, supermarket and a pharmacy.

Once more the ritual for swimming was carried out. But Maxwell soon signalled he wanted to be back on board as he found the water too cold.

While Rankin had managed to avoid the lens of any prying photographer, he had not paid any attention to the small motorised yacht that had first anchored out in the Bay of Marina del Atlantico, a strategic spot from which its four-man crew could watch the *Lady Ghislaine* making its way south for Maxwell's brief swimming excursion. The yacht was now cruising a little way off the coast as the *Lady Ghislaine* prepared to return to its designated mooring at Darsena Pesquera.

Aboard his own boat, fisherman Ernesto Krjus watched 'the smaller boat, which bore no name or flew no flag. It followed the *Lady Ghislaine* back up the coast.'

When the two boats reached the Marina del Atlantico bay, several local fishermen were puzzled. Later they were convinced the way the smaller yacht was manoeuvring, it was 'trying to get close but not so close to the big yacht', one of them later told a Spanish journalist, Miguel Rozas.

On board the smaller yacht the *kidon* now knew Maxwell had cancelled his plan to fly back to London in the morning. One of the *yahalomin* units stationed out at sea between Tenerife, the largest island in the archipelago, and Gran Canaria continued to monitor the communications traffic from the *Lady Ghislaine*. The second unit had conducted its own test. Using the converted laptop the two-man team had brought with them, they were able to send a transmission to the *Lady Ghislaine* that appeared to be an incoming call from London.

'Once the call had been acknowledged on the *Lady Ghislaine*'s bridge, it was terminated,' Ari Ben-Menashe would later claim.

Like Victor Ostrovsky, Ben-Menashe still had friends in Mossad. Both men accepted that their knowledge of what was happening on that November day would not be complete. The highest purpose of those directly involved – these small groups of Mossad officers in Tel Aviv and the *kidon* and *yahalomin* teams – was to ensure that their complicity remained hidden and, at worst, ambiguous. But equally both Ostrovsky and Ben-Menashe also knew that, while they could not fill in all the gaps, what they did learn could be taken as the truth. Others would later presume to ask how they knew such matters. But, like all serious questions, this should be approached obliquely. Both men had made part of their life in secret intelligence. While they worked in a world where falsity and truth are opposite sides of the same coin, their versions of events are similar regarding the essentials.

On board the *Lady Ghislaine* events had begun to gather momentum.

From the yacht's sun deck at 3 p.m., Maxwell used his mobile phone to call Kevin. He did not expect any good news and was, no doubt, all the more pleased to get it. Kevin had somehow managed to winkle £30 million out of Solomon Brothers, a smallish but prestigious bank. He had pledged collateral he did not possess: the MCC shares held by other banks.

In Headington Hill Hall, Betty was reading the speech for the Anglo-Israeli dinner. It would begin with an apology for her husband's absence. Then it would remind them what it meant to be a Jew in this troubled world, what his faith represented to him, what he wanted for Israel. Having read the speech, Betty telephoned Ian. She would like him to deliver it. Her son was a gifted public speaker, his timing and tone pitch-perfect. She feared that her French accent, so often a bone of contention with her husband in the last years, would not do justice to the words. Ian would serve his father well when he stood at the lectern in the Grosvenor Hotel in London. She would be there beside him, smiling and nodding the way she used to do when she had sat alongside her husband at other dinners.

On board the *Lady Ghislaine* Robert Maxwell was preparing for another dinner. To show his displeasure that the hapless Robert Keating had failed to produce lobsters for lunch, Maxwell had decided to have his meal ashore. A table had been reserved for him at Tenerife's finest hotel, the Mencey in the centre of Santa Cruz.

Dressed in a blazer, checked trousers and his American baseball cap, his sartorial trademark, and carrying his mobile phone, Maxwell walked down the gangplank to the waiting taxi. It was a few minutes after six in the evening when the bridge log noted 'owner ashore'.

From the moment he stepped into the magnificence of the Mencey dining room and was escorted by Sergio Rodriguez, the maître d', to his table, every movement of Robert Maxwell was later to become a matter of intense scrutiny.

The few unchallenged facts are: the restaurant was virtually empty; the hour was early for guests, who usually preferred the Spanish time of starting dinner from nine o'clock onwards. Rogriguez led Maxwell to a table in the corner of the restaurant furthest from the entrance. He sat with his back to the wall, his phone on the table in front of him. He ordered an asparagus mousse dip and a main course of hake with clams in a parsley sauce.

The wine waiter, Jose Dominguez Sanchez, served him a white burgundy.

When he came to refill Maxwell's glass, he noticed he had hardly touched his food. 'He looked thoughtful as if he was in another world,' the waiter recalled. Rodriguez hurried over to enquire if the food was cooked to Maxwell's satisfaction. Maxwell nodded and sipped his drink. 'His eyes kept going to the phone, then looking towards the door. I had the feeling he was either expecting a call or a visitor,' Rodriguez recalled.

After he had toyed with the main course, Maxwell pushed aside the plate and beckoned to Rodriguez. He wanted a cigar. The head waiter returned with a box of the hotel's finest Cuban cigars. Maxwell chose a medium-sized one. Rodriguez clipped its tip and lit it for Maxwell.

As the waiter withdrew, he noticed that Maxwell was once more dialling a number on his phone. He had done so several times during the meal.

'The guest seemed to be getting angry and was preoccupied,' Sanchez would later recall.

Maxwell once more beckoned the head waiter. He wanted the bill. Rodriguez produced it in the leather wallet that the Mencey reserved for that moment. Maxwell checked the amount and produced a bundle of pesetas from his own wallet. He placed the money inside the hotel wallet and hurried out of the restaurant.

Sanchez saw that not only had Maxwell left his half-smoked cigar smouldering in an ashtray, but had also forgotten to take his mobile phone. The waiter grabbed it and ran out of the hotel. He caught up with Maxwell as he was about to enter a taxi, handing over the phone.

Maxwell grunted his thanks. Sanchez heard him tell the taxi driver to take him to the Olimpio café. It was now 9 p.m.

The café was a ten-minute drive away. Its tables spilled out on to the pavement. Maxwell settled himself at one near the door. Though the café was busy, it was not full and waiters had time to note the huge man sitting at the table dialling on his phone. Mobile phones were still relatively new in Tenerife and the waiter who brought Maxwell a coffee and a cognac thought his customer must be very important to have such a phone. He also noted something else. 'This man looked at people passing all the time. He didn't look happy.'

The waiter had concluded this could be because there was no reply to the stranger's constant attempts to ring a number.

Maxwell abruptly stood up, put a handful of pesetas on the table and clambered back into a taxi.

He arrived at the *Lady Ghislaine*. The bridge log noted 'owner on board' at 9.45 p.m.

Rankin was on watch. Maxwell told the captain that he wanted to leave as 'soon as possible' for Los Cristianos. It was on the far side of Tenerife, almost at its southwestern tip.

Los Cristianos was close to the island's airport. Rankin wondered whether Maxwell planned to fly from there after he had enjoyed swimming in the sea at the resort; if so, Rankin was puzzled. At this time of year Los Cristianos would be filled with tourists seeking to escape the cold of Northern Europe.

It was a place where Maxwell could easily be spotted, resulting in photographers swarming around the *Lady Ghislaine*. But that was not Rankin's problem. His job was to carry out Maxwell's every lawful order; that was why he was paid almost £1,000 a week. His predecessors had forgotten that; to survive with someone like Maxwell, you needed to know exactly how far to go in offering advice.

'Los Cristianos it is, Mr Maxwell,' confirmed Rankin before making a note in the ship's log.

Rankin proposed the *Lady Ghislaine* should follow a leisurely route.

First they would sail up the coast of Tenerife to the top of the island. Then they should make for the northern end of Gran Canaria. Once there, the yacht would turn south, this time heading down past Las Palmas to the southern tip of Gran Canaria. From there they would head west, back towards Tenerife. That should bring them to Los Cristianos.

'How long will all this take?' Maxwell had asked.

'Twelve hours.'

'Good. Time for a good night's sleep,' Maxwell remarked. He had often said he slept really well only when at sea, rocked into slumber by the motion of the yacht.

Maxwell then went to his cabin.

On the bridge Rankin supervised the preparations for departure. The only problem he foresaw would be when he came back on watch at 6 a.m. next day. The southern sea around Tenerife was a route used by local ferries and the hydrofoil between the islands. There could also be restrictions in force in Los Cristianos because it was a favourite berth for whaling vessels. The large container-like ships were the mother craft for smaller fishing boats. They came from as far away as Russian ports to catch the abundant fish in the deep Atlantic.

At 10 p.m. the *Lady Ghislaine* was underway.

The stewardess Lisa Kordalski knocked on the door of Maxwell's stateroom thirty minutes later. He called for her to enter. She opened the door and remained in the doorway. She could see Maxwell at his desk through the open study door. Earlier she had turned down his bed and she saw that at some point he had lain on the cover, wrinkling it with his weight. She asked him if he wanted a nightcap. He said he didn't. Lisa walked over to the bed and quickly smoothed down the sheets and plumped the pillows. As she turned to leave, he told her to lock the bathroom door that was adjacent to the study. He had never done this before. She wondered why, but knew better than to ask. Having done so, to leave the stateroom she had to walk back across the bedroom and out through its main sliding door which led to the yacht's central corridor. As she began to walk down the corridor, she heard the lock turning inside the stateroom door.

Lisa again wondered what was going on. In the end she decided that if Maxwell wanted to lock himself in, it was none of her business. When she went to the bridge to tell Rankin her duties for the night were over, Lisa did not mention what Robert Maxwell had done.

The *kidon* yacht – flying no flag and displaying no nameboard, its only lights those required by maritime law to navigate – had also put to sea. In its cabin one of the team was crouched over a short-wave receiver waiting for the next short-burst transmission from either of the *yahalomin* units. The last one had been to alert the *kidon* the *Lady Ghislaine* was embarking on an overnight journey through some of the loneliest waters in the archipelago. Boat traffic would not begin to increase until the *Lady Ghislaine* was approaching Los Cristianos. That was still eleven hours away.

At 10.40 p.m. Ian Maxwell called the *Lady Ghislaine*. He was put through to his father. Ian was excited. The speech he had delivered had been well received; people from all over the Jewish Diaspora at the banquet has asked to be remembered and said how much they missed Maxwell. After a few minutes of describing the evening, Ian had concluded with words he would always remember.

'See you tomorrow, Dad.'

'You bet.'

There had been no talk of business. The universe of possible bankers to bail out MCC had shrunk to nothing. Friendships Maxwell had once counted on were gone – men who had sailed as his guests on the yacht, who had been frequent dinner companions at his penthouse. Ian had made no mention of any of those men. It had been a son reporting that he had not let down his father.

It was now 11 p.m.

Robert Maxwell called the bridge shortly afterwards and spoke to Rankin, who had still an hour to go before his watch ended.

'Notify me first before you put through any more calls.'

'Understood, Mr Maxwell.'

A short while later Rankin called down to say he had a Rabbi Feivish Vogel on the line calling from Moscow.

'Put him through.'

The rabbi was an old friend. He apologised profusely for disturbing Maxwell but he wanted his help to remove Jewish archives from the Lenin Library in Moscow; Rabbi Vogel felt their rightful home was in Jerusalem. Maxwell agreed and said he would try to arrange the matter.

At midnight First Officer Grahame Shorrocks relieved Rankin on the bridge. Having discussed their present course which put them on a heading towards Gran Canaria at a speed of twelve knots, Rankin issued one instruction.

'Call me if any craft shows up on radar within five miles.'

Like the request to Lisa Kordalski to lock the bathroom door and then Maxwell locking himself in, Rankin's instruction would also become the subject of endless speculation.

Rankin would never explain what had prompted him to issue the instruction to his junior officer. Shorrocks himself would have no clear recollection if he had asked Rankin what he had meant.

Again there are some facts not in dispute. The *Lady Ghislaine* was in calm water. Though the sky was almost without stars, a normal occurrence at this time of year, visibility was good. There were no crewmen on deck watch; there never were. The three security cameras were switched off; they always were at sea. The yacht was navigating on autopilot on a set course and speed. The two echo sounders and wind-speed indicator had all been called into play. The FX 4200 weather fax was switched on to alert of any weather change.

Had Rankin's order to Grahame Shorrocks been really no more than an ultra-careful captain who was determined not to lose his £50,000 a year job because he had not anticipated every possible eventuality – including that another boat showing up at a radar distance of five miles would pose any threat to the *Lady Ghislaine*?

There were two radars, the Furuno 1 and the Furuno 2, with a colour screen. Both were required to be switched on to provide an electronic alert around the *Lady Ghislaine*.

But Ari Ben-Menashe was convinced from all he would later learn that the equipment the *yahalomin* units carried would enable them to distort the signals the radars were receiving.

At 3 a.m. Second Officer Mark Atkins came up to the bridge to join Grahame Shorrocks. Atkins checked the gyro compass, the echo sounders and other monitoring equipment. The *Lady Ghislaine* was on a southerly course. Away on the starboard side was the landmass of Gran Canaria. At this hour only a few lights blinked ashore. Below them the ocean surged against the hull and the engines left a widening course in the yacht's wake.

*

The *kidon* yacht could have used the wake as a guide if they had not known exactly where the *Lady Ghislaine* was heading.

The night was darker, as it always was in the pre-dawn. On deck the *kidon* had put aside any pretence they were fishermen. Soon it would be time to work.

At 4.25 a.m. Second Engineer Leo Leonard came up onto the aft deck. He had checked that both engines were maintaining their consumption of 380 litres an hour and that the three Mercedes 100 kilowatt generators were set at their temperatures. Even in the cool of the night the engine room was a warm place to work.

Reaching the deck, he saw Robert Maxwell standing a few feet away.

'He was in his blue striped nightshirt in his favourite place on the starboard – the right-hand side near his stateroom door. With his left hand leaning on a stanchion and his back to the sea, he was looking towards the lights of Gran Canaria. From where Maxwell stood, the security cameras, even if they had been switched on, would not have shown him on the closed-circuit monitors on the bridge.

'No one knew that better than Maxwell. He had often used that spot to urinate over the side of the boat during the night or simply go on deck for fresh air.

'There were three cameras but none of them covered the area where Maxwell was standing. The bridge watch would not have been able to see. Neither would they have known if any intruder had boarded the boat.'

Spotting Leo Leonard leaning against a rail, Maxwell told the engineer he wanted the air conditioning turned up in his cabin.

'He didn't look at me,' Leonard recalled as he left the deck and went back to the engine room to carry out Maxwell's order.

It was now 4.30 a.m.

At 4.45 a.m. the bridge received a call from Maxwell. He told Mark Atkins his cabin was now too cold.

'Turn it up a degree or two,' Maxwell ordered.

'Straight away, Mr Maxwell.'

The brief exchange was the last Robert Maxwell would have with any crew member.

Sometime afterwards, Victor Ostrovsky would say, 'During the night of November 4/5, Mossad's problem was laid to rest in the salty waters of the Atlantic.'

It would be left to Ari Ben-Menashe, his one-time colleague in Israel's intelligence community, to explain how that had been achieved.

'At some time during his trip ashore in Tenerife the previous evening,

Maxwell had received the call he was waiting for. It originated from one of the *yahalomin* team.

'His caller told him that the packet he was expecting would be delivered to him between the hour of 4 a.m. and 5 a.m. He was to go on deck in that period and stand on the starboard side. The first time he went up, he encountered the ship's engineer. He sent him back down below. To make sure the engineer would not return on deck, Maxwell then called the bridge and had his cabin heating system adjusted.

'He knew he could not be observed from the bridge where he stood. He knew there was no deck watch. He knew no one would leave the bridge.

'Because of the surge of the sea against the hull and the noise of the engine, he did not hear the dinghy from the *kidon* yacht come alongside on the port side. There were three men in the dinghy. The fourth had remained on board the yacht to navigate it. The three men in the dinghy all wore frog suits; their faces were painted with a black water-resistant camouflage.

'Two of the frogmen used rubberised grappling hooks to come on board the *Lady Ghislaine*. The man in the dinghy dropped astern, having removed the grappling hooks. Because they were made of rubber they left no markings on the deck rail or hull.

'The two frogmen came on deck. One carried a waterproof pouch. From it he removed an already loaded syringe. Both men wore rubber-soled shoes. They reached Maxwell in a few strides. The *kidon* with the syringe plunged the needle into Maxwell's neck, just behind his right ear. The substance was a lethal nerve agent. It had been developed at the Institute for Biological Research in Tel Aviv.

'The two men gripped the body and lowered it over the side into the sea. They then followed into the water and were soon back on board the dinghy.'

What Victor Ostrovsky had called 'the *kidon* magic' had worked one more time.

That what had happened was incredible – of course. That Ari Ben-Menashe and Victor Ostrovsky expected to be traduced for their claims was a given.

Unlike those who would challenge them, both men had themselves direct knowledge of Mossad's methods. They knew what could be done. At the Mossad training school in Herzilia, Ostrovsky had been shown many examples of assassinations. For the *kidon*, boarding the *Lady Ghislaine* was not a problem: part of their training had involved climbing onto ships travelling at the speed the yacht was moving. They had been furnished with the crew's routine and would know the aft deck would be deserted. They had sat down with the scientists at the Institute for Biological Research and been told the right nerve agent to use and where to plunge the needle. They knew Maxwell's weight and height. He was tall and heavy but they were strong and fit and had trained in manoeuvring such a weight in moments over the side.

But they did not stand alone in saying what did happen on the aft deck.

There is first the testimony of the last man to see Robert Maxwell alive: Leo Leonard, the second engineer. Like most who follow his profession, he is a careful man in all he says and does. In his judgment, what had happened on the deck was no accident, no sudden heart attack. Without having spoken to Ben-Menashe or Ostrovsky, Leonard would later conclude: 'The wood-topped railings were too high and the wire railing where Maxwell liked to stand was just as much a protection. They would have stopped a bull going through.

'I think someone got on board during the night and did the job. I was in the Navy before I went on yachts. I know what you can do, especially in a calm sea at night. A professional assassin could have clambered on easily from a small craft that would not have shown up on radar, done what he had to and gone off. The killer would have taken the key from the stateroom to put off the time Maxwell was missing.'

It is, of course, still an extraordinary claim. But it becomes increasingly more credible when the words of Captain Gus Rankin are added. When Maxwell had gone overboard, he had been asleep in his cabin. Usually a man of few words, Rankin would later argue with considerable persuasion and knowledge of the sea and the *Lady Ghislaine* that what Ben-Menashe, Ostrovsky and Leonard had all outlined was manifestly feasible.

'The boat was moving along at 13/14 knots,' Rankin stated. 'That doesn't seem fast by driving standards. But you drop a can over the side and see how fast it disappears from you. It disappears rapidly. Plus, you've got the noise of the engines, the turbulence of the water and you've got a crew pretty much forward on the boat. With closed doors you're not going to hear at all. I think maybe the air conditioning call to the wheelhouse might have been a way of keeping the engineer away from the aft deck again.'

Had Maxwell gone out onto the aft deck to collect the package that Ben-Menashe alludes to? Had the mysterious call he had received previously been specific instructions as to when and where he was to appear on deck? Had Leo Leonard's presence sufficiently alarmed Robert Maxwell to make that call Rankin clearly thought was a diversion?

These questions would be at the forefront of the mind of an unchallengeable witness – Dr Iain West. He had a record of showing that what appeared to be a suicide or accident was in reality murder. Taking Ostrovsky's '*kidon* magic' as a prism, West had shown that a friend of Maxwell's, Dr Robert Ouko, Kenya's Foreign Minister, had not committed suicide a few months previously: the bullet had been fired from too far away for death to have been self-inflicted.

Soon West would be involved in the death of Robert Maxwell. For him there were four possible scenarios.

First, signs of incipient heart and lung disease are potentially lethal. But if Maxwell had died of either, I would have expected him to have fallen on the deck and remained there.

Secondly, he could have accidentally fallen overboard. But the sea was not rough; there were no abrupt changes of course and he would have had to do something quite active to fall over the side.

Thirdly, is suicide. Clearly his problems could cause a person to kill himself.

Fourth, there is the option he was murdered.

But, before any forensic conclusion could be drawn, the body of Robert Maxwell had to be found. His time of death, his exact number of hours in the water and much else would be forensically required.

NINETEEN

At 6 a.m. on 5 November 1991, Robert Keating was in the yacht's kitchen making the crew's breakfast. He also squeezed fresh orange juice and made a plate of smoked salmon sprinkled with caviar for Maxwell. Keating was certain he would find lobsters in Los Cristianos to make up for yesterday's failure to obtain them for Maxwell's lunch. He knew chefs had come and gone, fired on Maxwell's whim. But Keating really believed he was doing a good job: Rankin and the crew said they had never eaten better on-board food.

At 6.30 a.m., shaved and showered and dressed in crisp whites, Rankin was back on the bridge to relieve Second Officer Mark Atkins. He reported that it had been a quiet night and there were no log entries after he heard from Maxwell to adjust the heating in his cabin. The radar had not shown any craft within the five-mile radius Rankin had ordered he should be wakened about. Back on the bridge the captain had still not explained why he gave the order.

The island of Tenerife now showed as a blip on the radar. There were a number of other ships on the screen. All were in their designated sea lanes and well clear of the yacht's course. The weather fax reported that it was going to be another fine day with a calm sea.

Until Maxwell either called the bridge or buzzed the kitchen to have his breakfast served, the crew maintained a 'quiet watch' routine over the deck and through the corridors.

On the bridge Rankin responded to instructions from the harbour master's office at Los Cristianos. Private yachts were no longer permitted to anchor in the harbour, but out in the bay. To ensure this was complied with, a port authority launch patrolled the harbour.

Shortly after 9 a.m. Rankin was radioed that he would be anchoring to the southeast of the green starboard buoy that marked the entrance to the port. He told the deck hands to get the Mercruiser ready for any run ashore to collect supplies.

Thirty minutes later the *Lady Ghislaine* dropped anchor and the cruiser was lowered into the water.

Maxwell had still not come on deck. Their morning duties completed, captain and crew could only now wait for him to appear.

At 10.30 a.m. there was a call from Robert Pirie, a banker with Rothschild's. He asked to speak to Maxwell.

'Is this important enough to waken him?' enquired Rankin.

Maxwell was heavily in debt to the bank. Pirie was its president and chief executive in New York and had played a role in helping Maxwell to acquire Macmillan, the publishing conglomerate. It had been Pirie who had devised a slogan for T-shirts with the words 'we wonnit' emblazoned on the front. That night there had been champagne and lobsters in Maxwell's suite in the Waldorf Hotel. But those days were gone. Pirie needed to know when Maxwell was going to pay back Rothschild's.

Waiting to decide whether he should insist on being put through, Pirie wondered if the tycoon had on board the yacht any bottles of the hair lotion his barber specially imported from America to maintain the black sheen of Maxwell's hair? Pirie felt a twitch of sympathy for Maxwell. A man so vain must be under immense pressure. A good night's sleep would help him.

'Tell Mr Maxwell I'll phone back,' Pirie told Rankin.

At 11 a.m. there was another call from New York. It was John Bender, a senior vice-president at Macmillan, and their lawyer. Once more Rankin asked if the call was urgent.

'It is,' snapped Bender. He wanted to confront Maxwell about the latest reports. Maxwell had planned to sell off one of the Macmillan companies but the deal was stalling. He had arisen at 5 a.m. to call Maxwell. He had no sympathy for a tycoon who needed to lie-in.

'Very well, I'll put you through to Mr Maxwell,' said Rankin.

He dialled the stateroom bedroom. There was no reply. He tried the study. There was no answer. Finally he dialled the phone on its stand on the aft deck. It rang out.

He had not called the kitchen or the stewardesses to see if breakfast had been cooked and served to Maxwell. Neither did he have one of the deck hands check on the upper sun deck to see if Maxwell had gone up there to look out for any passing ships.

Rankin told Bender he would have to call back. He now dialled the kitchen and told Keating to meet him outside the study door, which led to Maxwell's private bathroom.

The captain had now begun to wonder if Maxwell had suffered a heart attack. If so, he would need Keating: he was the one man on board with first-aid experience. It was one of the reasons he had been hired. Rankin would never be able to explain his premonition that Maxwell had suffered a heart attack, except 'he was a big man and it could have happened'.

The two men made their separate ways to the study door. Rankin tried the handle. The door was locked. He banged on the door.

'Mr Maxwell, are you OK in there?' asked Rankin.

The captain knocked louder. Keating joined, knocking on the door.

'Mr Maxwell! Are you OK?' they chorused.

There was no response.

'Let's try the main door to his stateroom,' said Rankin.

They found the door locked.

'What's he up to?' asked Keating.

Rankin didn't answer. He used his pass key and entered the stateroom.

Rankin noted the time: 11.15 a.m. The two men moved into the master suite. The bed had been occupied, the sheets pushed back and the pillows rumpled. On a newspaper on the floor were two banana skins. Maxwell's blue, stained nightshirt was on the floor.

'He's not here,' said Keating.

But Rankin was already on his way out of the cabin back to the bridge. Atkins was on watch.

'Let's get a search going,' ordered Rankin. 'Maxwell's disappeared.'

'Disappeared? Where could he have gone to?' Atkins asked. The former policeman knew people did not just 'disappear' on a boat. Maxwell could only have gone overboard. While he hurried off to organise the crew, Rankin went to Leo Leonard's cabin, rousing the second engineer from sleep.

Leonard recounted how he had seen Maxwell on deck in the small hours in his nightshirt, and had gone back to adjust the thermostat setting for the master suite. Fifteen minutes later had come the call from the bridge to reset it.

Leonard joined the search. At some stage Lisa Kordalski mentioned the request to lock the bathroom door and hearing the key turn in the main door to the suite.

Rankin shook his head. Nothing made sense.

Up on the sun deck a crewman was scanning the sea with binoculars.

'He's out there! Swimming!' he shouted to Rankin on the aft deck.

The captain raised his binoculars and saw a dark-haired man swimming some distance away, heading for the beach.

'Boat crew to the cruiser,' ordered Rankin. But, even as the two deck hands scrambled to board the motorboat, Rankin stopped them. The figure in the sea was treading water as he headed up the beach. It was not Maxwell.

One by one the crew reported they had found no trace of Maxwell. For Rankin there were unanswered questions. Why had Maxwell locked himself in his suite? Had he come back on deck a second time? Surely he hadn't gone for a swim.

But right now answers to those questions were not important. If Maxwell was not on the yacht – then he must be in the sea. There was no way of telling when Maxwell had gone over the side.

At 11.45 a.m. Rankin returned to the bridge. He lifted the plastic cover on the emergency phone, pressed the red button underneath and dialled a three-digit code to send a 'Priority Three' call for 'Man Overboard'.

He gave the yacht's present position and what few details he had of their course before then. He added his name, rank and the yacht's satellite-phone call-back numbers.

He then called the local emergency station at Los Cristianos. The man who answered the phone spoke no English. Rankin slammed down the phone and called the only Englishman he knew, a shipping agent on the other side of the island. He told him what had happened – and asked the agent to call the authorities in Los Cristianos to alert them.

Rankin had still not called the port office in the ferry building only a few hundred yards from where the *Lady Ghislaine* rode at anchor. The office was open and there were several staff who spoke English and other languages: it was where all the visiting captains had to come ashore and report their arrival. The office routinely dealt with and had immediate access to the National Search and Rescue Service.

Finally, at 11.50 a.m. – almost forty minutes after he and Keating had first entered Maxwell's cabin – Rankin sent First Officer Grahame Shorrocks in the cruiser to raise the alarm at the port office.

Watching her boyfriend heading off, Lisa Kordalski bit her lip. Maybe if she had reported Maxwell's strange behaviour, some of this would not be happening.

At 12.02 p.m. Rankin placed his first call to England. He spoke to the Gulfstream pilot, Brian Hull.

'We've lost Maxwell. Who should I tell?'

'You'd better call Kevin Maxwell,' said Hull.

Instead, Rankin decided to send out an SOS on the Satcom network. It was picked up by the emergency service operator in Stavanger, Norway. The operator was explaining that the Canaries were outside his designated search-and-rescue area, when a voice interjected.

'Let me connect you to the New York Coastguard.' It was an American operator monitoring international distress calls.

Moments later a calm voice was asking the captain for details. The news that Robert Maxwell was missing had begun to spread across the world.

On the bridge Gus Rankin was using his charts and compass to circulate what had been the position of the *Lady Ghislaine* at 5 a.m. There was nothing to show that was when Maxwell had gone overboard. But to the captain it seemed a good starting point – given Leo Leonard had seen Maxwell alive thirty minutes before.

Meanwhile, the yacht had been cleared to enter the harbour and moor at the quayside. Atkins had also contacted the pilot, David Whiteman, at the island's airport. He was on his way by car to the harbour.

At 12.35 p.m. – a full ninety minutes after Maxwell's disappearance had been registered by the crew – Rankin phoned Kevin Maxwell in his office on the ninth floor of Maxwell House.

Rankin's voice was calm and controlled.

'I'm sorry to tell you your father has gone overboard during the night.'

'I take it you've searched the boat.'

'Everywhere. He's not on board. I've alerted all the emergency services.'

'Call me in five minutes.'

At 12.40 p.m., Rankin made the call. He was put on a speakerphone. He could hear Ian Maxwell in the background.

'I don't care what it costs. Rescue planes. Whatever is needed. Just find my father's body,' said Kevin.

It was the first time anyone had accepted they were looking for a body; that Robert Maxwell was dead.

'The only calls you take are from me. Or Ian. Understand, Captain Rankin?' said Kevin, a new crispness in his voice. For Rankin it was clear who was now in charge.

The *kidon* and *yaholomin* units were on their separate ways back to Israel. Allowing for plane connections, the *kidon* would reach Tel Aviv by nightfall. The *yaholomin*, having to return their boats to Rabat, would not reach Israel until the following day. By then the group of Mossad officers had heard the news.

At 1.34 p.m. on that November day, the country's ambassador in Madrid was having his first conversation with Prime Minister Yitzhak Shamir, breaking the news Robert Maxwell had disappeared at sea.

By 1.40 p.m. Spanish time, the search-and-rescue operation was up and running. It consisted of three helicopters, a Fokker aircraft and a tugboat. Using the coordinates that plotted where Rankin had said the *Lady Ghislaine* had been at 5 a.m., and working with local knowledge of the tides and wind drift, the helicopters and Fokker had begun a grid search pattern extending beyond Gran Canaria all the way to Los Cristianos. The tugboat had started a search along the coastline in case Maxwell had been washed into an inlet.

Local fishermen were alerted to keep a lookout from their boats. With the calls coming into both Tenerife and Gran Canaria, it was beginning to dawn on the local authorities that this was no ordinary tragedy. In Madrid the pressure had started. The first media calls from London had come.

*

In London Kevin and Ian told their mother. Betty took it calmly. She was beginning to display the same steely resolve that would characterise her in the coming days. Kevin called his eldest brother, Philip, who was in France. Within an hour he was on his way to meet up with Betty at Farnborough, where Brian Hull had prepared a flight plan to Tenerife. It had been decided by Kevin and Ian that Philip should travel with their mother. He spoke fluent Spanish and both brothers agreed there was no one better than Philip in a crisis.

Both brothers also had their eyes on the clock as they made calls to their brothers and sisters to break the news. They wanted to reach them before a reporter did. It was still early morning in San Francisco when Isabel heard. She could not remember what she said or did. 'It was just unreal – someone like Dad just didn't vanish like that,' she said later. Ghislaine, whose name was proudly displayed on the prow of the ship, was more practical. How was their mother coping? Told that Betty was going to Tenerife, Ghislaine said she would be there as fast as the first plane would carry her.

For Kevin and Ian there was another need to watch the clock creep round to 3 p.m. MCC shares were now nose-diving. So were those in Mirror Group Newspapers. As they watched the stock market screens in their office, millions more were wiped off their value. MCC had opened at 139 pence a share. By 2.58 p.m. in London, they stood at 121 pence, their lowest in eight years. MGN had also hit a new low, hovering at 77.5 pence a unit. With a minute to go before the City of London stopped trading, Kevin decided to ask the stock market for trading in both companies to be suspended.

At 3.05 p.m. the Press Association carried a news flash to all newspapers in Britain. 'Robert Maxwell missing at sea'. Reuters and the Associated Press of America relayed the message around the world.

At 4.45 that Tuesday afternoon, the Gulfstream 2 began its descent into Tenerife. From the cockpit, its pilot, Brian Hull continued to relay details he was picking up on the VHF radio of the sea rescue.

During the flight Betty had said little, sitting close to Philip, feeling the protection of his body. She had chosen a black dress and in her handbag was a Bible. Sitting behind them were a reporter, John Jackson, and photographer, Ken Lennox, from the *Daily Mirror*. Over the years they had become personal friends of Betty's, two of the few she had established on the newspaper, and she was glad of their company. The paper's editor, Richard Stott, had warned her that now the word was out there would be a media feeding frenzy on Tenerife and his staff were there to stop, as far as possible, the intrusion she would face. She was grateful.

The mood on board the Gulfstream was sombre: it reminded one of the *Mirror* men of what it must have been like when Jacqueline Kennedy had brought back the President's body to Washington – except that there was still no sign of Maxwell.

Philip had gone to the cockpit and spoken directly over the radio to the Spanish Air Sea Rescue Service in Madrid. They told him every ship in a thousand-square-mile area was searching.

After each titbit of news Betty sat there, eyes closed. 'My heart heavy, my body tense. I just prayed.'

Philip was back on the radio to Madrid. The weather in the area was becoming misty. The helicopters were reporting visibility down to a few yards. The search would soon have to be called off until morning.

Betty sat there trembling. The thought that Bob was out there in the Atlantic sea was too awful to bear. Suppose there were sharks or some other man-eating fish. She closed her eyes and prayed harder.

At 5.25 p.m. the cockpit radio crackled again. The Madrid rescue coordinator reported that a fisherman had spotted a body floating in the water.

Hull noted the coordinates: 27. 47. 6N, 19.06 W. He called back into the cabin.

'They have a sighting. It's about a hundred miles to the east of Tenerife – about twenty miles to the south of Gran Canaria.'

The words finally ended the last vestige of hope Betty realised she had been clinging to. Bob was gone.

She knew she would not see his features alive again. What, she wondered, would he look like in death?

The Puma helicopter pilot was close to having to turn back to refuel when he had received the sighting report. In minutes he was over the area. The winch man opened the Puma's sliding door and Jose Francisco Perdoma, the frogman, clipped his harness to the cable and crouched in the opening, eyes scanning the sea. He waved to the winch man to tell the pilot to descend. The helicopter's down draft began to flatten out the water round the body.

Fifty feet below, face upward, arms extended, feet together, Robert Maxwell looked as if he had been crucified on some invisible cross.

Perdoma made the sign of the cross before the winch man lowered him into the water. At sea level the down draft from the Puma's blades was considerable, so that the body was floating beneath the surface.

Perdoma made a quick estimate of the weight the winch would have to lift: about 310 pounds (140 kilos). Would the cable be able to hold such a massive dead weight?

There was a further problem. Normally Perdoma used a large basket into which he put a body before it was lifted up to the Puma. But Maxwell's size meant he would have to be placed in a harness.

Perdoma swam around the body after waving the helicopter to ascend to reduce the down thrust. The pilot hovered one hundred feet above the sea.

Free of the downward pressure, Robert Maxwell rose slowly to the surface, still with his arms extended. His eyes were open and his mouth slack.

Grasping the harness in one hand, Perdoma sank beneath the body and began to work the webbing into place. He put it first under the head, then, using one hand to swim, extended the harness down Maxwell's back to his large thighs. Next he hooked the webbing over the toes. Holding the rest of the harness, Perdoma surfaced. Now came the hardest part of all: manoeuvring the arms into the harness.

Above the frogman, the Puma's navigation lights were brighter as darkness closed in. Perdoma knew he would have only a few more minutes to complete his work.

He took one arm, stiff from rigor mortis, and forced it to Maxwell's side. Then he repeated the action with the second arm.

With the body now secured in the harness, Perdoma signalled for the Puma to descend. The winch man lowered his cable. Perdoma clipped it to the harness. With a great sucking sound the sea released its grip on Robert Maxwell. Slowly, the huge lifeless body, its skin glistening wet, was pulled up into the helicopter.

In forcing Maxwell's arms to his sides, Perdoma had unwittingly caused the first serious problem for the pathologists waiting ashore to conduct a post-mortem. The movement of the arms had broken the rigor mortis in Maxwell's body.

As the Gulfstream continued its descent into Canary Islands air space, Brian Hull tried to follow the excitable chatter in his headphones. The body was being taken to Gando Airfield, a Spanish military base. Soon Hull was told he could land there. There was something about a judge giving orders. Then came an English-speaking voice.

'Pilot of the Gulfstream. The British press magnate will remain on board the helicopter until you arrive. There are many people waiting.'

Hull acknowledged the message. The *Mirror* reporter John Jackson murmured to the photographer Ken Lennox that 'people waiting' translated to fellow journalists. They began to strategise how they were going to keep them away from Betty and Philip. Jackson went forward to consult with Hull. The pilot said he would call Gando and ask for permission to park as close as possible to the airport terminal. The voice in Hull's headset said the judge agreed to that. Whoever this judge was, Hull thought, he seemed to be running things.

At 8.30 p.m. Hull brought the Gulfstream down on to the runway at Gando and taxied towards buildings in the distance. As he came closer, he saw through the cockpit windows a group of people, many holding cameras. He called Philip into the flight deck.

'Nothing we can do,' said Philip. He returned to sit beside his mother. Betty, fingers entwined, felt she was still a stranger caught up in an event to which she was a spectator.

Jackson leaned forward and said he and Lennox would leave the aircraft first, then Betty, with Philip bringing up the rear. The three men would form a phalanx around her; Lennox knew Betty would be the one the photographers wanted for their 'grieving widow' pictures.

Betty was determined not to oblige them. In life they had hounded Bob. They were not going to have the satisfaction of seeing her cry.

She stepped briskly down the aircraft steps into a fusillade of flashguns. Her face was a mask. Out of the corner of her eye she saw a stretcher covered in a white shroud beside a helicopter.

'My heart lurched. My only thought was to follow the stretcher,' she remembered.

She asked if she could go over to the stretcher.

'Not yet, señora,' one of the men gathered around her murmured. 'He must be prepared.'

What could that mean? Had Bob been so badly damaged they were going try to make him presentable for her? Maybe that was the custom in Spain. She didn't know how matters were handled here.

'This way, señora,' murmured a voice. With Betty protected in the centre, the phalanx of Philip, the *Mirror* men and uniformed soldiers and police walked into a building.

Outside, cameras lit the night sky. Reporters continued to shout questions. Jackson had been right when he predicted it would be a media circus.

Inside, Betty and the others were taken to an office already filled with Spanish air force officers, standing against the walls. With them was a man in a lightweight suit: the British vice-consul who had come over from Las Palmas.

He shook Betty's hand and murmured condolences. Betty thanked him and then turned to face a major, who had risen from behind his desk. He stepped forward and gave her a hand kiss, his lips passing just above her extended hand. He acknowledged Philip and the two journalists with polite nods.

'When can I see my husband's body?' Betty had steeled herself for the moment she would actually acknowledge Maxwell was no longer a living person.

'Soon, señora. In the meantime maybe you would like to talk to the pilot who found your husband,' suggested the major.

She nodded. Questions had already begun to form in her mind during the flight. Why had it taken so long for the search to start? Kevin had said Rankin had called him after midday. All those planes and ships: why hadn't they been able to find Bob earlier? How long had Bob been in the water? Had anybody any idea how he died? Kevin had said Rankin thought it was a heart attack. How did the captain know that? He wasn't a doctor. And why hadn't Rankin been here to meet her?

As all the questions swirled through her mind, a tall sallow-faced man in the uniform of the Spanish National Rescue Service stepped forward. The major introduced him as Captain Jesus Fernandez Vaca, the pilot of the Puma.

The major turned to the others and suggested they should all join him in the corridor outside the office.

Betty gave a quick smile of thanks. She needed to be alone with the man who might be able to answer her questions. Vaca motioned her to a seat and sat beside her. For a moment they sat in silence. Then she turned to him.

'Do you speak English?'

'Yes, señora.'

'Good. I would like to ask you some questions.'

Vaca inclined his head, indicating he would do all he could to answer them.

'She had many questions and that was understandable,' Vaca would recall. She wanted to know every detail of the rescue: exactly where we had found the body and the exact condition it was in. She asked how long I thought it had been in the water and I said it was probably twelve hours. I said it was not possible for me to be more precise. She began to ask about my experience in the work of search and recovery, and I told her I had been doing this for twelve years. I had recovered many hundreds of bodies from the sea. I explained that no recovery was the same. She listened to me carefully, as if she was memorising everything I was saying. She had extraordinary self-control. Other relatives would have perhaps collapsed under the strain. But she was a strong woman.'

She thanked Vaca and looked towards the door as it opened to admit Luis Gutierrez Ruiz, the local judge who now had legal charge of Robert Maxwell's body. The judge was a commanding figure with a kindly face.

He bowed towards Betty. In broken English he said the body was now ready to view. He motioned for Philip to join her; the others must remain behind.

As she walked down the corridor, Betty's mind was filled with what Vaca had told her. One issue above all others returned. Vaca had estimated Bob had been in the water for around twelve hours. He had been found, according to the pilot, around 6 p.m. Rankin had told Kevin he had returned to the bridge of the *Lady Ghislaine* at 6.30 a.m. Given that Rankin would have performed his usual morning toilet, he would very likely have been awake when, if Vaca's timing was right, Bob had gone overboard.

Back on the bridge after a good night's sleep, why had Rankin not noticed anything? Bob had told her that 'captain on the bridge' meant that everybody was snap-eyed. There was also the question of daybreak. Vaca had said the first grey light of dawn came at this time of the year around 6 a.m., so there would have been sufficient light to see if Bob had gone overboard. That is if anyone had been looking back down the yacht, or beyond to its wake.

Equally puzzling was why Rankin hadn't come to the airport. He knew what time she was going to land.

But all such thoughts were banished from Betty's mind as she reached the end of the corridor. Judge Gutierrez Ruiz stood aside and motioned her towards an open door. Beyond, she could see the stretcher and the massive mound of the body beneath the sheet. For some reason she thought the shroud was made of canvas, and she wondered if that would be rough on Bob's skin.

Lined up, staring at her in silence, were three figures, two men and an attractive young woman. Sitting behind them in wooden chairs were several dark-suited officials, a middle-aged man in the olive uniform of the Guardia Civil and the vice-consul. The diplomat stepped forward and began to introduce the others.

'Mrs Maxwell, this is Dr Carlos Lopez de Lamela, the chief forensic pathologist.'

One of the white-coated figures inclined his head.

'And assisting him is Dr Luis Garcia Cohen.'

Another nod towards Betty from the second pathologist.

'And this is Dr Maria Ramos, who will be assisting as a pathologist,' intoned the vice-consul.

Betty nodded at the young woman while Philip frowned at the vice-consul to end any further introductions. The diplomat returned to his seat.

Betty moved closer to the stretcher. She stood silent and inwardly terrified at what she would see. Had 'her giant of a man' been mauled by sharks? Would the sea have left him bloated? She turned to Philip, uncertain what to do.

Dr Maria Ramos was at her side. She gently lifted the sheet, slowly uncovering Maxwell's face, then continuing to roll down the sheet to his waist. The pathologist stepped back. The seated men craned forward to get a better look. Philip moved closer to his mother. She glanced at him, and then turned back to the body.

For her, Maxwell was 'as he had been in life. His jet-black hair was slightly discoloured by the sun and the salt water. His face was at peace.'

Others in the room would say that Maxwell's hair showed traces of dye mixed with his natural greyness.

Betty continued to look down at her husband. Apart from traces of dried blood from his nose, his face was unmarked. She touched his cheek. It was icy cold. She traced her hand over his forehead. She put her own hand in his clenched fist. His fingers opened easily and were soft to the touch. 'It seemed strange but there was no sign of rigor mortis.'

No one had told her how the telltale sign of death had been broken in the struggle to get Maxwell on board the helicopter.

She stepped back, wishing everyone would leave the room and leave here alone with her husband. Even in death he seemed more of a physical colossus than in life. The more she looked, the more she could see a dignity and defiance about him, as if he now needed to fear no one, and no one could harm him any longer.

Why didn't all these people leave? Leave her to be with him? Leave her to note all the things she wanted to remember: the way his arms were slightly bent forward at the elbows, as if he were about to lever himself off this stretcher which was much too narrow to hold him? She ran her fingers over his face one more time. She turned. Dr Ramos was back beside her.

'Please would you remove the entire sheet? I want to see all of my husband.'

'Of course, señora,' whispered Dr Ramos. Slowly and carefully, she rolled down the sheet to expose Maxwell's entire body. Betty's eyes travelled down from the top of his head to the soles of his feet. 'His body was completely straight and his whole bearing was one of extreme dignity.'

There was no sound in the room apart from her soft footsteps as she moved from one end of the stretcher – from his head to his feet and then back again – staring and occasionally touching. Dr Ramos would always remember the 'quiet dignity of this remarkable lady. The pain was deep in her; the bravery was for all to see.'

Staring at his body, cold like marble – filled with her own inner grief, shock, fear, sadness, awe and perplexity – Betty knew the overriding feeling she had was one of love.

She loved him still.

By 10 p.m. Betty and Philip were on their way to Los Cristianos where the *Lady Ghislaine* was anchored. Much had happened since she had finally said her farewell to Maxwell with a lingering touch of her fingers against his cheek. Outside in the corridor, Dr Carlos Lopez de Lamela had enquired if Maxwell had been taking any prescribed drugs. She mentioned a heart-muscle relaxant. She asked the pathologist how her husband had died.

'I believe it was a heart attack,' came the reply.

How could he know? she wondered. What were the outward signs of a heart attack? And how could anyone be so certain after a body had been twelve hours in the water?

Perhaps sensing her questions, de Lamela said there would be an autopsy.

'How long will it take?' Philip asked.

'A few days to arrange everything,' said the pathologist. He turned to Betty. 'Would you like a British pathologist to attend?'

Betty looked at Philip. Neither had any previous experience of post-mortem procedures. But what would be the point of bringing a pathologist all the way from London? Surely the Spanish were competent to conduct an autopsy?

Besides, 'Bob was dead. No one could bring him back to life. All I wanted was to bury him as soon as possible.'

Then Judge Gutierrez Ruiz intervened. He told Betty there would have to be an enquiry into the cause of death. That could take place, at the earliest, next day in Las Palmas.

On that note they had left the building. Outside, the number of journalists had grown significantly. Helped by the two *Mirror* men and policemen, Betty and Philip reached the Gulfstream, its engines running. Hull took off for the short flight to Tenerife. He had taxis waiting and they sped out of the airport as more journalists were arriving.

During the drive Betty fretted about what the pathologist had said about a possible heart attack. She understood enough about the condition to know there are warning signs. Bob was careful about his health: he could have called for help if he had sensed trouble. If it had been one of those sudden massive coronary failures, then surely he would have collapsed and remained on deck, his body to be found later. So how had he gone over the side? Had he leaned against the rail when the attack happened? But the rails were level with his upper waist, from what she remembered. Given that his massive body weight centred on his stomach, he could not easily have toppled over into the sea. More likely he would have crumpled against the rail. But these, she realised, were only theories. She hoped to learn more when she reached the yacht.

Close to 11 p.m. they arrived at the *Lady Ghislaine*. On deck Rankin and the entire crew were lined up. One by one the captain introduced them. Each murmured their condolences; some were close to tears. Philip turned to the crew and said he would like to see them all in the main salon. He did not tell them why.

For a moment, Betty stood there again uncertain what to do. Some of the crew were unknown faces; Rankin she had not met before. He was watching her carefully. She looked about her, wondering where it had happened. Her memory had been right: the rails were waist high. She glanced down the aft deck. There were wires at the same height in place of the railings. But, if Bob had fallen against them, surely there would have been some mark on his body. But his chest had been as smooth as she had always remembered it. There were just so many questions.

She looked at Rankin. He indicated a plain-clothes man standing beside him.

'This is a police officer, Mrs Maxwell,' explained Rankin.

Betty nodded. She said she would like to go to her cabin.

'You mean Mr Maxwell's?' asked Rankin.

'Of course. Mine!' said Betty.

She was tired. It had been a long day. She didn't feel she had to explain to anyone where she wanted to sleep. Philip had gone down to the salon to interview the crew. Rankin turned to her.

'I regret, Mrs Maxwell, you will not be able to use the cabin. The police have sealed it. It's part of their investigation.'

Betty turned to the officer. 'How long will this investigation last?'

'It is finished, señora.'

She managed to hide her surprise. What sort of investigation had this been? And why had Rankin said she could not sleep in the cabin when the policeman had finished there? More unanswered questions. But Betty felt it was not the time to press. She just wanted to go to the cabin where Bob had last slept.

'Then I can use my cabin tonight?'

'Of course, señora. But the safe has been sealed.'

Like a hunting dog coming to point, Betty, despite her tiredness and the emotional strain of the past hour, was now alert.

'Sealed? Why is it sealed?' she asked.

'Because we could not open it,' said the policeman.

Betty stared at him, perplexed. Why seal the safe if it couldn't be opened? And why couldn't it be opened? Rankin had a key.

'The captain has the key,' she said.

The officer turned to Rankin for confirmation. Rankin shook his head.

'Señora Maxwell, Captain Rankin says he doesn't have a key.'

'That's correct, Mrs Maxwell,' said Rankin.

Betty's irritation increased. Maxwell had a rule that the captain should always have a copy of the key so that, when the boat was chartered, the safe could be used by whoever was in the master suite.

There was also a second key she kept in her jewellery box on board, in her dressing room.

'Come with me!' she commanded the police officer. Rankin followed. She already had formed an unfavourable impression of the captain: he was too casual in his manner, 'not giving the spruce naval impression of previous captains, not what you would expect to see commanding the *Lady Ghislaine*'.

Further, in the short time she had been on board, she felt the yacht 'did not seem quite shipshape'.

Reaching the cabin, she went to her dressing room, opened the jewellery box and produced a key to the safe.

'There! You can open the safe now,' she said to the officer. He replied he would need to leave that to his commander. He saluted and left.

Betty turned to Rankin and began to give orders. The *Lady Ghislaine* was to leave the harbour. It would be only a matter of time before the press arrived. Out at sea they would not be able to reach her or Philip. She looked around the stateroom.

What kind of investigation had gone on here? Everything was as she would have expected Bob to leave it. He was notoriously untidy, dropping his clothes to be picked up by others. She could see them scattered all over the bedroom. Shouldn't the police have taken them away for forensic examination? Wasn't that what usually happened? What other purpose could there be for the investigation? And why seal the safe? She still had the key in her hand. Maybe she should open it and see what was inside. But she would then be breaking Spanish law if she removed the police tape over the lock. That could bring more problems.

She went to Maxwell's bathroom and stood in the door. His swimming trunks were crumpled in a corner. She began to inspect the cabin more carefully. On the floor beside the bed was a pair of his undershorts and a sweatshirt. Nearby was a crumpled nightshirt.

'All this was perfectly normal. Bob liked to get up in the middle of the night to change his nightshirt. He would get clammy, so there were several shirts on hand for him,' Betty would recall.

Bathed and changed into summer clothes, she went in search of Philip, the two *Mirror* journalists and her Spanish lawyer, Julio Claverie. They were all settled into their cabins and ready for bed. She told them that if they required any food or drink they should buzz the duty stewardess, Lisa Kordalski. Betty then returned to her suite and phoned for Rankin to come and see her.

He arrived in a few moments, and again she was struck by his familiarity: the way he sat down without being invited and his offhand manner. She felt it did not auger well for their future relationship. But she needed answers to questions that perturbed her.

'When did you discover my husband was missing?' she began.

'Like I told Kevin, it was after I came here into the cabin.'

'What time was that?'

'Like I told Kevin, it was after the second phone call for Bob.'

'What steps did you take to find Mr Maxwell?'

Betty listened as Rankin told her about the boat search and the various steps he had taken to raise the alarm.

'What do you think happened to Mr Maxwell?' she asked.

'Well, I think he went up on deck, had a heart attack and fell over the side.'

'But you don't know for sure?'

'No, Mrs Maxwell. Nobody knows for sure because no one saw him go,' said Rankin. It was a stressful time for them both.

Betty went to the master suite and climbed into the large double bed she had once shared with Maxwell. In minutes she fell into an uneasy sleep to the noise of the steady surge of the *Lady Ghislaine* moving through the water.

In the main salon Philip had completed his interviewing of the crew. Most had been asleep at the time Maxwell had been seen on deck except the second engineer, Leo Leonard, and had been unable to contribute to solving how Maxwell had gone over the side. But there was the puzzling matter of his being found naked in the sea. While several of the crew confirmed he liked to swim in the nude, no one had ever seen him on deck late at night without any clothes on. At the time Leo Leonard had seen him, it had been cold enough for the engineer to be glad he was wearing his boiler suit.

Philip had begun to jot down his impressions, cross-checking answers, trying to formulate a list of questions to be followed up. From what the crew had said, there had been no police forensic examination of the wooden deck rail or the wire rail at the end of the aft deck. No one had examined the deck itself or the hull of the yacht for any evidence that Maxwell had hit it during his fall into the sea. None of the rudiments of a standard police investigation had been performed.

In the early-morning hours Betty awoke. She didn't know why, but something was troubling her. Then she remembered. In those times when her marriage was happy, Maxwell called her 'the guardian of my Jewish soul'. Well, she reminded herself, a guardian didn't sleep when there was important work to do.

She knew why she had awoken. A note. Not a suicide note – but one that explained to her what he was going to do. For a moment she lay in the darkness of the cabin, struggling to focus her thoughts. Suppose he had left a suicide note. But that was impossible. Bob was absolutely against suicide; he had said it was a coward's way out. No! He would never have killed himself. But maybe another kind of note? One that would explain everything? But what *was* everything? For so long he had cut her out of his life. But she was the guardian of his Jewish soul.

Betty switched on the bedside light and began to search the suite. First she checked the bedside drawers. No note. She looked under the mattress and in all 'those special places where he used to put his money or an important document'. No note. The more she searched, the more reassured she became. If he *had* planned to commit suicide, she knew in her heart he would have left her a note.

She checked his wardrobe, under every shirt, shorts and underpants. She looked in the pockets of his trousers, in his topcoats. She checked inside his shoes, inside his sock drawer. She checked beneath his handkerchiefs and his collection of baseball caps. Everywhere she looked, she still could not find a note.

Having conducted a thorough search of the bedroom and his dressing room, she went to his study. The desk was piled with paperwork. But there was no note among the faxes and documents. On the floor beside the desk were five leather pilot cases. She searched each one in turn. There was no note addressed to her. Having searched everywhere, she was certain of one matter. Maxwell had not committed suicide.

At 5 a.m. 6 November, Betty finally went to bed and fell into a dreamless sleep.

While Betty slept, the other players in the unfolding story were taking their place on stage. Some had already familiar roles: the reporters who had chronicled Maxwell's every financial twist and turn had been joined by the colour writers who were laying siege to Maxwell House and Headington Hill Hall: anyone who had a memory to offer could expect to receive cash. The obituary writers were dusting down their thick files. On the editorial floor in Maxwell House, he was still the hero who had saved the newspaper.

With the libel writs dying with Maxwell, Hersh and his publishers returned to the attack. They announced they would soon produce more evidence of Maxwell's link to Mossad. It would never transpire. Tracked down, Ari Ben-Menashe said he was certain Maxwell had been murdered by Mossad. The claim was lost in the welter of stories, all for the moment on the lines of what the *Daily Telegraph* wrote: 'The nation's headlines will be much poorer for his passing and the length of his journey from the place and circumstances of his birth demands respect from all of us who had to travel much less far to rise much less high.'

Having read it, Roy Greenslade would later write, 'This seemed to suggest that the end justified the means.'

These were the comments of outsiders, not privy to what was happening on the *Lady Ghislaine*.

Betty awoke at 10 a.m. on that Wednesday morning. The yacht had anchored off Darsena Pesquera near Santa Cruz.

Rankin was outside her cabin door. Betty sensed the captain was anxious about his own future. He asked her if he was still going to sail to New York.

'What on earth for?' she asked. 'I have no plans to go there.'

She told him after she returned to London he should take the yacht to its home port of Palma, Majorca.

'I'll need money for that,' said Rankin.

Betty did a quick mental calculation. She was prepared to refuel the yacht and pay the crew's salaries for the next two weeks. After that she would make a decision about the future of the *Lady Ghislaine*. She went back into the cabin and returned to Rankin with a bundle of English notes.

'There is ten thousand here.' She handed the bundle to Rankin.

Betty made her way to the observation lounge. Waiting there was Julio Claverie. Her plan had been to have him join in her questioning of Rankin. But that idea was blown away by Claverie's revelation. He now believed the Spanish autopsy would take up to a week.

'My husband is a Jew,' she said with quiet emphasis. The lawyer looked at her puzzled, wondering what that had to do with anything.

'As a Jew my husband has to be buried in the Orthodox tradition,' Betty said more forcefully. 'In Jerusalem. It was his wish and it will be kept.'

Claverie tried to fit what he was hearing into what he knew was the Spanish timetable.

'The latest he can be buried is next Sunday,' said Betty.

Claverie nodded. Sunday was still four days away. It was possible, though barely, to meet her deadline.

'Under the Orthodox tradition no burial can take place on the Jewish Sabbath. That means no body can be received into Israel after sunset on Friday,' continued Betty.

'Which means?' asked Claverie, still trying to see how matters could be resolved.

'Which means, Señor Claverie, that my husband's body will have to leave here at the latest on a plane on Thursday night or Friday morning.'

The lawyer blinked furiously.

'Señora Maxwell, that is just impossible.'

'But you will try?' encouraged Betty.

'I will try,' said the lawyer. Betty was proving as formidable as Robert Maxwell.

Throughout the morning the yacht had been inundated with phone calls from Kevin and Ian briefing Philip on the latest financial situation. There was some respite: the creditors had momentarily ceased searching for any financial bone they could gnaw on. In part this was because of the prevailing mood: world leaders were showering Maxwell House with eulogies. Maxwell was hailed as 'a great character who will be sorely missed' and received many similar panegyrics.

Kevin told Philip the momentary ceasefire would not last: already the first of dozens of bankers and brokers were calling to set up meetings. No longer having to go to his father for every decision, Kevin began to make his own solutions. He became chairman of MCC; Ian would become the head of Mirror Group Newspapers.

Throughout the night that Betty had searched for a suicide note, Kevin had been fighting off similar suggestions from his creditors: they feared killing himself had been the precursor to the collapse of Maxwell's empire.

At 11.30 a.m. on Wednesday, Julio Claverie led Betty and Philip into the office of Judge Gutierrez Ruiz. There followed a surreal conversation that lightened an otherwise difficult day.

The judge studied Betty and Philip for a long moment. Then he reached for one of the official forms on his desk. He looked first at Betty.

'You are Mrs Maxwell?' he asked.

Betty was nonplussed. She had already been introduced to the judge the previous evening when she had been waiting to view the body.

'Yes, I am Mrs Elizabeth Maxwell. I am also known as Betty.'

'What is your relationship with Mr Maxwell?'

'I am his wife.' She paused. 'I am his widow.'

'How long have you known Mr Maxwell?'

'We have been married for forty-six years. We were married shortly after we met at the end of the war.'

'The World War Two?'

'Yes, in Paris.'

The judge made another note.

'Was your husband in good health?'

'He was overweight and I had been told he had a pulmonary complaint,' Betty said. Philip once more translated for his mother. The judge made another note on the form. Claverie nodded as if all the questions seemed normal to him.

Judge Gutierrez Ruiz sat back in his chair and looked at Betty.

'How do you think he died, Mrs Maxwell?'

Once more Betty was nonplussed. She had been told Maxwell died from a heart attack. She had been told there would be an autopsy. How could she prejudge the outcome of that? She shook her head and said she had no idea how her husband died.

The judge nodded as if this were the answer he expected.

Back on board the *Lady Ghislaine* Betty found that her youngest daughter, after whom the yacht was named, had arrived in the Gulfstream. It had been piloted from London by Brian Hull, his second round trip in 24 hours. Hull had a message from Kevin: he was to collect all Maxwell's papers and return with them to London.

Betty and Ghislaine sat alone in the stateroom, deciding what Ghislaine's role would be. Her daughter was a charismatic figure, ideal for dealing with the press. The yacht had now returned to Santa Cruz and the quayside was filled with journalists. Ghislaine should be the one to tell them that all efforts were being made to complete 'formalities' on the island. Ghislaine would then answer questions.

In the meantime, Betty decided it was time to interview Rankin again, this time in the presence of Claverie. The place to do it would be in the dining room. It had been agreed Philip would not be present.

Betty and Claverie sat on one side of the table opposite Rankin. Betty wasted no time on small talk. Her first question set the tone of others to follow.

'Why did you wait so long to start the search?'

'I've told you, Mrs Maxwell, the moment I saw he was not in his cabin, I had the boat searched. Having established he was not on board, I raised the alarm with the appropriate authorities.'

'The chef, Mr Keating, has said he had been up at 4.25 a.m. and then again at 6 a.m. Why was that?'

'The first time he may have gone to the kitchen for a drink. He would be up at six to get breakfast ready.'

'And you reached the bridge at 6.30 a.m.?' Betty asked.

'Yes.'

Claverie now spoke. 'So we have this. The engineer saw Mr Maxwell at 4.25 a.m. The chef was up soon afterwards and then again at 6 a.m. You were on the bridge at 6.30. So sometime in a two-hour gap Mr Maxwell vanished. Have you any idea at all, any idea at all, how that could have happened?'

Rankin shook his head. He had no answer.

'What mood was my husband in?' Betty resumed.

'When I last saw him, he was in a good mood.'

'So he didn't look or sound suicidal?'

'No, Mrs Maxwell, he did not.'

Her questions continued. Later she remembered that she had asked, 'What did he eat? What had they talked about? Who phoned him last and when? I questioned him about the crew. Finally I asked the captain how he thought Bob died. Could he have slipped? Where from? I needed to find some truth in all this.'

Rankin could not provide it. Eventually she thanked him for his help and the captain left the room. Betty had sat there feeling 'a sense of malaise that is difficult to describe or explain'.

There had been nothing suspicious to her in Rankin's responses. But they had only made Maxwell's death seem, if anything, more incomprehensible.

Ghislaine emerged on deck, dressed in a skirt and halter top. She walked slowly to the rail and looked down at the massed journalists and photographers. They had come from all over the world, and more were arriving even as she watched. The only time she had seen such a media scrimmage had been when her father had bought the New York *Daily News*. They were shouting questions up to her in English, Spanish, French, German, and languages she did not even recognise.

She raised her hand, an imperious gesture she had seen her father use to quieten a media frenzy. It worked for her. When there was complete silence, she addressed the throng.

She gave a concise summary of what had happened and which members of the family were on board. Her elder brothers were in London dealing with their father's many business affairs. She could not yet say when her father's body would be free to leave the island. She gave a little shrug and smile: officials could not be rushed, not even here in Spain. She ended by saying on behalf of the family she would like to thank them all for their courtesy. When she had more information she would give it to them. As she turned to leave, a reporter shouted up at her.

'How did your father die?'

Ghislaine turned back to the rail. She looked down at the reporters. Cameramen zoomed in on her face, sensing she was going to say something important.

In a loud and clear voice she spoke.

'I think he was murdered.'

Part V
AUTOPSIES AND A FUNERAL

TWENTY

After Betty had viewed the body and left the air base, the corpse of Robert Maxwell was transferred to a waiting hearse and driven to the mortuary in Las Palmas. It was a small, featureless building adjoining a cemetery. During the night the corpse lay undisturbed in the autopsy room.

In the morning of Wednesday, 6 November, an attendant arrived to prepare for the post-mortem. When he saw the size of the body, he summoned two other attendants. Together they manoeuvred the corpse onto the steel autopsy table, which had a built-in weighing scale. The body lay on its back, staring sightlessly up at the strip lighting over the table.

The attendant noted on an official pad the body weight was 130 kilograms – almost 20½ stone, or 286 pounds. He ran a tape from the top of the skull to the soles of the foot. The overall length was 1.90 metres. It was the corpse of a giant: six feet four and a half inches.

It was one of the largest bodies the attendant had seen on the table. He entered the measurements on two other identical pads and placed them on a small table beside the entrance to the changing area. He had been told three pathologists would be performing the autopsy and he had laid out their garments in the cubicles.

The half-tiled walls, frosted-glass windows and the floor, made of a composite material, gave the room an antiseptic ambience that was deceptive. There was nothing in the room that was sterile.

The steel sinks stood against one wall. Against another was a steel working top running almost the length of the room. Above the working area were cupboards with glass-fronted doors, containing a variety of instruments and glass jars of all sizes for holding anatomical specimens.

The attendant began to remove from the cupboards the instruments the pathologists would need: scalpels, hooks, spatulas and bowls. He took these to the two trolleys standing on either side of the autopsy table and arranged them in a predetermined pattern. From a drawer under the work-top he pulled out a small circular saw and plugged it in to one of the several socket boxes in a wall. There was a high-pitched whine from the blade. Satisfied, he switched off the saw and placed it on the trolley, making sure the trailing cable was well clear of the table on which the body lay.

On the worktop was a weighing scale with a large pannier, the kind old-fashioned grocers still used to weigh potatoes. From under the worktop the attendant pulled out two medium-sized plastic drums and several steel buckets. He positioned the buckets in no special order on the floor. Into each one he poured a quantity of liquid from the drums. It was formalin, a preservative.

Preparations over, the attendant left the room.

The body, waxy and cold, was once more left in peace.

At noon, Dr Carlos Lopez de Lamela and his two assistants came out of the changing room. They all wore faded green surgical smocks and baggy pants. Over these they had donned impervious rubber aprons. Rubber gloves encased their hands.

Dr Maria Ramos had covered her hair with a surgical cap.

Dr de Lamela was the director of the Las Palmas Forensic Institute. A medium-sized, soft-spoken man, he had still to reach his fortieth birthday. But over the past ten years he had conducted hundreds of autopsies on tourists who had died in road accidents or drowned off one of the island's beaches. Usually the bodies had been quickly recovered and the pathological cause of death established beyond doubt.

Dr Luis Garcia Cohen, a taller and darker-complexioned man than de Lamela, was in his early thirties. They had worked together many times.

Dr Maria Ramos was younger than both men and even her shapeless garb could not disguise her femininity. She was an outstanding medical student, and her tutors had thought she would opt to become a surgeon. Instead she had chosen forensic pathology for a career.

They knew that this morning they would have five separate, yet interrelated, objectives: to conclude the cause of death for the death certificate; to establish the manner of death; to determine any contributory factors; to decide whether to continue the clinical study of the case in laboratory conditions; to investigate all problems of a physical, chemical, bacteriological, pathological and anatomical nature.

The central question they would have to decide was whether the body had been alive at the time of submersion. The scene of the drowning, the events leading up to it, eyewitness accounts and any clothing the deceased had been wearing – all played a significant role in determining the cause of death. De Lamela had once had a case of a man found floating in water at the foot of a cliff, and his open fly zip had led the pathologist to conclude the man had been trying to direct his stream of urine over the cliff when he stumbled and fell.

In this case there was no clothing or eye witness statements to guide him to what had happened in the critical moments leading up to the death of this huge figure on the autopsy table.

The precise length of time the body had been in the water would also play a significant part in any pathological finding. Sea water contains 3 per cent sodium chloride concentration. This allows fluids to be drawn from the blood into lung tissue, causing severe pulmonary oedema. The one advantage of dealing with a sea drowning is that putrefaction is slower, because the sea water retards bacterial growth.

These were some of the matters de Lamela and his assistants would have to consider as they picked up their notepads and made their way across the floor to the autopsy table.

From outside the tumult continued. Dozens of reporters and photographers had gathered, the latecomers seeking vantage points by standing on gravestones in the adjoining cemetery. Camera flashes constantly lit the inside of the room. Interspersed with the shouts of the journalists were orders from the police for them to stand back.

None of the pathologists had experienced such a situation. On their way to the mortuary their car radios had been full of the story of the death they were about to investigate. Ghislaine Maxwell's claim that her father had been murdered had been given support by Julio Claverie; the lawyer had said he was not prepared to rule out such a possibility.

In London Dr Joseph Joseph, Maxwell's personal physician would soon express his view that the death was 'suspicious'. In New York both Jules Kroll and Dr Rosenbaum would express similar reservations. Maxwell had called only a few days ago to set up a meeting with the detective and, in Kroll's experience, someone didn't do that if he was contemplating suicide. Rosenbaum was equally mystified: he had given Maxwell a clean bill of health. A person could still have a heart attack but Kroll and the doctor both knew in such cases the victim usually collapsed on the spot and did not have the strength to climb over a ship's rail and fall into the sea.

For the three pathologists the one certainty was that this was going to be the most important post-mortem they had ever conducted. The cameras of the world were trained on this small, insignificant building on the edge of a graveyard.

Privately Maria Ramos wondered why the body had not been brought to the Forensic Institute with its modern equipment, including a laboratory where chemical tests could be carried out on tissue samples. She could only assume that, as the mortuary was close to Gando Air Base, that had influenced the site of the autopsy.

Lamela led his two assistants on a slow walk around the table.

While Betty had noticed nothing untoward on the body, they were looking for more specific signs. Drifting bodies can often travel huge distances. Along the way they collect injuries: a peck from a seagull, a nibble from a fish, collision with a piece of debris. A clue would be evidence of bleeding around the wound. Usually a victim of drowning tends to bleed more readily and more profusely compared with a person who is already dead on entering the water. But, if a corpse had spent a lengthy time in the sea, even the most experienced pathologist often found it difficult to determine how a skin wound was made.

That the body had been found naked did not unduly surprise the pathologists. They knew from experience that many corpses are recovered either completely or partly nude as a result of several possibilities: there was the churning action of the waves pounding one against the other, or the ebb and flow of the current. Sometimes, in the struggle to stay afloat, a victim tries to remove clothing.

As they circled the body the pathologists were looking for lividity, when the blood drains from the upper layers of the skin. After a lengthy immersion it was not easy to confirm because the skin became waterlogged.

But the face showed no evidence of being fed upon by crabs or fish: the eyelids, lips, the top of the nose and ears were untouched. No algae had formed on these exposed parts that would have given them a black-green colour.

These initial observations formed part of their note-taking. All three recorded the scar tissue on the upper torso, noting it as the residue of surgery.

There were no visible injuries on the lower torso, the thighs and calves, except for some wrinkling between the toes.

Elsewhere the body did not show the skin shrinkage often found in a corpse that has been in the sea for some time. The best indication of time de Lamela had been given was that the body had been drifting in the water for around twelve hours. The conclusion was based on a short conversation with the pilot, Jesus Vaca, and the local police commander who had questioned the crew of the *Lady Ghislaine*.

The pathologist told the others that not only would an examination of the lungs, heart and stomach possibly provide a more accurate time frame, but also hopefully answer another vital question: had all life been extinguished by the time the body entered the water? If that was the case, they could rule out suicide.

For all his experience, de Lamela had no knowledge of dealing with this unique form of murder designed to simulate accidental drowning. Consequently, despite what he had heard on the radio that morning, homicide was a low possibility in his investigation. He was looking for something closer to what he had been told was the more likely cause of death: a heart attack leading to accidental drowning.

To establish that, he would, with the help of his assistants, be following definite pathological signs. Submersion is usually followed by a panicky struggle to reach the surface. Only when the body's energy reserves are depleted does the struggle subside and actual drowning commence. At this stage there are changes in the carbon dioxide in blood and tissues; in turn this causes stimulation of the respiratory centre in the brain, followed by inhalation of water. Coughing, vomiting and a swift loss of consciousness follows. Finally, there are irreversible changes in the brain. Drowning is then complete. A verdict of natural causes is the only one to conclude.

The three pathologists positioned themselves around the table, de Lamela on one side, his assistants on the other.

De Lamela began to run his gloved hands over the torso, squeezing muscle and fat, confirming that complete cellular and molecular death had occurred. Occasionally he flexed a joint. He looked under the armpits, between the toes and in the groin. As he worked, he dictated brief observations to Maria Ramos.

The pathologist took the circumcised penis in his hand: he was looking for a condition known as hypospafias, in which the urethra opens on the underside of the penis instead of in the centre. The defect is not uncommon but in this was case not present.

As he continued to palpate and prod, the wall-mounted telephone by the door rang. Cohen went to answer it. The caller was the clerk of Judge Isabel Olivia. She wanted de Lamela to know that, because the autopsy was taking place within her jurisdiction, she was taking judicial charge of the case. His report should come to her office first before anyone else in the judicial system saw it.

Back at the table Cohen related the message to de Lamela. He grunted. All three pathologists knew Judge Olivia. She was one of the most colourful judges in the islands: she wore miniskirts on the bench, flirted with the lawyers and enjoyed seeing her photograph in the local press and her name mentioned on the radio.

De Lamela led Ramos and Cohen back to the top of the table. He nodded for Ramos to take over; it was the only way she would gain more experience.

She buried her hands in the corpse's hair; it was slightly stiff with the residue from the salt water. She felt the scalp. There were no cuts.

Watched closely by de Lamela, Cohen peered closely up the nostrils and into the eyes. He saw nothing he would not expect to find from lengthy immersion in sea water.

Meanwhile, de Lamela had been inspecting each hand in the hope of finding some clue as to the length of time the body had been in the water.

But at best it would only be a rough guide, as he did not know where the body had entered the water and how close it had drifted inshore, and there was a significant difference in temperature at this time of year between that in deep sea and close to land. In cold water several days could elapse before the epidermis peeled from the fingers; in warmer water it could occur in hours. But again there was no clue to help de Lamela to come to a conclusion.

He returned to the top of the table. He prised apart the jawbones and peered inside the mouth.

'Lower teeth dentulous in the upper and this was compensated. But we should have a dental X-ray.' The pathologist's voice echoed off the tiled walls.

Maria Ramos walked from the table, past the body staring sightlessly at the ceiling, hands rigid at its sides, the massive stomach raised like a mound, toes pointing stiffly upwards.

She dialled the number of Judge Gutierrez Ruiz and explained the request for a dental technician to come to the mortuary. She listened for a moment, said, '*Si, comprende*,' and hung up.

She called to de Lamela. 'The judge says there is no time. He wants nothing to delay matters. The family wish the body to be released as soon as possible.'

De Lamela nodded. The local papers were already describing the body as that of 'the international celebrity tycoon'. The senior pathologist sensed there would be pressures going on behind the scenes he would never learn about. All he knew was that 'the widow, Mrs Maxwell, had struck me as a very determined lady'.

He suspected that may have played its part in Judge Olivia's becoming involved and, no doubt, the chief prosecutor for the islands would be wondering at what point he might usefully intercede. A case like this, de Lamela was coming to realise, was of a sufficiently high profile to attract all kinds of powerful figures.

Already Radio Tenerife had quoted the chief prosecutor as saying, 'Until the cause of death is completely clear, the body will not move from here.'

But in the next breath the law officer had also said that he understood 'the state of the body is concurrent with its having floated in sea water and there is no sign of violence.'

The prosecutor had not viewed the body. That kind of uninformed speculation did nothing to take away de Lamela's concerns about which kind of conclusion he came to would be most welcome.

His assistants helped to turn over the body. After they had done so, its great stomach flopped over the lip around the table that was there to prevent body liquids from dripping onto the floor. The trio continued to work as a single mind.

The external inspection continued. De Lamela carefully examined the base of the neck before tracing his gloved hands down each side of the spinal column. He had to feel quite deep for the vertebrae. He prodded the ribcage. He moved down to the buttocks, spreading the cheeks so that he could inspect the anus.

'Normal genitalia. Small external haemorrhoids,' he called out.

He ran his hands over the back of the thighs and then moved to the legs.

'No evidence of varicose veins,' he announced. Once more he examined the soles of the feet. Again, there was nothing untoward.

Meanwhile, standing on either side of the head, Cohen and Ramos had continued their external examination of the ears. Haemorrhaging from the middle ear was sometimes found in cases of drowning, the result of pressure changes. These can occur at a depth of as little as two feet.

It was Maria Ramos who next broke the silence.

'What do you make of this?' she called out. Her finger indicated a tiny puncture mark behind the right ear.

De Lamela and Cohen both peered closely at the spot.

'It could be a bite mark. A mosquito could have bitten him before he entered the water. Or maybe a fish nibble,' suggested Cohen.

The senior pathologist shook his head. 'A sting or a fish bite would usually cause more erytheme.'

Ramos pulled back the ear lobe, tightening the skin around the puncture mark.

The action had produced a slight contusion under the skin. They all peered one more time. De Lamela knew there were no reliable tests to allow for an unequivocal diagnosis of what could have caused the mark. The hole was too small to allow for sea water to have entered the body. However, whatever had caused it would, after this time, have dissipated in the bloodstream.

The only case he had heard of was where a similar mark had baffled an American pathologist: a drug addict had injected himself and collapsed from an overdose. To revive him, his friends put him in a bath of water. He had drowned in the process. But the body of this elderly man did not suggest he had been a narcotics user.

'Let's open him,' said de Lamela.

Maria Ramos positioned the head the way she knew de Lamela liked. Cohen used a pair of scissors to snip off patches of hair and quickly shaved the scalp with a razor, leaving a wide path running from ear to ear.

A cranial autopsy was always the first stage of a post-mortem. Incisions into lower areas, the chest or the abdomen would allow blood to escape from the brain and give a wrong clinical picture of its original condition.

De Lamela positioned himself over the exposed piece of scalp. It glistened whitely from the powerful overhead light.

Maria Ramos handed him a scalpel from the trolley. The senior pathologist made an incision extending from behind the left ear, up over the middle of the head to behind the right ear, ending close to the puncture mark de Lamela had dismissed as unimportant enough to warrant further investigation.

A trickle of blue-black blood followed in the wake of the blade. Cohen handed him a pair of retractors and de Lamela began to peel away the skin flaps from the incision. He worked steadily, not only following the textbook procedure, but relying on his own experience. Satisfied he had exposed a sufficient portion of the skull, he rolled the skin flap down over the forehead until it covered the eyes and the nose. When he stepped back from the table, his apron was speckled with blood.

He called for the electric saw. Cohen handed it to him. The pathologist switched it on; the sound of the blade changed pitch as de Lamela pushed it firmly against the bone. He began to execute one angle of a wide V-shaped cut, which would go inwards from the back of the neck. He paused periodically.

The human skull can be anything from one-quarter to three-quarters of an inch thick: he had no way of knowing the thickness until he completed the cut. Each time he resumed, a shower of fine bone dust sprayed the air. The room began to fill with an acrid aroma.

It took some minutes to make the first cut. De Lamela made an identical one starting from the forward side of the head. The smell of singed bone increased. He finally switched off the saw and handed it back to Cohen.

Maria Ramos passed de Lamela the elevators she had been holding. These were spatula-like instruments specially designed for the task. De Lamela used them to prise loose the segmented bone section from the rest of the head as if he were removing a skull cap.

Below lay the dura, the tough membrane covering the brain. De Lamela inspected the dura for signs of disease. He saw none. Ramos handed him a small scalpel and he nicked a corner of the membrane. Then, using pointed scissors, he cut the dura exposing the brain. All three carefully studied it. There were no visible signs of malformity.

Using a long-bladed knife, de Lamela snipped the nerves and blood vessels at the base of the skull, steadily loosening the brain from the roots that had linked it from birth to the spinal column. He then began to ease out the organ through the hole he had made in the skull, pausing from time to time for Cohen to cut free a remaining blood vessel or nerve.

Maria Ramos stood by with the pannier from the weighing scale on the worktop. She took the soft ball of greyish matter to be weighed.

'Five hundred grams,' she called out. An average weight. She began to slice pieces from the brain in a search for disease. She found none. She dropped the segments into one of the buckets of formalin.

Back at the table, Cohen replaced the bone and skin flaps in their original positions and neatly sutured along the line of the original incision de Lamela had made.

Ramos was back at the table to help turn the body once more over onto its back. Fluid slowly began to seep through the sutures, dribbling its way to the lip at the edge of the table and from there down a pipe to a drain in the floor.

Once again de Lamela reached for a new knife. He sank it expertly into the skin at the top of the breast bone and, using steady pressure, continued to cut down the entire middle line of the body, ending the incision at the upper edge of the pubic bone.

He used his hands to peel back the incision to reveal the ribcage. He changed places with Cohen, who stepped forward with a pair of surgical shears. With one powerful stroke he split the breastbone, neatly segmenting the ribs. Cohen and Ramos began stripping away the tough membranous sheath covering the ribs, opening a pathway to the heart and lungs.

For a moment they all peered into the cavity. Then Ramos put a gloved hand into the opening to hold aside a lung. De Lamela carefully severed the ligaments and blood vessels attached to the heart. He then lifted it out of the cavity.

Ramos took the heart over to the scale. It weighed 500 grams, an average weight. She snipped and peeled back the fibrous sac enclosing the heart until its surface glistened under the bright light. She examined the aorta: there was nothing alarming there. She turned her attention to the left and right coronary arteries. Again, there was no sign of any defect. Maria Ramos placed the heart in a bucket of formalin.

Outside, the tumult from the journalists had abated with the arrival of more police cars. Their pulsating strobe lights coming through the frosted glass windows bathed the room with a bluish glow.

Time had become a still more pressing matter. While they had been working, the attendant had taken another call. This time it was the local undertaker. He wanted to know when he could collect the body. He said he had been retained by Julio Claverie on behalf of the Maxwell family.

De Lamela also knew the status of the lawyer. In the islands' legal circles he was a powerful figure. The pathologist had told the attendant to inform the 'Director' that they would be finished by 3 p.m. No one ever called the undertaker anything but the 'Director'.

Beside him, Maria Ramos was dissecting the lungs. De Lamela reminded her that the presence of sea water was of no real significance: the presence of water became significant only when a person had drowned in fresh water. De Lamela examined the lungs. Again there was some sea water in each organ. But that too was of no real diagnostic importance: the water had probably entered the stomach after death.

Working as a team, with little conversation, the three pathologists examined the liver, prostate and spleen. Each organ showed no evidence of disease.

From time to time his assistants returned to place their hands inside the dark shell to bring out more entrails including the kidneys and bladder. Each was contained in its viscous sac. After dissection and examination, the organs were dropped into the buckets of formalin.

Ramos and Cohen carried some of the organs over to the table and placed them loosely in the chest and abdominal openings.

De Lamela then rapidly tie-stitched the long frontal incision he had made so as to hold the organs, swilling in blood, securely inside the body.

It had taken three hours to complete the post-mortem. De Lamela nodded to the attendant, who began to dial the number of the Director.

Outside, the clamour of the reporters had started up. They were demanding a statement from the chief pathologist on what he had found.

In that they would be disappointed. His report was for Judge Olivia alone.

Only later would serious questions be asked about what had happened during the autopsy.

There had been no staining or other chemical tests of the organs. These would have helped to establish the rapidity of post-mortem changes in the blood and tissues. The blood levels of adrenaline and noradrenaline rise under conditions of shock or stress. A full examination of tissue catecholamines could have helped to distinguish a case of sudden natural death – such as a heart attack or an accidental fall into the sea – as opposed to a murder designed to simulate natural causes.

That distinction could have been made, if at all, only at the autopsy while the body was being dismembered. Any later post-mortem examination would only leave unanswered questions because any forensic evidence would have been destroyed by the organs' immersion in formalin.

Given that, the findings of Dr de Lamela are remarkable. He concluded that death was due to heart failure. He also ruled out suicide because 'the deceased was a good swimmer'.

When they had read his findings, his peers in Britain and elsewhere dismissed them as meaningless.

It was left to the most junior of the autopsy trio, Dr Maria Ramos, to say, 'Murder at sea is always difficult when nothing fits what is expected, or fits too easily. After being in the water for many hours, it is easier to have the truth covered up – how the body came there.'

But now it was the turn of the Director to make the truth even harder to discover. Shortly after 3 p.m., the undertaker arrived to collect the mortal remains of Robert Maxwell from the mortuary.

*

By that Wednesday afternoon, Betty Maxwell had assembled a small coterie of advisers, lawyers mostly, who were constantly available to help and guide her through the legal maze in both the Canary Islands and Israel.

They were led by the family's long-trusted attorney, Samuel Pisar. Based in Paris, the attorney was an Auschwitz survivor who had become one of Maxwell's few confidants and probably his closest business adviser. He had helped pave Maxwell's entry into Israel's business community.

During his first call to Betty, Pisar bluntly asked if she was satisfied there was nothing suspicious about Maxwell's death. She had told him she had unresolved questions. He had made no comment but she sensed that her words troubled him. He told her the most important matter now was to arrange for the body to be transferred to Israel. He would instruct Claverie to handle the Spanish end of this while, in Jerusalem, Ya'atov Neeman, Maxwell's personal lawyer and the country's leading attorney – whose connections extended into the Prime Minister's office – would handle the funeral arrangements.

In the meantime a second Spanish lawyer, Jose Maria Armero, had also been retained. His task was to ensure that Judge Olivia did not delay the release of the body. She had already become a quotable source to the scores of journalists now on the island. She had told one reporter, 'This man's death is nothing special.' To another she had announced, 'I will decide when the body is moved.'

With limited experience of criminal investigation and no knowledge of the desperate financial straits Maxwell had been in before his death – let alone his phone calls to Mossad – the honey-blonde judge found herself the centre of constant media attention. Armero's task was to do anything to ensure that plans already under way to move the body out from her jurisdiction were not interfered with.

Betty had discovered that the two satellite phones on the yacht had become her 'main life in this godforsaken place'.

She used them constantly, one to make calls, the other to receive them. They came from Kevin and Ian, from Pisar in Paris, from friends all over the world. They wanted to know how she was coping and what they could do to help. The press were still on the quayside, constantly badgering Ghislaine for more details as to why she thought her father had been murdered. Executives from Mirror Group Newspapers asked if she would like them to fly out more reporters to keep their colleagues at bay. She said that was not necessary. The last thing she wanted was to see more journalists confronting each other.

Twice a day, morning and evening, Julio Claverie made his way through the media scrummage to board the *Lady Ghislaine*. Sometimes he brought good news, other times less so. Paperwork that he assured her would be cleared had, a few hours later, required more official signatures and legal stamping.

The latest call from Paris on that Wednesday afternoon had alarmed her. Pisar said he had spoken to both the Spanish lawyers to see if they had learned about the outcome of the post-mortem. Both had expressed concerns over what they were hearing – that there had been considerable pressure on the pathologists to get the autopsy finished as quickly as possible.

Betty was delighted with the news. It meant she could soon be moving Bob out of the Canaries.

Then once more had come disturbing news. Jose Armero had called to say that Judge Olivia wanted to see Betty and Philip in her office.

Meanwhile, Philip had been working his own phone, making lengthy calls to Ya'atov Neeman about his father's wish to be buried on the Mount of Olives in Jerusalem. Neeman had explained that it would require 'negotiations' with the relevant authorities and especially the cemetery administrator. The keeper of the hallowed ground rejoiced in the name of Chananya Chackov. Philip, in true Maxwell style, told the lawyer to do what it required. The negotiated fee for the plot was $5,000.

Betty was in her suite on the yacht preparing to go to see Judge Olivia when there was a call from London. It was the insurance broker representing Lloyds. He explained he was calling about the benefit of £20 million payable to her upon the accidental death of her husband. The broker told her two forensic pathologists representing Lloyds would arrive in Tenerife to carry out a further autopsy for Lloyds. The broker explained the insurers were concerned about media reports that Maxwell had died of a heart attack or had been murdered.

Ghislaine's claim that her father had indeed been murdered was now in wide circulation.

There were also, added the broker, claims he had committed suicide.

Shocked by the suggestion, Betty wondered what she should say. The broker continued to explain that, if suicide was found to be the case, then Lloyds would not have to pay out.

She wondered how two pathologists from London would be able to establish anything. But the broker had not finished.

'The pathologists intend to arrive in Tenerife this coming Saturday. They are two of the foremost in the world. Dr Iain West and his wife. They could—.'

Betty cut the broker off in mid-sentence.

'That's not possible! I am burying my husband in Israel. We will be flying his body there on Thursday or Friday!'

There was a moment's silence on the phone. She sensed the broker was consulting somebody. Then he was back on the line.

'Dr and Mrs West can fly to Israel in time to perform their post-mortem before the funeral.'

'I will get back to you,' said Betty. Having put down the cabin phone, she sat for a moment on the edge of the bed. Would this never end?

She called Ya'atov Neeman. 'He was reluctant to go for a second post-mortem. But I impressed upon him its importance. If Sam Pisar was hearing concerns about the autopsy done on Tenerife, then it was better to have a second one.'

There was also the not inconsiderable matter that if the second autopsy ruled out suicide, then Lloyds would have to pay out on the policy. Given the continuing bad news coming from Kevin and Ian in London about the near collapse of MCC and MGN, the £20 million would ensure she and the children would have a secure future.

'You must fix things,' Betty told Neeman. 'I can't stress how important this second autopsy will be for me.'

In Israel there was a strict law that a post-mortem could be performed only on the direct wishes of the closest next of kin, or if the authorities suspected the cause of death was murder or suicide.

Betty gave Neeman authority to act on her behalf to inform the Israeli authorities she had consented to a second post-mortem.

Then she set off with Philip to keep her appointment with Judge Olivia. Once more the quayside was lit by a blaze of flashguns as mother and son climbed into Jose Armero's car.

The body of Robert Maxwell had found a new, if only temporary, resting place. It was the preparation room of the funeral parlour to which the Director and his assistants had brought the corpse. In some ways it was not unlike the autopsy room: a sink, wall cupboards and a large steel table dominated it.

The purpose of what went on here was to restore the damage the pathologists had done: the dextrous hands of the Director would turn the body back into a semblance of the living.

Just as the room was similar to the autopsy room with its tiled and sterile look, so the Director's equipment was crudely imitative of those the pathologists had used: scalpels, scissors, needles and hooks were in place in orderly rows on a steel trolley. On another trolley was equipment never to be found in any autopsy room. There was a foot positioner, which resembled an old-fashioned stocks, a wooden block designed to hold the head and shoulders at the correct height, an arm and hand positioner to keep both limbs at a desired angle. There was also a selection of forms and lip supports for creating a suitable mouth.

The Director regarded himself as both an embalmer-cum-restorative artist and amateur surgeon. Some of his materials had come all the way from their American manufacturer – the Slaughter Corporation.

These included an astonishing array of chemicals, skin conditioners, cosmetics, creams, jellies, pastes, oils, powders and waxes. Each was designed to harden or soften tissue, to shrink it if swollen, to dry it if moist. There was a compound designed to make a joint more flexible so as to make its skin cover appear more natural. There were several fast-acting chemicals to make skin firm again and a preparation for solidifying a body cavity. There were solutions of dyed and perfumed formalin, glycerine, borax, phenol and alcohol. They were standard preparations to be found in any modern preparation room.

The Director, like an experienced practitioner in his business, had his own cosmetic kit of face creams and carefully mixed powders milled to make the skin velvety smooth. The kit included preparations labelled 'Restoration Wax', 'Lip Wax' and 'Lip Tint'. There was an aerosol of Leakproof Skin, a remarkable substance that ensured there was no seepage from a cadaver. There was a wax to remove frowns and a chemical to clean inside nostrils and an adhesive for permanently closing lips and eyes. The cosmetics were manufactured by Avon.

Before the Director used some or all of these, there was the matter of the choice of coffin.

He had been told by Claverie that the embalmed body would be flown to Israel for burial. The Director was determined that his handiwork would bear the most careful scrutiny. He would recommend two coffins, one inside the other. The inner casket would be made of lead and have a window over where the face would be visible so that a customs officer could peer through to verify it was the correct body. The outer coffin would be an altogether more elaborate affair, of mahogany decorated with gold-plated handles, the finest on sale. With all that clear in his mind, there was only one issue to settle: his fee.

The Director did not know that Jewish burial rites forbid embalming – and that all Betty wanted was a simple pine coffin. In Israel the body would be wrapped in a prayer shawl, a *tallith*, before it was lowered into the ground.

Having once again made their way through waiting reporters and photographers, Betty and Philip were shown into the office of Judge Olivia.

She rose from behind her desk, hand extended and smiling, motioning for them to be seated. Though Betty had seen photos of the judge in the newspapers, she looked even younger. Betty wondered how she could be in charge of such an important case. But permission for Bob to be taken to Israel would depend on this young woman.

For a few moments there was small talk: how unfortunate that Betty and Philip were visiting the island at such a sad time; if they should return there were so many beautiful places to visit. Betty smiled and nodded at this promotion for local tourism. Suddenly Judge Olivia was all business.

She began to ask questions about Maxwell's medical history and his alcohol consumption. Betty and Philip glanced at each other. Surely the autopsy would have established such matters.

'The police found a near-empty bottle of red Martini in his cabin. There were also two full ones.' The judge's words, to Betty, had an accusatory tone.

For the next two hours she questioned Betty about Maxwell's lifestyle, sounding more like a reporter for a celebrity magazine than a member of the judiciary. Betty answered her questions patiently. Finally she had a chance to ask the one most important question in her mind: what was the conclusion of the autopsy? Judge Olivia rose and walked to her desk. She looked down at a document. In what may have been her best courtroom voice, she pronounced the verdict was natural causes.

'The pathologists conclude your husband suffered a heart attack, slipped on the deck and fell into the sea,' she said.

'Then he can leave? We can all leave?' asked Betty.

'*Si, si.* Once the paperwork is complete, you may take your dear husband with you,' said Judge Olivia.

She came from behind the desk, shook their hands and led them to the door of her office. Outside in the corridor the media were waiting. Judge Olivia smiled into the cameras as she stood close to the widow and her son.

The Director was becoming frustrated. He had spoken to Julio Claverie several times about his fee. The lawyer had been reassuring.

'Just do what you have to do and all will be well,' Claverie had assured him.

The Director decided to take it a stage further. He called the *Lady Ghislaine* and spoke to Betty.

She was dumbfounded by his attitude. He told her he would not release the body until he was paid in full.

'You are not dealing with fly-by-nights,' she replied. 'You will be paid.'

But once more another call from Pisar had raised a familiar nagging concern that was always there at the back of Betty's mind. Pisar had again spoken to colleagues about the circumstances of Maxwell's death. There were just too many imponderables to leave them satisfied. Why had the police investigation of the yacht been so perfunctory? Why had a forensic team not been brought in to investigate? Why had officials in the Canaries been allowed to go unchallenged in their prejudgments that the death had been an accident? Why had the case been put in the hands of such a relatively inexperienced judge as Olivia? Why had the autopsy been held in a mortuary that did not have a backup laboratory, rather than conducted in the island's main Forensic Institute, where such facilities were available?

Why had not experienced detectives in Madrid been summoned? This was no ordinary person whose death was being investigated. This was a world-famous figure. Could it be that no one wanted a thorough investigation? For Pisar and his colleagues it was no secret that the Maxwell empire was financially struggling to survive. Had a decision been taken that it was best if he should be declared dead, ideally by his own hand so that the financial remains could be grabbed by whoever reached them first? Pisar knew that Maxwell had hired Kroll. He would not have done that unless he was fearful that powerful enemies were gathering to destroy him. But who were they? Pisar could not think beyond bankers. In spite of his close friendship with Maxwell, he had no inkling of his client's other secret life – as Israel's superspy.

The concerns expressed in Paris were ones that Betty would later come to share. But now, as darkness once more enveloped the yacht, she had other matters to distract her. She had to approve the arrangements under-way in Jerusalem for the funeral. She had to cope with phone calls from all over the world from mourners who wished to attend. Kevin and Ian were calling with news of fresh financial disasters; Kevin planned during the time he and his brother were in Israel for the funeral to find an opportunity to talk to Ya'atov Neeman about new possibilities of a loan.

After yet another reassurance from Claverie that his fee was safe, the Director set to work. He had snipped open the tie-stitch down the front of the body and fished out the organs, dropping them into large steel pails, pouring a powerful chemical over them. He then washed the body with warm water and soap. He worked quickly, knowing he had lost a great deal of time if he was to meet the deadline Claverie had given him. The body had to be ready and in its coffin by early Friday morning. He drained the blood out of the veins, leaving the body looking pale and waxy. He covered the face with a thick cream to protect the skin from any burns arising from any leakage of the powerful embalming fluid he pumped through the arteries. Almost miraculously the skin began to approach the pinkish colour of living tissue.

More importantly, any possibility of establishing the skills of those professionals – the *kidon* of Mossad – had been washed out with the blood.

Piece by piece over the next 36 hours, the agonisingly slow Spanish legal system released its paperwork to allow the body to leave its jurisdiction. The Gulfstream was impractical to carry the corpse. The pilot, David Whiteman, had solved the problem. He hired a Challenger plane: wide-bodied and with seating for nineteen passengers, it had a cargo area in the rear for the coffin.

A departure time had been set for 2 a.m. on Friday.

On Thursday afternoon, 7 November, Betty spent time alone in the cabin she had once so often shared with Maxwell. She put out of her mind the thought of any other woman who may have also slept there. She took her time packing, looked at treasured items, remembering when he had given them. The memories were bittersweet.

After dinner with Philip and Ghislaine, she slowly made her way up to the upper deck where Bob had so often sat, peering through his binoculars at passing ships, making his phone calls. Sitting in his chair, she could almost sense his presence.

From where she sat she could look back down on the aft deck where the second engineer, Leo Leonard, had been the last person to see him alive. What had happened on the deck afterwards? Once more the questions from the lawyers in Paris rose in her mind. Why had the police been so slipshod in their investigation? Was it because of that that they were now being so busy? They had finally questioned the crew and walked all over the yacht. She wondered what the point was? Any forensic clues had long been lost. Scores of hands had gripped the handrails, trampled all over the aft deck, endlessly retraced Bob's own final walk on to the deck. What was the point of it all *now*? It wouldn't bring Bob back.

As the night cooled, she began to walk slowly around the boat, going from salon to salon, each step filled with more memories: how she had chosen the décor, arranged the seating and lighting. She sat for a while in the observation lounge, caressing the cushions where Bob had sat.

In the dining room, a stewardess was putting away the crystal and silverware. Betty gently motioned her to leave and finished the job herself. More memories: of dinners they had shared alone in the cabin, he pouring the finest wines and raising his glass to her. He had always ended every toast by saying how much he loved her. Her mind filled with the resonance of his rich voice, his smile and the lips she had fallen in love with the first time she saw him.

She walked slowly up the internal staircase into his study. The pilot bags had been packed with all his papers and flown to London. Without them the study looked almost bare. Finally, she entered the bedroom. It had been stripped of all his clothes and personal items. It was just another suite 'with the soul taken out of it'.

Betty may have sat on the bed and cried then. She could never be quite sure.

More certain is that she would recall conducting a 'final, final' search of the cabin for any note he may have left her, hidden in a place he knew she would find. But there was not even a scrap of paper in his handwriting. It was as if he had never been there.

The Director stood over the double coffin, looking down at the body. The lips were ever so slightly parted, the merest hint of perhaps a smile, the upper lip protruding slightly to give a more youthful appearance. The head was supported high in the coffin, yet not so high that when it was lowered the lid would hit the nose.

But all this work would be for the Director alone to admire. Because the body would be flown out of the country, it would have to be covered with a sheet and tightly trussed after it had been inspected by a customs official. The shroud and robes were neatly placed inside the coffin.

At eleven o'clock on Thursday night the pilot Brian Hull called the *Lady Ghislaine* to say that time was running out to make the journey to Israel before the Sabbath.

Suddenly there was the sound of a car outside on the quayside. Only a few journalists were on hand to see Julio Claverie running up the gang plank.

Betty was already waiting for him.

'Señora, good news! Your husband is now, as we speak, being taken to Las Palmas airport!'

The Challenger was parked there.

Philip immediately called Hull with the news and was assured by the pilot that, if they took off within the hour, they would arrive on schedule.

By now the quayside was swarming with newsmen and police cars. Word had spread that the Spanish part of the drama was ending.

Claverie led Betty and Philip and Ghislaine off the boat. Rankin and the crew stood silently on deck, heads bowed. Betty did not once look back as she entered the car.

A police escort cleared the path of the lawyer's car. Two hours later Betty and her children settled in their seats in the Challenger cabin. More than once they glanced towards the back, where a door led to the cargo hold.

One of the pilots had explained that the coffin had not yet arrived.

Betty sat staring out of the cabin window. Had there been another last-minute hitch? Had some paper still not been correctly signed? Had the undertaker asked for a bigger fee? Had there been an accident? The questions came and went and came again into her mind.

Then, shortly before 3 a.m., the ground handling crew slowly manoeuvred the huge coffin into the cargo hold.

Moments later the Challenger was in the air.

Dawn was breaking on Friday, 8 November, as the plane entered Israeli airspace. From out of the rising sun came two Israeli fighter planes. They took up position on either side of the Challenger.

As its pilots looked at each other and wondered if they had entered restricted airspace, a voice crackled in their headphones.

'We are your official escort. We will escort you into Jerusalem.'

Robert Maxwell, Israel's superspy, was finally returning 'home' with the honour and respect only a head of state would command.

TWENTY-ONE

As the Challenger began its final approach into Jerusalem Airport on Friday afternoon, back in Tenerife, some of those who had been central figures in the drama for the past few days were finding it hard to let go.

The pathologist Maria Ramos told a journalist there was 'always the possibility of a substance being in the body we did not find'.

The pinprick behind Maxwell's ear still troubled her.

Judge Isabel Olivia announced she would have liked more time to pursue her enquiries, but, out of respect for the family and Jewish custom, she had agreed to release the body.

Soon a new and more expert opinion would emerge. Nick Baker worked for Camper and Nicholson, the agency that chartered out the *Lady Ghislaine* when Maxwell had not used it. Baker would express 'serious doubts that Maxwell toppled overboard. That would be as hard as falling off a cross-Channel ferry.'

Like Pisar and his Parisian colleagues and Kroll and Rosenbaum, Nick Baker also knew nothing of Maxwell's secret connections with Israel.

None of their views mattered to Betty at the moment, as the Challenger touched down.

As the aircraft came to a stop, Betty saw ten men in long black coats and hats step forward. They were *hevra kadisha* (literally 'holy brotherhood') who had come to carry the coffin out of the cargo hold.

Behind them came Ya'atov Neeman and a group of dark-suited men. Nearby a hearse was waiting, its back door raised.

Through the closed cabin door that led to the cargo area came murmured voices and grunts as the rabbis lifted the casket. It weighed four hundred pounds. A *tallith*, a prayer shawl, was draped over the mahogany coffin before it was slowly brought out of the hold and carried to the hearse.

As it drove away, Betty, Philip and Ghislaine came down the front steps

323

of the Challenger. Each was embraced in turn by Ya'atov Neeman and the senior airport officials.

'The second post-mortem will begin as soon as the British pathologists arrive,' whispered Neeman.

Since he had accepted the assignment from the insurers to represent them and Lloyds, who had underwritten the £20 million policy of which Betty was the sole beneficiary, Iain West and his wife, Vesna – also an experienced forensic pathologist – had been busy making preparations for going to Israel.

In the grisly world they worked in, the husband-and-wife team had become two of its stars. As head of the Forensic Medicine Department at Guy's Hospital, London, West was seen by his peers as a worthy successor to the great British pathologists of the century: Bernard Spilsbury, Francis Camps and Keith Simpson.

Like them he had made his reputation by solving some of the most sensational cases of the past decade: fatal crimes and mysterious deaths were his speciality. But there was more to West than helping Scotland Yard and other police forces to solve murders. He was also called upon by MI5 and MI6. He had dealt with agents and double agents who had died in Berlin and Vienna and other cities where spies roamed freely until they met an untimely end.

He never spoke about this side of his work except perhaps to Vesna, his attractive blonde Yugoslav wife, and then he would not have told her everything. Among much else, the Glasgow-born West, the son of an RAF officer, was punctilious about secrecy: on a sensitive case he often typed up his own findings.

But, having accepted the Maxwell assignment, he had consulted his contacts in Britain's two intelligence services. 'For him it would be the most natural thing to do. "Forewarned is forearmed" was more than a motto for him: it was his way of life,' said former intelligence officer, Colin Wallace.

Certainly, West and his wife, who would assist him at the autopsy, were as prepared as they could be.

They had studied the newspaper reports of Maxwell's death and the aftermath; much of it was repetitious and speculative. But there were hints in some of the stories that the huge financial pressure Maxwell had been under could have played its part in his fate.

'A man can take so much before cracking,' Iain West had once said, giving evidence in a court case.

The couple had spent hours with the insurers, Continental Insurance International, who held the actual policy, which a Lloyds syndicate had underwritten.

The Wests had been briefed on their assignment: they were to consider the 'likelihood' of Maxwell's having a previous history or heart disease, 'or other physical defect or infirmity'.

In his proposal form Maxwell had not listed any such problems. However, if the insurers could show he had been suffering from a heart complaint or any other life-threatening illness, at the time he had taken out the policy, then they could move to have it declared invalid. However, if the Spanish findings were correct and Maxwell had died from a heart attack and then fallen into the sea and accidentally drowned, under the terms and conditions of the policy payment would have to be made in full. Equally, murder would not nullify the policy but suicide would.

The verdict that Iain and Vesna West would come to would be accepted by the insurers.

West had checked who would be running the Israeli end of the post-mortem. He was reassured to learn it would be Professor Yehuda Hiss, director of the Institute of Forensic Medicine in Tel Aviv and the country's state pathologist.

Iain West knew both Hiss and the institute from the time he had secretly investigated the body of Georgi Markov, the Bulgarian dissident who had been murdered by the poisoned tip of an umbrella held by a Bulgarian secret service agent.

West's intelligence contacts had told him the institute was one of the places where *kidon* went to study how its pathologists went about their work: it enabled the *kidon* to develop methods whereby their own use of nerve agents would stand less chance of being discovered.

But there was a problem. All the commercial flights to Tel Aviv that would get Iain and Vesna West to Israel in time to take part in the autopsy before the funeral were booked.

Even with £20 million at risk, the insurers did not feel it justified their chartering a private plane to take the two pathologists to Tel Aviv.

There was only one solution. Iain West called Maxwell House and talked to Kevin. This was their second contact in a few hours. On the first one, Kevin had said he understood the Wests would have only a secondary role in the post-mortem. 'It will be run by the Israelis.'

West had not argued. Time enough to deal with such matters when he and Vesna arrived in Tel Aviv. Besides, Hiss was 'not the sort of chap to make things difficult', he had told Vesna.

Now, with time a factor, West was again calling Kevin. Could he and his wife fly with him to Israel?

'There are seats for two more passengers,' said Kevin.

Four hours later, about the same time the Challenger had landed in Jerusalem, the Gulfstream, filled with people, had West and his wife also on board. The others were going to mourn. The pathologists were on their way to work.

All Saturday evening limousines travelled from Tel Aviv's Ben-Gurion airport to the forecourt of the King David Hotel in Jerusalem. In one car sat Isabel and her husband, David, red-eyed from the long flight from San Francisco. Then came Helene and Michael from New York; they were the eldest children of Maxwell's sister. Another car brought another sister, Sylvia, arriving with her husband and three children; all those years ago Maxwell had located Sylvia in a refugee camp in postwar Germany and he had cared for her ever since. Then came Kevin and his wife, Pandora, with Anne, Philip's wife.

Other cars brought friends from England, mainland Europe and the United States.

Each was shown up to the presidential suite Maxwell had always occupied, which was now Betty's domain. Before anyone could enter the suite with their bunches of flowers, baskets of fruit and newspapers from all over the world reporting the latest details about Maxwell's death, they were subjected to a police security check.

Betty greeted each arrival with an embrace and kiss, glanced at the headlines, and handed over the fruits and flowers to hovering waiters. There was a buffet and soft drinks. In a corner of the suite fax machines poured out an endless stream of messages.

Some were for Kevin. Before leaving London he had asked Ya-atov Neeman to try to arrange a private loan of £24 million. He was offering stock in a Maxwell company, Teva. He had not told the lawyer, who had been his father's most trusted friend in Israel, that the shares were already pledged to several banks.

While Ghislaine and her sisters discussed what to wear to the funeral and used the suite telephones to book hairdressing appointments, Kevin and Neeman huddled with Iain and Philip to discuss business matters with Sam Pisar, who had flown in from Paris.

Betty had placed several calls to the French capital, where her daughter, Christine, was awaiting the birth of her third child in a few days. She was distraught at not being able to be at the funeral and Betty had spent time trying to comfort her.

In between, she had discussed with her other children the speech for the funeral service, and who should deliver it. Protocol required it would have to be one of her sons – ideally the eldest one, Philip.

But Betty had noticed that Philip was showing signs of increasing stress, the aftershock of the 'trials and tribulations' of Spain. She decided to postpone any decision on who would deliver the homily.

By now the suite had taken on the appearance of 'an Oriental bazaar',

Betty would recall. Telephones rang constantly. Newspapers arrived with each mourner. Groups stood around the buffet or strolled out onto the balcony to stare towards the Mount of Olives, where the next day Maxwell would be buried. There were a dozen and more animated conversations and sometimes muted laughter.

Into this highly charged atmosphere came reporters specially selected to interview Betty: the men from the *Mirror* group, *Ma'ariv*, and other Israeli newspapers. Flashguns lit the suite and microphones were tested before being pointed at Betty. No novelist would have dared introduce such a twist in what was supposed to be a solemn occasion. While the newsmen followed Betty around the suite noting her every word, the more discreet figures, the men of Mossad, arrived.

Nahum Admoni expressed his condolences and then left. Shabtai Shavit and Rafi Eitan followed. Few noticed them come and go. Betty had never met them before and she would not later recall them.

The great and the good of Israeli society continued to arrive, circulate, nibbling and sipping as they greeted the widow and her children. Teddy Kollek, the mayor of Jerusalem, was as effusive as always. There was Ehud Olmert, the Minister of Health, who, in those days Maxwell had first come to Israel, had stood beside him on a platform saying this was the man to do business with.

Finally, the gathering began to thin out. Then, at long last, after the last goodnight kiss, Betty was alone with her thoughts. Uppermost in her mind was what would happen to Bob after she saw the hearse drive away with the coffin.

While Betty prepared for bed, the second post-mortem was under way in the Institute of Forensic Medicine in Tel Aviv.

Iain and Vesna West stood around the brightly lit autopsy table with Yehuda Hiss and four other Israeli pathologists. With them was a medical secretary, a radiographer, who would also act as a stills photographer and video cameraman. Every word and every move would be recorded by him.

But, for the moment, the only sound was the rapid scratching of West's pen on a notepad. Like everyone else he had never quite seen anything like what lay on the autopsy table. The massive coffin with its twin casket had gone, never to be seen again. Now, West noted: 'The deceased was laid out on the mortuary table, encased in an outer wrapping of coarse muslin, marked "Maxwell R" with an indelible marker. It was tied round the ankles, upper thighs and lower chest.'

The body resembled a mummy in a poorly wrapped parcel.

The first still and video shots were taken as the mortuary technician began to cut loose the ties.

West noted: 'The face was exposed. There was an inner sheet of white muslin, stained with body fluids, covering the front of the body. The body was lying on a sheet of clear plastic and a white plastic body bag, cut open along the white zip.'

The air began to fill with a familiar smell: the acrid aroma of formaldehyde – so strong that the eyes of the onlookers began to smart.

Finally, the body was exposed in shadow-free overhead lights. The radiographer continued taking pictures, panning the video camera slowly over the corpse, adjusting the lens for close-ups of the head. West wrote: 'The head hair was brown, approximately 2.5 to 3 inches long, cut away at the temples. The eyebrows were bushy and appeared complete. The eyelashes were of moderate length.'

The radiographer put aside his camera and wheeled a portable X-ray machine into position above the head. He took film of the head, upper limbs and feet.

West saw there was no visible evidence of abnormality except from an old deformity at the base of the left thumb.

The aroma from the formalin was increasing. West told Vesna, 'This is getting to be extremely unpleasant.'

Around the table, the others nodded, their eyes smarting even more. Hiss said the Spanish undertaker had used neat formalin when it should have been diluted.

The body had been only partially embalmed.

West continued his careful inspection of the head. Meticulous observation was the key to his work. There were always a number of clues imperceptible to the untrained eye: a blemish, the state of the teeth, and a broken vein in the skin.

He stepped back to allow Professor Baruch Arensburg, the professor of anatomy at the institute, to carry out dental charting. He reported considerable decay of the teeth, some of which were missing.

Hiss and the others now continued their external examination. West wrote rapidly: 'Eyeballs slightly prominent due to decomposition. Face cleanly shaven. Body hair unremarkable.'

Small scars were noted on the left side of the penis and on the left thigh. Neither mark had been included in the copy of the Spanish autopsy report which had accompanied the body.

Hiss measured the sutured cut de Lamela had made to open up the body. Another pathologist removed the cotton wool and gauze the Director had used to seal the body orifices. West noted a 'fresh haemorrhoid in the anus and slight oedema in both ankles'.

One by one the pathologists continued to step away from the table because of the stench: a mixture of decomposition and embalming fluid, which left the corpse in various states of decay. The face was grey-green and there was red marbling on the chest and other parts of the body.

It was not in the condition any pathologist would want to be able to come to proper conclusions.

On they went, peering, measuring, discussing and writing. As well as West, Hiss's medical secretary was taking notes, logging every minute abrasion. Some were so small they required repeated inspection. It was after one such inspection that West noted:

Half-inch abrasion over the rim of the right ear, just below the tip of the ear. Half-inch abrasion on the helix of the right ear, and one inch reddening and pressure abrasion above the tragus and extending onto the ear with underlying deep bruising behind and in front of the right ear.

It was the area of the pinprick Maria Ramos had noticed in her examination, and where one of the *kidon* had injected his lethal nerve agent.

But, whatever that agent had been, Iain West and the other pathologists would never find it – no matter how hard they looked. The draining of the blood and then partial embalming had ensured it would not be found.

It was Hiss who made a discovery that would play a key part in his conclusion in what he thought had happened. The state pathologist dictated to his secretary:

At the dorsal side of the left shoulder, on the upper edge, an area of vertical abrasion is visible, extending parallel and linearly over a total area measuring 2.4cm x 10cm. Under the skin of the left shoulder, from behind, extending over the upper two-thirds of the scapula, there is a haemotoma, measuring approximately 6 x 9.5cm, with a blood accumulation of approximately 1.5cm thickness in the deltoid muscle, the infraspinatus and the teres minor, near the scapula, with tears of the muscle. In the muscles, underneath the subcutaneous adipose tissue of the back, on the mid-line and to the right, at a distance of approximately 58cm from the crown, haemotoma of a dark colour is clearly visible, measuring 4.5cm x 8cm with small longitudinal tears.

In plain language, the kind the insurers would understand, West noted that it meant that the left shoulder muscle had been quite badly torn.

The tear would become the evidence from which to develop a theory: that Maxwell had fallen into the sea while he was hanging onto the yacht and his excessive weight ripped the shoulder muscle, causing him excruciating pain, and forcing him to let go. From that would grow even more remarkable speculation: was he hanging on to the side of the *Lady Ghislaine* because he had been pushed, had fallen or had jumped from the deck and changed his mind halfway?

That last possibility would be offered by Chester Stern, the author of *Dr West's Casebook*, a collection of the pathologist's cases, in which the Maxwell case would be described as 'the mysterious death of a tycoon at sea'.

Certainly, on this Saturday night, the mystery was not resolved by what the pathologists discovered when they opened the body for internal examination.

With mounting disbelief, Hiss and West both noted: 'Heart: not found. Esophagus: not found. Stomach: not found. Bladder: not found. Endocrine organs: not found.'

The oesophagus, the gullet, a tube connecting the throat with the stomach, would have enabled tests to be done to establish if poison had been secreted.

The endocrine glands, which secrete directly into the bloodstream, are ductless glands found in the thyroid, parathyroid, kidneys, testes, duodenum and small intestines and thymus gland in the neck. Again, these could have been tested for traces of poison.

The absence of the stomach meant there was no way to measure its capacity and the condition of its mucous lining in the small muscle, which is affected by various factors, including the emotional state of the person.

The presence of the bladder would have enabled checks to be made for congenital deformity, or evidence of any sudden injury caused by a fall.

The pathologists wondered what had gone on in Spain. 'It was bizarre,' Hiss said.

West confined himself to another note: 'There had been no proper examination of the arms, back, face and areas under the skin.' After a moment, he added, 'This should have been more than a standard post-mortem.'

Meanwhile, one of the Israeli pathologists had drawn their attention to a large haemorrhage at the back of the skull. Hiss and West checked their copy of the Spanish autopsy report. There was no mention of the haemorrhage.

How was this possible? Even a medical student would not have missed such a massive blood clot. What made matters worse, conditions around the table had become almost intolerable from the powerful aroma of formalin. It was like tear gas, remarked West. Hiss had managed a smile. That was something the Israelis knew about.

Vesna West recalled, 'Your eyes, nose and respiratory tract became affected quickly.'

Hiss cut the stitches de Lamela had used to suture the back of the scalp. West noted: 'The dura had been stripped and was lying loose inside the skull, with fixed haemotoma. A thick coating of coagulated, fixed blood was present.'

The Spanish pathologists had left blood in the skull vault and the funeral director had not drained it off when he put in embalming fluid. It had mixed with blood into a hardening compound, creating the effect of what resembled the massive haemorrhage.

The brain had also not been found. It had been put in formalin and sent by de Lamela to Madrid.

More discoveries were being made. There were only pieces of the lung to be found soaking in the formalin/hardening compound inside the chest cavity.

West confined himself to a headshake towards his wife and Hiss. This had not only been a post-mortem to tax his skills but also his patience.

What had been going on in Spain?

As the post-mortem drew to a close, Hiss continued to dictate his findings to his secretary.

Abrasions of the right auricle with contusions around the acoustic meatus; small abrasions at the nose apex; haemotomata and tears of the posterior of the left shoulder muscles, along with abrasions of the overlaying skin. Haemotomata and muscle tears around and to the right of the lower thoracic spine; small bleeding in the psoas muscle on the right; contusion in the upper extremity.

Abrasions, haemotomata on the body of Mr Maxwell are compatible with an involuntary fall into the sea.

For preparing a final opinion, we requite the protocol from the first autopsy, histological sections and the results of toxicology and biological tests (including water sample from the drowning area).

The damage to the shoulder muscles could just as easily have been caused by the *kidon* dragging the body across the deck and manoeuvring it over the side of the yacht.

But there was no time for any test to prove or disprove that was what had happened. As in Tenerife, time had become a consideration in the second autopsy. The pathologists would have to complete their work ready for the corpse to be prepared and driven to Jerusalem. With any number of vital organs not available to them, and those that had been dumped in the chest cavity left in a combination of formalin and hardening compound, the pathologists had difficulty reaching meaningful pathological conclusions.

Nevertheless, the state pathologist of Israel was staying with the conclusion that Robert Maxwell, still a heroic figure to Jews everywhere, had somehow fallen off the boat by accident.

It was 5 a.m. when Hiss led the others out of the autopsy room. The team had spent twice as much time as their Spanish colleagues inspecting and dissecting what they could. But for all their efforts they had found nothing.

Anything possibly indicating a crime, West told his wife, had 'through a combination of decomposition and embalming been obliterated'.

The mortuary technician began to prepare the body for burial.

In the early hours of Sunday, 10 November, one of the employees in the Forensic Institute placed a telephone call to a Tel Aviv number. The caller reported on what the state pathologist had concluded. The man who received the call thanked him and hung up. He then made other calls. The group of Mossad officers Ostrovsky referred to now knew there would be no difficult questions to explain. The *kidon* had once more worked their magic.

Betty woke early that Sunday. Dressed and made up, she walked on to the suite's balcony. The sun was rising over Jerusalem, the city Bob had loved above all others. Now it would for ever be his home.

She turned towards the Mount of Olives, hallowed ground for Jew and Christian alike. His grave was being prepared somewhere on that famous of all hillsides. It was there that King David had fled across its ridge while escaping from the Absolomites. For a time it had been known as the Hill of Corruption after Solomon had built pagan altars on its slopes until King Josiah had destroyed them. And it was across its ridge that Christ had made his way to Lazarus, and later came down on the back of a donkey to make his triumphal entry into Jerusalem. It was there, too, his disciples had prayed the night he was arrested, and where the Risen Christ had appeared to them.

Now, as Betty looked out, the words she had learned at Sunday Bible class came back. 'He was taken up before their eyes and a cloud hid him from their sight.'

Bob had been taken from her without a chance for her to see him again. They had not even said goodbye the last time they had spoken on the phone to discuss her role in that Anglo-Israeli banquet.

The chimes of the suite's door broke her reverie. Ya'atov Neeman, the pale colour of his face emphasised by the black suit he wore, had arrived. He had done much to ease the arrangements through the labyrinth of Israeli legal formalities. But he had saved the best until now.

'I have good news, Betty,' he said in that gentle voice she always loved to hear. 'It is to be a state funeral. Yitzhak Shamir has ordered it. Bob will lie in state in the Hall of Nations.'

Betty was overcome. The terrible darkness that had enveloped her for days had lifted a little. Israel was paying the highest honour it could. Only its presidents and prime ministers were usually accorded this farewell.

'Please thank the Prime Minister,' she said.

'You can yourself. He will be there. They will all be there,' said Neeman. 'I will make sure of that.'

And, one by one, they had agreed. Even those who had contributed, each in his own way, to the assassination of Robert Maxwell – Israel's superspy.

At noon Betty led the family out of the King David to the line of black limousines parked in the hotel's forecourt.

On the short drive she was stunned to see the streets lined with people, standing in silence, many with their heads bowed in prayer.

The cars pulled up outside the Hall of Nations, one of the most imposing modern buildings in the city. Before she stepped out of her car, Betty pulled down her veil to hide her face from the waiting cameramen; the balconies of the hall were crammed with their colleagues.

Betty ignored them all as she led her family to a side room. Neeman had arranged for the body to be there, lying on a stretcher, and covered with a *tallith*. It was their last chance to say goodbye to a husband and father.

They then led eight pallbearers back into the main hall. The body was positioned between six tall candles, each on its stand, flames flickering in the charged atmosphere.

A fusillade of camera flashes from the balcony lit the hall. In their own way, wrote a reporter, 'The press world he had dominated was also saying its farewell to a man who had been one of the most photographed on earth.'

It was crass – but also somehow appropriate.

One by one, Israel's leaders stepped forward. First it was President Chaim Herzog, his fulsome words echoing round the hall. Next came the diminutive figure of Prime Minister Yitzhak Shamir. His hoarse voice echoed the words of the President, as did those of the opposition leader, Shimon Peres – the man who had been present when Robert Maxwell had been propositioned by Nahum Admoni to become a spy for Israel.

But there would be no mention of that today. No mention that somewhere in the congregation were the leaders of Mossad, past and present, and other senior figures from the Israeli intelligence community. There were generals and businessmen. And bankers, the same men who had spurned Maxwell's increasingly desperate pleas for help. In their own way too, they had helped to murder him.

Betty, not knowing, shook them all by the hand as they filed past her and her children. The line was endless, so many faces she did not recognise, and some only vaguely. Perhaps the most moving moment, one she would treasure all her life, was when a group of children, the survivors of the Chernobyl disaster, filed past. In a halting voice, the first child said they were all there to say goodbye to the one man who had made it possible for them to have treatment for their leukaemia in the best hospitals in Israel. That was the moment Betty felt it hard to hold back her tears.

After an hour, a long hour, it was time for prayers. Betty did not understand the words, but their tone and the slow lament that followed was another memory she would cherish.

Samuel Pisar then recited the Kaddish, the prayer for the dead. He said it with the emotion of a man who understood what it was like to be a Jew like Robert Maxwell when six million Jews had perished in the gas chambers of Nazi Germany.

Once more Chaim Herzog walked to the podium. His voice ringing with emotion, he spoke of how Maxwell 'had scaled the heights of human endeavour. Kings and princes waited on him. Many admired him. Many disliked him. But few were indifferent to him.'

Now it was the turn of Philip Maxwell to express what he and his siblings felt about their father. Pale and trembling slightly, he began.

'Dear Dad. Publisher and patriot, warrior and globetrotter.'

He listed all his father's many accomplishments: among them, he was a multilinguist, a newspaper magnate, chairman of a football club.

The pallbearers stepped forward, big powerful men, and lifted the stretcher. The chief rabbi went to the podium. Grouped around him were lesser rabbis. His voice deep and resonant, he reminded his listeners what Robert Maxwell had once said: 'I was born a Jew and I will die a Jew.'

At those words, a young rabbi ran from the ranks of the other priests shouting and gesticulating at the mourners.

Betty was stupefied. Then other rabbis dragged away the protester. The hall was filled with angry cries over such scandalous behaviour. No one would ever know what had driven the rabbi to interrupt the last rites for Robert Maxwell.

On the Mount of Olives the gravediggers had opened up a huge hole, packing its sides with planks to stop earth from pouring back into the cavity.

Police patrolled the cemetery wall to keep out journalists, who perched on the wall like carrion birds, talking to each other in almost as many languages as Maxwell spoke.

It was late afternoon, the winter sun already beginning to drop behind the Mount of Olives, when Betty, with Iain and Kevin on either side, made her way through the hundreds of silent mourners, to the grave.

Shimon Peres stepped forward. His few words were carefully considered: 'He is closing the circle of a life that knew want and plenty, danger and grandeur, but never surrender and despair.'

He paused and looked around the mourners before his eyes settled on Betty. Then, in a loud, accented but firm voice, Peres spoke again.

'He has done more for Israel than can be said here today.'

*

The final moments now took on a momentum that had not changed down the centuries. The gravediggers brought the stretcher to the edge of the hole. One of them climbed down into the cavity. Four of the mourners gently lifted the *tallith*, holding it horizontally to shield the corpse from the eyes of the family. The gravediggers slowly tilted the stretcher so that the naked body began to slide into the opening. Below the rim a gravedigger guided it until the corpse lay flat on the earth. The *tallith* was now held over the hole so no one could see what was happening below. Slabs of Jerusalem stone, hewn for this purpose, were lowered to the man in the pit. He placed them one by one over the body until the hole had become a grave. The man was then helped out of the grave. It had all been done in complete silence.

The gravediggers turned and faced the family, extending their shovels. Each family member dug his or her spade into the mound of fresh earth and let it fall over the slabs. After a while the grave was closed.

Watching the final moments was a sallow-faced man. It was Andrei Lukanov. He let a handful of soil slip through his fingers onto the grave. A moment later, a man who had become his enemy repeated the process. Then deliberately turning his back on Lukanov, Ognian Doinov, the keeper of many of Maxwell's most recent secrets, walked away into the gathering dusk.

Still not knowing who either man was, or the part they had played in Robert Maxwell's life, Betty made her own way from the grave. All she wanted now was peace, to be gone from here, to be left alone with her memories.

One of the gravediggers placed a small white marker on the grave. It bore Robert Maxwell's name in Hebrew.

An hour or so later, with David Whiteman at the controls, the Gulfstream cleared Israeli airspace and set course for London. On board, there was, for the first time that day, open laughter and the sound of champagne bottles being popped. The solemnity of a Jewish funeral had given way to an Irish wake.

Betty was pleased. Bob would have wanted it no other way. There was always a tomorrow.

Iain West was back in London. While Hiss had delivered his verdict, West was not yet prepared to close the case.

Part VI
FINAL POST-MORTEM

TWENTY-TWO

Iain West's initial report to the insurers and the Lloyds underwriters was succinct. By contrast, in the Spanish autopsy there had been no diagnostic tests on the heart and other organs; partial embalming had only compounded matters. By West's high standards, what had happened in Tenerife made his job harder.

While the Tel Aviv post-mortem had been more professional, within the limits of what was forensically available in the ways of organs, it still in his view had not produced a conclusive verdict, one that would be unchangeable in a court of law as to how Robert Maxwell ended up in the Atlantic.

In his report Hiss had spoken of 'an involuntary fall' and the cause of death as drowning. West pointed out that conclusion could be interpreted in two ways: either Maxwell had fallen accidentally into the water or he had ended up in the sea against his will – the 'involuntary fall' clause in the Israeli state pathologist's verdict.

The questions the insurers hoped West would resolve remained unanswered. Was it accidental death? Had Maxwell been suffering from a serious heart condition that led to his death – a condition he had not revealed when he had signed the policy? In the latter case, the policy would be nullified.

But if he had been suffering from a life-threatening illness *after* he had signed the policy, and had not then informed the insurers, it could still be cancelled. The premium on the policy was £60,000 a year, and for the past twelve years Betty had paid it herself – from the time her marriage had been in trouble. The money for the premium had come from the personal allowance Maxwell had paid her. If the insurers could show that he had subsequently developed a serious medical condition, then, they would successfully argue, they believed she must have known about it. The policy could then still be nullified.

West well understood the mindset of the insurance world. It would be his task to ensure they did not have to pay out.

He told them what he planned. He had returned from Tel Aviv with tissue samples from Maxwell's body. He would subject them to a variety of forensic tests, one of which was highly controversial: it was to establish the presence of diatoms in the body. They are silicon-coated algae found in sea water, and their presence would go a long way to showing that Maxwell must have been alive when he entered the water, and that drowning had been the cause of death. Diatoms would enable West also to distinguish between drowning and pulmonary oedema found in heart disease.

But West knew this diagnostic tool had, for the past century, been the subject of a fierce debate within forensic science.

The equally eminent pathologist Werner U Spritz, author of a textbook West respected, *Guidelines for the Application of Pathology in Crime Investigation*, had repudiated the test.

Diatoms for diagnosing drowning at autopsy are widely used in most European countries, but in the United States the search for diatoms in the body remains mostly unaccepted as a diagnostic tool. The portal of entry of diatoms into the blood was believed to be via the lungs, through microscopic tears of alveolar walls that occur in the process of forceful water inhalation. It was after the diatom method for the diagnosis of drowning was established in Europe that it began to spread to North American collegial medical departments, but in 1963 we questioned the validity of this method by the recovery of diatoms in the liver and in organs of other individuals who had died of causes other than drowning.

Spritz further rejected the test by asserting that meteorologists had known for years about the presence of diatoms in the air.

Nevertheless, West began to conduct the test in his laboratory at Guy's Hospital in London. He had arranged for three litres of sea water to be flown from the area where the body had been pinpointed by Rankin as the most likely place it had gone overboard. Sealed in a sterile container, the water was in a condition as close as possible to when it had been scooped out of the Atlantic. But, against that, West had no idea what the precise sea temperature had been when Maxwell had gone over the side of the yacht.

He noted: 'It is perfectly possible that if he fell into the water and managed to float for a while, that drowning could have been exacerbated by the effects of diminishing body temperature.'

But, after days of testing, West could still not come to a definite conclusion that a heart attack had led to drowning. But he would not give up.

On 23 December 1991, Iain and Vesna West flew to Madrid with a

Spanish-speaking interpreter. They went to the Madrid Toxicology Institute, where they had arranged to examine samples from the first autopsy in Tenerife. They were shown organ and tissue samples stored in formalin.

West noted: 'The heart had been very extensively dissected and most of the heart muscle reduced to small blocks of tissue.'

It was agreed that they could take samples back to London for microscopic study. Once more they examined the autopsy report de Lamela had signed.

Iain West told his wife, 'In the Spanish judgment, the cause of death is not totally clear.'

West and his wife now set about analysing the samples they had brought back from Spain. They also pored over the plans and photographs of the *Lady Ghislaine*, focusing on the aft deck and its rails. West once more noted:

Sudden heart failure may induce breathlessness and it is possible he would have been leaning against the rail on the lower deck in order to breathe more easily. In this instance he is likely to be leaning so that his body is behind the rail with his hands grasping it tightly. This would have assisted his breathing.

Inconclusive though the observation was, it would have placed Maxwell in an ideal position for the *kidon* to strike.

But the two pathologists, armed with whatever evidence they had, were moving towards a different conclusion.

'If he had suffered a heart attack coincidentally while leaning over the rail, he would have fallen into the water and we do not believe he could have received the injuries to his back,' West wrote.

He did consider the possibility that Maxwell's torn shoulder muscles could have been caused by the body being pulled along the deck, and over the side of the yacht. He found it 'unfortunate' there had been no proper crime-scene examination of the yacht in Tenerife – no footprints, dusting for fingerprints or anything of that nature.

It left him saying, 'I can't dispute the possibility of murder.' But forensically he had nothing to support that and West was not in the business of speculating without that support. The furthest he would go would be to ask and answer his own question: 'Could he have been killed and thrown into the water? The answer is yes, but I think it very unlikely.'

The frustration of not being able to be more definitive is there in those words.

To conduct a test would have required a body of similar height and weight to Maxwell. It would then be necessary to drag it over a deck and lift it over rails identical to the ones on the *Lady Ghislaine*. Indeed, such a rough test had been conducted by the former editor of the *Daily Mirror*, Roy Greenslade. He later wrote how he had found a yacht with

> railings approximately the height of those on the *Lady Ghislaine*. I interviewed two former crew members. We tried to fall over. It appeared unlikely Maxwell could have done so, even with his bulk and top heaviness which made his centre of gravity different from ours.

The enterprising pop-journalism investigation did not take into account that Maxwell's 'bulk' and 'top heaviness' did not fit the facts: his massive waistline would have been mostly *below* the *Lady Ghislaine*'s rail, making it in reality much *harder* for him to fall overboard.

But Iain West had no body available for a more scientific test and there was already enough controversy. Somehow a copy of the video tape of the Tel Aviv autopsy ended up in the offices of the French news magazine *Paris Match*. It concluded Maxwell had been 'brutally beaten up before [being] thrown into the sea'. West had furiously rebutted the allegation, insisting that, if such evidence had been present, he would have informed Scotland Yard.

No doubt concerned that further stories would appear, Iain and Vesna West began to write their final conclusions over Christmas 1991. They offered a 'a number of possible scenarios' to explain the troubling injuries to Maxwell's shoulder muscles.

a. If he was hanging onto the rail of the boat and trying to prevent himself from falling into the water, then it is possible that in such a large and unfit man, the muscular effort to hoist his body back into the boat would cause the damage seen here.

b. If he balanced and fell over the railing but managed to grab the railing as he fell, then it is possible he would have torn the muscles affected here. It is difficult to see, from the available evidence, how such an accidental fall could have occurred on a smooth sea unless the deceased had been leaning over the rail. The arrangement of the railings suggests that if he had tripped or slipped on the deck, then it is impossible he would have fallen overboard.

c. These injuries would not be seen if an individual allowed himself to deliberately topple over the side. If, however, the deceased had deliberately climbed over the railing so that he stood on the protrusion of the outer hull, it is possible he could have slipped from this while holding onto the railing with his left hand. This could well account for him hanging for a short while by that hand and for the injuries that were found.

It is difficult to conceive of a reason for anyone to carry out an action of this type, except with the intent of self injury, whether as the result of an impulse or as a more carefully planned act.

Surrounded by caveats and the careful words of two experienced pathologists who suggested scenarios designed no more than to draw fact out of darkness and for whom the art of informed conjecture was anathema, and given their remit to content themselves only with the forensic evidence available, Iain and Vesna West had concluded that suicide was at most not more than a scenario, and in no way could be considered a final verdict.

It was indeed difficult to accept that Robert Maxwell, who had hired Jules Kroll to investigate his enemies, who had believed Mossad would save him, who had been in a 'good frame of mind' shortly before he vanished, according to the yacht's captain, would have committed suicide. The image of a 286-pound man being able to climb onto the outer hull beggars belief.

The Wests' own sense of being baffled was there in the final words of their report:

We are in a position not uncommonly seen in second post-mortem examinations, of not having a clearly defined cause of death. Whilst the deceased did suffer from cardiac disease and we cannot exclude it as a factor in his death, we are of the opinion that the most likely cause of death is drowning.

But:

It is impossible to rule out homicide. Homicide will remain impossible to exclude from a purely pathological point of view.

Support for that came from other issues that need to be settled. How did the *kidon* unit get on board to commit the assassination that Dr West finds impossible to exclude? Both Ben-Menashe and Ostrovsky would have confirmed that part of *kidon* training is to perform such a manoeuvre at sea. The *Lady Ghislaine* was not travelling at full speed. The *kidon* boat would have been ahead of it on an intercept course – which may go some way to explaining the concern Rankin had of wanting to be alerted if any boat came within five miles.

At some point on that course, the *kidon* would have entered their dinghy with its powerful, muffled engine. As it approached the yacht the helms-man would have cut the engine and allowed the dinghy to drift until it was alongside the *Lady Ghislaine*. The rubber-sheathed grappling irons would have secured the dinghy to the handrail long enough for the *kidon* to climb on board.

Even if the security cameras were on, the areas where Maxwell liked to stand, from previous observations by the crew, were a blind spot. The cameras were, of course, not on: they never were at sea. They were primarily intended to alert the crew of any intruders trying to board when the yacht was tied up in harbour.

The later repeated claim that Maxwell jumped/slipped/fell to his death – the root of the claim that he committed suicide – does not stand any serious scrutiny. West does not say that Maxwell committed suicide. He merely cannot discount it. However, the suicide theory can be rejected for the following reasons. If Robert Maxwell jumped into the sea, he would have to be facing *outwards*. That would mean his hands were in front of him, making it physically impossible for a man of his bulk to have manoeuvred in midair and try to grab onto the boat. Again, what would he have tried to grab onto? The hull of the *Lady Ghislaine* had no protrusion. If he fell forward, it would have been physically impossible for him to have twisted in mid-fall/jump/slip to grab onto the rail. His massive body weight would have propelled him into the water. The time from his jump/fall/slip from the deck into the sea would only have been seconds. It is on those grounds that the suggestion, widely reported later, that suicide was how he died can now be laid to rest.

West's report went to the insurers and underwriters. Betty Maxwell did not receive a copy but she read press leaks that it identified the cause of death as suicide. Betty was perplexed. She had spoken to Iain West on the phone after his return to London from the Tel Aviv autopsy. He had not said to her that suicide would be his verdict. In fact, according to Betty Maxwell, his view appeared to concur with that of the Israeli state pathologist, Dr Hiss, that death had been due to drowning after an 'involuntary fall'. Betty had understood that to mean accidental death. Hiss had told her the insurers would have to pay her the £20 million.

The only thing she could now do was go back to Tel Aviv to see Dr Hiss. Perhaps he could resolve the confusion. Isabel Maxwell clearly remembers what transpired when her mother went back to Israel.

'Dr Hiss showed great compassion. He went over in great detail with her what they found during the autopsy which was practised in front of Dr West, his wife and three Israeli pathologists – as recorded in a video with the exchange of conversations. Both Dr West and Dr Hiss agreed on the conclusions which would be published. Dr Hiss published his report a few weeks after the autopsy had taken place and sent it to my mother and he told her himself on her second trip to Tel Aviv that he was astounded to read what Dr West had published, which did not tally with what had been the consensus of opinion at the time of the autopsy of both parties.'

*

For weeks after Iain West had sent his report to the insurers, Betty Maxwell heard nothing. Her fears grew. She later expressed them (to the authors) in a remarkable claim:

'When the insurers feared that the verdict of suicide might be overturned, then they said that I had signed a false declaration, i.e. that my husband was in good health and lied to them. They tried to make another case, playing both sides against the middle. Then they said they would at least give me back my premium on the insurance I had covered personally for twelve years. But they also invoked the same reason that I had lied to refuse to pay that sum. At that stage I was advised by my lawyers to abandon the case as the atmosphere in the country was so bad because of the pension funds.'

Betty would have been happy for the policy millions to have been paid to the receivers to compensate those workers who lost their savings in her husband's pension-fund swindle.

But she had other matters to contend with. In the spring of 1992, she discovered that Maxwell's organs were still in sealed jars and containers in Madrid. With the help of Ya'atov Neeman she had them released and buried with his body. What especially distressed her was 'that the Spaniards had also kept his brain'.

Then came the news from Lloyds that they were not going to pay her a penny.

But there was more pain for her to endure. Kevin and Ian had been questioned by a Parliamentary Select Committee over the missing pension funds, the first stage to their eventual arrest (and subsequent acquittal). The penthouse in Maxwell House had been emptied of all its possessions; even his collection of baseball caps had been taken by the receivers. Headington Hill Hall had been similarly stripped.

Betty had tried and failed to find one lawyer in the country who would try to make the insurers pay up. She would become convinced 'that pressures were exercised, perhaps not so much against me but against finding anything that would exculpate my husband from being a total villain, and therefore they blackened his reputation so that the guilty men in the City could escape justice. I could tell you a hair-raising story about the actions of British intelligence services in the case and, in particular, that they made files disappear from the official archive. And what about the disappearance of the stewardess's film?'

She was referring to the photographs taken by Emma, the Gulfstream's stewardess who had been invited on board the *Lady Ghislaine*. Emma had given the film to Betty as a memento of Maxwell. Betty had asked Isabel to take it to Maxwell House so that it could be developed in the *Mirror*'s darkroom.

'The photographic technician was astonished. When he unwrapped the film he discovered that someone had spliced it inside and removed most of the film. What was left was blank. It was just another puzzle. It meant, according to the technician, that someone had opened the film, removed what they wanted, and resealed it. But why? What had it contained for someone to do that? The stewardess said she had kept it around her person. She couldn't understand how someone could have got access to it,' said Isabel Maxwell.

Had the *kidon* monitoring the *Lady Ghislaine* seen her photographing other yachts in the harbour and feared she might have snapped them?

The assassination of Robert Maxwell completed a succession of related deaths, all as skilfully planned and all of which, unlike Maxwell's, remain to this day mysterious.

Like him, those men had operated in or around the world of intelligence with its close ties to arms and drug dealers, economic espionage and often terrorism. Just as a new form of spy emerged in the wake of the Cold War, so has a new kind of terrorist: often highly educated and provided with equipment that matches that which his hunters possess.

In October 2001, a month after the destruction of the Twin Towers in New York and the attack on the Pentagon in Washington by al-Qaeda suicide bombers, it emerged that the man who controlled them, Osama bin Laden, had acquired a copy of the still highly secret Promis software.

The version of Promis provided to bin Laden came from a former FBI agent, Robert Hanssen. For years he had been a Russian spy inside the FBI. He had passed over the latest version of Promis to his handlers in Moscow. They had sold on a copy to Simeon Mogilevich for a reputed sum of $3 million. He had sold it on to bin Laden for an undisclosed price.

Promis currently provided the most dangerous terrorist on earth with the ability to monitor the efforts to track him down, and access to databases on specific targets. Bin Laden could also use the software for electronic banking transactions and money-laundering operations much more sophisticated than anything Robert Maxwell had devised. The Promis software in Bin Laden's hands was equipped with artificial intelligence and developed in parallel to the world's banking systems to track money, stock trades and other financial dealings.

The discovery that bin Laden had the software created havoc within the global intelligence community. The FBI, MI5 and MI6 and Germany's BND were among the agencies that stopped using their version of Promis – fearing bin Laden had already used his version to access their own hard drives.

The tangled saga of Promis that continued to involve Bill Hamilton in law-suits in which he charged the US government with complicity in the theft of his software had also attracted the attention of a journalist, Danny Casolaro.

Danny Casolaro was one of those young men journalism produces from time to time: ambitious, energetic, determined to make his own name – and a trifle naïve. Recklessness and a need to sound mysterious about his contacts completed the broad brushstrokes of a character who had begun to believe he could fill all the gaps in the complex story of Promis. He already had a title for the story: *The Octopus*. It would uncover the missing link, still unresolved, in Iran–Contra.

He would include the October Surprise – the alleged trade-off authorised by Ronald Reagan of a vast sum of money for the Iranian mullahs in exchange for their setting free the American diplomats held hostage in Teheran, the release to be timed for the day Reagan entered the Oval Office. Casolaro also believed he could show, as never before, the role of the Bank of Commerce and Credit International (BCCI) as the world's largest money launderer. The bank's services had been used by Robert Maxwell, the godfathers of crime in the Eastern Bloc, Mossad, the CIA and Middle East terrorists like Abu Nidal. The Iranian Revolutionary Guard even had an account in the London branch of BCCI.

For Danny Casolaro, if he could prove any of that, he would have his place in one of the newsrooms of mainstream news gathering.

Casolaro had diligently built his case. Over months he had amassed an impressive amount of documentation filled with the names of CIA and Mossad agents and those of leading arms dealers. The most important documents never left his side. Like Robert Maxwell, he carried with him everywhere he went a briefcase filled with them. One document included a copy of a cheque made out to one of the arms dealers for $4 million.

Yet, for a reporter who saw himself as a hard-nosed investigator, Casolaro was something of a romantic: he raised Arabian horses and quoted poetry. He would turn up on a date wearing a tuxedo and carrying roses; sometimes he wore a gilded tin hat. Three weeks before his death he asked a girlfriend, Wendy Weaver, 'Will you kiss me when I am dead?' He told Bill Hamilton, the president of Inslaw, he 'was close to the truth, but was kinda scared'. He told his brother, a doctor, 'If I die and they say it's an accident, don't believe them.'

Was this more of the self-dramatisation Casolaro was certainly capable of? Or had he somehow picked up an inkling that his life was in danger? Over the months, his contacts within the Washington intelligence community had developed. He had, he told Wendy, 'met a lot of spooky people'.

Could one be the person he had come to meet on that afternoon of 10 August 1991, in a motel that specialised in small conventions, a place where people came and went unnoticed?

After he had checked in at the Martinsburg Hotel in West Virginia, Casolaro went to his room, left his briefcase and overnight bag and walked the few yards to the motel bar. The dimly lit area was furnished with the kind of cheap and chintzy decor that characterises such places.

Later, a cocktail waitress remembered Casolaro talking to 'a man who looked Middle Eastern'. She could not identify him beyond that – and the man would never be traced.

Hours later, Casolaro was discovered in his bathroom, lying naked in the bath. The bloodstained water had slopped over the floor. His eyes were still open, staring up at the cheap cottage-cheese textured ceiling. Both his wrists had been slashed, each one ten times in precisely the same place.

When the police came they found only his overnight bag. It would be hours before they learned his briefcase was missing. Like the man in the bar, it would never be located.

In a drawer of the bedroom desk, police found a note. It read, 'Please forgive me for the worst possible thing I could have done. Most of all I'm sorry to my son. I know that deep down inside God will let me in.'

They checked the writing on Casolaro's hotel registration form. It matched.

'Another poor devil who couldn't cope,' one policeman said to another.

All else would flow from that, as far as the Martinsburg Police Department investigation went.

But others were less certain it was a simple suicide. Dr Tony Casolaro, a quiet-spoken specialist in pulmonary medicine, plunged into his dead brother's world. He spent weeks talking to everyone he could. He was driven by the memory of the last time he had seen Danny: 'He was just so excited and upbeat about the way his investigation was going. Suicide would have been the last thing on his mind.'

So how did he explain the suicide note?

'My brother was big, a tough guy, fearless. But he, like everyone, had an Achilles' heal. In his case it was his son. He lived for him after his divorce. In my view somebody had stood over Danny in that hotel bedroom and made him write the suicide note by telling Danny if he did not, there was someone holding his son who would kill the child. That would be enough to make Danny cave in. Where his son was concerned he could never have resisted that kind of pressure.'

How had his killer manoeuvred Danny into the bath?

'They had told him that unless he did exactly what they told him, his son would die.' Dr Casolaro believed 'one or more persons are involved in the fake suicide'.

There is no way to prove or disprove that theory. It would have needed an Iain West to explain how usual it is for a person to slash each wrist carefully with precision the same number of times when committing suicide.

Like Robert Maxwell, Danny Casolaro had not shown the slightest hint he was going to take his own life. Hours before he had gone to the motel to keep his appointment, Wendy Weaver remembered 'his high spirits and quoting to me some lines from a poem – "the gold-hatted high-bouncing lover" – that

Scott Fitzgerald used as the epigraph to *The Great Gatsby*. He was in a great mood. I had already warned him that this story he was working on was no adventure. It was traumatic. But he was obsessed with it.'

It would be left for *Time* to ask, but not to be able to answer, the question: was Danny Casolaro murdered because he was 'The Man Who Knew Too Much'?

Certainly the Martinsburg police did not think so. They failed to follow up the statement Dr Casolaro gave them that his brother had told him he had been getting 'these strange phone calls saying that he was going to die'.

A neighbour had told police investigators she had been checking on Danny Casolaro's house while he was at the motel and the phone rang. A voice said, 'You're dead, you sonofabitch.' That call – a man's voice – came hours after the body had been found in the bath.

An FBI agent gave reporters an unattributable briefing that Casolaro was 'getting into areas that were very dangerous – very dangerous and we told him so'.

A more powerful voice concurred. Former United States Attorney-General Eliot Richardson, usually circumspect, who was trying to push the government to settle with Inslaw over the theft of Promis, went on the record.

'I believe there is strong evidence to show that Casolaro was deliberately murdered because he was close to uncovering sinister elements in what he called *The Octopus*.'

It was sufficient for the Senate Judiciary Committee, which had begun to look at the background to the Promis theft, to announce that it had discovered that Danny Casolaro had several conversations, prior to his death, with a man identified by the FBI as having 'ties with organised crime and the world of covert intelligence'.

Those links involved Eastern Bloc figures with whom Robert Maxwell had developed ever-deepening connections. In turn those links had extended to Cyrus Hashemi, Amiram Nir and many others. To try breaking that chain could have led to those 'sinister elements', which one of the most respected lawyers in the United States had identified, requiring the end of Danny Casolaro's life.

The man the FBI had identified as having such links, one of the shadowy figures who had drifted into Casolaro's life, was already a convicted felon, found guilty of 'solicitation of murder'.

Increasingly the death of Danny Casolaro took on the intrigue of film noir. But nothing could budge the Martinsburg police investigators from their original belief that this was suicide.

In January 1991 they announced their final verdict: a self-inflicted death. Their only piece of evidence was the hotly disputed suicide note.

They could offer no reason why a young man who only hours before his death had been cheerful, had no record of mental instability, had no financial worries, was in a stable relationship, and believed he was about to bag that one big story, the journalistic equivalent of discovering the lost treasure of the Incas, had undressed, run his bath, sat in it and calmly slashed each wrist ten times on his own volition.

Andrei Lukanov had returned to Sofia from the funeral of Robert Maxwell a worried man. It was not only the presence of Ognian Doinov at the graveside that had unsettled him. One of his contacts in Darzhavna Sigurnost, the still feared Bulgarian secret service, had said he should take greater care with his personal protection.

In Maxwell's absence, Lukanov used his political influence and his Moscow connections to continue as before. Multi-Group, the organisation Maxwell helped to found, had emerged as a vehicle for privatising every profitable part of the Bulgarian economy.

Ivo Janchev, with his intelligence connections in Sofia and Moscow, had helped expand Multi-Group's interests in Macedonia, where the authorities were determined to prevent money laundering.

But the early 1990s in Eastern Europe saw the rise of competing syndicates, each forming alliances with businesses run by men Vladimir Kryuchkov had put in place, or by the leadership of the KGB's successor.

Russia wanted to ensure that, whatever joint projects were in place, they had their men on the boards of the companies involved. Lukanov had always been one of Moscow's men but the wily politician had also played both sides against the middle. Like Maxwell he had learned that 'my enemy's enemy is my friend' when it came to straight profit.

A world even more complex than that of the Maxwell era had developed in Bulgaria and Moscow with Multi-Group, Orion and other conglomerates fighting to establish their power bases with links to other East European countries.

In 1995, Lukanov became boss of TopEnergy, a joint Bulgarian–Russian project aimed at breaking the monopoly of Turkey's US-backed stranglehold on Russia's flow of oil and gas through the Bosphorus.

The move pleased Moscow but not people within Multi-Group, which had a large investment in the project. For them Lukanov had become a liability because he had made too many enemies in the Bulgarian political establishment and in new syndicates like Orion. Before long, Lukanov's political battles, going back to his 'palace revolt' days when he overthrew Zhivkov, came back to haunt him.

There were many people now in Bulgaria waiting for an opportunity, in true Balkan fashion, to exact revenge. In Moscow, there was unhappiness that their man in Sofia was creating problems for TopEnergy. Old enemies in the Bulgarian Communist Party were determined that Lukanov should not succeed in his new post even if that meant stymieing the potential of the Bulgarian–Russian energy project.

To make matters worse, his associate Ivo Janchev was playing with fire in developing projects for Multi-Group in Macedonia, with his own interests in mind. That was also causing problems, and those came to a head when an attempt was made to assassinate the Macedonian President, Kiro Gligorov, in October 1995.

Macedonian and Greek newspapers pointed the finger at Multi-Group, claiming it had reacted to Gligorov's strategy to reduce the power of syndicates such as Multi-Group. Speculation was rife and the evidence for such claims questionable. Nevertheless, Janchev's name was mentioned in Macedonian secret service files as one of the figures behind the attempted assassination. Again, it was based on unnamed sources, but it was dangerous for those organisations in which Janchev had a prominent role.

Janchev heard about the rumours through his intelligence connections and publicly denounced those who were spreading them.

'Something like that is far away from our line of business,' he said in his capacity as director of the Macedonian office of Multi-Group.

Six months later, on 12 April, Ivo Janchev's body was found hanging in a toilet in the Bistrica International Management Center, which Maxwell had first bought for a paltry sum.

While the police declared it suicide, Lukanov and Janchev's former colleagues in Darzhavna Sigurnost thought otherwise. They privately launched an investigation but the findings have never been made known.

Lukanov now knew that even he was not safe. Friends in the Bulgarian secret service again warned him and offered him protection. He rejected it. Instead he hired a driver and two bodyguards. He paid them well, the only way he knew to keep their loyalty.

'Like Maxwell, I will also be murdered,' he told close friends in mid-September 1996.

Two weeks later, he had set up a meeting in the Sheraton Hotel, where almost a decade before he had laid out his plans before Maxwell in a private dining room – the onset of Maxwell's descent into the world of crime in Eastern Europe.

Now the meeting he was going to have was for a different purpose. It was to meet a *katsa* sent by Mossad's new director, Danny Yatom, to brief him on the latest activities of the Bulgarian and Russian intelligence services. Though Lukanov did not have his high-level connections, he still believed what he would pass on would be valuable. He also hoped it would be an opportunity to damage the standing of his enemies. At the end of their meeting, the *katsa* had told Lukanov that Mossad had established there was a clear and present danger to his own life. In return for all he had done after Maxwell's death, Mossad was prepared to spirit Lukanov out of Bulgaria.

He was advised that the sooner he left the better. No one should be told. He should take as little as possible with him. His nearest relatives could come later.

Several days later, on 1 October, Andrei Lukanov walked out of his apartment in the Iztok suburb of Sofia. He expected to see his driver and the two bodyguards in their usual position: parked at the kerbside, the driver behind the wheel, the bodyguards standing either side of the open back door of the limousine.

They were not there. As Lukanov hesitated, a man stepped out of an adjoining doorway. At point-blank range he fired three bullets from a Russian-made Makorov 9mm pistol into Andrei Lukanov's head and chest. He died instantly.

It would be left to Marin Markovski, Bulgaria's prominent criminal lawyer, to make the link with the assassination of Robert Maxwell.

'The connection is that both murders were related to political and financial issues. I am not saying the murders of Maxwell and Lukanov were one and the same thing, but both murders were interwoven politically and financially.'

Markovski had not been alone in naming Maxwell in the same context as Lukanov. The Bulgarian Minister of the Interior, Bogomil Bonev, went further in attacking the Maxwell legacy. In March 1998, referring to claims that 'money from the pension funds of the British millionaire Maxwell, the Central Committee of the Communist Party and secret services, were used to fund Multi-Group', Bonev said the Interior Ministry would 'investigate all unlawful privatisation deals of Multi-Group'. They would also investigate 'suspicious murders of the officials of the Group.'

He was referring specifically to the 1994 death of Miho Mihov in the town of Lovech; the director of the branch of the Credit Bank had shot himself in the head.

Two years later 'the corpse of Ivo Janchev' was found hanging in the toilet at Bistrica.

Then there were other 'suicides' of Sasho Danchev and Peter Boychev. All these men had long-standing links to organised crime. They had all been involved in Robert Maxwell's activities.

By the end of the 1990s, Multi-Group had begun to change its image from those early years. It wanted to rid itself of the tainted Lukanov–Maxwell era and erase the bad publicity that surrounded its activities. It took on the look of an international corporation with men at the top who were now visible.

*

Edmund Safra had been one of Robert Maxwell's closest friends. Safra had personally allowed money to be funnelled through his bank from Eastern Europe.

'When Safra realised the bureau [FBI] was moving in,' John O'Neil recalled, 'he did a deal. He agreed to keep the bureau informed of what moved through his bank to the Bank of New York, which had been targeted by Russian and Bulgarian crime syndicates. Safra didn't like the heat on him, so he agreed to help the bureau.'

But, when Safra announced he was going to sell his bank for $9.8 billion in 1999, he also attracted powerful enemies.

In December of that month, Safra was in his penthouse, one as secure as Maxwell's, in the Belle Epoque building on Monaco's exclusive Boulevarde Ostend. Some time during the night masked intruders had entered the penthouse. A male nurse, one of two Safra kept permanently available to tend his needs – an American – raised the alarm. The female nurse and her elderly patient locked themselves in a bathroom.

Safra used his mobile phone to contact his wife, asleep in her bedroom in another part of the spacious penthouse. She assured him help was on the way.

When police and firemen broke down the bathroom door they found Edmund Safra and the nurse dead from smoke inhalation. The cause of the fire and how the intruders made good their escape was never established. They had not been captured on the penthouse surveillance cameras.

From the day he had walked out of Robert Maxwell's hotel suite that wintry morning in Canada after years of money laundering for Maxwell as the front man of Earl Brian's company Hadron, Janos Pasztor had led a charmed life. While Earl Brian had finally ended up in a California jail for earlier scam operations, Pasztor had managed to stay one step ahead of John A Belton, the determined stockbroker.

Belton had wanted Pasztor as his principal witness in a case he was bringing against the Bank of Montreal, who had purchased Nesbitt-Thompson in 1987. Belton believed the bank was still responsible for the substantial damages he and his clients had suffered as a result of what he called 'The Maxwell Channel' – the interlink between Robert Maxwell, Rafi Eitan, Earl Brian and Janos Pasztor.

Slowly but surely, with the single-minded purpose of a true obsessive, Belton had amassed every detail of Pasztor's life, including his colourful sexual life.

'He had taken up with a nude dancer, a hooker. He even paid for her to attend a special school for ladies. He took her on a world tour and signed over his house to her. She cleaned him out financially and left. I found all that out', Belton's voice was filled with pride as he recounted his sleuthing.

By the spring of 2000, he believed Pasztor was 'a broken man – ready to spill the beans on Earl Brian, Robert Maxwell and Rafi Eitan. The Maxwell Channel was about to start broadcasting.'

But months later Belton's optimism took a surprising turn. Janos Pasztor had taken on a new lease of life.

'I was in touch with people close to him and suddenly I heard that he seemed to be enjoying life again. He had got over the hooker. He was enjoying life and he loved playing tennis every day. It was a metamorphosis even I could not quite understand.'

Nonetheless Belton heard through contacts that 'Pasztor might just be willing to turn over a new leaf and provide me and the Canadian courts and the RCMP with the information we all needed.'

On 15 October 2000, Pasztor, following his now daily routine, played a game of tennis. But later that day he complained of not feeling well – attributing it to flu symptoms. A visit to his doctor confirmed this diagnosis and he began a course of antibiotics.

Three weeks later on 3 November, unable to rid himself of the flu he thought he had, he checked into hospital. This time he complained of a 'slight chest pain'.

Two days later he was dead. The cause of death was listed as lung cancer. For John A Belton 'it had all the hallmarks of the death of Cyrus Hashemi in London. Pasztor held the key to so much. I had solid information that he was ready to blow the lid off it all. He knew about Mossad, Maxwell and their role in Promis and money laundering. He was also the man who could finger Earl Brian.'

Belton would remain convinced 'from intelligence' he received that 'Pasztor met Maxwell in New York the week before Maxwell was murdered'.

If that is the case, it could be explained by Maxwell's desire to get at money Pasztor had secretly transferred for him into offshore accounts. Another hypothesis that Belton offered is that Maxwell may have asked to see Pasztor to tell him one more time to 'keep his mouth shut'.

Jonathan Moyle was another journalist following the same complex trail of Promis that Danny Casolaro had travelled. By March 1990, it had taken him to Santiago, Chile, to investigate the activities of Cardoen Industries, one of the country's leading arms manufacturers. The young and relatively inexperienced reporter was looking for proof to confirm what he had been told in London by an MI6 contact: that Cardoen had supplied both Iran and Iraq with arms. The boss of the company was Carlos Cardoen.

An FBI source had told Moyle that Cardoen had been actively involved in helping Maxwell sell the doctored Promis software to Chile's intelligence service. Maxwell, Promis and the Iran–Contra affair had been magnetic links Moyle could not resist. From his hotel suite in Santiago he had begun to make telephone calls.

Suddenly they stopped. When a maid went to clean the suite she found Moyle inside a closet. He was hanging by his shirt with a pillowcase over his head. A later forensic examination found a needle mark on his leg. The pathologist who conducted the autopsy suggested he had been sedated and then force-fed the drugs found in his stomach.

No hotel employee had seen any person come to or go from the suite. Attempts by the family to have the Chilean authorities conduct a proper criminal investigation were rejected. The death was registered as 'unsolved'.

Carlos Cardoen disappeared from Chile. In 2002 he remained on the FBI's most-wanted list. His whereabouts are unknown.

The residue from the assassination of Robert Maxwell would continue. By 2002, the figure of $10 billion would be estimated to be the amount plundered from Bulgaria during and after the Maxwell period. The country's national debt was placed at $9 billion.

Much of the paper trail of Maxwell's dealings in Eastern Europe has been shredded or mysteriously disappeared from official files – including company registration data. Maxwell had not been alone in realising the need to hide his complicity.

However, in 1996, the Maxwell name surfaced once more in Sofia but this time it was his son, Iain. Sofia District Court deleted Iain's name from the board of managers of Informvest – a company his father had established. Other names deleted from the board included Stoyan Georgiev Denchev, Brian Arthur Coll and John Bonn.

Documents linking Robert to the eventual collapse of the Bank of Agricultural Credit had by then vanished.

In August 2000, that CIA director George Tenet decided it was time to put pressure on the governments in Sofia and Moscow to deal with organised crime. He travelled to both capitals.

'The evidence had been available for years that organised crime had its roots in the Soviet Bloc and linked up with our indigenous crime syndicates in the US,' John O'Neil confirmed. 'Tenet's predecessor, John Deutsch, had told Congress about it. Few people took note until it hit us hard. The Russians were laundering their money through banks in New York and other states. Some crime bosses were using Israeli passports to get into the country to avoid INS scrutiny.'

In Sofia, Tenet was blunt. He told the Bulgarian Interior Ministry that it had better deal with the problem. He warned that Bulgaria's application to join NATO and the European Union could be in jeopardy if it did not comply with his demand.

While Tenet travelled on to Moscow, the Bulgarian government acted. Eight Yugoslav businessmen had their right to enter Bulgaria withdrawn and five businessmen, born in the former Soviet Union – holding Russian, Israeli or Greek citizenship – were expelled from the country.

One was Michael Chorney, who many years earlier had impressed Maxwell. Now 49, and a major shareholder in banks – Roseximbank and Neftinvestbank, two that Maxwell once used – and the largest shareholder in Mobitel, Bulgaria's only GSM operator, Chorney felt he had been singled out unfairly. He charged the Bulgarian government with yielding to unreasonable pressure from the Americans. He had, he said, been a scapegoat. From his new home in Israel, Chorney later wrote an open letter to the Russian and Israeli governments, declaring himself a patriot of both countries, and offering to help in the fight against international terrorism.

'There are documents in the Russian Interior Ministry that could allow Israel to consider me Russian mafia,' he added, pleading for a review of his status in both countries.

'We are Israeli patriots. We did not come here to Israel to launder money or invest in prostitution or drugs. We are here to help the Jewish people build a bridge between Israel and Russia. Russian businessmen are the strategic wealth of Israel in its fight,' Chorney added.

He went on to condemn 'certain politicians and the media for calling me the godfather of the mafia'.

One of the first things Chorney had done on arrival in Israel was to visit the grave of Robert Maxwell.

On 13 February 2000 at 6.15 p.m. in the Donau Hospital, Vienna, Ognian Doinov, Maxwell's bagman, died of cancer.

During a prolonged illness he had dictated his memoirs to his wife – the references to Maxwell infused with the same fawning praise he had heaped on the tycoon in his lifetime. Doinov admitted he was the conduit through which Maxwell dealt with Eastern Europe and had continued to serve his dead mentor long after from his base in Vienna. His legacy was like that of Andrei Lukanov, whom he had come to hate. Doinov had also raided the coffers of his own country.

Dr Iain West died of an illness in 2001 but Professor Yehuda Hiss subsequently became the subject of a judicial and police investigation in Israel.

After 400 hundred body parts belonging to 81 dead family members were discovered in his Forensic Institute, calls were made for his resignation. Body parts – organs, feet, hands, bones – had been removed from corpses without permission. The skull of a soldier killed in the 1990s was discovered in a display cabinet in the institute. Anaot Maor, chairman of the Knesset science committee, had demanded the immediate suspension of Hiss.

A Health Ministry investigation of the facility was launched as well as an investigation by the Attorney-General, Elyakim Rubenstein. A report written by a former judge, Aryeh Segelson, two doctors and several other health professionals concluded, 'Hiss and his workers violated the concept of honouring the dead.'

Hiss, who gave evidence to the committee, was accused in the report of giving 'confusing and contradictory answers'.

In January 2002, despite growing demands from the Movement for Quality Government to have him removed from his post, Hiss remained Israel's state pathologist.

The Maxwell family have suffered terribly from Robert Maxwell's assassination and the subsequent revelations about his life. For Betty Maxwell the tragedy was perhaps greatest. She had been there for him from the first day she met her, but what he left her was financial chaos. In her heart she knew he had not committed suicide, or died of a heart attack. The autopsies had not addressed her real fears that he was murdered.

Her most important task after his death had been to fight for her sons, charged with complicity in their father's crimes.

Kevin and Iain were arrested in their London homes in June 1992, handcuffed and driven to a police station next to the *Mirror* newspaper building in central London. Fingerprinted and questioned, they were later released on bail. Betty had managed to encourage friends to help her raise the £500,000 bail bond for Kevin and £250,000 for Iain.

In September 1992 Kevin Maxwell was declared bankrupt by the liquidators of Bishopsgate Management. The debts were put at £405 million, the largest in British bankruptcy history.

Headington Hill Hall suffered an invasion of assessors from the receivers of her husband's estate with orders to auction off the contents. Betty would have to find a new home. She managed to persuade them to let her buy her own piano and some family heirloom portraits. However, Maxwell's Military Cross, which he had won for gallantry on the battlefield, was put on sale. Friends later bought it back and presented it to her.

A Department of Trade and Industry report excoriated Kevin for his role in the pension-fund scandal, but it also delivered a swingeing indictment of the bankers and financiers who had lived off Maxwell's commission payments while ignoring his dishonesty. There was no mention made of Arthur Andersen, the world's largest accounting firm, charged with winding up Maxwell's worldwide enterprises. The company would later be at the centre of the Enron scandal in the United States. They had also been the accountants of Multi-Group in Bulgaria.

'Arthur Andersen accounting sold off viable companies for nothing,' said Isabel Maxwell.

In the Maxwell story, accountants were among the hyenas that picked on the carcass. If companies ended up being asset-stripped, the man who had been best at it had been Robert Maxwell.

In 2001, Kevin Maxwell's imposed three-year bankruptcy ended. He had blamed a tyrannical father for many of the decisions he had taken. Now Kevin was free to open a bank account again. The London *Daily Telegraph* reported that for several years Kevin had been a consultant with Nordex, trading in finance and construction in Russia and its satellites. Isabel Maxwell remained in San Francisco, a successful president of an Internet company and a tireless worker for an Israeli charity. Ghislaine, who had always been the family member in the headlines, continued to feature in the gossip columns of newspapers and magazines from New York to Paris and Rome. Philip, who had interviewed the crew of the *Lady Ghislaine*, avoided media scrutiny, as did Christine, who lives in France.

Betty Maxwell, now over 80 years of age, continued her charitable work and devoted much of her time to giving talks on the Holocaust. Whatever her husband had done, she would not allow one aspect of his memory to diminish. He had been, after all, a survivor of the Holocaust and there were few of those from that part of Europe where he had been born.

He had also, though she had never known it, been Israel's superspy.

TWENTY-THREE

On 24 September 1997, two suntanned young men got off a flight in Amman, the capital of Jordan, and took a taxi to the city's Continental Hotel. To anyone watching they were typical tourists.

At the hotel check-in they produced Canadian passports, smiled at the desk clerk and falsely signed their names as Barry Beads and John Kendall. The stamps on their passports showed they had already been to Athens, Paris and Rome.

These men were *kidon* and they were in Amman to carry out a mission personally approved by their Prime Minister, Binyamin Netanyahu. Earlier that summer two Hamas suicide bombers had struck in a Jerusalem marketplace, killing fifteen and injuring 150 persons. Netanyahu had promised they would be avenged.

That retribution was now in the hands of the *kidon*.

On 9 September Hamas had struck again, wounding two Israeli body-guards of the Israeli Attaché at the newly opened Israeli embassy in Amman.

Three days later Netanyahu invited the Mossad director, Danny Yatom, to his home for lunch. The Prime Minister wanted to know how the Mossad chief in Jordan had failed to anticipate the attack on the Amman embassy.

Yatom told him Mossad had identified one of Hamas's key operational officers. He was now in Amman. He was Khalid Meshal and he ran the Hamas office in Jordan. He had been travelling to Arab capitals but he was now back in the country.

'Then go and knock him down. Knock him down! Tell your people in Amman to do that!' said Netanyahu.

Yatom squinted behind his spectacles. Killing Meshal in Amman would jeopardise the accord with Jordan reached with the previous Prime Minister, Yitzhak Rabin. It would be better to wait and kill Meshal in some other Arab country.

'Excuses! That's all you give me. Excuses!' Netanyahu is alleged to have shouted. 'I want action. I want it now.'

Now the *kidon* were in place to do just that.

They had been briefed and shown photographs of their target, Khalid Meshal, fully bearded and strong-looking. Amman station reported he was a devoted father of seven children and lived close to the palace of King Hussein.

Outwardly he was little known beyond the Islamic fundamentalist movement. But he had tasked Hamas suicide bombers.

Now in the hotel, the *kidon* meticulously went over their plan. They would be part of an eight-man team. The hit would be carried out in broad daylight. There would be six *katsas* in the backup squad. The *kidon* would use an aerosol filled with a nerve agent they had brought with them from the Institute for Biological Research.

The next day, the two *kidon* – Barry Beads and John Kendall – met other members of the team.

The following morning, 26 September, the *kidon* had breakfast in their rooms and then went down to the lobby.

At 9 a.m., Beads signed for a blue Toyota rental car and Kendall for a green Hyundai.

An hour later Meshal was being driven to work by his chauffeur. In the back of the car were three of his children, a boy and two girls.

As Meshal's car entered Amman's Garden District, his chauffeur said they were being followed. Meshal picked up the car phone and rang police headquarters. The chauffeur, his eyes in the rear-view mirror, relayed the number of a blue Toyota – Bead's car – and Meshal passed it on to the police.

Meshal's children meanwhile were looking out of the rear window waving at the Toyota. Beads ignored them. At that moment Kendall's Hyundai pulled in front of Meshal's car just as the three vehicles were caught in a line of traffic.

Minutes later Meshal received a return call from police headquarters confirming the Toyota was registered to a Canadian tourist. There was nothing to worry about.

At 10.30 a.m., the chauffeur pulled into Wasfi Al-Tal Street and parked. A crowd had gathered outside the Hamas office, among them Beads and Kendall.

Meshal was half out of the car pausing to kiss his children, when Beads stepped forward as if to shake his hand. Kendall was at his shoulder fumbling with a plastic bag.

'Mr Meshal?' asked Beads pleasantly.

Meshal looked at him puzzled. At that moment Kendall produced the aerosol and tried to spray its contents into Meshal's left ear.

The Hamas leader recoiled and began wiping his lobe.

Kendall tried again to spray the nerve agent into Meshal's ear. By now the crowd understood what was happening. Dozens of hands reached out to grab the Mossad agents.

'Run!' Beads shouted in Hebrew to Kendall.

The two *kidon* sprinted towards the blue Toyota parked some way up the street, the crowd in pursuit. Meshal's chauffeur reversed their car to block their path to the Toyota.

Meshal was staggering, moaning, partly supported from falling by some of the crowd. Others were screaming for an ambulance.

In the mayhem, with Beads sprawled beside him, still clutching the half-used aerosol, Kendall barely managed to escape being run over by Meshal's chauffeur. Finally they got into the Toyota.

By now, the Mossad backup team had arrived. One of them shouted to Beads and Kendall to transfer to his car. But another car driven by one of the crowd blocked their path. They were cornered. Realising there was nothing they could do, the backup team drove away.

Beads and Kendall were seized by police, who had just arrived. They were taken to the city's central police station. Then they produced their Canadian passports and protested their innocence. The arrival of Samih Batihi, the formidable Jordanian counterintelligence chief, ended that ploy. He had just spoken to the Mossad station chief in Amman.

Batihi ordered the two *kidon* to be locked in cells and not harmed.

Meshal, meanwhile, was in hospital on life support to stabilise his heart and lungs.

Later that day, Binyamin Netanyahu received a phone call from King Hussein telling him the two Mossad agents had made a full confession and copies of it were on the way to US Secretary of State, Madeleine Albright. The king's many words ended with a demand that Mossad should provide an antidote for the nerve agent used on Meshal.

Within the hour an antidote was flown in an Israeli military plane to Amman and administered to Meshal. He began to recover quickly.

Kendall and Beads were handed over, minus their Canadian passports, to the Canadian embassy in Amman. From there they were driven across the Allenby Bridge into Israel.

Their time with the *kidon* was finished. For them the 'magic' had failed.

Some time later, Victor Ostrovsky would confine himself to one judgment: 'The method used in the failed attempt in Jordan was essentially the one which had worked in the assassination of Robert Maxwell.'

Notes and Documents

The death of Robert Maxwell attracted more media coverage than any other one at sea. It eclipsed the space devoted to the death of the Hollywood producer, Thomas Ince, who had been a guest on board the *Oneida*, a yacht every inch as luxurious as the *Lady Ghislaine*, and owned by an earlier newspaper tycoon, William Randolph Hearst, a man Maxwell admired. On a summer day in 1924, Ince had joined the guests on the *Oneida*. They included Charlie Chaplin, the newspaper columnist Louella Parsons and the actress Marion Davies, Hearst's lover.

Off the coast of San Diego, Ince suddenly died. He was cremated within hours; there had been no autopsy. The police verdict for the cause of death was cardiac arrest following 'an acute attack of indigestion'. The rumour mills of Hollywood said Hearst had shot Ince after he discovered him in bed with Davies, and in return for her silence, Louella Parsons received a huge contract. The story became part of the film world's legends.

On 28 November 1981, the actress Natalie Wood disappeared off the yacht *Splendour*. She had been having dinner with her husband, Robert Wagner, and the actor Christopher Walken. No one saw her go overboard. Next day her body was found floating nearly a mile away – a jacket covered her nightdress. The yacht's dinghy was found nearby. There were reports that Wood had used it to row away. The coroner's verdict was one of accidental death after she had slipped and fallen overboard during the night.

While both deaths have continued to be discussed from time to time, the fate of Robert Maxwell has remained a constant source of fascination to the print and electronic media. The focus of that interest has been on his financial affairs. These have been usefully chronicled in two books by the investigative author and journalist, Tom Bower. Both *The Outsider* and *Maxwell: The Final Verdict*, are an excellent recounting of how Maxwell managed to manipulate the City of London and Wall Street. He deserves credit for being the first writer to confront Maxwell when he was alive and able to protect himself with writs. Roy Greenslade's *Maxwell* and *Death of a Tycoon* by Nick Davies provide glimpses of how Maxwell ran his newspaper and publishing empire.

But none of the books deal with the central themes of the book we set out to write. The questions we asked ourselves were numerous.

What other financial relationships did Robert Maxwell have that went beyond those described by Bower, Greenslade and Davies – and the writers of endless articles? None of them barely moved outside the confines of London and Wall Street.

But what about his connections with the Soviet Union? Our months of research in the Western media showed that almost nothing had been written beyond brief mentions of Maxwell's trip behind the Iron Curtain into the heartland of the Cold War. What exactly had he done there?

What about his relationship to Israel? Maxwell had proclaimed his faith with pride, and rightly so. But was that all his relationship was – a wealthy Jew paying homage to his spiritual home? Bower devotes fewer than thirty pages to Maxwell's relationship with Israel in his *The Final Verdict*. Was that all it deserved?

What about the Maxwell family? Betty Maxwell and the children had been traduced in the eyes of many, charged and convicted of being found guilty by association. Was that really the truth? Even a casual perusal of the copious clippings on the family showed that there was a continuous recycling of the same alleged quotes. Some, like Isabel, had clearly never been interviewed. Would she talk to us? If so, would she act as our guide into the family?

Then there were the circumstances around the death of Maxwell. Much had been written about it. But the key elements, the autopsy reports, which could show the cause of death, or at least eliminate some of the possibilities, had clearly never been seen by any outsider. Could we access them? What other documentation could we obtain? To answer those questions would be crucial. There were also other considerations. Seymour Hersh had raised a storm with his allegations that Maxwell worked for Mossad. But he had not said in what capacity, or exactly how Maxwell had been employed. Would we be able to find out?

Many of the questions we knew could only be answered, or not, by research. We both understood the complex business of primary and secondary sources, on- and off-the-record conversations, and recreating a moment with the use of memoranda, documents, letters, diaries and contemporaneous notes. We both know that memories can play tricks, especially when the frame of the story encompasses a strange period, somewhere between recent history and fading memories that could depend on news clips to refresh them. As with our previous books, we knew we would have to be on guard against attempts to spin the story in one direction or another.

As well as the usual research tools – official records, memoranda, a wide variety of published material – we would need to get to the unpublished data. Without that we would not able to move far beyond the published record.

That we were able to do so we owe, above all others, to one man.

John P O'Neill changed this book with his contribution to our knowledge of the globalisation of organised crime and Maxwell's seminal role in it.

The FBI's foremost counterintelligence expert, John O'Neill was an executive agent in the New York Federal Bureau. He understood how major East European crime figures had learned from Maxwell the way to launder money and manipulate the world of international finance.

Equally JP, as he was sometimes called by his friends, detected the dangers lurking in Afghanistan long before al-Qaeda surfaced as the major terrorist organisation in the world. He had studied the post-Soviet–Afghan war and warned that former mujahedeen had linked up to form a new terrorist organisation.

'These guys are a serious threat. They are confident because they believe they defeated one of the greatest armies on earth – the Soviets. The problem for us is that many of them are from different countries and the linkage between them is well hidden,' O'Neill stated.

That was years before the 11 September attacks in 2001 on America, and no one listened.

'People have forgotten the first attack on the World Trade Center. It is as if that was a one-off. When you think like that you are vulnerable,' he told close friends.

In 2001, John O'Neil decided that his time pursuing a lonely course in the bureau, which he had done for years while trying to get people to listen, was over.

'I'm thinking of going into the private sector. That's where the real money is.' he remarked in June 2001.

It was time to talk to a close friend and look for alternative employment. The man he turned to was Jules Kroll of Kroll Inc., the top private investigative agency in the world. 'John was the best,' said Kroll.

There was a big job going and Kroll knew J P O'Neill was the man for it. It would eventually give John $300,000 per annum – the kind of money he needed to finance his complex and lavish lifestyle. It would also give him prestige.

'I got John the job as head of security at the World Trade Center,' Jules Kroll told us.

That was at the end of August 2001.

On the evening of 10 September 2001, John O'Neill went out on the town to celebrate his new status and the wealth it would bring him. First there were drinks in Windows on the World atop the World Trade Center, where he was now the security boss. Then it was on to Elaine's bar-restaurant on Upper East Side for dinner, where he talked about terrorism and the 1993 attack on the World Trade Center. Later he took friends to Stage 3 at the China Club.

One friend later recalled his saying, 'At least on my watch I can say there was never an attack on New York City.'

The next morning, 11 September, he was in his new office on the 34th floor of the World Trade Center by 8.45.

After the first plane struck he phoned several friends.

He was last seen outside the Trade Center looking up before running back in. His body was found five days later under the rubble of the Twin Towers.

His contribution to this book was enormous and began several years ago when he first talked about organised crime, citing the Maxwell factor as a significant turning point in the way East European criminals operated. He had not seen a direct link between organised crime and terrorism but believed that sooner or later one would occur.

'If there is big money in it, organised crime will supply the product. They have well-established routes through which to channel fissile materials. Just because they are not doing it now does not mean they won't. Many of the people running crime syndicates have come out of East European intelligence services like the KGB and Bulgaria. Those guys know how to hide their traces. They have been trained to do it, for Chrissake. When Vladimir Kryuchkov was KGB chief he put his people into the private sector before the collapse of the Soviet monolith and they are still there in every European country and here in the United States. You only have to look at what Maxwell was about. He designed the financial model and the Soviet lot brought their expertise to it,' said O'Neill.

He saw the intelligence on the flow of money from Eastern Europe and had no doubt that some of those involved had used not only aliases to enter the US, but also Israeli passports, to do deals with indigenous crime organisations such as the Gambino and Gotti families and the Russian Mafia based in Florida and Brighton Beach in New York.

'The fact that some of these people were Soviet Jews is no comment on Israel – criminality and race are separate – but the problem began with men like Maxwell and Lukanov and was passed on to men like Mogilevich and Ivo Janchev, to name but a few. Many of these guys have been able to hide behind big bank accounts or politicians and state officials they bought in the countries where they have their operations. Organised crime may not have direct links with terrorism in the minds of some analysts, but just give it time. These people have no scruples. They're just as likely to fly a consignment of missiles to Iran as a plane load of coke out of Colombia into Florida. They are sophisticated and wealthy. Money can buy the silence of important people. It talks, believe me. Their laundering of money is hard to trace and terrorists have learned from organised crime – from the Maxwells of this world,' John O'Neill remarked in one of his conversations punctuated by brief absences from the table while he took another call from a friend who was a source or a source who was a friend.

The revelations about John Goodwin Tower came from three sources: CIA, FBI and MI6, coalescing in the words of John O'Neill, 'When Tower became involved with Maxwell he came to the attention of all those agencies. You've got a senior political figure who's a national security risk. We're not talking about a nobody – Tower was across a lot of sensitive stuff. Next thing reports are hitting people in London and Washington that he's in the company of the wrong people – intelligence agencies were interested and had files on both Tower and Maxwell. There was one helluva problem. Tower had a lot of powerful friends. But there he was using his reputation to open doors to Sandia for Maxwell. You can't take down a guy like Tower without clearance from the top – we're talking White House. He was opening doors for Maxwell that should have remained closed. I don't want to go too deeply into this but it didn't go unnoticed and I'm not gonna speculate about why or who. It was clear Tower was bought by Maxwell but that would not have been enough to go after him. As I see it, Tower had to know who he was dealing with, especially Maxwell's business associates in the Eastern Bloc. You may want to look at why we never followed up on Maxwell after the Sandia episode. That should have set off alarm bells – and again when Tower joined one of Maxwell's companies and spent time in Bulgaria. You might also want to look at Maxwell's Israeli contacts and ask if he had a godfather in Mossad. Tower was a national security risk. With his background he was mixing in bad company. It goes deep, that's all I'm gonna say about it. Be careful where you tread on this one. For some people it may be a very sensitive issue,' said John O'Neill, making it clear from the look on his face that he would say nor more on the issue.

Isabel Maxwell's contribution to this book began on 24 January 2000, and in the following five months she provided important insights into the Maxwell family and documents not seen by other writers.

Cautious at first, she eventually became a source of vitally important information, supporting her many hours of conversation with a steady flow of emails. Through her, the interfamily relationships became clearer, as well as many previously unresolved questions. She had a lawyer's crispness in her responses, never straying from the point of a question. At the same time she was able to provide more information about her brothers and sisters, who, until then – apart from Kevin and Iain – had really been no more than names in the Maxwell pantheon. Sometimes Isabel would be in her home in San Francisco when she called or wrote; at other times she would be with her mother in England, or in Israel doing work for the charity Soroka. This book is all the better for her frank and honest contribution. Unlike her father, whom she clearly adored, she did not gild the truth.

It was through her that her mother, Betty, also provided a rare insight into her life with Robert Maxwell, her belief that his death had never been properly investigated and her continued fear that sinister forces were at work in destroying critical evidence that could have confirmed his assassination.

Isabel's prior reluctance to talk to writers about her father's death is explained by her admission in one of the first of many emails that she had had 'enough publicity to last me a lifetime and I do not seek it'.

Despite her previous reticence, however, a rare interview she had given in Israel could be found online, in which she dismissed the belief that her father had committed suicide: 'I don't intend to spend the rest of my life trying to rehabilitate my father's reputation or to find out who killed him, if it was murder.'

Like the rest of her family, she had been unable to escape the publicity they attracted before and after her father's death. Often journalists confused her with her younger sister, the outspoken socialite Ghislaine, who counted among her friends Prince Andrew.

Tall, sophisticated and very private, Isabel had made her own way in the world long before her father had become the focus of negative publicity on both sides of the Atlantic. Highly articulate, with an Oxford degree, she had taken her father at his word that his children would 'not inherit a penny'. After marrying Dale Jerassi, the son of a millionaire Bulgarian inventor, she moved with him to San Francisco in 1981. When that marriage ended she remarried a hi-tech inventor and got involved in an Internet business.

As a child she had rarely seen her father and that did not change much when she was married.

'I am willing to put myself out there for causes I believe in but otherwise I guard my privacy fiercely. Money is not my driver either,' she wrote to us on 26 January 2002.

Those who knew her well could testify to the truth of that statement. She was committed to her job as president of CommTouch, an Internet company, and her charity work for Israel. She was also very protective of her mother, Betty, believing she had been harshly judged by everyone who had written about Robert Maxwell. When it came to describing her relationship with her father she did not shirk from revealing the truth – difficult though that was for her.

'He was brutal in his manner, scary in delivery, or in nondelivery, angry, ruthless – he did not brook cowards, timidity, stupidity, laziness, mental laziness... I can speak from personal experience of what it was like to be "out in the cold" with him – he cut me off for six months for a perceived "infraction of the heart" I will call it, which as a young adolescent was one of the most scary things a parent could do to his child.'

Nonetheless, she loved her father.

'I love and miss him – the good parts – and I am not ashamed to say who I am and that he is/was my father,' she wrote.

Privately, she harboured a feeling that perhaps her father had been murdered but it had been easier over the years to tell herself it was an accident. Then someone approached her and led her to believe that she may not have been mistaken in her suspicions about her father's death.

During a trip to Jerusalem, an elderly man phoned her in her hotel room.

'He told me he was a researcher at the Holocaust Museum and he had documents to prove my father had been murdered. I don't know how he got my number. He said his name was Ben Moshe,' she told us in January 2002.

She had not followed up on that lead or agreed to meet the caller. She felt it was not something she felt she alone could investigate. She told Ben Moshe to phone an 'important person I knew but he never did'. Yet it remained in her mind, just like all the other doubts she had about her father's death. She had last seen her father on 5 August 1991 at her brother Iain's marriage celebration.

'He had beautiful hands for such a big man, my father. He said to me, "You're a very nice person, Izzy." It was a special moment because it was human.'

During her initial correspondence she said she had sources she could not name. One in particular she described as 'the important person'. When asked if her father had expressed concerns about his life in the months before his death, she replied that he did.

'Near the end I know he did. He expressed them in a particular way to that same "important person" because that person told me,' she said.

When we asked about David Kimche, the former deputy director of Mossad, Isabel said he had always been a close friend of the family.

Throughout those months we came to know her, she increasingly helped solve difficult questions about her father's life but she always made clear that no approach should be made to other members of her family. She alone would handle enquiries that related to one or other of her siblings. In April 2002 she encouraged her mother Betty, now eighty, to answer our myriad of questions about her late husband. When asked about the crew of the *Lady Ghislaine*, Betty Maxwell provided the following written response through Isabel:

It was the first time it was an entirely American-chosen crew. God knows who vetted them? I am certain that by that time, your father put his trust in anyone he fancied but the people who did care for him and loved him. It seems strange since at the time he seems to have been particularly worried about who was 'after him'.

By 'after him' she meant his business enemies. Both Isabel Maxwell and her mother were at all times forthright in their responses to questions, never seeking at any stage to divert our investigation or to insist that it follow a path determined by them. Betty Maxwell, in her own book, aptly named *A Mind of My Own*, had shown she had just that. Beautifully written, it did not set out to try to hide any of the monstrous qualities of her husband. One thing she hoped for in providing material to us was that we would not shrink from pointing the finger at 'the other guilty men' – the financiers, bankers, and the men of Arthur Andersen, the global accountants who would profit from the collapse of the Maxwell empire.

Isabel also provided us with details of the *Lady Ghislaine*: its layout and how Betty had given its staterooms a personal touch. Through Isabel the yacht became a boat we knew well. We, of course, were not the only ones to have experienced that feeling: we learned that the *kidon* had also spent many hours studying the plans of the layout they had obtained.

Perhaps the most valuable contribution Isabel Maxwell and her mother made was in providing us with copies of the three autopsy reports and the story of how Betty Maxwell was left to deal with the London insurers. The post-mortem reports and Betty Maxwell's own account of how they were conducted provided vital insights into the assassination of Robert Maxwell and the inability of pathologists to establish the truth.

Victor Ostrovsky, Mossad's biggest whistleblower, now lives in Phoenix, Arizona. To visitors at his local art gallery, where his work is on sale, he is a painter. He even sells his fine prints on an online website.

The past is never far behind him, as we discovered when we spoke to him. He was nervous but when he understood what this book was about, he was central to our understanding of what went on within Mossad in the events leading up to the assassination of Robert Maxwell.

He had every reason to be worried about his former Mossad employers in Tel Aviv. As he explained to us, they had set out to destroy him – even making it impossible for him to get publishing deals and driving him from Canada.

Painting eventually became his means of living. It came naturally to him, just as spying had done. A serious man with a strong jawline and dark eyes, he produce work that is colourful and evocative of some of the French Parisian painters of the 1920s.

As a child in Canada he had lived in the same street as the famous Israeli painter, Giladay. On his way to and from school, Victor would stop to marvel at Gilady sitting outdoors with his brushes paint and easel. The painter's vibrant images left a lasting impression. But Victor Ostrovsky had no desire at that time to paint. Instead he joined the Israeli Defence Forces and eventually Mossad.

Nowadays he is reluctant to talk about the past but he did for this book, insisting, however, that he would not name names. No matter what his disagreements were with Mossad, he would not name those directly involved in planning and carrying out Robert Maxwell's assassination. Nevertheless, he provided valuable material on the cabal in Mossad HQ's operational section who decided Maxwell had to die.

Our final telephone call with Victor Ostrovsky was brief. He sounded agitated and nervous – understandable for a man who, more than any other, had betrayed the inner secrets of Mossad. Perhaps he felt he always had to look over his shoulder and be careful with his words. People in the Israeli intelligence community have long memories and resentment towards him ran deep.

Like his mentor, the painter Gilady, he no doubt hopes that he will be remembered for what he now places on canvas. But the mark he left on the tapestry of Israel's secret history was indelible.

The *kidon* whom we can only identify as Efraim deserves our deepest appreciation. After weeks of delicate negotiations, during which we became certain he was running his own checks on our backgrounds, he agreed to meet with us. That first meeting was in Amsterdam, Holland. We met in a café opposite the city's railway station. He was polite but distant to begin with.

In that first meeting he made no attempt to justify what he had done. We never asked, neither did we press him, for his motive for breaking silence. We agreed to meet later. In all there were several meetings. Each time he told us a little more about how *kidon* worked and provided details we had until then not suspected. They closely matched what Victor Ostrovsky and Ari Ben-Menashe had said. Efraim said he knew of them only by name. They had left Mossad before he had joined.

A number of other people combined to provide the details of Maxwell's involvement with Mossad. Bill Hamilton, the feisty president of Inslaw, provided the FBI documents (see documents section beginning on page 383) that confirm evidence of Maxwell's sale of the Promis software to the Sandia Laboratories at Los Alamos and the lengthy investigation by the FBI into his activities.

Colin Wallace, a former senior British intelligence officer, was able to confirm that both MI5 and MI6 had also for some years monitored the activities of Maxwell, both in Britain and the Soviet Union.

In Israel those connections enabled pertinent questions to be put to Rafi Eitan at his home in a north Tel Aviv suburb.

Some he answered as he stood over his small furnace out behind his home, blowtorch in hand, shaping a piece of rusty pipe he had salvaged into a piece of sculpture. Others he dealt with as he sat in his living room, often gesticulating as he made a point. Like the movements of his hands, he had an expressive way of talking. But there was something about him that was also a little chilling. In mid-sentence he would stop and stare at us, asking a question of his own we became familiar with. 'Why do you ask that?' After we had explained, giving him more time to weigh a proper response, it would come in a short, sharp burst of accented English. At those moments it was not hard to see him walking into Bill Hamilton's Inslaw company or briefing Ari Ben-Menashe, or talking to Robert Maxwell on where next to sell Promis software.

He had aged and filled out since those days when he had been a key member of Mossad operations, sitting in on *kidon* meetings. But his mind was as sharp as ever. Like all good spymasters he volunteered nothing. But he answered all our questions in a straightforward manner. The only time he showed any anger was when asked about Ari Ben-Menashe and Victor Ostrovsky. He regarded them as having betrayed the trust Mossad had put in them. But he did not deny the many claims they made, which are reflected in our book, just as Rafi Eitan's own central role in running Mossad is also dealt with. Eitan asked for no guarantees or payment and he received neither. On some occasions he was taped; on others he preferred to speak without being recorded. For a man of advanced years he was surprisingly specific and well able to recall the minutiae – who said what, when and where.

He would be embarrassed to be called a prime source, but he was.

Over a period of two years Ari Ben-Menashe constantly provided information about Maxwell and his activities for Mossad. In dealing with Ben-Menashe there was always going to be a problem. Since his arrest, trial and acquittal, Ben-Menashe had become a controversial figure. He had been savaged – there is no other word for it – by a Washington Senate Committee investigating the background to the theft of Promis. And, it must be said, his testimony over the years on certain matters has shifted, sometimes at the speed of quicksand. He is fast-talking and clever, and is never far away from his last headline. But, given that, what he has said about Maxwell has proved to be truthful.

There are certain important factors about Ben-Menashe. The case in the US court collapsed against him. Ben-Menashe was able to prove to the satisfaction of the court that he was not a low-level operative but a person of seniority in the Israeli intelligence community. He received affidavits of full support from two serving senior members of that community, which confirmed his status.

Victor Ostrovsky assured us that Ben-Menashe was a credible witness in terms of the Robert Maxwell story and not a low-level operative. Despite the harsh attacks on Ben-Menashe, there have been other experienced writers who continue to speak out in favour of his credibility.

He has been granted Canadian citizenship after a rigorous investigation into his background, and currently runs a political consultancy in Montreal. In the early months of 2002 it attracted unfavourable world media attention when it was discovered to be implicated in secretly filming the leader of Zimbabwe's Opposition Party to discredit him in the run-up to the country's election, which saw the return to power of the despot, Robert Mugabe.

Meir Amit and others who had served Israel's intelligence services were in the twilight of their lives when we contacted them. Nevertheless, like Eitan, they were prepared, for the most part, to answer questions.

Amit's initial interview took place in his surprisingly small office on Jabotinsky Street, in the Tel Aviv suburb of Ramat Gan. Ageing had not taken anything away from his intimidating bearing; it was not hard to see why his peers in the Israeli intelligence community said he was still probably the finest director-general Mossad ever had. He never answered any question without giving it full consideration. Some he would not answer; many more he did. From time to time he was interrupted by his secretary – who had once worked for him in Mossad – stepping into the office to say there was an important caller on the line. Meir Amit would break off, take the call, speak in Hebrew, put down the phone and then resume his answer to us at exactly the point he had left off. It was a trait that John O'Neill also had.

David Kimche was more difficult to interview. He wanted a list of questions beforehand. In the end, when we did sit with him in his spacious home in Tel Aviv, he was careful in all he said. But he was still revealing. Asked why he had attended the trial of Kevin and Iain Maxwell, on an almost daily basis, he sat silent for a long moment. Then in a quiet voice he replied, 'The sins of the father should never be visited on the children. I was not there for Robert Maxwell: I was there for his fine sons.'

Then he moved on to paint a portrait of the time in which Robert Maxwell had operated and Kimche had held the Lebanon 'account' for Mossad. It enabled us to understand better why Maxwell had been such a superspy for his spiritual home.

Eli Cohen gave us a number of insights into what it had been like to be a Mossad *katsa*. Through him, sitting in his garden in the Judean hills, close to Nazareth, we began to grasp the details of Mossad's way of working – including the way it used its *kidon*. Cohen had himself killed for his country. He said he was not proud of that – but it had been essential at the time.

Inevitably, there were some interviews in which the participants agreed to talk after an undertaking that they would not be identified. Others agreed to speak because they felt it was time that the truth about Robert Maxwell should finally emerge. What was interesting was that almost all of them did not see him as a greedy businessman, but as a heroic figure who tried to help Israel. Some went so far as to say he had been betrayed by those who could have helped him.

For their readiness to help, they have our gratitude – the more so because the government of Israel did not cooperate in answering our questions.

John A Belton, the intrepid sleuth and former stockbroker, provided us with access to his extensive archive and recordings of telephone calls with some of the major players in this book.

Tall, strong and fearless, Belton had every reason to be concerned about his own safety. He got closer than most to what he called the Maxwell Channel. His house, tucked away in a remote part of the Montreal countryside, was known only to close friends, or so he thought. Bullet holes remain where a gunman fired through a window into his drawing room.

In another room files are stacked from floor to ceiling. There is a desk with two ashtrays overflowing and boxes of telephone recordings. Meticulous in everything he has done, Belton was one of the victims of the Maxwell Channel. Like his Nesbitt-Thompson clients, who were scammed by Earl Brian and Janos Pasztor, he also lost huge sums of money. Those, added to the money he had spent over the years on his personal investigation and in court battles with the Bank of Montreal, have left him less than the rich man he had been before Eitan, Pasztor and Maxwell came into his life.

His contribution to this book was immense.

No other investigative authors had sat down with Jules Kroll to discuss his dealings with Robert Maxwell. Yet, as Jules Kroll pointed out to us, he had been quoted extensively and inaccurately in many publications and newspapers articles.

On the day of our interview with him, he arrived in the conference room of his plush offices on Madison Avenue in Manhattan looking like an immaculately dressed Wall Street executive. Tall, with white hair and a welcoming smile, he did not resemble the supersleuth of legend. He quickly relaxed into a chair and spoke with the confidence, preciseness and openness of a man who had impressed juries and judges in New York courts during his years as a district attorney.

Now he was sitting atop one of the most formidable and respected private security agencies in the world. Like many others who had met Robert Maxwell before his assassination, Jules Kroll was equally astonished by later reports that Maxwell had committed suicide.

'I don't think his actions in hiring me, knowing I had investigated him on four occasions, were the actions of a man about to commit suicide. I got the call through our joint legal intermediary – the week before Maxwell died – that he wanted a meeting with me the following week.'

The chairman of Kroll Inc. was no less forthright with us in his judgment of Maxwell.

'I had no illusions about his character but I had admiration for his success,' said Kroll in his usually calm and authoritative way.

His statements enabled us to correct inconsistencies about the crucial meeting he had with Maxwell before the tycoon was murdered.

Two investigative journalists with extensive knowledge and sources in Eastern Europe were important to our unravelling the complex web of dealings Maxwell had in the Soviet Bloc and in Russia and Bulgaria after the collapse of Communism.

Nickolai Petrov, an economist and journalist with international experience, was able to trace important linkage involving Maxwell's companies. Rumyana Emanilidu, based in Bourgas on the Black Sea, used her sources in criminal underworld to provide crucially important data. In New York, the writer and journalist, Violeta Kumurdjieva acquired research material vital to the project and translated classified documents, including some that we had obtained but could not source to individuals concerned for their safety.

One of those documents from the official archive in Sofia was a transcript of a conversation between Robert Maxwell and the country's President, Todor Zhivkov, on 1 March 1985.

The document states that Maxwell did not wish to have an interpreter and pointed out 'he knew Bulgarian pretty well'.

The meeting between the two men had followed the visit of the British Foreign Secretary, Geoffrey Howe – the first visit of a British foreign minister since Bulgaria was liberated from the Turks in 1878.

The archive paper stated that, several times during his conversation with Todor Zhivkov, Maxwell said he could 'exert pressure on Margaret Thatcher' to visit Bulgaria.

Then Thatcher was at the height of her political power. She would later go on record to describe Maxwell as a 'remarkable man'.

The transcribed conversation has Maxwell using the same open flattery he would employ many times in meetings with Zhivkov and other Communist leaders. He told him he was 'a born revolutionary, a born statesman and a born party leader'.

Another line in the archive document, following a sales pitch to allow him to develop hi-tech industries in the country, has Maxwell making the following statement to Zhivkov:

'I do not know of any other political personality outside Mrs Thatcher who could see the broad picture of applying hi-technology in virtually every aspect of modern life as you do.'

A former member of Multi-Group, now living abroad after the murder of his friend, Andrei Lukanov, described for us the inner world of Multi-Group and men like Maxwell, Janchev and Mogilevich. That source was an invaluable link to a period when documents had been deliberately shredded to hide the roles of the main participants. Quietly spoken with impeccable English, he outlined the connection between Maxwell and the emerging Multi-Group. He had feared most for his own life when Lukanov was shot dead.

'I thought I could be next on the list so I got out,' he told us over drinks during one of our meetings. 'A lot of people were scrambling for power – not only in Multi-Group but between them and emerging syndicates like Orion. There was also the Moscow connection. It had always been there. The Russians, all former KGB – now Mafia – wanted Lukanov to head up a joint Bulgarian venture but people in Orion felt that he liked to play both ends against the middle and that didn't suit their interests. They may have hired the Russians Mafia to organise the hit on him. Andrei knew the risks in this game. He knew that someone as powerful as Maxwell had been murdered so nobody was safe. When you play in that world of politics, finance and secret alliances, you had better watch your back.'

At one time this particular source had also been in the employ of both the KGB and the Bulgarian secret service, Darzhavna Sigurnost.

Through him, we were able to reconstruct many conversations between Maxwell, Lukanov and Doinov and between Maxwell and the KGB chief, Vladimir Kryuchkov.

Help was also provided by two former members of the KGB still based in Moscow and working in the private sector. They asked for their names to be withheld because, in their words, 'Much of the private sector remains in the hands of former KGB colleagues and loose talk in Russia can lead to an untimely end even for people with previous intelligence connections.'

They had worked closely with Kryuchkov and had seen his file on Maxwell and Lukanov, including transcripts of his meetings with both men. They said they were convinced those files were subsequently erased as part of a deal with Mossad – 'a quid pro quo for something Boris Yeltsin wanted from the Israelis and their support in encouraging the Americans to get the International Monetary Fund to economically underpin his regime'.

The Bulgarian lawyer Marin Markovsky and some of his colleagues, who preferred their names to be withheld because of the power of organised-crime syndicates in their country, gave us important documents and their analysis of the roles of Maxwell, Lukanov and Doinov.

We met the former Bulgarian secret service general, Georgi Ormenkov, in an apartment in the Mladost suburb of Sofia. In his mid-sixties, he possessed a sharp, analytical mind. He had been in charge of the investigations into the death of the dissident Georgi Markov and the attempt on the Pope's life by the Turk, Mehmet Ali Agca.

He understood the roots of organised crime and the global threat it posed. Something of a Cold War warrior, he articulated with clinical precision his solution for dealing with the godfathers.

'I would identify them, put the teams together and in one swoop round them up. They would be transferred to an island. There they could set up a republic, a democracy, whatever they wished, but they would never get off the island. Food would be sent in and all access from the island sealed.'

The journalist Nick Davies was exceedingly friendly and open when he spoke to us from his home in England. He rejected claims that he had been running guns through ORA, the company based at his London home in the mid- to late-1980s. When asked about Maxwell's use of drugs like Halcion, he did not shrink from declaring that Maxwell had been a habitual user.

On the question of how Maxwell died, he also had his own theory.

'Undeniably suicide. In the shit financially, he couldn't take the ignominy of it.'

Davies told us he had information that 'Maxwell laid on the first $1 billion from West Germany to Moscow. He was working for the KGB but he was also the unofficial Israeli representative in Moscow because Israel had no formal diplomatic status there. He was the go-between.'

When we asked Davies in that telephone call about the relationship between Maxwell and David Kimche, the former Mossad officer, Davies had a ready answer.

'Kimche was very important to Maxwell – no doubt – very important. Through Kimche Maxwell had direct access to the Israeli Cabinet. Maxwell through his contact with Kimche was proving himself to Israel.'

And what about Maxwell's millions?

'Maxwell was clever at concealing stuff – Swiss bank accounts and all that money in Bulgaria.'

Would Maxwell's former secretary, Andrea Martin, talk to us?

'She doesn't talk to anyone. No way.'

What did the Maxwell family really think of his book, *Death of a Tycoon*, considering the fact that he sometimes had Maxwell's trust?

'The family thought I did a good reporting job.'

We wondered how Davies had reached that conclusion when Betty Maxwell made it clear to us she thought the book was deeply flawed – but then Davies had a way of presenting his own truths.

Would he answer further questions from us? In his inimitable style, he saw no reason not to help.

We then emailed him a lengthy series of questions, beginning with the statement that we 'understood that you were much more deeply involved in the Maxwell story than we had at first imagined'.

He never replied to the questions.

Of all the journalists we spoke to in the United States, Murray Weiss, a senior crime writer with the *New York Post*, proved the most valuable. It was through him that we learned about the *Lady Ghislaine* stewardess, Lisa Kordalski. His material written about the yacht and the crew gave us a clear picture of life on board. Murray is writing a book on the life, career and death of J P O'Neill, one of the major sources for this book.

Through Murray were learned about the problems the chef Robert Keating had in satisfying Maxwell's every catering whim; the care Lisa Kordalski took to anticipate his every wish; the routine on the bridge and below decks. This, and other vital information, helped us piece together the atmosphere on board as the yacht sailed to her place in maritime history.

In February 1992, the *Lady Ghislaine*, with Captain Gus Rankin on the bridge, quietly slipped her moorings in Palma, Majorca, which had always been her home port, and sailed for Antibes on the French Riviera.

The yacht had been up for sale for over a month at $19 million but there had been no takers. Now it was hoped in Antibes it would catch the eye of a billionaire in one of the playgrounds of the rich. Someone with the money to spend $1 million a year just to run it.

On board in the weeks after Maxwell had been assassinated, Rankin confided to some of the crew that he would write his own story. He even, he claimed, had been negotiating with a big publisher and he expected to make a 'small fortune'.

When asked how the death of Maxwell on his watch might affect his career, he had given one of his brooding smiles and said, 'It's going to look brilliant on my résumé, isn't it?'

Rankin, in the aftermath, had learned how to handle the media and never failed to provide good news copy, laced with his dry humour.

'All I know is that Mr Maxwell could have been more considerate and died in his bed.'

It was not until August 1992 that the *Lady Ghislaine* was sold to a

Middle Eastern businessman for $15 million. He then renamed it to erase its infamous reputation.

Rankin, a US citizen, returned to his home at Pocahontas in the backwoods of Arkansas.

By 2002, the man who once said 'the Maxwell thing will never go away' had not written his story of the events on the *Lady Ghislaine*.

Instead he had decided to profit from the experience while still immortalising the yacht Maxwell so loved. Like Victor Ostrovsky, Rankin took an interest in art – yacht paintings by the marine artist Harry Clow. Clow had painted the *Lady Ghislaine* and wanted Rankin's signature on each of the 350 limited-edition prints he produced. Rankin duly obliged.

If he could not, as he believed, escape the publicity, he might as well benefit from it.

The Gulfstream 4, Maxwell's favourite plane on which he made his last flight from Luton to Gibraltar, was sold to a US buyer for $19 million,

The 1976 Gulfstream 2, which had impressed Communist leaders on Maxwell's trips behind the Iron Curtain, was declared unsaleable.

His Aerospatiale Twin Star helicopter, seen so often lifting off from the roof of Maxwell House, was bought for $400,000.

But perhaps the most bizarre purchase in the sell-off of Maxwell's penthouse possessions – they raised £430,000 – was his shredder. It was sold for £400 to an unnamed buyer. The *Daily Star* newspaper tried to purchase Maxwell's loofah, but the receivers withdrew it from sale.

Barbara Honegger, an author and writer/researcher at the US Naval War College became a significant source for us. Thanks to her mother, we managed to track her down – not an easy task since she nowadays keeps a low profile after sensational claims she made about Irangate. She established the connection for us with Richard Brenneke and his CIA background. She also gave us material on Maxwell's role in the arms-to-Iran fiasco.

We owe a special debt to the renowned American forensic pathologist, Werner U Spritz and his book, *Medical Investigation of Death: Guidelines for the Application of Pathology in Crime Investigation*. Also to John Harbinson, state pathologist of the Irish Republic, for providing us with written guidelines on complex autopsy issues. We are also indebted to Dr Alfred Rosenbaum, the distinguished New York radiologist, for talking to us about his diagnosis of Robert Maxwell. Dr Rosenbaum helped clarify issues relating to Maxwell's health. He had given him clean bill of health weeks before Maxwell was assassinated. He had also established for us a connection between Henry Kissinger and Maxwell. Whether Kissinger and Maxwell had business dealings remains one of several mysteries concerning the two men.

Rupert Allason, also known by the pen name Nigel West – is an expert on the intelligence world and responded to many of our questions and offered his own thoughtful perspectives on the Maxwell story, including his role as a Member of the British Parliament in exposing Maxwell as a Mossad spy and Nick Davies's connection to Ari Ben-Menashe. It had been Rupert Allason, along with a fellow MP, who made it possible for the British media to avoid strict defamation laws and report the allegations made by Seymour Hersh about Israel's superspy.

The complex world of international money transfers involving the CIA and organised-crime families became that much clearer from a study of the documentation of Richard J Brenneke, the CIA operative who had been in overall charge of the agency's secret money-laundering operations. It was a world that none of the other writers on Maxwell's life had ever entered. Brenneke not only made clear to us the technicalities of the whole-scale transfers of billions of dollars, but also the problems of those trying to track them. He had pieced together the jigsaw of evidence to show the interplay of companies Maxwell had controlled and governments like those of Bulgaria and Hungary – a world where the stakes and tensions were always high and the issue of payback always in the background. The world Brenneke described was not only one of villains and dark forces, but of men like Maxwell, who had made a Faustian pact to ignore the moral issues.

FBI documents detailing the agency's investigation into Robert Maxwell and his sale of software to the Sandia Laboratories, one of the most secret in the Los Alomos complex, the heart of America's nuclear defence arsenal. Many of the documents are still so sensitive that to this day they remain redacted.

THE WHITE HOUSE
WASHINGTON

October 7, 1988
(Date)

TO: FBI, LIAISON

FROM: ARTHUR B. CULVAHOUSE, JR.

SUBJECT: FBI Investigations

Subject's Name: MAXWELL, ROBERT

Date of Birth: 10/6/23   Place of Birth: _____

Present Address: _____

We request: _____ Copy of Previous Report

            X   Name Check _____ Expanded Name Check

            _____ Full Field Investigation TO IRS TO FBI

            _____ Limited Update

The person named above is being considered for:

            _____ White House Staff Position

            _____ Presidential Appointment

            X   ACCESS

Attachments:

            _____ SF 86 1   2

            _____ SF 87, Fingerprint Card

            _____ SF 86, Supplement

Remarks/Special Instructions: BUSINESS ADDRESS
                Publisher
                Mirror Group Newspaper Ltd.
                Holburn Circus
                London ECIPIDQ
                United Kingdom
                PPT#: B 252462

ALL INFORMATION CONTAINED
HEREIN IS UNCLASSIFIED
DATE 12-13-95

62-5-68126

B7C

143

1　2

7/19/84　　　　　　SECRET　　　　　　ROUTINE

*F143*RR SF AQ*DE HQ H0143 *H*YS*R 192033Z JUL 84

FM DIRECTOR FBI

TO FBI ALBUQUERQUE [105C-3262] ROUTINE

FBI SAN FRANCISCO　ROUTINE

BT

S E C R E T

ROBERT MAXWELL DBA PERGAMON INTERNATIONAL; ▇▇▇ 00: ALBUQUERQUE

THIS COMMUNICATION IS CLASSIFIED "SECRET" IN ITS ENTIRETY.

RE ALBUQUERQUE AIRTEL TO FBIHQ JUNE 13, 1984.

SF DIVISION CONDUCTED A ▇▇▇▇▇▇▇▇▇▇▇▇▇▇▇▇

ON DEMAND INC., 2112 BERKELEY WAY, BERKELEY, CALIFORNIA, FROM

▇▇▇▇▇▇▇▇▇▇▇▇▇▇▇▇▇▇▇ WHEN IT WAS PLACED IN A

CLOSED STATUS.

SF PROVIDED PERTINENT INFORMATION REGARDING INVESTIGATION

OF INFORMATION ON DEMAND INC. TO ALBUQUERQUE VIA SF AIRTEL DATED

JUNE 29, 1984.

FDW: ▇▇ (2)　7/19/84　4425/5　4587

PAGE TWO DE HQ 0143 S̶E̶C̶R̶E̶T̶

(s) b1

C BY: S̶0̶6̶; DECL:OADR

BT

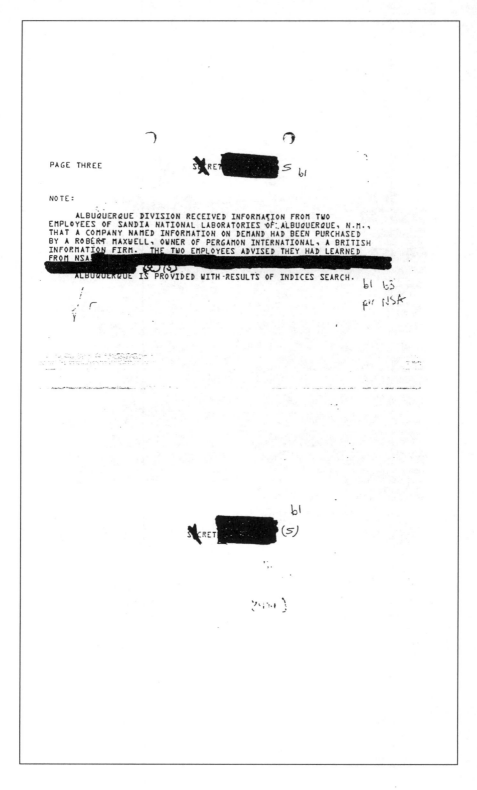

PAGE THREE   S̶ CRET   S bl

NOTE:

    ALBUQUERQUE DIVISION RECEIVED INFORMATION FROM TWO
EMPLOYEES OF SANDIA NATIONAL LABORATORIES OF ALBUQUERQUE, N.M.,
THAT A COMPANY NAMED INFORMATION ON DEMAND HAD BEEN PURCHASED
BY A ROBERT MAXWELL, OWNER OF PERGAMON INTERNATIONAL, A BRITISH
INFORMATION FIRM. THE TWO EMPLOYEES ADVISED THEY HAD LEARNED
FROM NSA

    ALBUQUERQUE IS PROVIDED WITH RESULTS OF INDICES SEARCH. bl b3

    fpr NSA

S̶ CRET   (s)

bl

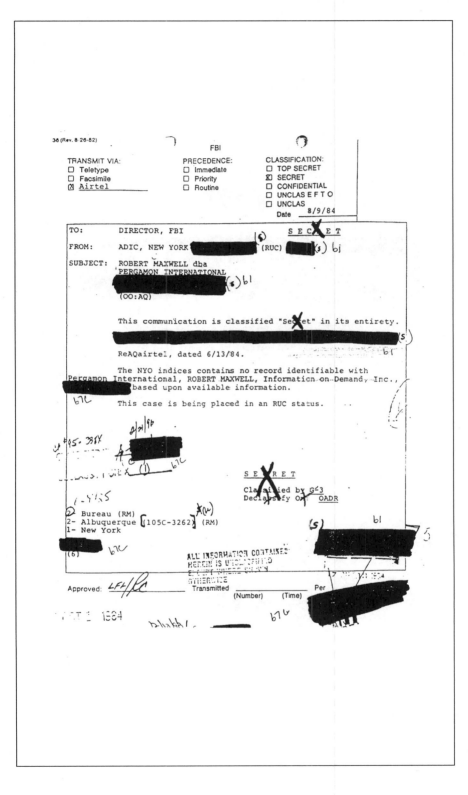

36 (Rev. 8-26-82)

FBI

TRANSMIT VIA:
☐ Teletype
☐ Facsimile
☒ Airtel

PRECEDENCE:
☐ Immediate
☐ Priority
☐ Routine

CLASSIFICATION:
☐ TOP SECRET
☒ SECRET
☐ CONFIDENTIAL
☐ UNCLAS E F T O
☐ UNCLAS
Date 8/9/84

TO: DIRECTOR, FBI   S E C R E T

FROM: ADIC, NEW YORK ███████ (RUC) ████ (s) bi

SUBJECT: ROBERT MAXWELL dba
PERGAMON INTERNATIONAL
████████████ (s) bi
(OO:AQ)

This communication is classified "Secret" in its entirety.
██████████████████████████████████ (s)

ReAQairtel, dated 6/13/84.   bi

The NYO indices contains no record identifiable with
Pergamon International, ROBERT MAXWELL, Information on Demand, Inc.,
based upon available information.

b7C

This case is being placed in an RUC status.

S E C R E T
Classified by G-3
Declassify On: OADR

105-385X

2- Bureau (RM)
2- Albuquerque [105C-3262] (RM)
1- New York

(6)   b7C

ALL INFORMATION CONTAINED
HEREIN IS UNCLASSIFIED
EXCEPT WHERE SHOWN
OTHERWISE

Approved: LFL/RC _____ Transmitted _____ Per
                              (Number) (Time)

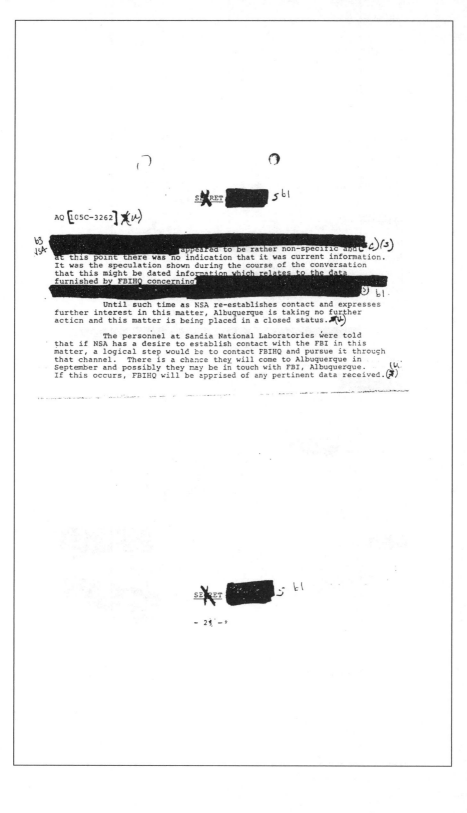

SECRET

AQ [105C-3262]

appeared to be rather non-specific and at this point there was no indication that it was current information. It was the speculation shown during the course of the conversation that this might be dated information which relates to the data furnished by FBIHQ concerning

Until such time as NSA re-establishes contact and expresses further interest in this matter, Albuquerque is taking no further action and this matter is being placed in a closed status.

The personnel at Sandia National Laboratories were told that if NSA has a desire to establish contact with the FBI in this matter, a logical step would be to contact FBIHQ and pursue it through that channel. There is a chance they will come to Albuquerque in September and possibly they may be in touch with FBI, Albuquerque. If this occurs, FBIHQ will be apprised of any pertinent data received.

SECRET

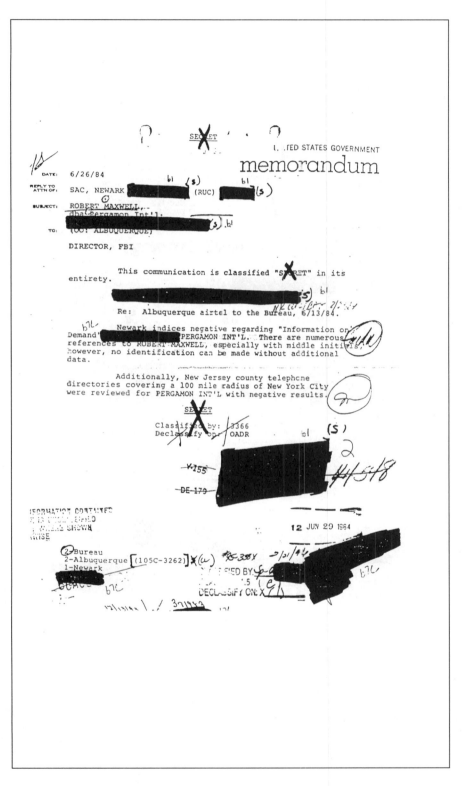

SECRET

UNITED STATES GOVERNMENT

memorandum

DATE: 6/26/84

REPLY TO
ATTN OF: SAC, NEWARK _____ (RUC) _____

SUBJECT: ROBERT MAXWELL,
dba Pergamon Int'l:
_____

TO: (OO: ALBUQUERQUE)

DIRECTOR, FBI

This communication is classified "SECRET" in its entirety.

Re: Albuquerque airtel to the Bureau, 6/13/84.

Newark indices negative regarding "Information on Demand" _____ PERGAMON INT'L. There are numerous references to ROBERT MAXWELL, especially with middle initials, however, no identification can be made without additional data.

Additionally, New Jersey county telephone directories covering a 100 mile radius of New York City were reviewed for PERGAMON INT'L with negative results.

SECRET

Classified by: 3366
Declassify on: OADR

X-155
DE-179

12 JUN 29 1964

2-Bureau
2-Albuquerque [105C-3262]
1-Newark

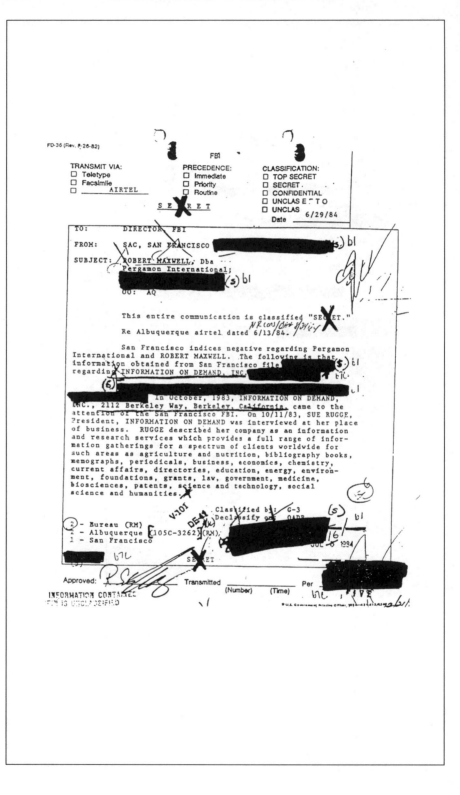

FD-36 (Rev. 8-26-82)

FBI

TRANSMIT VIA: PRECEDENCE: CLASSIFICATION:
☐ Teletype   ☐ Immediate   ☐ TOP SECRET
☐ Facsimile   ☐ Priority   ☐ SECRET
☐ _____AIRTEL_____   ☐ Routine   ☐ CONFIDENTIAL
                                                    ☐ UNCLAS E☐T O
                       S E C R E T   ☐ UNCLAS
                                                    Date 6/29/84

TO: DIRECTOR, FBI

FROM: SAC, SAN FRANCISCO ████████████████ (s) b1

SUBJECT: ROBERT MAXWELL, Dba
           Pergamon International;
           ██████████████████ (s) b1
           OO: AQ

           This entire communication is classified "SECRET."
           Re Albuquerque airtel dated 6/13/84.

           San Francisco indices negative regarding Pergamon
International and ROBERT MAXWELL. The following is that
information obtained from San Francisco file ████████████ (s) b1
regarding INFORMATION ON DEMAND, INC.

           In October, 1983, INFORMATION ON DEMAND,
INC., 2112 Berkeley Way, Berkeley, California, came to the
attention of the San Francisco FBI. On 10/11/83, SUE RUGGE,
President, INFORMATION ON DEMAND was interviewed at her place
of business. RUGGE described her company as an information
and research services which provides a full range of information gatherings for a spectrum of clients worldwide for
such areas as agriculture and nutrition, bibliography books,
memographs, periodicals, business, economics, chemistry,
current affairs, directories, education, energy, environment, foundations, grants, law, government, medicine,
biosciences, patents, science and technology, social
science and humanities.

                              Classified by: G-3
                              Declassify on: OADR   (s) b1

② - Bureau (RM)
  1 - Albuquerque (105C-3262)(RM)
  1 - San Francisco

                         S E C R E T

Approved: _____ Transmitted _____ Per _____
                                  (Number) (Time)

SECRET

AQ [105C-3262]

94704, with Telephones (415) 644-4500 and (800) 227-0750. The president of this firm is a woman known as SUE RUGGE. The nature of this firm is that it is a firm which has compiled data base information and for a fee will provide them to customers. The data base information relates to a wide variety and to the best of their knowledge is not classified in any manner. However, it includes information concerning government and various available means of tapping government information data bases. The information provided by the Sandia employees was received from employees of the National Security Agency (NSA) and has to do with the purchase of Information On Demand, Inc., by one ROBERT MAXWELL, the owner of Pergamon International, a British information firm. According to NSA,

The information received from these Sandia employees is

computerized data bases on behalf of the Soviets.

        Albuquerque indices are negative regarding Pergamon International, ROBERT MAXWELL, Information On Demand, Inc.

        According to the Sandia employees, there is a New Jersey Pergamon International Office; however, they did not know where it was located.

LEADS

NEW YORK CITY DIVISION

        AT NEW YORK CITY, NEW YORK

        Search indices regarding Pergamon International, ROBERT MAXWELL, Information On Demand, Inc.

NEWARK DIVISION

        AT NEWARK, NEW JERSEY

        Will check indices as set forth for New York Office.

SECRET

- 2 -

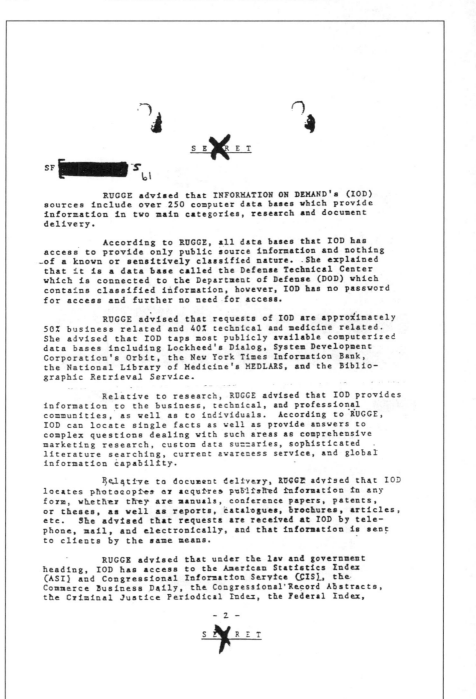

S E X R E T

SF ▇▇▇▇▇ ˢ₆₁

     RUGGE advised that INFORMATION ON DEMAND's (IOD)
sources include over 250 computer data bases which provide
information in two main categories, research and document
delivery.

     According to RUGGE, all data bases that IOD has
access to provide only public source information and nothing
of a known or sensitively classified nature. She explained
that it is a data base called the Defense Technical Center
which is connected to the Department of Defense (DOD) which
contains classified information, however, IOD has no password
for access and further no need for access.

     RUGGE advised that requests of IOD are approximately
50% business related and 40% technical and medicine related.
She advised that IOD taps most publicly available computerized
data bases including Lockheed's Dialog, System Development
Corporation's Orbit, the New York Times Information Bank,
the National Library of Medicine's MEDLARS, and the Biblio-
graphic Retrieval Service.

     Relative to research, RUGGE advised that IOD provides
information to the business, technical, and professional
communities, as well as to individuals. According to RUGGE,
IOD can locate single facts as well as provide answers to
complex questions dealing with such areas as comprehensive
marketing research, custom data summaries, sophisticated
literature searching, current awareness service, and global
information capability.

     Relative to document delivery, RUGGE advised that IOD
locates photocopies or acquires published information in any
form, whether they are manuals, conference papers, patents,
or theses, as well as reports, catalogues, brochures, articles,
etc. She advised that requests are received at IOD by telephone, mail, and electronically, and that information is sent
to clients by the same means.

     RUGGE advised that under the law and government
heading, IOD has access to the American Statistics Index
(ASI) and Congressional Information Service (CIS), the
Commerce Business Daily, the Congressional Record Abstracts,
the Criminal Justice Periodical Index, the Federal Index,

- 2 -

S E X R E T

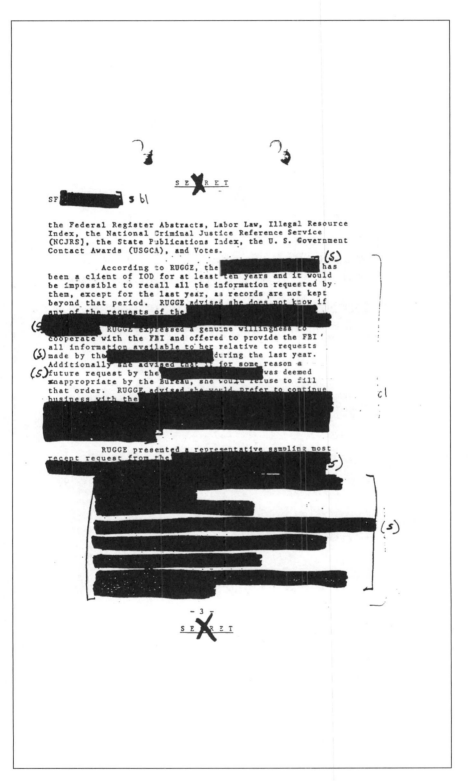

SE╳RET

SF ███████ **3** 61

the Federal Register Abstracts, Labor Law, Illegal Resource
Index, the National Criminal Justice Reference Service
(NCJRS), the State Publications Index, the U. S. Government
Contact Awards (USGCA), and Votes.

According to RUGGE, the ████████████████ has (S)
been a client of IOD for at least ten years and it would
be impossible to recall all the information requested by
them, except for the last year, as records are not kept
beyond that period. RUGGE advised she does not know if
any of the requests of the ████████████████
(S)████████████ RUGGE expressed a genuine willingness to
cooperate with the FBI and offered to provide the FBI
all information available to her relative to requests
(S) made by the ████████████ during the last year.
Additionally she advised that if for some reason a
(S) future request by the ████████████ was deemed
inappropriate by the Bureau, she would refuse to fill
that order. RUGGE advised she would prefer to continue
business with the ████████████████████████

RUGGE presented a representative sampling most
recent request from the ████████████

-3-
SE╳RET

AQ [105C-3262] (u)

<u>SAN FRANCISCO DIVISION</u>

<u>AT SAN FRANCISCO, CALIFORNIA</u>

Will search indices as set forth for New York Office.

<u>REQUEST OF THE BUREAU</u>

Requested to search indices regarding the firms and individuals as set forth in the New York lead.

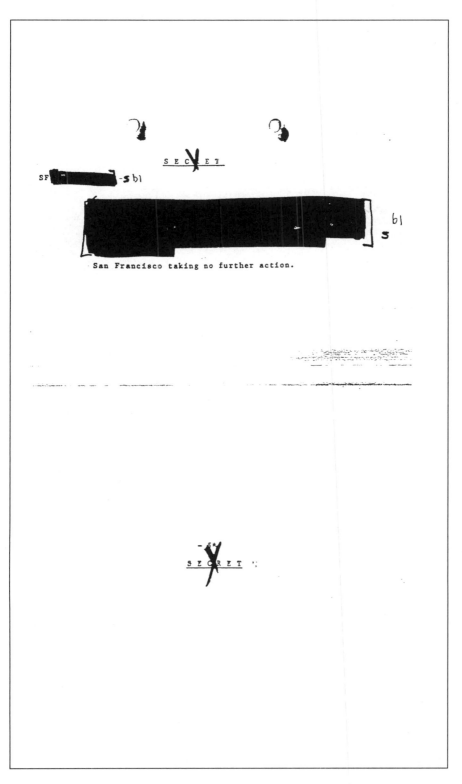

San Francisco taking no further action.

The Second Autopsy

It was prepared by Dr Iain West and his wife, Dr Vesna West (née Djurovic). It differed from the previous post-mortem findings – and leaves open the question of murder.

Courtesy:
Betty and Isabel Maxwell

DEPARTMENT OF FORENSIC MEDICINE
GUY'S HOSPITAL
(UNIVERSITY OF LONDON)

Dr. LE. WEST, M.B., Ch.B., F.R.C.Path., D.M.J.
Dr. R.T. SHEPHERD B.Sc., M.B., B.S., M.R.C.Path., D.M.J.
Direct Telephone Line 071-407 0378 / 071-403 1118)
(Fax: 071-403 7292)

UNITED MEDICAL AND DENTAL SCHOOLS
GUY'S AND ST. THOMAS'S HOSPITAL
LONDON BRIDGE, SE1 9RT
TELEPHONE: 071-955 5000 Ext: 3118 / 3119

6th January 1992

At 10.15 pm on Saturday 9th November 1991 at the Institute of Forensic Medicine, Tel Aviv, Israel we performed a post mortem examination on the body of

Robert Maxwell aged 68 yrs

The identification was confirmed by Mr. B.G. Sims, Forensic Odontologist, at 11.30 am on 15th November 1991.

Also taking part in the examination were:

Dr. Jehude Hiss, Director of the Forensic Institute,
Dr. Birtolon Levy, Forensic Pathologist, Tel Aviv,
Professor Baruch Arensburg, Professor of Anatomy, Tel Aviv,
Dr. Vesna Djurovic, Forensic Pathologist from the Department of Forensic Medicine, Guy's Hospital.

Present at the post mortem examination were:

Dr. Esther Daniels Phillips, Forensic Pathologist, Tel Aviv.
Mr. Eliezek Lipstein, Mortuary Technician,
Miss Edna Bares, secretary to Dr Hiss.

Photographs, x-rays and a video recording of the post mortem were carried out by Mr. Naim Batsri.

Photographs and the video recording of the exterior of the body and an x-ray skeletal survey were performed prior to the post mortem examination.

EXTERNAL APPEARANCES

The deceased's was laid out on the mortuary table, encased in an outer wrapping of coarse muslin, marked "Maxwell R" with an indelible marker. It was tied around the ankles, upper thighs and lower chest. The face was exposed. There was an inner sheet of white muslin, stained with body fluids, covering the front of the body. The body was lying on a sheet of clear plastic and a white plastic body bag, cut open along the white zip.

Upon removal of the wrappings, x-rays were taken of the deceased's head, upper limbs and feet. These showed no evidence of abnormality apart from some old deformity of the 1st left metacarpophalangeal joint, at

DEPARTMENT OF FORENSIC MEDICINE
GUY'S HOSPITAL
(UNIVERSITY OF LONDON)

Dr. I.E. WEST, M.B., Ch.B., F.R.C.Path., D.M.J.
Dr. R.T. SHEPHERD B.Sc., M.B., B.S., M.R.C.Path., D.M.J.
Direct Telephone Line 071-407 0378 / 071-403 1118)
(Fax: 071-403 7292)

UNITED MEDICAL AND DENTAL SCHOOLS
GUY'S AND ST. THOMAS'S HOSPITAL
LONDON BRIDGE, SE1 9RT
TELEPHONE: 071-955 5000 Ext: 3118 / 3119

Marks of Identification

The head hair was brown, approximately 2½-3" long, cut away at both temples. The eyebrows were bushy and appeared complete. The eyelashes were of moderate length.

The eyeballs were slightly prominent due to decomposition. There were no petechial haemorrhages in the conjunctivae.

The face was cleanly shaven. There was considerable decay of the teeth, some of which were missing. Dental charting was performed by Prof. Arensburg.

The body hair was unremarkable.

There was a stretched 5" scar in the right iliac fossa and a 1¼" scar just above the root of the penis, on the left side. A violaceous 1¼" scar on the upper outer left thigh. Scar on back of left chest.

Disease and deformity

There were minor papillomas on the inner upper left thigh and right side of the lower abdomen, above the pubis.

The anus showed skin tags and a fresh haemorrhoid.

Slight oedema of the ankles.

Post mortem changes

There was a transverse sutured post mortem incision, in the form of a shallow letter "V", passing between the shoulders, measuring 10" in length and then extending down the midline to the pubis (pelvis), over a distance of 31".

A further 9½" sutured post mortem incision was present over the right thigh. The femoral vessels on that side were cut and tied off and the cavity, formed by post mortem dissection, was filled with formalin powder.

A sutured post mortem incision extended from the superior part of the root of the right ear, across the scalp, to the lower left temple, just in front of the root of the ear.

There was a 2¼" sutured post mortem incision on the back of the right

DEPARTMENT OF FORENSIC MEDICINE
GUY'S HOSPITAL
(UNIVERSITY OF LONDON)

Dr. I.E. WEST, M.B., Ch.B., F.R.C.Path., D.M.J.
Dr. R.T. SHEPHERD B.Sc., M.B., B.S., M.R.C.Path., D.M.J.
Direc: Telephone Line 071-407 0378 / 371-403 1118)
(Fax: 071-403 7292)

UNITED MEDICAL AND DENTAL SCHOOLS
GUY'S AND ST. THOMAS'S HOSPITAL
LONDON BRIDGE, SE1 9RT
TELEPHONE: 071-955 5000 Ext: 3118 / 3119

The mouth and nostrils were plugged with cotton wool and gauze; the packing of the right nostril had penetrated the nasal lining and the tissues of the right upper lip, causing a small amount of post mortem red discoloration in the adjacent soft tissues.

The scrotum was distended and the penis retracted due to embalming.

There was minimal wrinkling of the pads of fingers and skin of feet.

CHANGES OF DECOMPOSITION

Green, grey-green and red discoloration, due to decomposition of the face, particularly the forehead, right cheek and jawline, left upper eyelid and nose.

Band of green discoloration, with marbling, on the right anterolateral chest. Green discoloration of the left pectoral region, the right lower quadrant of the abdomen and right flank.

Marbling over the left pectoral region. Prominent green discoloration and marbling over the back of the trunk. Areas of blistering, containing dark red fluid, over the back of the trunk, along the pressure areas.

Green discoloration of the both upper arms and forearms with considerable skin slippage over the back of forearms and hands.

Faint green discoloration over the upper right thigh and both hips. Green discoloration and marbling over the back of the right thigh and early marbling of the back of the lower legs.

All the skin discoloration was due to decomposition.

Marks of Injury

(Includes externally visible injuries and those revealed by dissection.)

Head & Neck

1/20" punctate abrasion, ¼" above the mid right eyebrow.

An area of purple/red discoloration extending from outer right nostril onto the cheek, below right lower eyelid, measuring 1 3/4" by up to 1¼".

In line with the previous mark and extending obliquely upwards and to the right was a further reddened area, with slight overlying abrasion, measuring 1" x ¼". It ran across the upper cheek to terminate below the

DEPARTMENT OF FORENSIC MEDICINE
GUY'S HOSPITAL
(UNIVERSITY OF LONDON)

Dr. I.E. WEST, M.B., Ch.B., F.R.C.Path., D.M.J.
Dr. R.T. SHEPHERD B.Sc., M.B., B.S., M.R.C.Path., D.M.J.
Direct Telephone Line 071-407 0378 / 071-403 1118)
(Fax: 071-403 7292)

UNITED MEDICAL AND DENTAL SCHOOLS
GUY'S AND ST. THOMAS'S HOSPITAL
LONDON BRIDGE, SE1 9RT
TELEPHONE: 071-955 5000 Ext: 3118 / 3119

Punctate abrasion below right lateral nasal bone.

1/8" and 3/16" abrasions between the nostrils.

Two punctate abrasions above the right corner of the mouth.

5/16" and ¼" linear abrasions on right jawline, 2" outside and between 1" and 2" below right corner of mouth.

Interrupted linear abrasion below right angle of jaw, over a distance of 5/8".

15/16" narrow linear abrasion on central forehead, 1¼" above eyebrow, coinciding with the line of opening of the skull vault performed at the previous examination.

3/4" x ¼" abrasion on central forehead, 2" above eyebrow, and a 1/10" punctate abrasion below its left hand end.

1/8" abrasion at the junction of the left nostril and cheek.

5/8" x ½" abrasion below and outside left nostril with a fine 3/8" x ¼" abrasion below inner lower left eyelid.

½" abrasion over the rim of the right ear, just below the tip of the ear. ¼" abrasion on the helix of the right ear and 1" reddening and pressure abrasion above the tragus and extending onto the ear with underlying deep bruising behind and in front of the right ear.

Trunk

1½" x 2" punctate intradermal bruise, immediately below the previously mentioned post mortem wound on the back of the right shoulder, together with some reddish discoloration over an area measuring ¼" x 2½". The underlying bruising was confined to the skin, and did not extend into the deep tissues.

Areas of punctate red marking, 1¼" x 1¼" and 1" x 1½", on the back of the left shoulder, behind and above the posterior axillary fold.

5/8" x 3/8" post mortem abrasion on the right lateral chest, 7" below the axilla.

1¼" areas of blue discoloration on the lower back, 4" above the sacroiliac joint.

DEPARTMENT OF FORENSIC MEDICINE
GUY'S HOSPITAL
(UNIVERSITY OF LONDON)

Dr. I.E. WEST, M.B., Ch.B., F.R.C.Path., D.M.J.
Dr. R.T. SHEPHERD B.Sc., M.B., B.S., M.R.C.Path., D.M.J.
Direct Telephone Line 071-407 0378 / 071-403 1118)
(Fax: 071-403 7292)

UNITED MEDICAL AND DENTAL SCHOOLS
GUY'S AND ST. THOMAS'S HOSPITAL
LONDON BRIDGE, SE1 9RT
TELEPHONE: 071-955 5000 Ext: 3118 / 3119

2" x 1½" reddened area in the midline of the lower back, at the level of the sacroiliac joints.

Dissection of the skin of the back showed an extensive 5" x 2" area of haemorrhage along the fibres of the left infraspinatus muscle. Some of the muscle fibres were torn and the haemorrhage involved most of the muscle. There was no bruising of the overlying soft tissues.

5" x ½" extensive haemorrhage into the muscles adjacent to the left side of the spine, extending from the 12th thoracic vertebra to the level of the 4th and 5th lumbar vertebra. There were torn muscle fibres associated with the haemorrhage. There was no bruising of the more superficial soft tissues.

Arms

On the outer right arm, starting 9" below the point of the shoulder was a 3 3/4" x up to 5/8" abrasion, ending just above the elbow, with haemorrhage in underlying subcutaneous tissues.

Behind and below the above abrasion were a group of four linear abrasions, measuring between 3/4" to 1", with a less convincing underlying haemorrhage.

On the left lateral arm, 6" below the point of the left shoulder, was a 1" x 3/4" deep and intradermal bruise. The underlying subcutaneous tissues were altered by embalming; no bruising could be sen on dissection.

On the outside of the lower left deltoid (outer shoulder), starting 5¼" below the point of the left shoulder, was a 3¼" x ¼" linear intradermal bruise terminating 8" above the point of the elbow. There was no visible underlying haemorrhage. The subcutaneous tissues were decomposing.

Legs

1¼" subcutaneous bruise outside the right knee, immediately above the head of the right fibula, 19½" above the heel.

½" graze over the upper third of the right shin, 13" above the heel, with a very slight underlying bruise.

3/4" x 1" subcutaneous bruise on the outer aspect of the left calf, 11" above the heel. This was not visible on the skin.

1" bruise on the front of the left shin, 15" above the heel, with an

DEPARTMENT OF FORENSIC MEDICINE
GUY'S HOSPITAL
(UNIVERSITY OF LONDON)

Dr. I.E. WEST. M.B., Ch.B., F.R.C.Path., D.M.J.
Dr. R.T. SHEPHERD B.Sc., M.B., B.S., M.R.C.Path., D.M.J.
Direct Telephone Line 071-407 0378 / 071-403 1118)
(Fax: 071-403 7292)

UNITED MEDICAL AND DENTAL SCHOOLS
GUY'S AND ST. THOMAS'S HOSPITAL
LONDON BRIDGE, SE1 9RT
TELEPHONE: 071-955 5000 Ext: 3118 / 3119

INTERNAL EXAMINATON

Scalp:	Collection of coagulated, fixed blood over the back of the head, dissecting into the nape of the neck. No visible bruising to the scalp.
Skull:	The skull was slightly thicker than normal, measuring 1cm in the frontal region, 0.6cm in the temporal region and 0.8cm in the occipital region. It showed slight hyperostosis. The dura had been stripped and was lying loose inside the skull, with fixed haematoma adherent to the outer and inner layers. A thick coating of coagulated, fixed blood was present over the posterior cranial fossa and occipital squama. The brain was absent.
	Minimal haemorrhage inside the middle ears.
Face:	Injury to the subcutaneous tissues around the right ear as described. No other injury identified.
Mouth:	The tongue had been left in situ together with the hyoid bone, epiglottis and distal carotid arteries.
	Examination showed the hyoid bone to be intact. Some formalin fixed blood was present on the right side of the neck around the internal carotid artery.
Neck:	The thyroid cartilage together with the proximal part of the trachea and adjacent soft tissues was found within the abdominal cavity. There was some post mortem flattening of the thyroid and cricoid cartilages, both of which were intact. A grey white area of slight abrasion, approximately 3mm in length, was noted on the inner aspect of the right vocal cord.
Trunk:	The chest and abdominal cavity contained the dissected organs and had been flooded with formalin liquid.

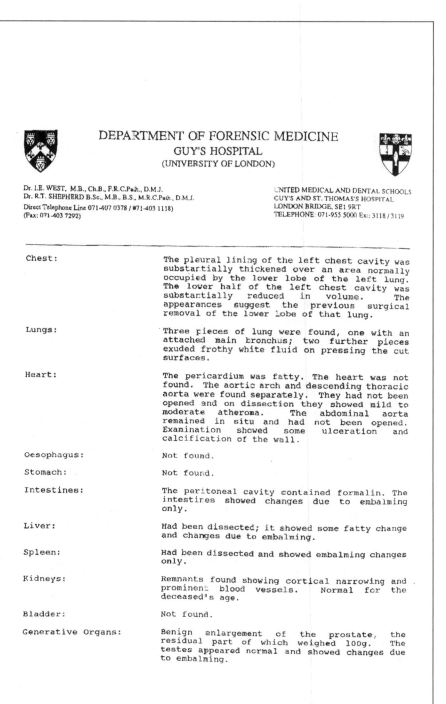

DEPARTMENT OF FORENSIC MEDICINE
GUY'S HOSPITAL
(UNIVERSITY OF LONDON)

Dr. I.E. WEST, M.B., Ch.B., F.R.C.Path., D.M.J.
Dr. R.T. SHEPHERD B.Sc., M.B., B.S., M.R.C.Path., D.M.J.
Direct Telephone Line 071-407 0378 / 071-403 1118)
(Fax: 071-403 7292)

UNITED MEDICAL AND DENTAL SCHOOLS
GUY'S AND ST. THOMAS'S HOSPITAL
LONDON BRIDGE, SE1 9RT
TELEPHONE: 071-955 5000 Ext: 3118 / 3119

Chest:	The pleural lining of the left chest cavity was substantially thickened over an area normally occupied by the lower lobe of the left lung. The lower half of the left chest cavity was substantially reduced in volume. The appearances suggest the previous surgical removal of the lower lobe of that lung.
Lungs:	Three pieces of lung were found, one with an attached main bronchus; two further pieces exuded frothy white fluid on pressing the cut surfaces.
Heart:	The pericardium was fatty. The heart was not found. The aortic arch and descending thoracic aorta were found separately. They had not been opened and on dissection they showed mild to moderate atheroma. The abdominal aorta remained in situ and had not been opened. Examination showed some ulceration and calcification of the wall.
Oesophagus:	Not found.
Stomach:	Not found.
Intestines:	The peritoneal cavity contained formalin. The intestines showed changes due to embalming only.
Liver:	Had been dissected; it showed some fatty change and changes due to embalming.
Spleen:	Had been dissected and showed embalming changes only.
Kidneys:	Remnants found showing cortical narrowing and prominent blood vessels. Normal for the deceased's age.
Bladder:	Not found.
Generative Organs:	Benign enlargement of the prostate, the residual part of which weighed 100g. The testes appeared normal and showed changes due to embalming.

DEPARTMENT OF FORENSIC MEDICINE
GUY'S HOSPITAL
(UNIVERSITY OF LONDON)

Dr. I.E. WEST, M.B., Ch.B., F.R.C.Path., D.M.J.
Dr. R.T. SHEPHERD B.Sc., M.B., B.S., M.R.C.Path., D.M.J.
Direct Telephone Line 071-407 0378 / 071-403 1118)
(Fax: 071-403 7292)

UNITED MEDICAL AND DENTAL SCHOOLS
GUY'S AND ST. THOMAS'S HOSPITAL
LONDON BRIDGE, SE1 9RT
TELEPHONE: 071-955 5000 Ext: 3118 / 3119

Endocrine Organs:	Not found.
Other Organs:	Small area of haemorrhage inside the right psoas muscle. No detectable rib fractures.

Samples of recovered organs were preserved by Dr. Hiss for histological examination. Part of the left femoral shaft was retained by us for diatom investigation.

Following our return to London we obtained the dental records from a representative of the deceased's family. In our presence Mr. B.G. Sims compared the dental records of Robert Maxwell with x-rays taken of the deceased during the post mortem examination in Tel Aviv. He comfirmed to us that the body which we had examined was that of Robert Maxwell.

Examination of the deceased's bone marrow, in our laboratory, indicated no diatoms to be present but examination of 2.2 litres of seawater handed to us by Mr. Roger Rich showed that very few diatoms were present in the water. We were informed that the water had been taken from the area near to where the body had been found.

We have subsequently examined copies of some of the deceased's medical records, photographs and plans of the Lady Ghislaine, a chart showing where the deceased had been found and copies of the relevant sections of the log of the Lady Ghislaine.

At 1.00 pm on 13th December 1991, Dr. V. Djurovic and I, together with Miss Maria Amvrosiou (interpreter) attended the National Institute for Toxicology in Madrid where the Director, Dr. Sanchez, showed us soft tissue samples and organs of Robert Maxwell, which had been retained by the Spanish authority. Where appropriate the organs had been preserved in formalin liquid and the containers sealed and labelled. The contents corresponded to the exhibits list that we were shown by Dr. Sanchez. The heart and lung had been retained at the initial post mortem examination and then subsequently dissected. The dissection of the brain appeared to have been carried out in the normal manner for a neuropathological examination, the brain being sliced and then tissue samples being removed for microscopic examination.

The heart had been very extensively dissected and much of the heart muscle reduced to small blocks of tissue.

In addition to the heart and brain, sections of lung had been preserved by freezing and pieces of the other body organs had been retained in formalin. They had been dissected and subsequently examined under the microscope.

DEPARTMENT OF FORENSIC MEDICINE
GUY'S HOSPITAL
(UNIVERSITY OF LONDON)

Dr. I.E. WEST, M.B., Ch.B., F.R.C.Path., D.M.J.
Dr. R.T. SHEPHERD B.Sc., M.B., B.S., M.R.C.Path., D.M.J.
Direct Telephone Line 071-407 0378 / 071-403 1118)
(Fax: 071-403 7292)

UNITED MEDICAL AND DENTAL SCHOOLS
GUY'S AND ST. THOMAS'S HOSPITAL
LONDON BRIDGE, SE1 9RT
TELEPHONE: 071-955 5000 Ext: 3118 / 3119

Whilst in Madrid we carried out a naked eye examination of these tissues and subsequently at Guy's Hospital carried out a microscopic examination of sections prepared from these tissue samples.

MACROSCOPIC EXAMINATION

Naked eye examination of the following tissues was possible:

Lungs, trachea (windpipe) and bronchi (air passages):

> Examination of the residue of the lungs shows areas of substantial fibrous thickening of the pleura consistent with previous pulmonary surgery. The lungs showed changes due to emphysema and chronic bronchitis.

Heart:
> Dissection was so extensive that the heart could not be anatomically reconstructed and the total heart weight was, according to the subsequently obtained report of the Spanish pathologists, approximately 500 gms. The thickness of the left ventricle at its mid lateral wall varied between 1.8cm and 2cm. The right ventricle was hypertrophied and up to 0.8cm in thickness. The mitral valve showed some minor nodular degeneration of its leaflets, a common finding in this age group. The right coronary artery showed some dilatation with irregular thickening of its wall but was patent. The left circumflex artery had not been completely dissected and showed no significant atheromatous stenosis.
>
> Examination of the remains of the anterior descending branch of the left coronary artery showed generally mild atheromatous stenosis with a single area of 50% stenosis in the mid anterior descending branch. We could find no evidence of potentially lethal stenosis of any of the coronary vessels and no evidence of coronary thrombosis.
>
> The root of the aorta contained some atheromatous plaques, the extent of which was normal for the deceased's age. We could detect no abnormality in the remains of the atrial chambers of the heart.

Brain:
> The brain had been sliced after fixation. The cerebral vessels were congested and showed up to 50% atheromatous stenosis in branches of the Circle of Willis. We could detect no evidence of cerebral thrombosis. The cerebral cortex was normal in appearances and thickness, measuring between 4-5mm. The white

DEPARTMENT OF FORENSIC MEDICINE
GUY'S HOSPITAL
(UNIVERSITY OF LONDON)

Dr. I.E. WEST, M.B., Ch.B., F.R.C.Path., D.M.J.
Dr. R.T. SHEPHERD B.Sc., M.B., B.S., M.R.C.Path., D.M.J.
Direct Telephone Line 071-407 0378 / 071-403 1118)
(Fax: 071-403 7292)

UNITED MEDICAL AND DENTAL SCHOOLS
GUY'S AND ST. THOMAS'S HOSPITAL
LONDON BRIDGE, SE1 9RT
TELEPHONE: 071-955 5000 Ext: 3118 / 3119

The ventricles were symmetrical and normal in size. We could detect no macroscopically visible infarct.

There was slight thickening of the arachnoid membrane covering the surface of the cerebral hemispheres. This thickening was within normal limits for his age.

HISTOLOGICAL EXAMINATION

Brain: Patchy perivascular oedema with some congestion of cerebral vessels. Corpora amylacea present but in numbers commonly found at this age. Mild thickening of the arachnoid. No evidence of infarction, haemorrhage or neoplasm. The cerebral vessels showed no detectable thrombosis. There was patchy cerebral atheroma.

Heart: Multiple sections of both ventricles were viewed. There was patchy interstitial fibrosis in the left ventricle but no scarring from a previous substantial infarct. The coronary circulation showed up to 50% stenosis by atheroma although the majority of vessels showed only mild atheromatous stenosis with occasional areas of calcification. No visible thrombosis. The myocardium showed patchy oedema but no detectable infarct. Occasional aggregates of chronic inflammatory cells in myocardium (an occasional finding in otherwise normal hearts). No evidence of myocarditis or cardiomyopathy. The right ventricle showed some hypertrophy. There was a normal degree of fatty infiltration of the right ventricular myocardium. Some chronic inflammatory cells in epicardium probably related to previous pulmonary surgery.

The heart showed a moderate degree of interstitial fibrosis consistent with a degree of damage due to previous ischaemia. There is nothing, however, to indicate a recent ischaemic episode.

Lungs: Variable picture in sections. Some sections showing fibrous thickening of the pleura were associated with considerable interstitial fibrosis of pulmonary tissues with quite marked thickening of alveolar walls with chronic inflammatory cell infiltrate in the interstitium. No evidence of pneumonia. Other sections show emphysematous changes, both chronic and acute, the acute being consistent with the terminal rupture of alveolar walls due to the presence of fluid in the small air
Eosinophilic staining fluid was present in many

DEPARTMENT OF FORENSIC MEDICINE
GUY'S HOSPITAL
(UNIVERSITY OF LONDON)

Dr. I.E. WEST, M.B., Ch.B., F.R.C.Path., D.M.J.
Dr. R.T. SHEPHERD B.Sc., M.B., B.S., M.R.C.Path., D.M.J.
Direct Telephone Line 071-407 0378 / 071-403 1118)
(Fax: 071-403 7292)

UNITED MEDICAL AND DENTAL SCHOOLS
GUY'S AND ST. THOMAS'S HOSPITAL
LONDON BRIDGE, SE1 9RT
TELEPHONE: 071-955 5000 Ext: 3118 / 3119

There was congestion of the pulmonary vessels. The pulmonary arteries showed some medial hypertrophy. No evidence of pulmonary emboli.

The appearances are those of a degree of chronic obstructive airways disease, ie chronic bronchitis and emphysema. There was also pulmonary fibrosis of a moderate degree affecting part of the lung substance, presumably the left lung, although we have no means of identifying from which lung these pieces of tissue had been taken by the Spanish pathologists.

Liver: Shows a moderate degree of fatty change, mainly small droplet, with an increase in periportal fibrous tissue. The portal tracts contained increased numbers of chronic inflammatory cells. No detectable active hepatitis although chronic inflammatory cells were scattered throughout the hepatic lobules. The appearances suggest alcohol induced fatty change associated with early cirrhosis.

Kidney: Marked autolytic changes, particularly in tubules. The glomeruli appeared normal.

Prostate: Showed marked benign enlargement.

Trachea: Showed no significant abnormality apart from changes of autolysis.

We understand that the deceased was left handed.

We have now studied a photocopy of the post mortem report prepared for the Spanish authorities by the pathologists in Tenerife. The report is in Spanish and some of the pages have been poorly copied with areas of text being illegible. We have not as yet received replacement copies of the pages in question.

Some additional information is available from the Spanish report and this can be summarised as follows:

a)   The report mentions a number of minor external injuries and attributes most of them to injuries caused during recovery from the sea.

b)   There is evidence of a greater degree of coronary artery narrowing than could be determined from our examination of the heart. This

DEPARTMENT OF FORENSIC MEDICINE
GUY'S HOSPITAL
(UNIVERSITY OF LONDON)

Dr. I.E. WEST, M.B., Ch.B., F.R.C.Path., D.M.J.
Dr. R.T. SHEPHERD B.Sc., M.B., B.S., M.R.C.Path., D.M.J.
Direct Telephone Line 071-407 0378 / 071-403 1118)
(Fax: 071-403 7292)

UNITED MEDICAL AND DENTAL SCHOOLS
GUY'S AND ST. THOMAS'S HOSPITAL
LONDON BRIDGE, SE1 9RT
TELEPHONE: 071-955 5000 Ext: 3118 / 3119

microscopic examination of parts of the heart. The accuracy of any assessment of coronary artery narrowing depends upon the vessels, which are under assessment, being cut perpendicularly to their long axis. They found areas of 95% stenosis or narrowing in the diagonal branch of the left coronary artery and 50% in the anterior descending branch. They found 40% and 70% stenosis in the left circumflex and the right diagonal branches. The posterior descending had 40-60% narrowing. The heart weight was reported at approximately 500gm.

These assessments appear to have been made from blocks of the heart towards the peripheral parts of these vessels as, except for the stenosis noted in the anterior descending branch, we could find no such levels of coronary artery disease. It is clear that the Spanish have retained the pertinent blocks of tissue.

c)   The actual description of the appearances of the right lung are almost classical of death due to drowning, although one may see this change, less commonly, induced by marked pulmonary oedema as the result of acute heart failure.

d)   Bleeding from the ear canal was noted at post mortem examination. This is a somewhat non-specific finding but is seen with deaths from drowning.

e)   Some aspirated gastric contents were found in the airway. This is not uncommonly seen and very difficult to interpret. It is not uncommonly found as a post mortem artefact caused by moving the body after death. It can also occur as the result of falling into water, the impact causing regurgitation of gastric contents. There is, however, no evidence, from our examination of the lungs, to indicate that vomit has been inhaled in life.

f)   Essentially the Spanish pathologists have concluded that the cause of death is not totally clear. They consider the most likely scenario to be his pre-existent ischaemic heart disease and are uncertain as to the role of submersion in water. In essence, they cannot exclude death from drowning and, from study of their report, their opinion on heart disease appears to be based on probabilities as there is no evidence of acute disease of the heart or its vessels. We could not find any formal pathological cause of death.

CONCLUSIONS

These conclusions are based on our post mortem examination of the

DEPARTMENT OF FORENSIC MEDICINE
GUY'S HOSPITAL
(UNIVERSITY OF LONDON)

Dr. I.E. WEST, M.B., Ch.B., F.R.C.Path., D.M.J.
Dr. R.T. SHEPHERD B.Sc., M.B., B.S., M.R.C.Path., D.M.J.
Direct Telephone Line 071-407 0378 / 071-403 1118)
(Fax: 071-403 7292)

UNITED MEDICAL AND DENTAL SCHOOLS
GUY'S AND ST. THOMAS'S HOSPITAL
LONDON BRIDGE, SE1 9RT
TELEPHONE: 071-955 5000 Ext: 3118 / 3119

examination, the Spanish report and the study of all the circumstantial evidence which is available to us to date. We have not seen the complete report prepared by the Spanish authorities. The findings of the Police may be of relevance in this respect, particularly in regard to the actions undertaken by their Scene of Crime personnel.

Based on the information currently available to us we have come to the following conclusions:

1. Robert Maxwell was a heavily built man who was very substantially overweight for his height.

2. The deceased suffered from some degenerative disease which was normal for his age, ie changes noted in the brain, kidneys, aorta, and prostate.

3. He had evidence of old ischaemic myocardial damage without anything to suggest a previous substantive myocardial infarct. There was evidence of coronary artery narrowing of a degree which is commonly found in individuals of this age and of a degree which can be diagnosed as being the cause of a sudden death.

    There was microscopic evidence of previous patchy scarring of the heart muscle but none of the areas examined showed that the deceased had suffered a substantial previous heart attack or myocardial infarct. It is likely that the scarring represents a degree of ischaemic heart disease which is not uncommonly found in men of this age, particularly in individuals who are grossly obese.

    We found no evidence to indicate that the deceased had suffered a thrombosis of the coronary circulation, nor was there evidence of a recent myocardial infarction or heart attack.

    It is, however, the case that many individuals in this age group die suddenly of heart disease where there is no detectable myocardial infarct or thrombosis. Death may be due to the sudden development of a lethal cardiac rhythm or a sudden loss of blood supply to part of the heart may occur which causes death to supervene before the pathological changes become apparent. It is frequently difficult to diagnose a myocardial infarct within the first few hours after it has developed unless one utilises certain special staining procedures. In this instance, unfortunately, we were unable to utilise this special staining method owing to the interference by

DEPARTMENT OF FORENSIC MEDICINE
GUY'S HOSPITAL
(UNIVERSITY OF LONDON)

Dr. I.E. WEST, M.B., Ch.B., F.R.C.Path., D.M.J.
Dr. R.T. SHEPHERD B.Sc., M.B., B.S., M.R.C.Path., D.M.J.
Direct Telephone Line 071-407 0378 / 071-403 1118)
(Fax: 071-403 7292)

UNITED MEDICAL AND DENTAL SCHOOLS
GUY'S AND ST. THOMAS'S HOSPITAL
LONDON BRIDGE, SE1 9RT
TELEPHONE: 071-955 5000 Ext: 3118 / 3119

the formalin fixation employed to preserve the heart in Spain. It is also clear that the Spanish pathologists did not employ these diagnostic techniques although they would have been in the ideal situation to do so as they had full access to the heart before it was fixed in formalin and could therefore undertake the tests on fresh heart muscle.

In cases of sudden cardiac death where no thrombus or infarct is found it is accepted, in pathological circles, that a significant degree of atheromatous coronary artery narrowing must be present. In order to diagnose potentially lethal stenosis one would expect to find areas where at least some 70-80% of the normal vessel lumen has been obliterated by disease. The greatest degree of stenosis that we found was 50%. The Spanish report indicates areas of greater stenosis which appeared to be in the peripheral parts of the arteries, particularly the left diagonal branch. The diagonal branch is generally a small branch of the left coronary artery but on occasions can supply substantial areas of the heart.

In men over the age of 65 sudden death may occur with a lesser degree of narrowing but where the coronary circulation has become quite heavily calcified. Death then usually occurs in a situation where the demand on the heart suddenly rises, the calcification under these circumstances preventing the normal dilatation of the vessels and leading to ischaemia or lack of oxygen in the face of an increased workload to the heart.

There are less common causes of sudden death due to coronary artery disease such as dissection or spasm. We found no evidence of dissection of the coronary vessels. Spasm is impossible to diagnose post mortem but rarely occurs unless there is some provoking cause, such as the use of drugs such as cocaine or sudden severe stress. In the latter instance it is frequently speculated upon as a potential cause of death but can rarely be proved.

The degree of fibrosis found in the deceased's myocardium is not uncommon for his age and may be seen in individuals who have no clinical symptoms or signs of ischaemic heart disease and have died as a result of totally unrelated causes such as homicide, suicide or accident.

In summary the deceased's cardiac status is such that he has undoubtedly suffered from a degree of ischaemic myocardial damage but there is no evidence to indicate that this is more than a potential cause of death. There is nothing to show that it is a probable or even likely cause of death.

DEPARTMENT OF FORENSIC MEDICINE
GUY'S HOSPITAL
(UNIVERSITY OF LONDON)

Dr. I.E. WEST, M.B., Ch.B., F.R.C.Path., D.M.J.
Dr. R.T. SHEPHERD B.Sc., M.B., B.S., M.R.C.Path., D.M.J.

Direct Telephone Line 071-407 0378 / 071-403 1118)
(Fax: 071-403 7292)

UNITED MEDICAL AND DENTAL SCHOOLS
GUY'S AND ST. THOMAS'S HOSPITAL
LONDON BRIDGE, SE1 9RT
TELEPHONE: 071-955 5000 Ext: 3118 / 3119

The behaviour of individuals who suffer from sudden severe heart disease is quite variable. Some may drop dead virtually immediately in which case they tend to slump down. If the deceased had fallen into the sea as a result of heart disease then he would have had to have been already leaning well over the rail in order to lose his balance. It is much more likely that heart disease would have caused him to collapse onto the deck of the boat. It would appear that it would have been impossible for him to have rolled from the deck into the sea.

Sudden heart failure may induce breathlessness and it is possible that he would be leaning against the railing on the lower deck in order to breathe more easily. In this instance he is likely to have been leaning so that his body was behind the rail with his hands grasping it tightly. This would have assisted his breathing by bringing into play the secondary muscles of respiration such as those in the shoulders and chest wall. The secondary muscles would not have been brought so effectively into play if he had been leaning so that his trunk was over the rail.

It is also improbable that a man who is collapsing due to sudden ischaemic heart disease would have been capable of grasping an object tightly and hanging onto that object to the extent that he tore muscles in his back. If he had suffered a heart attack coincidentally whilst leaning well over the rail he would have fallen into the water and we do not believe that he could have received the injuries found to his back.

4. Examination of the deceased's lungs indicated that he had suffered from chronic airways disease, in the form of bronchitis and emphysema, and that there was a significant degree of scarring or fibrosis of the lung. The extent of such scarring is difficult to assess as we did not see the lungs in their intact state and were only able to examine the tissue once it had been cut into small pieces.

It would appear, from the microscopic examination, that the majority of the fibrosis was in the left lung. This, together with his obesity, would account for the episodes of breathlessness and he could well have been breathless at rest. There is pathological evidence of a strain on his heart due to his lung disease with enlargement of his right ventricle and changes in the lungs due to pulmonary hypertension. The bronchitis and emphysema would also have predisposed him to recurrent chest infections. Chest infections which might follow a cold for instance, would have

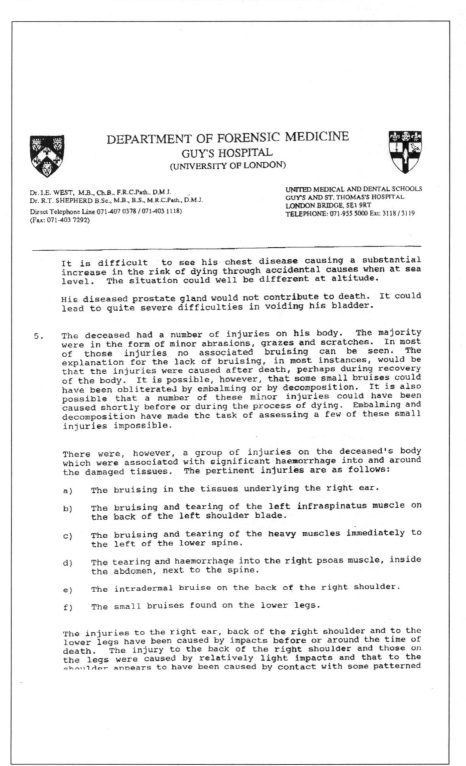

DEPARTMENT OF FORENSIC MEDICINE
GUY'S HOSPITAL
(UNIVERSITY OF LONDON)

Dr. I.E. WEST, M.B., Ch.B., F.R.C.Path., D.M.J.
Dr. R.T. SHEPHERD B.Sc., M.B., B.S., M.R.C.Path., D.M.J.

Direct Telephone Line 071-407 0378 / 071-403 1118)
(Fax: 071-403 7292)

UNITED MEDICAL AND DENTAL SCHOOLS
GUY'S AND ST. THOMAS'S HOSPITAL
LONDON BRIDGE, SE1 9RT
TELEPHONE: 071-955 5000 Ext: 3118 / 3119

It is difficult to see his chest disease causing a substantial
increase in the risk of dying through accidental causes when at sea
level. The situation could well be different at altitude.

His diseased prostate gland would not contribute to death. It could
lead to quite severe difficulties in voiding his bladder.

5.   The deceased had a number of injuries on his body. The majority
were in the form of minor abrasions, grazes and scratches. In most
of those injuries no associated bruising can be seen. The
explanation for the lack of bruising, in most instances, would be
that the injuries were caused after death, perhaps during recovery
of the body. It is possible, however, that some small bruises could
have been obliterated by embalming or by decomposition. It is also
possible that a number of these minor injuries could have been
caused shortly before or during the process of dying. Embalming and
decomposition have made the task of assessing a few of these small
injuries impossible.

There were, however, a group of injuries on the deceased's body
which were associated with significant haemorrhage into and around
the damaged tissues. The pertinent injuries are as follows:

a)   The bruising in the tissues underlying the right ear.

b)   The bruising and tearing of the left infraspinatus muscle on
      the back of the left shoulder blade.

c)   The bruising and tearing of the heavy muscles immediately to
      the left of the lower spine.

d)   The tearing and haemorrhage into the right psoas muscle, inside
      the abdomen, next to the spine.

e)   The intradermal bruise on the back of the right shoulder.

f)   The small bruises found on the lower legs.

The injuries to the right ear, back of the right shoulder and to the
lower legs have been caused by impacts before or around the time of
death. The injury to the back of the right shoulder and those on
the legs were caused by relatively light impacts and that to the
shoulder appears to have been caused by contact with some patterned

DEPARTMENT OF FORENSIC MEDICINE
GUY'S HOSPITAL
(UNIVERSITY OF LONDON)

Dr. I.E. WEST, M.B., Ch.B., F.R.C.Path., D.M.J.
Dr. R.T. SHEPHERD B.Sc., M.B., B.S., M.R.C.Path., D.M.J.
Direct Telephone Line 071-407 0378 / 071-403 1118)
(Fax: 071-403 7292)

UNITED MEDICAL AND DENTAL SCHOOLS
GUY'S AND ST. THOMAS'S HOSPITAL
LONDON BRIDGE, SE1 9RT
TELEPHONE: 071-955 5000 Ext: 3118 / 3119

It is possible that the legs received injuries in the water by being knocked against floating objects or the hull of the boat. Bruises of the type found on the legs could be caused for anything up to two hours after death.

The bruising under the right ear suggests a more substantial impact to the side of the ear and in that context it is likely that the abrasions of the outer ear are associated with the underlying bruising.

The tearing and bleeding into the muscles on the back of the left shoulder and into the muscles adjacent to the spine have not been caused by direct impacts to these areas but have resulted from sudden physical stress being applied to the muscles, causing them to stretch and tear. In our opinion these injuries have not been caused after death. The degree of haemorrhage is such that causation in the immediate post mortem period can be excluded. The pattern of tearing of these muscles suggests that the deceased has, at some point, been hanging on to an object with his left hand with all of his weight being carried by that hand. This could occur, for instance, in a person who is hanging vertically from a rail with his body freely suspended.

There are a number of possible scenarios where these types of injuries may be received:

a)   If he was hanging on to the rail of the boat and trying to prevent himself falling into the water then it is possible that, in such a large and unfit man, the muscular effort required to hoist his body back onto the boat could cause the damage seen here.

b)   If he overbalanced and fell over the railing but managed to grab the rail as he fell then it is possible that he would have torn the muscles affected here.

   One must look at this, of course, in the context of the ability of a man of his size, age and state of health, being able to carry out this type of action. One must also consider the ways in which an individual could accidentally fall from this boat. It is, we think, difficult to see, from the available evidence, how such an accidental fall could have occurred on a smooth sea unless the deceased has been leaning well over the rail.

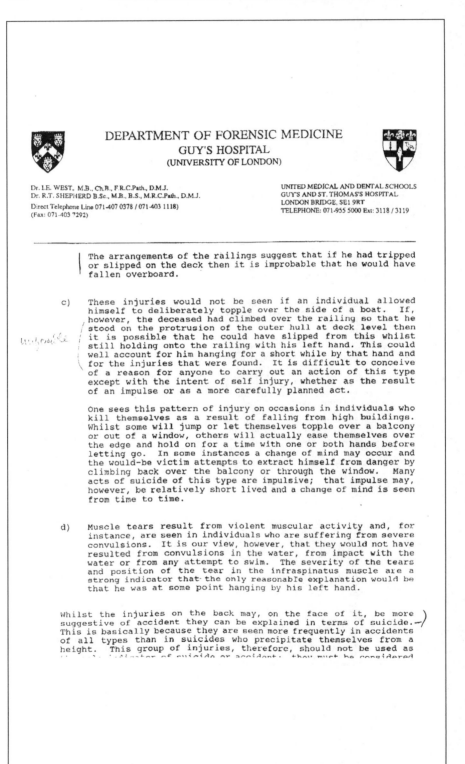

DEPARTMENT OF FORENSIC MEDICINE
GUY'S HOSPITAL
(UNIVERSITY OF LONDON)

Dr. I.E. WEST, M.B., Ch.B., F.R.C.Path., D.M.J.
Dr. R.T. SHEPHERD B.Sc., M.B., B.S., M.R.C.Path., D.M.J.
Direct Telephone Line 071-407 0378 / 071-403 1118)
(Fax: 071-403 7292)

UNITED MEDICAL AND DENTAL SCHOOLS
GUY'S AND ST. THOMAS'S HOSPITAL
LONDON BRIDGE, SE1 9RT
TELEPHONE: 071-955 5000 Ext: 3118 / 3119

The arrangements of the railings suggest that if he had tripped or slipped on the deck then it is improbable that he would have fallen overboard.

c)   These injuries would not be seen if an individual allowed himself to deliberately topple over the side of a boat. If, however, the deceased had climbed over the railing so that he stood on the protrusion of the outer hull at deck level then it is possible that he could have slipped from this whilst still holding onto the railing with his left hand. This could well account for him hanging for a short while by that hand and for the injuries that were found. It is difficult to conceive of a reason for anyone to carry out an action of this type except with the intent of self injury, whether as the result of an impulse or as a more carefully planned act.

One sees this pattern of injury on occasions in individuals who kill themselves as a result of falling from high buildings. Whilst some will jump or let themselves topple over a balcony or out of a window, others will actually ease themselves over the edge and hold on for a time with one or both hands before letting go. In some instances a change of mind may occur and the would-be victim attempts to extract himself from danger by climbing back over the balcony or through the window. Many acts of suicide of this type are impulsive; that impulse may, however, be relatively short lived and a change of mind is seen from time to time.

d)   Muscle tears result from violent muscular activity and, for instance, are seen in individuals who are suffering from severe convulsions. It is our view, however, that they would not have resulted from convulsions in the water, from impact with the water or from any attempt to swim. The severity of the tears and position of the tear in the infraspinatus muscle are a strong indicator that the only reasonable explanation would be that he was at some point hanging by his left hand.

Whilst the injuries on the back may, on the face of it, be more suggestive of accident they can be explained in terms of suicide. This is basically because they are seen more frequently in accidents of all types than in suicides who precipitate themselves from a height. This group of injuries, therefore, should not be used as

DEPARTMENT OF FORENSIC MEDICINE
GUY'S HOSPITAL
(UNIVERSITY OF LONDON)

Dr. I.E. WEST, M.B., Ch.B., F.R.C.Path., D.M.J.
Dr. R.T. SHEPHERD B.Sc., M.B., B.S., M.R.C.Path., D.M.J.
Direct Telephone Line 071-407 0378 / 071-403 1118)
(Fax: 071-403 7292)

UNITED MEDICAL AND DENTAL SCHOOLS
GUY'S AND ST. THOMAS'S HOSPITAL
LONDON BRIDGE, SE1 9RT
TELEPHONE: 071-955 5000 Ext: 3118 / 3119

the boat, the presence of disease, drugs, alcohol and obviously the presence or otherwise of any motive and ancillary evidence of suicide.

It is impossible to exclude homicide. There are no injuries on the deceased which indicate that he has been assaulted, but even a man of this size, particularly one who is unfit, could easily be pushed into the sea without leaving injuries which were characteristic of an assault. Homicide will remain impossible to exclude from a purely pathological point of view.

The tests conducted in Spain indicate that the deceased had not been drinking prior to his death and the samples tested contained no traces of any controlled or prescribed drugs. His tissues contained trace quantities of a cold remedy which would not have affected his state of mind. It would not have made him more liable to an accidental fall.

We found nothing to indicate that he has tripped or accidentally stumbled against some object on the deck. There was no damage around the ankles or the lower legs of the type that might suggest such an accident. Such an accident would be unlikely to cause him to fall overboard unless the sea is rough.

There was no evidence of any acute, physically detectable, disorder of the brain which might have led to sudden alteration in behaviour.

6.   The presence or otherwise of fluid in the deceased's lungs is not diagnostic of drowning. Fluid could have come from the sea or from his circulation in the form of pulmonary oedema. Where diatoms are present in water then it is usually possible to distinguish between pulmonary oedema and drowning, as these diatoms, in cases of drowning, will be carried into the body organs whereas they will be absent in death due to pulmonary oedema. If, however, the sea water contains very scanty numbers of diatoms it is frequently the case that none can be found in the body organs, even in incidents of proven drowning.

The pattern of alveolar rupture, as seen on some of the microscope sections, would, however, suggest some acute obstruction of the airway; these findings are more typical of drowning than of

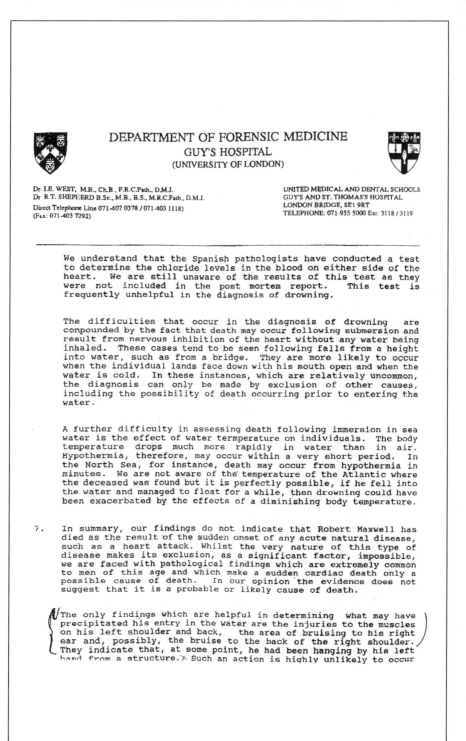

DEPARTMENT OF FORENSIC MEDICINE
GUY'S HOSPITAL
(UNIVERSITY OF LONDON)

Dr. I.E. WEST, M.B., Ch.B., F.R.C.Path., D.M.J.
Dr R.T. SHEPHERD B.Sc., M.B., B.S., M.R.C.Path., D.M.J.
Direct Telephone Line 071-407 0378 / 071-403 1118)
(Fax: 071-403 7292)

UNITED MEDICAL AND DENTAL SCHOOLS
GUY'S AND ST. THOMAS'S HOSPITAL
LONDON BRIDGE, SE1 9RT
TELEPHONE: 071-955 5000 Ext: 3118 / 3119

We understand that the Spanish pathologists have conducted a test to determine the chloride levels in the blood on either side of the heart. We are still unaware of the results of this test as they were not included in the post mortem report. This test is frequently unhelpful in the diagnosis of drowning.

The difficulties that occur in the diagnosis of drowning are conpounded by the fact that death may occur following submersion and result from nervous inhibition of the heart without any water being inhaled. These cases tend to be seen following falls from a height into water, such as from a bridge. They are more likely to occur when the individual lands face down with his mouth open and when the water is cold. In these instances, which are relatively uncommon, the diagnosis can only be made by exclusion of other causes, including the possibility of death occurring prior to entering the water.

A further difficulty in assessing death following immersion in sea water is the effect of water termperature on individuals. The body temperature drops much more rapidly in water than in air. Hypothermia, therefore, may occur within a very short period. In the North Sea, for instance, death may occur from hypothermia in minutes. We are not aware of the temperature of the Atlantic where the deceased was found but it is perfectly possible, if he fell into the water and managed to float for a while, then drowning could have been exacerbated by the effects of a diminishing body temperature.

7. In summary, our findings do not indicate that Robert Maxwell has died as the result of the sudden onset of any acute natural disease, such as a heart attack. Whilst the very nature of this type of disease makes its exclusion, as a significant factor, impossible, we are faced with pathological findings which are extremely common to men of this age and which make a sudden cardiac death only a possible cause of death. In our opinion the evidence does not suggest that it is a probable or likely cause of death.

The only findings which are helpful in determining what may have precipitated his entry in the water are the injuries to the muscles on his left shoulder and back, the area of bruising to his right ear and, possibly, the bruise to the back of the right shoulder. They indicate that, at some point, he had been hanging by his left hand from a structure. Such an action is highly unlikely to occur

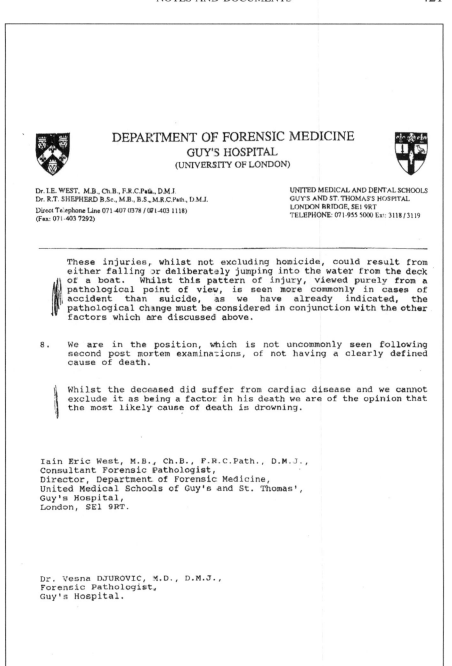

DEPARTMENT OF FORENSIC MEDICINE
GUY'S HOSPITAL
(UNIVERSITY OF LONDON)

Dr. I.E. WEST, M.B., Ch.B., F.R.C.Path., D.M.J.
Dr. R.T. SHEPHERD B.Sc., M.B., B.S., M.R.C.Path., D.M.J.
Direct Telephone Line 071-407 0378 / 071-403 1118)
(Fax: 071-403 7292)

UNITED MEDICAL AND DENTAL SCHOOLS
GUY'S AND ST. THOMAS'S HOSPITAL
LONDON BRIDGE, SE1 9RT
TELEPHONE: 071-955 5000 Ext: 3118 / 3119

These injuries, whilst not excluding homicide, could result from either falling or deliberately jumping into the water from the deck of a boat. Whilst this pattern of injury, viewed purely from a pathological point of view, is seen more commonly in cases of accident than suicide, as we have already indicated, the pathological change must be considered in conjunction with the other factors which are discussed above.

8. We are in the position, which is not uncommonly seen following second post mortem examinations, of not having a clearly defined cause of death.

Whilst the deceased did suffer from cardiac disease and we cannot exclude it as being a factor in his death we are of the opinion that the most likely cause of death is drowning.

Iain Eric West, M.B., Ch.B., F.R.C.Path., D.M.J.,
Consultant Forensic Pathologist,
Director, Department of Forensic Medicine,
United Medical Schools of Guy's and St. Thomas',
Guy's Hospital,
London, SE1 9RT.

Dr. Vesna DJUROVIC, M.D., D.M.J.,
Forensic Pathologist,
Guy's Hospital.

The final page from the second autopsy in Israel.

It was prepared by State Pathologist Hiss.
It would leave many unanswered questions.

Courtesy: Betty and Isabel Maxwell

- 13 -

Interim Expert's Opinion :

On basis of the results of the autopsy performed on the
embalmed body, and following the previous autopsy of
Mr. Robert MAXWELL, I hereby give my expert's opinion, that
his death was most probably caused by drowning.

1.   The traumatic injuries which were summarized in the
     previous paragraph, are the result of blunt injuries
     and were caused antemortem.

2.   Abrasions, contusions and hematomata on the body of
     Mr. Maxwell, are compatible with an involuntary fall
     into the sea.

3.   For preparing a final opinion, we require the protocol
     of the first autopsy, histological sections and the
     results of toxicological and biological tests
     (including water sample from the drowning region).

Jehuda Hiss, M.D.
Director

Extract from original briefing paper prepared for his clients, Inslaw, by Elliot Richardson, former Attorney-General of the United States for the Senate Judiciary Committee investigating the theft of Promis software – and the role of Robert Maxwell.

FOR BACKGROUND
PURPOSES ONLY

Memorandum to the Record
December 22, 1999
Page 13

Until his arrest by the U.S. Navy in November 1985 for espionage for Israel, Pollard was a civilian intelligence analyst at the Navy's Anti-Terrorism Alert Center in Suitland, Maryland. According to press accounts of the Pollard case, Pollard was using a computer terminal on his desk at this U.S. Navy intelligence facility to search computerized databases of U.S. intelligence agencies for information that he had been directed by Rafi Eitan to steal for Israel.

Eitan used Israeli intelligence officials stationed in the Israeli embassy in Washington, D.C. to liaise directly with Pollard on espionage assignments to Pollard, a circumstance that matches Eitan's description of the way in which Israeli intelligence exploited PROMIS databases in U.S. Government agencies.

When Eitan made his admissions about governments to which Maxwell had sold PROMIS, Eitan neglected to admit sales of PROMIS that Robert Maxwell made to U.S. Government agencies, as reflected in the following paragraphs.

The FBI conducted a foreign counterintelligence investigation of Robert Maxwell, doing business as Pergamon International in New Mexico in 1984, for the sale of computer software products "including but not limited to the PROMIS computer software product." The words in quotation marks were the words that INSLAW used in its Freedom of Information Act (FOIA) request that prompted the FBI to produce a copy of the above-mentioned foreign counterintelligence investigative report. The FBI redacted most of the text in the copy of the report it sent to INSLAW, citing the need to protect U.S. national security secrets.

The portions of the investigative report that the FBI did not delete for national security reasons reveal, however, that the FBI office in Albuquerque, New Mexico was the office of origin for the investigation, that FBI sources for the investigation included two employees at the Sandia National Laboratory in New Mexico, and that these two FBI sources had expressed concern about Maxwell's sale of PROMIS because another company owned by Maxwell was simultaneously selling unclassified U.S. Government data to the Soviet Union.

According to several apparently unrelated sources in the U.S. intelligence community, each of whom has provided information to INSLAW that has proved to be consistently reliable, Maxwell's sales of PROMIS in New Mexico in 1984 were to the Los Alamos National Laboratory and the Sandia National Laboratory, and the aggregate dollar value for the sales to the two U.S. national nuclear weapons laboratories in 1984 exceeded $30 million. In the normal commercial world, such a large software license dollar amount would indicate a large number of copies of PROMIS and/or a large number of staff who would have access to the PROMIS software.

Beginning in the late 1960's, "much of the United States' primary analysis of nuclear intelligence had been shifted from the CIA to the design and engineering laboratories for nuclear

Memorandum to the Record
December 22, 1999
Page 14

weapons at Los Alamos and Sandia" in New Mexico, according to Seymour Hersh's expose on Israel's nuclear arsenal, which is entitled *The Samson Option*. Moreover, the Los Alamos National Laboratory reportedly designs nuclear warheads for missiles on board U.S. nuclear submarines, and the Sandia National Laboratory does the engineering work to "weaponize" those designs by implementing them into the delivery systems of the nuclear submarines. Finally, the Los Alamos National Laboratory also develops artificial intelligence software for the automated analyses of intelligence information, according to the testimony of Brian Bruh, then Director of a U.S. Treasury Department intelligence agency known as FinCEN, before the House Appropriations Subcommittee on Treasury, Postal Service, and General Government of March 9, 1993.

The following circumstances suggest that Robert Maxwell's sale of PROMIS to the U.S. Government in New Mexico in 1984 included the first PROMIS licenses for internal use within the U.S. intelligence community, *i.e.*, the sale of the VAX 11/780 version of PROMIS for operation on board U.S. nuclear submarines:

- The year when Maxwell made his sale to the U.S. Government in New Mexico, *i.e.*, 1984, coincides with the year of the first internal deployment of PROMIS within the U.S. intelligence community;

- The CIA engineered the decision to use PROMIS as the standard database software within the U.S. intelligence community, used the submarine version of PROMIS as the first deployment of the U.S. intelligence community's new standard version of PROMIS, and had long ago begun to rely on the Los Alamos National Laboratory and the Sandia National Laboratory for much of the United States' nuclear intelligence work;

- As explained more fully later in this memorandum, Brian probably initially planned to have Hadron make the sales of PROMIS to the U.S. intelligence community but Brian probably could not use Hadron to make the initial sales in 1984 for the following reason: Independent Counsel Jacob Stein was that year investigating Attorney General-Designate Edwin Meese's failure to disclose certain business ties with Earl Brian and searching for evidence of whether Meese had influenced the U.S. Government to award any contracts to companies controlled by Brian;

- Eitan admitted that Israeli intelligence had successfully penetrated PROMIS databases in unidentified U.S. Government agencies as part of its espionage against the United States, a feat that would be more feasible if Eitan and Maxwell were directly involved in PROMIS sales to U.S. Government agencies;

Memorandum to the Record
December 22, 1999
Page 15

- Eitan directed Maxwell's sales of PROMIS while serving simultaneously as Israel's spymaster for Jonathan Pollard, and Pollard carried out his espionage assignments for Eitan, in part, by accessing computerized databases in the U.S. intelligence community;

- The submarine version of PROMIS supported nuclear targeting, and Eitan used as Pollard's controller, Israeli Air Force Colonel Aviem Sella, who was reportedly one of Israel's top nuclear targeting experts; and

- The inclusion of licenses for copies of PROMIS for every U.S. nuclear submarine could help explain why Maxwell allegedly obtained such a large aggregate amount of PROMIS license fees, *i.e.*, over $30 million, for the sales in New Mexico in 1984.

The reason that Rafi Eitan used Colonel Aviem Sella, "perhaps Israel's top air force expert in nuclear targeting and the delivery of nuclear weapons," as Pollard's controller was that "new missile targets inside the Soviet Union," "for Israel's own "advanced Jericho missile system," "required increased intelligence" "and Sella's mission was to help Pollard gather the essential information and then evaluate it," according to Seymour Hersh's book in Israel's nuclear arsenal entitled *The Samson Option*. According to Hersh, "Israel would need the most advanced American intelligence on weather patterns and communications protocols, as well as data on emergency and alert procedures."

The U.S. Department of Justice "took, converted, stole" the VAX 11/780 version of PROMIS from INSLAW through a campaign of "trickery, fraud and deceit" during the winter and spring of 1983, according to the fully litigated findings of fact of two federal courts, the U.S. Bankruptcy Court for the District of Columbia in January 1988 and the U.S. District Court for the District of Columbia in November 1989. The House Judiciary Committee, in its September 1992 Investigative Report, *The INSLAW Affair*, independently confirmed the government's theft of PROMIS, almost 18 months after the U.S. Court of Appeals for the District of Columbia had overturned the decisions of the two lower federal courts on a jurisdictional technicality, without addressing the merits of the dispute.

In February 1983, early in the Justice Department's campaign of "trickery, fraud and deceit," the Justice Department sent Rafi Eitan to INSLAW for a demonstration of the VAX 11/780 version of PROMIS, although the U.S. Justice Department falsely introduced him to INSLAW as Dr. Ben Or of the Israeli Ministry of Justice in Tel Aviv. INSLAW did not discover the real identify of its Israeli visitor until the House Judiciary Committee revealed in its Investigative Report, *The INSLAW Affair*, almost 10 years later, that the Justice Department had documented the transfer of some version of PROMIS to a Dr. Ben Or of Israel in May 1983. That was only a few weeks after the Justice Department had taken delivery from INSLAW of the VAX 11/780 version of PROMIS.

FOR BACKGROUND
PURPOSES ONLY

Memorandum to the Record
December 22, 1999
Page 17

Independent Counsel explained that his decision resulted from his inability to find any evidence that Meese had influenced the award of federal contracts to Brian.

Allowing Robert Maxwell, an Israeli intelligence contractor, to make the first sales of PROMIS in 1984 for internal use within the U.S. intelligence community may have allowed Brian to circumvent the problem caused by the Independent Counsel's 1984 investigation of Meese's relationship to Brian, while satisfying Brian's determination to profit from sales of PROMIS, but it could also have jeopardized vital U.S. national security interests. One illustration of the risk to U.S. national security interests relates to the W-88 nuclear warhead, the most advanced nuclear warhead in the U.S. arsenal. The Los Alamos National Laboratory completed the design of the W-88 in 1984 for future deployment on Trident II nuclear submarines. No later than 1988, the People's Republic of China had acquired the specifications to the W-88 from an unknown source. If Los Alamos included in a PROMIS database specifications for the W-88 nuclear warhead, Rafi Eitan may have been able to use Pollard to steal such specifications. The Government of Israel has been an important source of the People's Republic of China's acquisition of advanced military technology, according to a recent Congressional Investigative Report on Chinese espionage entitled *The United States House of Representatives Select Committee on U.S. National Security and Military/Commercial Concerns with the People's Republic of China* dated January 3, 1999.

The prosecution of Jonathan Pollard in 1986 and 1987 for espionage for Rafi Eitan and Israel would, under the circumstances, have presented both political and institutional conflicts of interest to the Meese Justice Department. Such conflicts of interest may explain the facts summarized in the remaining paragraphs of this memorandum.

In October 1986, both Meese and his Deputy Attorney General, Arnold Burns, discussed the INSLAW case with Leonard Garment, then a Senior Partner at Dickstein, Shapiro and Morin, the law firm that had filed INSLAW's lawsuit against the U.S. Department of Justice for the theft of the VAX 11/780 version of PROMIS several months earlier. The Justice Department disclosed these communications in sworn answers to INSLAW's interrogatories in 1987. Garment, however, never disclosed the communications to INSLAW.

Earlier that same year, the Government of Israel had hired Garment to represent Israeli Air Force Colonel Aviem Sella, the nuclear targeting expert whom Rafi Eitan used as Pollard's controller.

Garment had a luncheon meeting with Deputy Attorney General Arnold Burns on October 6, 1986 during which Burns complained of INSLAW's strategy in the litigation against the Justice Department, and implied that a settlement might be forthcoming if INSLAW's litigation strategy were to change, according to the September 1989 Investigative Report of the Senate Permanent Investigations Subcommittee. One week after the luncheon meeting, Dickstein, Shapiro and Morin

Memorandum to the Record
December 22, 1999
Page 18

fired the partner in charge of the INSLAW case, according to the same Senate report. About two months after that, the law firm sent a letter to INSLAW giving INSLAW the choice of abandoning its claims for PROMIS license fees or finding new litigation counsel.

Garment initially maintained to the press that his October 1986 discussions with Meese were about a foreign policy issue involving Israel rather than about INSLAW, according to an April 4, 1988 interview of Garment published in *Barron's Financial Weekly*, entitled "Rogue Justice -- What Really Sparked the Vendetta Against INSLAW."

Select Bibliography

Bonavia, David, *The Chinese: A Portrait* (Harmondsworth, England: Penguin Books, 1989).

Bower, Tom, *Maxwell: The Outsider* (Harmondsworth, England: Viking Penguin, 1992).

Bower, Tom, *Maxwell: The Final Verdict* (Hammersmith, London, England: HarperCollins, 1996).

Black, Ian and Morris, Benny, *Israel's Secret Wars: A History of Israel's Intelligence Services* (London, England: Futura Publications, 1992).

Davies, Nick, *Death of a Tycoon: An Insider's Account of the Fall of Robert Maxwell* (New York, NY: St Martin's Press, 1993).

Greenslade, Roy, *Maxwell: The Rise and Fall of Robert Maxwell and his Empire* (Secaucus, NJ: Birch Lane Press, 1992).

Maxwell, Elizabeth, *A Mind of My Own: My life with Robert Maxwell* (New York, NY: HarperCollins Publishers, Inc., 1994).

Ranelagh, John, *The Agency: The Rise and Decline of the CIA* (Kent, England: Sceptre Edition, Hodder and Stoughton Limited, 1987).

Stern, Chester, *Dr Iain West's Casebook: The chilling investigations of Britain's leading forensic pathologist* (London, England: Werner Books, Little Brown and Company (UK), 1996).

Thomas, Gordon, *Gideon's Spies: The Secret History of the Mossad* (New York, NY: Thomas Dunne Books, St Martin's Press, 1999).

Thomas, Gordon, *Seeds of Fire: China and the story behind the attack on America* (Tempe, AZ: Dandelion Books, Dandelion Enterprises, Inc., 2001).

Tomlinson, Richard, *The Big Breach: From Top Secret to Maximum Security* (Moscow: Narodny Variant Publishers, 2000).

West, Nigel, *MI5 1945–72: A Matter of Trust* (Kent, England: Coronet Books, Hodder and Stoughton Limited, 1992)

Index